John Fletcher Williams

A History of the City of Saint Paul

And of the County of Ramsey, Minnesota

John Fletcher Williams

A History of the City of Saint Paul
And of the County of Ramsey, Minnesota

ISBN/EAN: 9783337225247

Printed in Europe, USA, Canada, Australia, Japan

Cover: Foto ©ninafisch / pixelio.de

More available books at **www.hansebooks.com**

A HISTORY

OF THE

CITY OF SAINT PAUL,

AND OF THE

COUNTY OF RAMSEY,

MINNESOTA.

By J. FLETCHER WILLIAMS,

SECRETARY OF THE MINNESOTA HISTORICAL SOCIETY; COR. SEC. OF THE OLD
SETTLERS ASSOCIATION OF MINNESOTA; SEC. OF THE RAMSEY
COUNTY PIONEER ASSOCIATION, &c., &c.

[COLLECTIONS OF THE MINNESOTA HISTORICAL SOCIETY: VOL. IV.]

SAINT PAUL:
PUBLISHED BY THE SOCIETY.
1876.

PREFACE.

This work was prepared at the request and advice of a number of friends, who believed that the writer had the material at hand and the opportunity to prepare it, better than any one else who was likely to undertake it. There seemed, too, a necessity for such a work. The old pioneers of our city and State were, one by one, passing away, and the events of our early history, if not soon gathered and placed on permanent record, would be lost. The *names* even, of those who first planted their cabins on the site of our city, were fast becoming lost and forgotten; and their worthy acts, their labors, their adventures, the privations and struggles of frontier life, and other events in the earliest days of our city, were rapidly fading from the memory of the little group of pioneers who survived. Even what manner of men they were, whence they came, their personal history, particulars which will interest those who come after us more, perhaps, than they do the present generation, were matters known to so few, and scattered in fragments among widely distant households, it was almost a sealed book to some of the pioneers themselves.

It needed, therefore, some one who was, by occupation and taste, *interested* in such a work to perform it—since it was certain to be both laborious and unremunerative—some one who would hunt up from the various sources the lost and forgotten threads which, little by little, might be woven into the record of the founding and early days of our goodly city. It was this work that, in a rash moment, I was induced to undertake, little foreseeing into what a labyrinth of troubles I was about to plunge. (At first, however, I should say, only a *pamphlet* was projected.)

It is now fully ten years since I began collecting material and data for these chronicles—and it was fortunate that I began the work then. I secured, in writing, the minute statements of some of the earliest pioneers of our city, who have since gone to their reward, and which, if not recorded by me then, would probably have been lost. Among

these were GUERIN, PIERRE GERVAIS, BEAUMETTE, SIMPSON, HARTS-
HORN, ROBERT, FORBES, HOYT, J. R. BROWN, and others, all of whom
were among the earliest residents here, and took a prominent part in
the pre-territorial period of our history. Coming to Saint Paul at
quite an early day myself, it was my good fortune to be well acquainted
with nearly all the early settlers—scores of them since deceased—and,
being in an occupation which enabled me to do so, was accustomed to
secure from them and write up for publication, little sketches, historical and biographical, about the early days and early men of Saint Paul.
Thus I collected and preserved from loss, a considerable amount of
materials for history, and became generally familiar with the subject.

I have since visited and secured the minute statement of every living
pioneer of our city, (besides the deceased ones mentioned,) whose address I could ascertain, if within any accessible distance—and also the
families of many who died before I began the work—securing also the
statements, in writing, of those I was not able to visit. To do this
has required not a little travel—sometimes journeys of considerable
length and expense. But I am repaid by the satisfaction of knowing that I left no known source unexplored, that would throw light on
my subject, or develop material. A large number of letters were written also, and circulars sent out, asking information, and I conversed
widely with our old settlers, from time to time, on various points.
These facts are not mentioned in a boastful way, but simply to enable
the reader to judge whether the author has performed the task under-
taken with the thoroughness and fidelity which was requisite—or,
rather, has endeavored to do so.

That the work is correct in every particular, he does not claim.
Among so many hundred names, dates and statements of facts, it would
be a miracle if errors are not found. Of the imperfections of the work
no one is more sensible than the writer—yet, in view of the many difficulties which surrounded him, he is entitled to the leniency of critics.
The task of one who writes a local history during the lifetime of the
actors, is an unenviable one. He must depend for many facts upon the
memory of those actors or their friends, no two of them, perhaps,
agreeing on the same statement, or in the exact amount of prominence
due to each. Where these oral statements are the only sources of information, any one can realize the troubles that environ a writer who
endeavors, with impartiality and candor, to build a faultless structure
on such shifting quicksands!

To the earliest years of our history, the pre-territorial period, and
up to the organization of the city, the most space and minuteness was
given. But the events of those years were so imperfectly recorded, if
recorded at all, as to be inaccessible to the great mass of our present
citizens, and almost forgotten by the old pioneers themselves. The
living witnesses were fast disappearing, and what they knew and could

remember of that period must be first cared for. After 1854, there were several daily papers, directories, and other means of recording history and its actors, which did not exist before. It was the *earliest* pioneers and *oldest* settlers who most needed the biographer and historian. Those of a later day are amply cared for in other ways. Hence, when the work was about half printed, finding that it threatened to largely overrun its intended size and cost, the later years were of necessity condensed to a simple record of important facts. Some 200 pages of manuscript, prepared with considerable labor and cost, were thus cut out—among other things, the entire census roll of the men of 1857.

It was my intention to have given many more portraits and biographies of pioneers of our city, and of men who have been prominent in public or professional life, &c.—one hundred, at least, were hoped for, but there were difficulties that prevented it. The publication, not long ago, of a "Historical Atlas," almost destroyed the desirableness of this feature, and quite recently the city has been flooded with the circulars of publishers from abroad, proposing to issue more works of that kind. In the face of such schemes, any legitimate work, purely in the interest of history, and *not* for profit, has but little chance of success, and I was compelled to forego much of what I had hoped to secure. Some, doubtless, supposed this work was also designed as a speculation. This does me injustice. It was projected and completed solely from a taste for historical research, a feeling of pride in the subject, and an endeavor to honor the memory of our pioneers and pioneer days, and without the slightest desire of profit. As an evidence of this, it will be observed that the copyright, even, has been given to one of our deserving institutions, so that not a penny of the receipts can enure to the writer. But if the labor and outlay incurred by him has in any satisfactory degree accomplished what was intended—if this work shall prove of any value or interest to those for whose pleasure and information it was written—then he will feel amply repaid for both.

Were I to mention those who have kindly aided me in my researches, and furnished information and other aid, it would embrace almost the entire roll of our old settlers. To one and all, I return my grateful thanks, regretting only that I have so imperfectly performed the task they confided to me.

J. F. W.

Saint Paul, January 6, 1876.

CONTENTS.

ILLUSTRATIONS.

PORTRAITS.

VIEWS.

ERRATA.

Page 282, 9th line, for " Tremont," read " Fremont."
Page 390, for " Henry J. Howe," read " Henry J. Horn."

Ｈｉｓｔｏｒｙ ｏｆ Ｓａｉｎｔ Ｐａｕｌ,

AND RAMSEY COUNTY.

CHAPTER I.

THE PRE-HISTORIC PERIOD.

IN WHICH IS MORE ROMANCE THAN HISTORY—THE CREATION OF THE WORLD—
GEOLOGICAL CHANGES—HOW SAINT PAUL LOOKED A MILLION YEARS AGO—THE
MOUND BUILDERS AND THEIR WORKS—ORIGINAL AND ABORIGINAL IDEAS—IM-
IN-I-JA SKA—THE RED MAN—THE SCENERY OF THE INDIAN PERIOD—PAST AND
PRESENT.

THE changes which the settlement of the Northwest by the
whites have wrought in this region, are truly wonderful,
even in a country that has shown so many instances of remarkable progress as America. Many a reader of these pages, yet
on the sunny side of forty, can remember when the great valley
of the Upper Mississippi was known only to a few adventurous
traders and explorers. On the school-boy's map over which he
pored in his far eastern home, not over thirty years ago, it was
put down as an "unknown region, inhabited by Indians and
buffaloes!"* Fort Snelling and the Falls of Saint Anthony
may have possibly been indicated, or the outlines of "Carver's
Claim," but beyond this all was vague and uncertain. Indeed,
as late as 1849, when the Territory of Minnesota was organized,
and the bill creating it located its capital at "Saint Paul,"

---

* The "National Geography," published in 1845, and widely used in schools at that
period, in describing this section of the country, says: "A large portion of this region
is *unknown*, and occupied by Chippewas, Menominees and other Indians. Wild rice,
growing in the marshes, furnishes a considerable portion of their food. The soil is
fine, and there are rich mines of iron, lead and copper."

2

people examined their maps for it in vain. It was vaguely supposed to be " somewhere near Saint Anthony's Falls," and that was all the light that geographers or newspaper writers of that day were able to throw upon its location.

The record of these wonderful changes—which have transformed this wilderness of yesterday, comparatively, into a garden of fruitful fields and busy cities, with railroads and factories, and churches and colleges—which have built up a prosperous empire, populous with civilized and educated people, where were only the few wandering bands of a pagan and savage race before—seems more like a tale of enchantment than a sober history. The scenes shift so rapidly, the phantasmagoria almost bewilder us. Literally—

> With smoking axles hot with speed, with steeds of fire and steam,
> Wide-waked To-day leaves Yesterday behind it like a dream;
> So from the hurrying trains of life, fly backward far and fast,
> The mile-stones of our fathers, the landmarks of the past.
> And in the tales our fathers told, the songs our mothers sung,
> Tradition, snowy-bearded, leans, on Romance, ever young.

PAST AND PRESENT.

Nor is this remarkable, for it is within the memory of men still young, when most of the site of Saint Paul was a tangled jungle—a morass—a wilderness of trees and bushes, and rocks, and long swamp grass and reeds—a spot almost inaccessible except for muskrats and aquatic fowl. As late as 1855, or possibly a more recent date, wild ducks were shot by the Indians on marshes where now stand some of our most durable blocks of warehouses. Where the muskrat built his queer " house," or the fox burrowed in the rocks, and wild fowl bred undisturbed in the tangled reeds of the slough, or the dense jungle, are now the homes of 40,000 people, many of them built in the highest style of elegance, and furnished with every appliance of comfort that human ingenuity and taste can devise, or wealth procure. Where the " medicine man" performed his barbarous incantations, now is reared the walls of colleges and schools in which a science more profound is taught, and the best learning of the age. And where the rude worship of the *Wakan* was performed, with its mystic rites and ceremonies,

now rise stately temples dedicated to the true GOD, in which
the mild religion of the Prince of Peace is taught to the people who have supplanted the pagans of that day. In a word,
upon the spot so recently wrested from the savage that the
smoke of his lodge-fire almost yet lingers in the vale, has
arisen, like the palace of ALADDIN, the work of enchantment,
a great, opulent, prosperous, populous city, with its wharves,
shipping, railroads, factories, granaries and business warehouses, schools and churches, and all the institutions of the
highest civilization of the age.

It is our task to chronicle these wonderful changes.

In writing our history, perhaps we may as well begin at

THE CREATION OF THE WORLD!

But here ensues a difficulty at the very outset, for while a
historian should always be very particular and accurate as to
dates, there is considerable disagreement among writers as to
the date of that event. MOSES' chronology would place it at
about 6000 years ago, while recent French savans are confident
of the great antiquity of the globe, and assert its age anywhere
from half a million to several million years. It is evident, then,
that Saint Paul is a place of great antiquity!

Originally, say those savans, the globe was a mass of molten
granite. The cooling process was beyond doubt a slow one,
and the crust just under our feet did not become hard enough
and cool enough to rest any superstructure on, for perhaps
many thousands of years. Perchance ages passed while it was
a rough, ragged, repulsive mass of granite—the skeleton of
the future earth. Abrasion and erosion ground the surfaces of
the mass into powder. Oceans swept over it. Chemical
changes operated on it. Next our sand rock, or the saccharoid
sandstone was laid up. This singular formation underlies the
whole limestone of the Upper Mississippi valley, from Saint
Peter to Rock Island. Then came the Magnesian Limestone,
of which our bluffs are composed.* Here fossil life begins.

---

* In the valuable work of OWEN, [" Geological Survey of Iowa, Wisconsin and Minnesota,"] is given an examination of the formation at and near Saint Paul. He says:
"At Fort Snelling the sandstone is one hundred and fourteen feet thick; it is here of

The Reptilian age came on. The Icthyosaurus, the Ptero-
dactyl, the Iguanodon and Plesiosaurus, and other huge mon-
sters wallowed and splashed in the muddy water, which in
time hardened into splendid building stone, worth $1.25 per
cord. Then came on the "Glacial Period." The edges of
the limestone strata along Dayton's Bluff and West Saint Paul,
are ground smooth and polished by the sliding of the icebergs,
on their way down from the north. The Mississippi of that
day could not have been the stream of the present time. Then
it must have flowed from bluff to bluff. Baptist Hill, a huge
pile of rocks and boulders, and gravel and sand, was evidently
deposited, like a great sand-bar, by a whirl or eddy of the wild
waters and icebergs. Perhaps the stream wore its way through
the limestone rock for many miles, since the Falls of Saint

---

a pure white color, composed of loosely cemented grains of quartz. Above this we
have 22 feet of fossiliferous limestone, with numerous organic remains, similar to those
at the Falls of Saint Anthony. The fossils of the upper beds are mostly casts, but the
moulds often show the structure of the original surface. Many of the fossils have a
coating of sulphuret of iron, which gives a bright metallic appearance.

"The best section of these rocks that we have observed in Minnesota is at a bluff half
a mile below Fort Snelling,. The section here is as follows :

		Feet.
1.	White sandstone, without fossils, in thick beds	92
2.	Soft argillaceous marlite of a blue color, in which no fossils were discovered	5
3.	Ash-colored limestone, clouded with blue, full of fossils. These layers effer- vesce freely with acids, and contain nearly 65 per cent. of carbonate of lime. They will probably afford the best rock for burning into lime of any of the beds in the neighborhood. Thickness	15

[The composition of this rock is as follows :

Carbonate of lime	64.85
Carbonate of magnesia	13.75
Insoluble matter	12.40
Alumina, oxide of iron and manganese	7.50
Water	1.25
Loss	0.25
	100.00]

4. Ash-colored, argillaceous, hydraulic limestone, in thin layers, sometimes with
    a conchoidal fracture. It effervesces slightly with acids, and disintegrates
    rapidly when exposed to the weather 5
5. Grayish, buff-colored, highly magnesian limestone, with numerous casts of
    fossils, &c.

"About half a mile above Saint Paul, near the entrance of a small cave, the sandstone has an elevation of only 14 feet above the river level, and on it rests 11 feet of
shell limestone.

"At Saint Paul, the strata again rise. Here the cliffs are from 70 to 80 feet high, of
which the lower 65 feet consists of white sandstone, the remainder being shell limestone. About one mile below this point the hills recede from the river."

Anthony have receded several hundred yards even since the white man settled here. But the Glacial Period passed. Its duration cannot be estimated. Vegetation appeared. The earth rejoiced in scenes of beauty. Mammals came. Man—rude and uncouth, the cotemporary of the mammoth and cave bear—appears on the scene. The Age of Flint, then of Bronze, the Era of 'the Mound Builder, and the Red Man succeeded—each an indefinite period—terminated by the advent of the white explorer. From this on, the milestones of history are plainly visible.

THE MOUND BUILDERS.

The first human inhabitants (unless DARWIN's theory be true) who occupied this spot, were of that mysterious race known as the " Mound Builders." Who and what they were, whence they came, their history and ultimate fate, are wrapped in an impenetrable mystery, that will perhaps always baffle the most industrious scrutiny of antiquarians. Many plausible theories concerning them have been advocated by writers. It is generally agreed that they were a simple and somewhat ingenious race, who subsisted partly by cultivating the earth and partly by the chase, and were more civilized than the Red Race who subsequently occupied this region. By what means they disappeared—whether by war, or famine, or disease, or partly by all those causes—will never be known, but it is beyond doubt that they disappeared centuries ago.

The only memorials of their existence that have survived are the mounds that lie scattered about, generally (and erroneously) called *Indian* Mounds, though the Indians deny that their race erected them, asserting, " our fathers found them here when they first possessed the land." A number of these mounds have been found on the site of Saint Paul, mostly on Dayton's Bluff. Several of them are very large, showing that the Mound Builders must have lived for some time on this spot, and in considerable numbers. The mounds in this city are evidently of great age. Several of them have been excavated at times by antiquarians, and human remains, beads, pottery, and other relics of the pre-historic races discovered. Occasionally the stone axes, chisels, arrow-heads, and other implements of the aboriginal dwellers here are found in the soil of our city. They are curious remains of this race.*

The object of these mounds has never been satisfactorily explained. Some regard them as memorials, others as sepulchral, and some as religious or sacrificial altars. Whatever they are, they possess absorbing interest, and carry back the imagination to the period of the lost race who built them, and to the time when they dwelt on the very spot occupied by our own hearth-stones. As a recent writer has aptly said :

"Lonely, storm-beaten and freshet-torn, they stand nameless and without a history in this generation—silent, yet convincing illustrations of the ephemeral character of the nomadic races which for centuries peopled this entire region, and, departing, left behind them neither letters nor monuments of art—nothing, save these rude earthmounds, and occasional relics, to give assurance of their former existence.

"In the twilight of what by-gone and unrecorded century were these tumuli built? Whence came, and who the peoples that lifted them from out the bosom of our common mother? Served they as friendly refuge in seasons of freshet and of storm? Were sacred fires ever kindled upon your summits? Within your hidden depths do the brave and honored of your generation sleep that sleep which knows no waking until the final trump shall summon alike the civilized and the savage to the last award? Or are ye simple watch-towers, deserted of your sentinels—forts, abandoned of your defenders? We question, but there are no voices of the past in the ambient air. We search among these tombs, but they bear no epitaphs. We gaze upon these monuments, but they are inscriptionless."

WILLIAM CULLEN BRYANT's beautiful poem, "The Prairie," refers thus to the Mound Builders :

> "Are they here—
> The dead of other days? And did the dust
> Of these fair solitudes once stir with life,
> And burn with passion? Let the mighty mounds
> That overlook the rivers, or that rise
> In the dim forest, crowned with tall oaks,
> Answer.

---

*One of the handsomest stone axes ever found in the Northwest was picked up by EUGENIO A. JOHNSON, C. E., in the ravine near the City Hospital, and presented by him to the Historical Society.

"A race that long has passed away
Built them! A disciplined and populous race,
Heaped, with long toil, the earth, while yet the Greek
Was hewing the Pentelicus to forms
Of symmetry, and rearing on its rock,
The glittering Parthenon. These ample fields
Nourished their harvests. Here their herds were fed,
When haply by their styles the bison lowed,
And bow'd his maned shoulder to the yoke.
All day, this desert murmured with their toils,
Till twilight blushed, and lovers walked and woo'd
In a forgotten language, and old tunes
From instruments of unremembered form,
Gave the soft winds a voice.

"The red man came—
The roaming hunter tribes, warlike and fierce,
And the Mound Builders vanished from the earth.
The solitude of centuries untold
Has settled where they dwelt. * * * All is gone—
All, save the piles of earth that hold their bones—
The platforms where they worshipped unknown gods—
The barriers which they builded from the soil,
To keep the foe at bay. * * *
Thus change the forms of being. Thus arise
Races of living things, glorious in strength,
And perish."

THE ABORIGINAL PERIOD.

Following the era of the Mound Builders, came the "Aboriginal Period,"—erroneously so called—or the period when the Red Race, or Indians, were in possession of this region, and probably all the continent of 'America, when it was discovered by the Northmen in the eleventh century. The nation which occupied this spot, and the region immediately about it, from the earliest period concerning which any traditions of the Red Man exist, was the Dakota or Sioux, one of the most populous of the Indian Nations of North America. There were numerous villages of that Nation in this vicinity at a very early day, and it appears to have been a favorite locality for them, on account of natural advantages, and the abundance of game. As late as the time of CARVER's visit this was the case. The towering cliffs, or "bluffs," of white sandstone which overhung the river, formed a prominent landmark for the Indians as they paddled up or down in their canoes, and it was known to them from time immemorial as *Im-in-i-ja Ska*, i. e., White Rock, and to this day is so called in their tongue.

The scenery, before the hand of the white man marred its wild, quiet beauty, must have been picturesque in the extreme. Then the bluffs were crowned with majestic trees, and the bottom lands above and below and opposite the city, were a dense jungle, where the primeval forests* grew in unchecked luxuriance. Here the deer, the bear and the buffalo roamed freely, disturbed occasionally by the wily Indian, whose skin teepee was frequently pitched in the bottom-land along the margin of the river. Standing on the edge of the high plateau, or second table, say where the bridge now starts, the eye would then have wandered over a sea of foliage on the bench below, through which rolled the calm and placid river, unvexed by anything except the " squaw's birch canoe." Civilization had not then come with its burning force, changing and marring the natural face of creation, but instituting new forms of beauty —planting in the solitude a busy, populous city, with its din and noise, and smoke and clang of factory and mill, and the scream of engine and steamer.

" Here lived and loved another race of beings." On the upper plateau of our city they hunted the deer and bear and bison ; speared the muskrat in its marshes, and shot the beaver in its streams. The quiet river bore their canoes. Under the old century-mossed trees in the glen their group of skin teepees stood. Their songs of festivity ,echoed in the vale ; anon it rang with the demon yells of their scalp-dance, or the shrieks of a victim tortured to death. The Indian lover wooed his dusky sweetheart with a flute serenade, or whispered sweet tales of love by moonlight. Anon they joined in death-combat with the wily Chippewa, and the soil beneath our feet may have once been reddened with the life-blood shed in those fierce battles.

---

* In 1854, Mr. R. O. SWEENY counted the rings on a large tree that had been cut down near the upper levee, and found *over six hundred annual rings*, indicating an age of over six centuries. Primeval indeed.

But it is not necessary here to speak at length of the Red Race who once occupied this spot. Their history, customs and character are too well known and too thoroughly recorded to need incorporation into this work. They seem doomed • to disappear before the settlement of the white man, and, however lightly they may be regarded by those who have mingled with them on the frontier, there is something sad in the way they have been dispossessed of their ancestral heritage by the pale-faced intruder. Truthfully are they represented as lamenting :

> " They waste us—aye, like April dew,
> In the warm noon we shrink away,
> And fast they follow as we go,
>   Towards the setting day,
> Till they shall fill the land, and we
> Are driven into the western sea!"

At the period of which we write they were at least untainted by the vices the white man introduced among them, and whatever natural nobility of character may be claimed for them by their eulogists, must have then been displayed. The white people, since St. Paul was settled, do not seem to have admired them greatly, though many who read this book may entertain for them the romantic regard of LONGFELLOW and COOPER.

CHAPTER II.

THE DISCOVERY OF THE NORTHWEST.

THE JESUIT MISSIONARIES AND THEIR EXPLORATIONS—MARQUETTE AND JOLIET
VISIT THE UPPER MISSISSIPPI—LA SALLE AND HIS ACTS—FATHER HENNEPIN
SENT TO THE SIOUX REGION—HIS ADVENTURES AMONG THAT NATION—HE
DISCOVERS AND NAMES SAINT ANTHONY'S FALLS—SUBSEQUENT DISCOVERIES
AND EXPLORATIONS—CESSION OF THIS REGION TO GREAT BRITAIN.

THE Northwest was early claimed by the French through
the right of discovery, and its first explorers were of
that nation. Religious zealots have ever led the vanguard of
discovery, and, in accordance with this rule, we find that many
years before even the traders had dared to traverse the wilds of
the Northwest, a class of men of that remarkable Order founded
by IGNATIUS LOYOLA—the Jesuits—had explored much of the
country around the Lakes and the headwaters of the Mississippi, sent hither to plant the banner of the Cross among the
aborigines, and win them to its mild religion. Its missionaries, inspired with a sublime heroism in the cause of CHRIST,
visited these wilds, endured incredible toils and privations,
and, with a fortitude that never faltered, even in the face of
peril and death, carried the precious words of the Gospel to
the savages of the wilderness. History records no devotion
more sublime. Many of them now wear the martyr's crown,
but their sufferings and toils were not in vain. To no sect or
order could such a work have been more properly confided.
Says MACAULAY : "Before the Order had existed a hundred
years, it had filled the whole world with memorials of great
things done and suffered. There was no region of the globe
in which Jesuits were not to be found. They wandered to
countries which neither mercantile avidity nor liberal curiosity
had ever impelled any stranger to explore. Yet, whatever
might be their residence, whatever might be their employment,
their spirit was the same—entire devotion to the common cause,

implicit obedience to the central authority. None of them had chosen his dwelling place or his avocation for himself. Whether the Jesuit should live under the Arctic circle or under the Equator—pass his life collating MSS. at the Vatican, or in persuading naked barbarians in the southern hemisphere not to eat each other—were matters which he left, with profound submission, to the decision of others. If he was wanted at Lima, he was on the Atlantic in the next fleet. If he was wanted at Bagdad, he was toiling through the desert with the next caravan. If his ministry was needed in some country where his life was more insecure than that of a wolf, he went without remonstrance or hesitation to his doom." Bishop Kip pays them this just tribute: "Amid the snows of Hudson's Bay—among the woody islands and beautiful inlets of the Saint Lawrence—by the council fires of the *Hurons* and of the *Algonquins*—at the sources of the Mississippi, where, first of all the white men, their eyes looked down upon the Falls of Saint Anthony, and then traced down the course of the bounding river as it rushed onward to earn its title of 'Father of Waters'—on the vast prairies of Illinois and Missouri—among the blue hills which hem in the salubrious dwellings of the *Cherokees*, and in the thick cane-brakes of Louisiana—everywhere were found the members of the 'Society of Jesus.'"

The reports and letters of these devoted Heralds of the Cross to their superiors. (*Jesuit Relations, and Lettres Edifiantes et Curieuses,*) contain the earliest reliable historical and descriptive data relating to the Northwest, and are rare and valuable. From them we glean the meagre details of the earlier explorations in the Northwest, and the

PROGRESS OF DISCOVERY TOWARDS THIS REGION.

GABRIEL SAGARD, in 1624, visited the tribes on Lake Huron, and in 1641 Fathers JOGUES and RAYMBAULT reached as far as the Sault Ste. Marie. Here they first heard tidings of the Dakotas. PAUL DE JEUNE, a Jesuit Missionary, is perhaps the first writer who mentions them with any distinctness, about the same date. He says they were called by the voyageurs, "The People of the Lakes." The Iroquois war ensued.

however, and further exploration was arrested for several years.
At length, in 1658, two daring traders penetrated to Lake
Superior, wintered there, and brought back accounts of a fero-
cious tribe who dwelt on "a great river" to the west. These
accounts incited the Jesuit Fathers at Quebec to dispatch a
missionary to the tribe mentioned. Father RENE MESNARD,
(or MENARD,) an aged priest, was selected, and set out in the
autumn of 1660, penetrating that fall as far as Chegoimegon
Bay on Lake Superior. The next spring he crossed the country
from Lake Superior to Black River Falls, Wisconsin. Here,
or near here, it is supposed, he was lost in the forest. His
cassock and breviary, long afterwards preserved among the
Dakotas as medicine charms, afforded the only clue to his fate.
In 1665, Father CLAUDE ALLOUEZ, the successor to MESNARD,
reached La Pointe, and, erecting a chapel, established a permanent mission among the Ojibwas.

SECOND DISCOVERY OF THE MISSISSIPPI.

DE SOTO had discovered the Mississippi in 1541, but the
discovery was never used, and was well nigh forgotten. Over
a century had passed, when it was again to be discovered from
the north. JEAN NICOLLET, an interpreter and Catholic, in
1639, advanced on a mission to one of the strange tribes of the
west [Winnebagoes] so far that he discovered the Wisconsin
River, and, floating down it, heard from the Indians of a "great
water," only three days' journey beyond, which he inferred was
the sea. While Father ALLOUEZ was preaching to the Ojibwas, on Lake Superior, he heard these accounts of a powerful
nation, called by that tribe the *Naudowessioux*, meaning, in
the Ojibwa tongue, "enemies," and of a mighty stream called
the *Mese Seepi*, signifying, "Great River." Returning to
Quebec soon after, he spread the reports of this great river, and
M. TALON, Intendant of New France, became interested in the
subject. He resolved to endeavor to discover this great stream,
so as to reap the honors of such a feat, but owing to the trouble
and delays incident to carrying an expedition into the far wilderness, it was not until 1673 that anything practical was effected.
    LOUIS JOLIET, of Quebec, once a priest, but at that time a

fur-trader, agreed to undertake a voyage to the unknown river. With him was associated Father JACQUES MARQUETTE, a Jesuit priest, then a missionary among the Hurons, admirably fitted, from his influence among the Indians, to aid the enterprise, and who has been thought by some to have been the real originator of the expedition. They set out from Michilimackinac, Father MARQUETTE's missionary station, on May 13, 1673, accompanied by five Frenchmen and two Algonquin Indians. They proceeded to Green Bay, thence up the Fox River to the portage, and on June 10 launched their canoes on the Ouisconsin. MARQUETTE and JOLIET proceeded thence alone. For seven days they floated down this river, and, on the 17th, chanting the *Exaudiat* and *De Profundis* in thankfulness to God, they glided out on the broad bosom of the " Great River."

The two explorers continued their journey down the Mississippi, until, about the middle of July, they reached the mouth of the Arkansas. Here they began to retrace their voyage, and, returning by the Illinois River, soon floated into Lake Michigan through one of the branches. JOLIET returned to Quebec to become famous for his discovery. MARQUETTE pursued his missionary labors along the western lakes for two years longer, and, on the 16th of June, 1675, died at the age of thirty-eight.

LA SALLE'S EXPEDITION.

No effort to follow up the discovery of MARQUETTE and JOLIET seems to have been made for fully five years. ROBERT CAVALIER, SIEUR DE LA SALLE, a descendant of a noble Norman family—once a Jesuit, but then a fur-trader of Montreal—resolved, if possible, to prosecute still further the discovery of the Mississippi, and laid his views before Count DE FRONTENAC, then Governor of New France. Imbibing somewhat of the enthusiasm of LA SALLE, but unable to fit out such an expedition, FRONTENAC sent him to France, with credentials that would ensure him aid at Court. COLBERT, the Prime Minister of LOUIS XV, kindly listened to LA SALLE's scheme, and procured for him authority to prosecute his plan, as well as other honors. LA SALLE also enlisted Chevalier DE TONTI, and about thirty colonists, to accompany him. The expedition arrived at Quebec September 15, 1678. A vessel was built, and LA SALLE started on his voyage, but was compelled to put into winter quarters near Niagara Falls. In the spring of 1679 he built and launched another vessel above the Falls. It was called the Griffin. The expedition again set sail on August 7. and arrived at Green Bay on October 8. The Griffin was loaded with furs and sent homeward. with instructions to return at once. But she never returned, a storm on Lake Erie having sent her and her cargo to the bottom. Meantime, having left a part of his force in a small fort near the mouth of St. Joseph's River, he proceeded with the rest to the Illinois River, where he built a fort, which, in view of the discouraging circumstances surrounding him, he named *Creve-Cœur*, [Broken Heart.]

While here he resolved to make another effort to explore the Mississippi, and on February 28, 1680, dispatched

FATHER LOUIS HENNEPIN,

with two companions, on a voyage of discovery. Perhaps no one could have been selected better fitted for such a mission. He had all the ambition and daring of a knight-errant. He was born in Flanders about the year 1640. He entered holy orders while young, but was always afflicted with a burning passion for travel and adventure. He relates that he used to hide himself behind the doors of taverns, to listen to the sailors narrate their adventures, and longed to visit strange lands. This at last led him to get leave of his superiors to go to Canada. He came over on the same ship which bore back LA SALLE in 1675, and then, most probably became acquainted with LA SALLE and his plans. PARKMAN describes his dress: "With sandaled feet, a coarse gray capote. and peaked hood, the cord of SAINT FRANCIS about his waist, and a rosary and crucifix hanging at his side." Such was the first white man who was to look upon the Falls of Saint Anthony.

HENNEPIN'S ADVENTURES.

HENNEPIN set off, as stated before, on February 28. His canoe was heavily laden with goods sent by LA SALLE as pres-

ents to the Indians. For companions and oarsmen he had two
Frenchmen, named Accau and Du Gay. Floating down the
Illinois River to its mouth, which they reached on the 12th of
March, they commenced their toilsome journey up the Mississippi. Game was abundant, and they fared well. On the 11th or
12th of April, HENNEPIN says they stopped in the afternoon to
repair their canoe, when a fleet of Sioux canoes suddenly swept
into sight, and in a moment they were surrounded by 120 naked
warriors. HENNEPIN placated them with presents of tobacco,
when they explained to him that they were on their way to
attack the Miamis. HENNEPIN caused them to understand that
the Miamis had gone across the Mississippi, beyond their reach.
At this they showed signs of sorrow, and finally stated that
they would retrace their way up the river, and that HENNEPIN
and his companions must accompany them. To this he agreed,
as they had thus far expected to be murdered, while it allowed
him to continue his explorations. Slowly the Indians and their
prisoners paddled their way up the Mississippi, HENNEPIN
and his companions still tormented with fears for their safety.

THEY ARRIVE AT THE SITE OF SAINT PAUL.

On the 30th day of April, or the 19th day after their captiv-
ity, HENNEPIN's captors arrived at what is most probably the
site of the present city of Saint Paul. He describes it as a little
bay or inlet, five leagues below the Falls of Saint Anthony,
grown with alders or rushes. This description seems to point
to the little bay at the mouth of Phelan's Creek, which is about
that distance below the Falls, and would be a very convenient
point for the Indians to land and set out on their journey overland to Mille Lac. Here, he says, the Indians broke his canoe
to pieces, and hid their own among the reeds. They then
divided amongst them the baggage and effects of the Father,
even taking his priestly robes, whose ornaments allured their
covetousness. They then set out on foot for their village,
which was near Mille Lac, and arrived there about May 5th.

Here HENNEPIN was adopted into the family of the Chief,
AQUIPAGUETIN, and lived with him in his lodge on an island
in the Lake. His account of his life among the Indians is
entertaining, but space forbids its narration here.

In September, the Indians set out on their annual hunt, and left HENNEPIN and his companions at liberty to go where they pleased. ACCAU preferred to remain with the Indians, and consequently HENNEPIN and DU GAY set off alone down the Mississippi River in a small canoe.

HE DISCOVERS THE FALLS OF SAINT ANTHONY.

About the first of October, they arrived at the Falls of Saint Anthony, being beyond doubt the first white men to gaze upon that spot. His description of the Falls is very brief, but tolerably accurate. He named them, he says, in honor of Saint ANTHONY, of Padua. They portaged around the Falls, meeting several Indians who were making sacrifices to the Spirit of the Waters. Launching their canoe below the Falls, they continued their journey, and, after a variety of adventures, reached the Jesuit station at Green Bay.

HENNEPIN'S SUBSEQUENT CAREER.

From thence he proceeded to Montreal, and, soon after, to Europe. "Providence," he writes, "preserved my life that I might make known my great discoveries to the world." He published an account of his travels, and afterwards, for some reason, put out a new edition, with a lying account of his exploration of the Mississippi to its mouth in 1680. This has detracted from the fame he otherwise would have had, and, though twenty editions of his work have been printed, in six different languages. HENNEPIN died at last in obscurity. In the Northwest, which he was so instrumental in discovering, something has been done to his memory. A town in Illinois, and a flourishing county of our own State, carry the name of the Franciscan priest to posterity.

THE MISSISSIPPI RIVER.

Though HENNEPIN referred to the River as the *Meschasipi* and *Meschasebe*, he nevertheless endeavored to bestow upon it the name of "Saint Louis," in honor of the King of France. MARQUETTE and JOLIET christened it *La Riviere de Conception ;* LA SALLE named it "the Colbert," after the Prime

Minister of the King; but none of these names have been retained, and that by which it was first known to the Algonquins two centuries ago, with slight modifications, still adheres to it.

But what a mighty change these two centuries have wrought. The route over which HENNEPIN then traveled was an unknown wilderness. Now it is dotted with populous and busy cities. The Anglo-Saxon, " the dominal blood of the world." with religion as its pillar of cloud by day and fire by night, has wrought this great change. As the Star of Empire lightens the Western sky, it gleams over fruitful valleys and opulent cities. In its track are borne the banners of the Prince of Peace; along its course flourish the Arts and Sciences, while the country blossoms as the rose.

DISCOVERIES SUBSEQUENT TO HENNEPIN.

The discoveries made by HENNEPIN undoubtedly attracted considerable attention to this region, and diligent efforts were made to take formal possession of it in the name of France. In 1689, NICHOLAS PERROT, a French officer, erected a fort on Lake Pepin, and, planting the arms of France on a cross, took formal possession of this region. Other forts were built, and the exploration of the country pushed. LE SUEUR ascended the Minnesota River in the fall of 1700, and established a fort, which he named *L'Heullier*, on the Blue Earth River, near the mouth of the Le Sueur, where there is a deposit of a sort of mineral which he mistook for copper ore.

CESSION OF THE COUNTRY BY FRANCE.

Before much further explorations were made, the "French War," between Canada and the Colonies, ensued, and prevented further progress of settlement in the Northwest for some years. It was not until the Treaty of Versailles, in 1763, by which all of the territory comprised within the limits of Wisconsin and Minnesota, east of the Mississippi, were ceded to Great Britain, that the way seemed opened for further discoveries. It needed only an adventurous spirit to take advantage of the fact, and introduce to the notice of the world the vast empire of the Northwest.

3

CHAPTER III.

JONATHAN CARVER AND HIS EXPLORATIONS.

Some Account of Carver—His Object in making the Journey—His account
of his Adventures—He discovers the "Great Cave"—Makes a Treaty
with the Sioux—And receives a Grant of Land—Subsequent fate of
the purported Land Grant—The Northwestern Territory Organized.

THE man for that work at length arrived.   It was brother
JONATHAN CARVER, a keen Yankee from Connecticut—
not indeed with a stock of wooden nutmegs and cheap clocks.
but with his eye open for a good speculation of any kind.
History must record him as the progenitor and founder of the
noble order of real estate speculators who have flourished here
since, and the first man to originate a "land grant."

SOME ACCOUNT OF CARVER.

JONATHAN CARVER was a grandson of WILLIAM JOSEPH
CARVER, of Wigan, in Lancashire, England, who was a captain in the army under King WILLIAM, and served in the
campaign against Ireland with such distinguished reputation.
that the Prince was pleased to reward him with the government
of the Colony of Connecticut, in New England. JONATHAN was
born in 1732, at the town of Canterbury. Connecticut.   His
father, who was a Justice of the Peace. died when he was 15
years of age.   It was designed to educate him for a physician,
but his spirit of enterprise and adventure could not brook the
close study necessary to acquire the profession, and he chose
the army instead.   He therefore purchased an ensigncy in a
Connecticut regiment, and soon, by good conduct, rose to the
command of a company during the "French War."   In the
year 1757, he was present at the massacre of Fort William
Henry, and narrowly escaped with his life.

CARVER'S OBJECT IN MAKING THE JOURNEY.

Having served through the war with credit and distinction.

.the peace of Versailles, in 1763, left Capt. CARVER without occupation. It was then that CARVER conceived the project of exploring the newly acquired possessions of Great Britain in the Northwest. In the preface to his book he says:

CAPTAIN JONATHAN CARVER.

" No sooner was the late war with France concluded, and peace established by the Treaty of Versailles, in the year 1763, than I began to consider (having rendered my country some service during the war) how I might continue still serviceable, and continue, as much as lay in my power, to make that vast acquisition of territory, gained by Great Britain, in North America, advantageous to it. It appeared to me indispensably needful, that Government should be acquainted, in the first place, with the true state of the dominions they were now become possessed of. To this purpose I determined, as the next proof of my zeal, to explore the most unknown parts of them, and to spare no. trouble or expense in acquiring a knowledge that promised to be so useful to my countrymen. I knew that many obstructions would arise to my scheme from the want of good maps and charts. * * * These difficulties, however, were not sufficient to deter me from the undertaking, and I made preparations for setting out. What I chiefly had in view, after gaining a knowledge of the manners, customs, languages, soil, and productions of the different nations that inhabit the back of the Mississippi, was to ascertain the breadth of that vast continent, which extends from the Atlantic to the Pacific Ocean, in the broadest part between 43 and 46 degrees northern latitude. Had I been able to accomplish this, I intended to have proposed to Government to establish a post in some of those parts about the Straits of Annian, which, having been first discovered by Sir FRANCIS DRAKE, of course belong to the English. This, I am convinced, would greatly facilitate the discovery of a northwest passage, or a communication between Hudson's Bay and the Pacific Ocean; an event so desirable, and which has been so often sought for, but without success. Besides this important end, a settlement on that territory of America would answer many good purposes, and repay every expense the establishment of it might occasion. For it would not only disclose new sources of trade, and promote many useful discoveries, but would open a passage for conveying intelligence to China, and English settlements in the East Indies, with greater expedition than a tedious voyage by the Cape of Good Hope, or the Straits of Magellan, will allow of. That the completion of the scheme I have had the honor of first planning and attempting will sometime or other be effected, I make no doubt. Whenever it is, and the execution of it carried on with propriety, those who are so fortunate as to succeed will reap, exclusive of the national advantages that must ensue, emoluments beyond their most sanguine expectations, and, whilst their spirits are elated by their success, perhaps they may bestow some commendation and blessings on the person that first pointed out to them the way."

HE SETS OUT ON HIS TRAVELS.

CARVER set out on his journey from Boston, in June, 1766. He proceeded to Mackinac, then the most distant British post, arriving in August.

"Having here (he says) made the necessary dispositions for pursuing my travels, and obtained a credit from Mr. ROGERS, the Governor, on some English and Canadian traders who were going to trade on the Mississippi, and received also from him a promise of a fresh supply of goods when I reached the Falls of Saint Anthony, I left the fort on the 3d of September, in company with these traders. It was agreed that they should furnish me with such goods as I might want for presents to the Indian chiefs during my continuance with them, agreeable to the Governor's order."

CARVER pursued the usual route to Green Bay, ascended the

Fox River, made the portage to the Wisconsin, and, descending that stream, entered the Mississippi on October 15. The
traders who were with him loft him at Prairie du Chien, opposite to which village, at "Yellow River." they took up their
quarters. CARVER here "bought a canoe, and, with two servants, one a French Canadian, and the other a Mohawk of
Canada." started up the Mississippi River.

Without giving too much space to CARVER's voyage, we
must now come to his arrival at the present site of Saint Paul.
and his description of

"THE GREAT CAVE,"

(under Dayton's Bluff,) which he thus describes in his work :

"About thirty miles below the Falls of Saint Anthony, at which I
arrived the tenth day after I left Lake Pepin, is a remarkable cave of an
amazing depth. The Indians term it *Wakan-Teebe*, that is, 'The Dwelling of the Great Spirit.' The entrance into it is about ten feet wide.
the height of it five feet. The arch within is near fifteen feet high, and
about thirty feet broad. The bottom of it consists of fine, clear sand.
About twenty feet from the entrance begins a lake, the water of which
is transparent, and extends to an unsearchable distance; for the darkness of the cave prevents all attempts to acquire a knowledge of it. I
threw a small pebble toward the interior parts of it with my utmost
strength; I could hear that it fell into the water, and, notwithstanding
it was of so small a size, it caused an astonishing and horrible noise,
that reverberated through all those gloomy regions. I found in this
cave many Indian hieroglyphics, which appeared very ancient, for time
had nearly covered them with moss, so that it was with difficulty I
could trace them. They were cut in a rude manner upon the inside of
the walls, which were composed of a stone so extremely soft that it
might be easily penetrated with a knife—a stone everywhere to be found
near the Mississippi. The cave is only accessible by ascending a narrow.
steep passage that lies near the brink of the river.

"At a little distance from this dreary cavern, is the burying place of
several bands of the Naudowessie Indians; though these people have
no fixed residence, living in tents, and abiding but a few months on
one spot, yet they always bring the bones of their dead to this place;
which they take the opportunity of doing, when the chiefs meet to hold
their councils, and to settle all public affairs for the ensuing summer."

This was CARVER's first visit to the now celebrated cave.
After leaving it, he proceeded on to Saint Anthony's Falls,
which he minutely describes in his volume of travels, accom-

panying it by a copperplate engraving from a drawing made by himself on November 17, 1766.   He afterwards took a short trip up the Mississippi River, as far as the "Saint Francis River," beyond which point, he says, it had never been explored, and thus far only by Father HENNEPIN and himself.

HIS JOURNEY UP THE SAINT PETER'S RIVER.

On the 25th of November, CARVER returned to his canoe, which he "had left at the mouth of the River Saint Pierre," [Minnesota,] and ascended that stream.   About forty miles from its mouth, he says, he "arrived at a small branch that fell into it from the north," which, as it had no name that he could distinguish it by, he called "Carver's River," which name it bears to this day.

HE WINTERS AMONG THE NAUDOWESSIES.

On the 7th of December he arrived at the most westerly limit of his travels, and, as he could proceed no further that season, spent the winter, a period of seven months, among a band of Naudowessies encamped near what is now New Ulm. He says he learned their language so as to converse in it intelligibly, (though white men who have learned this language declare that to be impossible,) and was treated by them with great hospitality.   In the spring, he returned to the cave.   His account of this is as follows :

THE RETURN TO THE "GREAT CAVE."

"I left the habitations of these hospitable Indians the latter end of April, 1767, but did not part from them for several days, as I was accompanied on my journey by near three hundred of them, among whom were many chiefs, to the mouth of the River Saint Pierre.   At this season these bands annually go to the 'Great Cave,' before mentioned, to hold a grand council with all the other bands, wherein they settle their operations for the ensuing year.   At the same time they carry with them their dead for interment, bound up in buffalo skins."

It was on this visit to the cave that CARVER made the alleged Treaty with the Indians, and received from them the celebrated deed of land.   His account of it is as follows :

"When we arrived at the 'Great Cave,' and the Indians had deposited the remains of their deceased friends in the burial-place that stands adjacent to it, they held their great council, into which I was admitted, and at the same time had the honor to be installed and adopted a chief of their bands. On this occasion I made the following speech which was delivered on the 1st day of May, 1767 :

· CARVER'S SPEECH TO THE INDIANS.

" My brothers, chiefs of the numerous and powerful Naudowessies! I rejoice that, through my long abode with you, I can now speak to you (though after an imperfect manner) in your own tongue, like one of your own children. I rejoice, also, that I have had an opportunity so frequently to inform you of the glory and power of the great King that reigns over the English and other nations; who is descended from a very ancient race of sovereigns, as old as the earth and the waters; whose feet stand upon two great islands, larger than any you have ever seen, amidst the greatest waters in the world; whose head reaches to the sun, and whose arms encircle the whole earth; the number of whose warriors is equal to the trees in the valleys, the stalks of rice in yonder marshes, and the blades of grass on your great plains; who has hundreds of canoes of his own, of such amazing bigness, that all the waters in your country would not suffice for one of them to swim in; each of which have great guns, not small like mine, which you see before you, but of such magnitude, that a hundred of your stoutest young men would with difficulty be able to carry one. And they are equally surprising in their operation against the King's enemies when engaged in battle; the terror they carry with them, your language lacks words to express. You may remember, the other day, when we were encamped at *Wadupaw-menesoter*, the black clouds, the wind, the fire, the stupendous noise, the horrible cracks, and the tumbling of the earth which then alarmed you, and gave you reason to think your gods were angry with you; not unlike these are the warlike implements of the English when they are fighting the battles of their great King.

" Several of the chiefs of your bands have often told me in times past, when I dwelt with you in your tents, that they much wished to be counted among the children and the allies of the great King, my master.

" You may remember how often you have desired me, when I return again to my own country, to acquaint the great King of your good disposition toward him and his subjects, and that you wished for traders from the English to come among you.

" Being now about to take my leave of you, and to return to my own country, a long way toward the rising sun, I again ask you to tell me whether you continue of the same mind as when I spoke to you in council last winter; and as there are now several of your chiefs here who came from the great plains toward the setting of the sun, whom I have nevèr spoken with in council before, I ask you to let me know if you are willing to acknowledge yourselves the children of my great master, the King of the English.

"I charge you not to give heed to bad reports, for there are wicked birds flying about among the neighboring nations, who may whisper evil things in your ears against the English, contrary to what I have told you; you must not believe them, for I have told you the truth.

"As for the chiefs that are about to go to Michilimackinac, I shall take care to make for them and their suits a straight road, smooth waters, and a clear sky, that they may go there and smoke the pipe of peace, and rest secure on a beaver blanket under the shade of the great tree of peace. Farewell!"

Whether any such grandiloquent speech as the above was really made by CARVER on the occasion or not, has frequently been doubted. It is probable, however, that he made them a short address, in such imperfect Dakota as he could command.

To this speech CARVER gives the reply of the principal chief, speaking, as the orator asserted, for the eight bands of the nation. He professed to believe CARVER's account of the King and his power, and desired CARVER to tell him that they "wished to be counted among his good children," and have traders sent among them.

THE PURPORTED DEED.

At this council was given the famous deed of land to CARVER, which reads as follows:

"To JONATHAN CARVER, a chief under the most mighty and potent GEORGE the Third, King of the English, and other nations, the fame of whose warriors has reached our ears, and has been now fully told to us by our *good brother* JONATHAN, aforesaid, whom we rejoice to see come among us, and bring us good news from his country.

"We, chiefs of the Naudowessies, who have hereto set our seals, do by these presents, for ourselves and heirs forever, in return for the many presents and other good services done by the said JONATHAN to ourselves and allies, give, grant and convey to him, the said JONATHAN, and to his heirs and assigns forever, the whole of a certain tract or territory of land, bounded as follows, viz.: From the Falls of Saint Anthony, running on the east bank of the Mississippi, nearly southeast, as far as the south end of Lake Pepin, where the Chippewa River joins the Mississippi, and from thence eastward, five days' travel, accounting twenty English miles per day, and from thence north six days' travel, at twenty English miles per day, and from thence again to the Falls of

Saint Anthony, on a direct straight line. We do, for ourselves, heirs, and assigns, forever, give unto the said JONATHAN, his heirs and assigns, forever, all the said lands, with all the trees, rocks, and rivers therein, reserving the sole liberty of hunting and fishing on land not planted or improved by the said JONATHAN, his heirs and assigns, to which we have affixed our respective seals.

> " At the 'Great Cave,'
> " May 1st, one thousand seven hundred and sixty-seven.
> " HAW-NO-PAW-GAT-AN, his ⋉ mark,
> (picture of a beaver.)
> " OTOH-TON-GOOM-LISH-EAW, his ⋉ mark,
> (picture of a snake.)"

It is a somewhat singular fact that CARVER nowhere mentions this deed in his writings. Why its existence was suppressed by him, can only be conjectured. It seems not to have been made public until after his death. JOHN COAKLEY LETT-SOM, who wrote the biography of CARVER for the third edition of his travels, says he (LETTSOM) had the original deed in his possession.

CARVER, after making the purported treaty with the Indians, returned to Prairie du Chien, and thence proceeded to Lake Superior, and spent some time in exploring that region, returning to Boston by way of Sault Ste. Marie, Detroit, and Niagara Falls. He arrived in Boston in October, 1768, "having been absent from it on this expedition two years and five months, and during that time traveled near 7,000 miles."

CARVER'S SUBSEQUENT HISTORY.

He soon after sailed for England, made known his discoveries, and claimed a reimbursement from Government. His petition was referred to the " Lords Commissioners of Trade and Plantations." They required him to surrender up the manuscript of a book he had nearly ready for the press, for which, with his other expenses, they allowed no reimbursement. He finally re-wrote his work from his original journals and papers, and it was published in 1769.

It is hardly possible that he realized much money from his book, as we hear of him a few months after this, in very indigent circumstances. His health also declined. In 1779, he secured a position as clerk in a lottery office, from the gains of which he eked out a scanty subsistence for a few months. Disease soon ensued, however, and he actually died of want in London, January 31, 1780, aged 48 years.

SUBSEQUENT HISTORY OF THE PURPORTED DEED.

CARVER, as we before mentioned, does not speak in his work of the deed said to have been given May 1, 1767. It was not until after his death that it was brought to light. CARVER had married during his sojourn in England, (although he had a wife and five daughters in Connecticut at the time,) and by this second wife had one daughter, named MARTHA. She was raised by Sir RICHARD and Lady PEARSON. When she grew up, she eloped with, and married a sailor, whose name seems to be now unknown. A mercantile firm in London, thinking that money could be made by securing the title to the alleged grant, secured from the penniless couple, a few days after their marriage, a conveyance of the grant to them, for the consideration of one-tenth the profits. The merchants dispatched an agent named CLARK to go to the Dakotas, and obtain a new deed, but on the way CLARK was murdered in New York, and the speculation for the time fell through.

In the year 1794, the heirs of CARVER's American wife, in consideration of £50,000, conveyed their interest in the Carver Grant to EDWARD HOUGHTON, of Vermont. In the year 1806, Rev. SAMUEL PETERS, who had been a Tory during the Revolutionary war, alleged, in a petition to Congress, that he had also purchased of the heirs of CARVER their right to the grant.

In 1821, Gen. LEAVENWORTH, pursuant to a request of the Commissioner of the Land Office, inquired of the Dakotas in relation to the grant, and reported that the land alleged to be granted " lies on the east side of the Mississippi." The Indians do not recognize or acknowledge the grant to be valid, and they, among others, assign the following reasons :

" 1. The Sioux of the Plains never owned a foot of land on the East side of the Mississippi.   *   *   *   *   *   *
" 2. The Indians say they have no knowledge of any such chiefs, as those who signed the grant. They say if Capt. CARVER did ever obtain a deed or grant, it was signed by some foolish young men who

were not chiefs, and who were not authorized to make a grant. Among the Sioux of the River there are no such names.*

"3. They say the Indians never received anything for the land, and they have no intention to part with it without a consideration. * *

"4. They have, and ever have had, the possession of the land, and intend to keep it." * * * * * * *

On January 23, 1823, the Committee on Public Lands reported to the Senate on the claim of CARVER's heirs, at some length. They argue that the purported grant has no binding effect on the United States, and give very satisfactory and conclusive reasons therefor—at too great length, however, to include in this paper. The prayer of the petitioners was, therefore, not granted.

It is certain that CARVER's American heirs always supposed, (and are said to this day to assert,) that they had a good title to the grant in question. Some of them have visited Saint Paul in their investigations of the subject.

Numerous deeds for portions of the land were made at various times by CARVER's heirs or their assignees. In 1849, and a few years subsequent, when real estate agents throve in the infant city of Saint Paul, very many of these deeds were received by land dealers here, to " locate." Several of them are among the MSS. in the Library of the Historical Society.

SUBSEQUENT HISTORY OF THE CAVE.

After the visit by CARVER, the cave remained unentered by the white man for nearly half a century. PIKE tried in vain to find it in 1806, but its entrance was stopped up. Maj. LONG succeeded in gaining an entrance to it in 1817. FEATHER-STONHAUGH, in 1835, found the entrance again closed up with debris. NICOLLET explored it in 1837, however, and says CARVER's description of it was " accurate." Indeed, it is so accurate, that, at the present day, if one wished to describe it, he could do no better than use CARVER's own language.

---

* CARVER only once, in the body of his work, mentions the chiefs whose signatures and "family coat of arms" are appended to the deed. On page 380, speaking of Indian nomenclature, he says: Thus, the great warrior of the Naudowessies was named, *Ottahtongoomliskeah*, that is, "The Great Father of Snakes;" *ottah*, being in English, father; *tongoom*, great; and *liskeah*, a snake. Another chief was called *Honahpawjatin*, which means, "A Swift Runner Over the Mountains."

Carver's Cave is now the most interesting relic of antiquity in this region. Unfortunately, the spirit of progress and improvement has no veneration for historical associations, and the Saint Paul and Chicago Railroad, which runs along the bank of the river directly by the mouth of the cave, will doubtless ere long dig down the bluff, and thus destroy the cave. The centenary of CARVER's treaty with the Naudowessies was duly observed on May 1, 1867, by the members of the Minnesota Historical Society. They paid a visit to the cave in the daytime, and held a reunion in memory of CARVER at their rooms in the evening. The proceedings were printed in pamphlet form, subsequently, at the expense of GEO. W. FAHNESTOCK, of Philadelphia, an estimable gentleman of historical tastes, (now deceased,) who was present.

CARVER'S PROPHESIES CONCERNING THIS REGION.

CARVER was a man of keen perceptions and shrewd foresight. He hints in his work at the possibility of a ship canal from the Mississippi River to the Lakes, and was sanguine that this region would ultimately become populous and wealthy. He says:

"To what power or authority this new world will become dependant, after it has arisen from its present uncultivated state, time alone can discover. But as the seat of empire, from time immemorial, has been gradually progressing toward the west, there is no doubt but that at some future period, *mighty kingdoms will emerge from these wildernesses, and stately palaces and solemn temples, with gilded spires reaching the skies, supplant the Indian huts, whose only decorations are the barbarous trophies of their vanquished enemies.*"

Already events were transpiring, which led to a more rapid fulfillment of his vision, than perhaps he himself even anticipated. The disputes between the Colonies and England were fast culminating in open rebellion. While CARVER was absent in England, the

REVOLUTIONARY WAR

broke out, and all progress toward the settlement of this region was stayed for the time. The war virtually terminated in 1782, and, by the Treaty of Paris, 1783, the territory east of the Mississippi River was ceded and yielded up to the United States, which now took its place among the nations of the earth. On March 1, 1784, Virginia, which claimed what was afterwards known as the Northwest Territory, ceded all that district to the United States, and, three years later, the famous "Ordinance of 1787" was enacted by Congress, creating the "Northwest Territory."

THE NORTHWEST TERRITORY.

This vast domain, comprising the present noble States of Ohio, Indiana, Illinois, Michigan, Wisconsin, and Minnesota east of the Mississippi, was probably the finest body of land, of equal extent, on the globe. At that time there were scarcely a dozen settlements of whites in the whole domain. Its present population must be over 10,000,000. Wonderful has been the transformation of this great empire from barbarism to civilization, and in the brief space of 88 years. It has scarcely, if at all, a parallel in the world's history.

Civil government was soon after established over the Territory, and it began rapidly to settle up. On May 7, 1800, Indiana Territory was created, embracing all of the previous Northwest Territory except the present State of Ohio, and, in 1805, Michigan Territory was formed, whose southern boundary ran from the Maumee Bay, on Lake Erie, westerly to the Mississippi River. Minnesota (east of the Mississippi) remained attached to Michigan until the formation of Illinois Territory in 1809, when it was included in the bounds of the latter, and so continued until 1819, when Illinois became a State. This region then fell again into the arms of Michigan Territory, and continued there until Wisconsin Territory was formed in 1836.

CHAPTER IV.

THE FIRST SETTLEMENT OF MINNESOTA.

EXPLORATION BY LIEUT. PIKE—HE SELECTS THE SITE FOR FORT SNELLING—RED
RIVER COLONY FOUNDED—TROOPS ORDERED TO "SAINT PETER'S"—THEY BUILD
FORT SNELLING—JOSEPH R. BROWN—RED RIVER REFUGEES SETTLE HERE—
ARRIVAL OF FIRST STEAMBOAT—EARLY MAIL SERVICE — GOVERNMENTAL
CHANGES—SKETCHES OF TWO PIONEERS, II. II. SIBLEY AND N. W. KITTSON.

THAT portion of Minnesota west of the Mississippi, as
mentioned before, had, by the "Louisiana Purchase,"
(December 20, 1803,) come into the possession of the United
States, and President JEFFERSON took prompt steps to extend
the authority of the United States over the domain acquired,
and to make an exploration of the same. Lieut. Z. M. PIKE,
U. S. A., was the officer selected to visit this region, expel the
British traders, and make alliances with the Indians. He
ascended the Mississippi River in a batteau in the month of
September, 1805, and arrived at the encampment of J. B.
FARIBAULT, an Indian trader, a mile or two above Saint Paul,
on September 21. On the 23d he held a council with the
Sioux at Mendota, and obtained from them a grant of land nine
miles square, for military purposes, which has since been known
as the Fort Snelling Reservation. Lieut. PIKE remained all
winter in Minnesota, and returned to Saint Louis in the spring.

THE RED RIVER SETTLEMENT.

In the year 1812, the Earl of SELKIRK, having obtained a
grant of land from the Hudson Bay Company, near the confluence of the Assiniboine and Red Rivers, established a colony
of Scotch settlers upon it, and subsequently a colony of Swiss
were induced to settle there. The colony suffered various
hardships for many years, from floods, frosts, grasshoppers,
&c., and were at times almost on the verge of starvation. In
1827, a party of the Swiss who had immigrated to Red River,

abandoned the colony, and established themselves near Fort Snelling, as will be noticed more fully a little further on.

The cession of land procured by Lieut. PIKE at the confluence of the Saint Peter's and Mississippi Rivers, in 1805, had been for the purpose of erecting a United States Fort. The matter was allowed to rest, however, for some years. The planting of SELKIRK's Colony on the borders of the United States, called attention to it again, and resulted, in 1819, in the establishment of a military post at the point named.

TROOPS ORDERED TO MINNESOTA.

On February 10, 1819, an order was issued by the War Department, concentrating the Fifth Regiment of Infantry at Detroit, under Lieut. Col. LEAVENWORTH, with a view of proceeding west. Portions were detailed to garrison Prairie du Chien and Rock Island, and the remainder were to proceed to establish a post at the point called "Saint Peter's," (since known as Mendota,) which was to be the headquarters of the regiment, and of Lieut. Col. LEAVENWORTH, its commander. He remained some time at Prairie du Chien, to organize "Crawford County," which had been created by the Legislature of Michigan Territory, on October 16, 1818. Its boundaries were as follows: On the east by a line running north and south from the portage of the Fox and Wisconsin Rivers, and extending to Lake Superior, thence westward to the Mississippi River.

He found great difficulty in securing enough persons qualified to fill the county offices.

The expedition up the Mississippi was made in keel-boats, and so low was the water that the party did not reach Mendota until September 24th. Rude huts for barracks were at once erected, in which the first winter was passed amid much discomfort. Many of the soldiers died from scurvy. The following August, Col. SNELLING took command of the post, and the erection of "Fort Saint Anthony" was commenced. On September 10th, 1820, the corner stone was laid with appropriate ceremonies, but the next winter had to be passed in their cantonments at Mendota again. The lumber for the buildings was cut on Rum River by the soldiers. The fort was not so far completed as to be occupied until the fall of 1822. It was, by recommendation of Gen. SCOTT, subsequently called "Fort Snelling," in honor of its builder.

MAJ. LAWRENCE TALIAFERRO.

In order to properly conduct relations with the Indians of this region, President MONROE also resolved to send hither an Indian Agent, to permanently reside at or near the new military post. Lieut. LAWRENCE TALIAFERRO,* an officer of the regular army, was selected for this duty, and commissioned on March 27, 1819. He proceeded at once to his post, and continued to fill that office for twenty years, resigning it in 1840.

CONDITION OF THE COUNTRY IN 1820.

The establishment of Fort Snelling (as it was *afterwards* known) attracted considerable attention to this region, and was an important event for the Northwest. Up to that time this region was almost unknown. A few traders had penetrated here and there through what is now Minnesota, but its geography was to the country at large a sealed book. Its great lumbering resources were almost unknown. It was not until 1822 that the Government saw mill was built at Saint Anthony Falls. The same year a permit was granted by Maj. TALIAFERRO to a man named PERKINS, from Kentucky, to erect a saw mill on one of the branches of the Menominee River, Wisconsin—the first mill erected by private parties in the Northwest. Indeed, only in 1822 was Minnehaha Creek—now in one of the most thickly settled parts of the State—explored by JOSEPH R. BROWN, then a soldier at Fort Snelling, and was long afterwards called by his name.

---

* LAWRENCE TALIAFERRO was born in Virginia, February 24, 1794. His ancestors were Italians, who settled in Virginia in 1637. TALIAFERRO enlisted in the war of 1812, when only 18 years of age, and rose to the rank of Lieutenant. When the army was reduced to a peace footing at the close of the war, he was retained as a First Lieutenant. On retiring from the Indian Agency, in 1840, he returned to his home at Bedford, Pennsylvania, where, in 1857, he was appointed Military Storekeeper, and filled that post until 1863. He died January 22, 1871, in his 81st year. While at Fort Snelling he kept à minute diary of events, now in possession of the Historical Society, and from which the writer has drawn valuable facts.

JOSEPH R. BROWN.

first frame, and first stone building in Minnesota. He assisted in staking out the first road from Fort Snelling to Prairie du Chien ; driving the first wagon over it, and the first from Mendota to Lac qui Parle. He built the first house in the present limits of Stillwater and Hastings, &c., &c. During his long and eventful life he suffered many reverses of fortune, but was always cheerful and full of energy. He died in New York City, whither he had gone on business, on November 9, 1870. Brown county was appropriately named in honor of him.

IMMIGRATION FROM RED RIVER.

Prior to the year 1827, there was no agriculture carried on in the entire State, except small gardens and limited fields attached to the trading posts here and there. In the year named, a number of Swiss families—who had been, several years previous, misled by the lying emigration agents of Lord SELKIRK into settling on the Red River—after suffering great hardships, were finally compelled, to avoid actual starvation, to leave the colony and come to Fort Snelling, where, it had been stated to them, they would be allowed to settle. They were kindly received by Col. SNELLING, the commander of the post, and permission given them to settle on the Reservation, near what was afterwards known as the "Saint Louis House," on the west side of the Mississippi, a little above the fort. Here they opened farms, erected dwellings, and, having brought cattle with them, soon became prosperous and comfortable farmers. In this colony were ABRAHAM PERRY, LOUIS MASSIE, and other patriarchs, some of whom, as will be seen a little further on, were among the earliest settlers of Saint Paul, Pig's Eye, Little Canada, Mendota, Saint Anthony, Stillwater, and other of the oldest towns in this region. Up to 1836, nearly 500 persons had left the Red River Colony and came to Fort Snelling, in search of new homes, and several large parties came subsequently. A few of them went on to Wisconsin, Illinois and Missouri, and some to Vevay, Indiana, (a Swiss settlement,) but most of the refugees settled in this region, and their descendants hereabouts are a numerous class. Most of the early residents of Saint Paul were Red River refugees, as we shall show a few pages further on.

Thus the first agricultural immigrants into Minnesota—the vanguard of that vast army that in later years poured over it—came from the " frozen north"—a sort of Nor' man invasion of a peaceful kind.

ARRIVAL OF THE FIRST STEAMBOAT.

During the year 1823, another event occurred of great importance to the Northwest. It was the arrival of the first steamboat, the " Virginia," from Saint Louis, loaded with stores for the fort. Her dimensions were: length, 118 feet; width, 24 feet; and draught, six feet. She was four days in getting over the Rock Island Rapids, an obstacle which it had been supposed would always prevent steamers from navigating the Upper Mississippi. As this was the first steamboat ever seen by the Dakotas in this neighborhood, their fright was extreme. They mistook it for some supernatural *monster*, and fled to the woods and hills, with their hair and blankets streaming in the breeze.

The success of the " Virginia" in reaching the mouth of the Saint Peter's, opened the Upper Mississippi to steam navigation, the mightiest agent in making the then wilderness blossom as the rose. Up to May 26, 1826, fifteen steamers had arrived at Fort Snelling, and they became more frequent after that.

SIOUX AND OJIBWA WARFARE.

The ancient feud of the Dakota and Ojibwa Nations, led to frequent encounters, some of them in this neighborhood. In 1826, a party of 200 or 300 Ojibwas, from the Upper Mississippi, came to Fort Snelling on a visit, and encamped near Pickerel Lake, across the river from this city. The Dakotas, learning of their presence, soon rallied and attacked them, killing in cold blood a number of women and children, who could not escape. The same autumn, at Fort Snelling, a party of Dakotas, after being hospitably entertained by some Ojibwas encamped there, and promising peace and good will, treacherously fired into the wigwams of the latter at night, killing several. Col. Snelling, the commandant, compelled the Dakotas to surrender the guilty men, and they were handed

over to the relations of the murdered Ojibwas for punishment.
Four of them were compelled to "run the gauntlet," i. e.,
allowed a few feet start, and, at a given signal, the Ojibwas
were to fire on them. They were in this manner shot down,
and their bodies mutilated.

These barbaric orgies were repeated from year to year, for
some time. The liquor sold to the Indians by traders was
mostly the cause of this, and every effort was made by the
authorities to break up the traffic, without success.

MAIL SERVICE—1820–49.

During the first three years, the mails for the garrison were
carried by soldiers, from Prairie du Chien. In the summer they
made the trips two or three times during the season, with keel-
boats or canoes, also bringing supplies for the garrison. In
the winter the trip was one of hardship and danger, occupying
many days. The whole distance to Prairie du Chien was
generally traversed on the ice, in a sort of sledge drawn by
dogs or a Canadian pony, and called a *train du glace*. Excepting probably an encampment or two of Indians, there was
no sign of a human habitation from Fort Snelling to Fort
Crawford, (Prairie du Chien,) and during the trip the mail
carriers and their animals must subsist as best they could. This
sort of winter transportation was kept up until stage service
was established in 1849. In May, 1823, the first steamboat
arrived at Fort Snelling, and thenceforward steamboats carried
the mails generally to that post, until a regular packet line
was established to Saint Paul, in 1847.

Of course, winter service in those days was irregular. For
instance, in one of TALIAFERRO's journals, kept at Fort Snelling,
now in the archives of the Historical Society, we find it noted
that on January 26th, 1826, there was much rejoicing over the
arrival of two officers "from below," who had returned from
a furlough, *bringing the first mail received for five months!*
In May, 1832, a soldier at Fort Crawford, named JAMES
HALPIN, was detailed by Col. ZACHARY TAYLOR, then commander of that post, to carry the mail from Fort Crawford to
Fort Snelling. A small pouch of mail was all there was to

carry, and he made the journey on foot, the round trip occupying generally two weeks. He carried the mail a whole year. There was not a human habitation on his whole route, unless he fell in with a teepee of Indians.

GOVERNMENTAL CHANGES.

In 1836, the Territory of Wisconsin was organized, comprising all of Michigan Territory west of the Lake. This, of course, included what is now Minnesota east of the Mississippi. Saint Paul, or what is now Saint Paul, thus fell in the jurisdiction of Crawford county, Wisconsin—an extended existence of Crawford county, Michigan. For several years it was represented in the Territorial Legislature of Wisconsin as follows:

	Council.	*House.*
1836	No member.	James H. Lockwood, James B. Dallam.
1837-8	No member.	Ira B. Brunson, Jean Brunet.
1838	George Wilson.	Alex. McGregor.
1839	George Wilson.	Alex. McGregor, Ira B. Brunson.
1839-40	Joseph Brisbois.	Alex. McGregor, Ira B. Brunson.
1840 (extra)	Chas. J. Learned.	Alex. McGregor, Ira B. Brunson.

In January, 1840, " Saint Croix County," as will be noticed a little further on, was created by the Legislature, out of Crawford county. It comprised all that territory west of a line running northward from the mouth of Porcupine River, on Lake Pepin, to Lake Superior. Most of the representatives subsequently lived in what is now Minnesota :

	Council.	*House.*
1840-1	Charles J. Learned.	Theophilus La Chapelle, Joseph R. Brown.
1841-2	Charles J. Learned.	Theophilus La Chapelle, Joseph R. Brown.
1842-3	Theophilus La Chapelle.	John H. Manahan.
1843-4	Theophilus La Chapelle.	John H. Manahan.
1845	Wiram Knowlton.	James Fisher.
1846	Wiram Knowlton.	James Fisher.
1847	B. F. Manahan.	Joseph W. Furber.
1847 (ext.)	B. F. Manahan.	Henry Jackson.
1848	B. F. Manahan.	Henry Jackson.

ESTABLISHMENT OF MISSIONS.

The various missions among the Chippewas and Sioux of Minnesota, were established during the period from 1830 to 1840. EDMUND F. ELY, (now of Santa Barbara, California,) and Rev. WM. R. BOUTWELL came in 1833 ; Revs. S. W. and G. II. POND in 1834 ; Revs. THOS. S. WILLIAMSON and J. D. STEVENS in 1835 ; Revs. S. R. RIGGS, ALFRED BRUNSON and DAVID KING in 1837 ; and Rev. S. SPATES in 1839. &c. More than half of the above band of self-sacrificing men are still residents of our State.

THE "PECULIAR INSTITUTION" IN MINNESOTA.

Connected with the operations of the missions in this locality, is a fact so curious that it deserves insertion here. During the early days of Fort Snelling, some of the officers were owners of slaves, whom they kept as their body or household servants. "DRED SCOTT," who afterwards became historical, owing to the decision of the Supreme Court of the United States—generally known as "the Dred Scott Decision"—was a slave of Surgeon EMERSON, at Fort Snelling, about this date, and married a negro woman belonging to Maj. TALIAFERRO, while at the fort. When Rev. Mr. BRUNSON established his mission at Kaposia, in 1837, he found himself unable to do much owing to his entire ignorance of the Indian tongue, and at once set about finding an interpreter. The only one he could secure was a young negro named JAMES THOMPSON, owned by an officer at Fort Snelling, and who was willing to sell him for $1,200. "JIM" talked Sioux first rate, and was religiously inclined, so that Father BRUNSON concluded to buy him if he could be secured. He accordingly wrote to some friends at Cincinnati the circumstances, and the amount necessary was soon raised and forwarded to him. "JIM" was purchased, his "free papers" secured, and he was soon interpreting the gospel to the pagans at Kaposia. Mr. THOMPSON now lives in St. Paul. This is, so far as has been recorded, the only sale of a slave which ever took place in what is now Minnesota.

Father BRUNSON yet resides in Prairie du Chien—a hale,

active pioneer of 83, and preached in Saint Paul during the past autumn.

THE PROGRESS OF SETTLEMENT.

During the period—or decade—from 1830 to 1840, there set-tled in what is now Minnesota, some of our oldest pioneers—names now honored and widely known. NORMAN W. KITT-SON came in 1832; HENRY H. SIBLEY in 1834; WILLIAM H. FORBES, MARTIN McLEOD and FRANKLIN STEELE in 1837; HENRY M. RICE and WILLIAM HOLCOMBE in 1839, &c. The Lake Superior region was early settled by WILLIAM A. AIT-KIN, the MORRISONS, and others. CHARLES H. OAKES lo-cated there in 1825, and Dr. CHARLES W. BORUP in 1831, both these gentlemen becoming residents of our city in a sub-sequent year.

During these years, this region was likewise visited by sev-eral distinguished savans and travelers—FEATHERSTONHAUGH, SCHOOLCRAFT, MATHER, NICOLLET, FREMONT, CASS, CAT-LIN, and others. Their published accounts aided in making the Upper Mississippi region better known, and undoubtedly tended to hasten the treaties which extinguished the Indian title to portions of the present State.

Sketches of three of the pioneers of this period are appended to this chapter, and another (Hon. H. M. RICE) will be found in Chapter XV.

NORMAN WOLFRED KITTSON

was born at Sorel, Lower Canada, March 5, 1814. He is a grandson of ALEXANDER HENRY, the celebrated explorer and traveler, who journeyed through the Lake Superior, Manitoba and Saskatchewan districts as early as 1776, and whose pub-lished travels are very scarce and valuable. In May, 1830, being then only 16 years of age, Mr. KITTSON engaged as an employee of the American Fur Company, and in that capacity came to the Northwest. From the summer of 1830 to 1832, he was stationed at the trading post between the Fox and Wis-consin Rivers. During the latter year, he was sent to the headwaters of the Minnesota, and from thence went to the Red Cedar River, in Iowa.

In 1834, he came to Fort Snelling, where he was engaged in the sutler department until 1838, in the fall of which year he returned to Canada, and remained until spring. On his return, (1839,) he began business on his own account, as a fur-trader, near what was then called " Cold Spring," just above Fort Snelling. He continued here until 1843, when he entered the American Fur Company, as special partner, having charge of all the business on the headwaters of the Minnesota, and along the British line. During that year he fixed his headquarters at Pembina, and commenced collecting furs there and shipping them in Red River carts to Mendota. This was the origin of a very large trade between Saint Paul and the Red River settlement, a few years later, which will be found more fully dwelt on in a subsequent chapter.

In 1854, Mr. KITTSON entered into partnership with the late WILLIAM H. FORBES, in St. Paul, in the general Indian trade supply business. Their establishment, called " The Saint Paul Outfit," was widely known at that time. This year, Mr. KITTSON came to reside at Saint Paul permanently, although it might almost be said that his residence dates back to 1843, as he had owned property here since that day, and was here a considerable share of his time. In 1843, as will be found more fully narrated under that year, Mr. KITTSON, purchased a claim which eventually proved very valuable, and was, in 1851, laid out as " Kittson's Addition," now one of the handsomest portions of our city.

In 1851, Mr. KITTSON was elected a member of the Council of the Minnesota Legislature from the Pembina District, and re-elected in 1853, serving four sessions in all, viz.: 1852, 1853, 1854, 1855, in which he took a prominent and useful part. In order to attend these sessions, in mid-winter, Mr. KITTSON was compelled to walk on snow-shoes the whole distance, or ride in a dog-sledge—a trip of great hardship, exposure and danger. Two of these trips, at least, he made on snow-shoes. Some account of these winter journeys will be found in the proper place.

NORMAN W. KITTSON.

In 1858, Mr. KITTSON was elected Mayor of Saint Paul, since which time he has not been in public life.

During that year, the firm of FORBES & KITTSON was dissolved. Mr. KITTSON continued his Red River trade until 1860. He soon after accepted the position of Agent of the Hudson's Bay Company, and established a line of steamers and barges on the Red River, which has grown into quite a corporation, now called the "Red River Transportation Company," with headquarters in Saint Paul, and operating several steamers and barges.

Mr. KITTSON is the oldest living pioneer of our State, with but one exception. In his 43 years' residence he has witnessed and taken part in changes which fall to the lot of but few men during an ordinary lifetime. Although over 60 years of age, Mr. KITTSON is as active, strong, and elastic in body as most young men of our day, and is constantly absorbed in an exacting and harassing business. He enjoys the esteem of a wide multitude of friends, who hope that far distant may be the day when, at one of our "Old Settler" reunions, the name of NORMAN W. KITTSON will be added to the list of those who have left us.

HENRY HASTINGS SIBLEY.

Every new community, and, to a great extent, every new State, receives from its first pioneers and prominent organizers, the impress which decides much of its future tone and spirit. Hence, the value of having society in every new State *started* in the right direction by men who can mold the "plastic elements" for good. Minnesota was peculiarly fortunate in having for its leading pioneers men of broad views, liberal culture and elevated character. and the effect of their influence is plainly traceable in the future successful course of our State, and the good name it bears abroad as a commonwealth, where education and religion are universal, and law and order are respected. How much of this we owe to the men who, with no selfish ends, but, actuated only by devotion to principle and the public welfare, and an unfaltering trust in the triumph of right, laid the foundations of our State, created its institutions, framed

its first laws, executed its first offices, and gave the first bent
to its usages—we can now scarcely estimate. Posterity must
indeed point to their names with gratitude and honor, far exceeding even that evinced by those of the present generation,
because to these the events (in some of which they may have
participated) are too recent and perhaps too much colored with
the passions or prejudices that are inseparable from our human
organization, to place an impartial estimate on motives, and
actions, and results. By such a rule as the above, the name
which heads this sketch, is one that must always occupy a
foremost place in the history of our State.

HENRY H. SIBLEY was born at Detroit, Michigan, February
20, 1811. His father, Judge SOLOMON SIBLEY, a native of
Massachusetts, was one of the most prominent pioneers of the
Northwest, settling in Ohio in 1795, and in Michigan in 1797,
from which he was a member of the first Legislature of the
"Northwest Territory" in 1799 ; a delegate to Congress in 1820 :
Judge of the Supreme Court from 1824 to 1836 : United States
District Attorney, &c. He died in 1846, universally lamented.
Judge SIBLEY married at Marietta, Ohio, in 1802. Miss SARAH
W. SPROAT, daughter of Col. EBENEZER SPROAT, a distinguished officer of the Revolution, and grand-daughter of Com-
modore ABRAHAM WHIPPLE, of the Revolutionary Navy. Her
parents and grand-parents were all pioneers of Ohio, so that
the subject of this sketch was, by ancestral influence, predisposed
to such a life of pioneer adventure as he was destined to lead.
Mrs. SIBLEY died at Detroit, January 22, 1851. Mrs. ELLET,
in her work, "Pioneer Women of the West," remarks that she
was a woman of unusual personal beauty, and rare mental
accomplishments.

II. H. SIBLEY received an academical education when young,
and subsequently enjoyed two years' private tuition in the
classics, from Rev. R. F. CADLE, one of the pioneers of education in the Northwest. His father had wished him to adopt
his own profession, but, after studying law sometime, he became convinced that his natural inclination would lead him to
more active and stirring life. His father very sensibly told him
to pursue his own inclinations in this respect—"a decision,"

H. H. Sibley

said a writer, referring to the fact, " that gave to Minnesota her honored pioneer—one whose history is so interwoven with her own that to write the one is almost *ipso facto* to record the other."

About the age of 17, young SIBLEY went to Sault Ste. Marie, and was engaged there in mercantile operations for about a year. In 1829, he went to Mackinac, and entered the service of the American Fur Company as clerk. He remained at that post five years. In 1834, Mr. SIBLEY, then 23 years of age, was admitted as a partner in the American Fur Company, of which RAMSEY CROOKS, father of Col. WILLIAM CROOKS, of this city, was President, and the late H. L. DOUSMAN and Joseph ROLETTE, Senior, of Prairie du Chien, were also partners, and was to have charge of the trade above Lake Pepin, as far as the British line, with headquarters at Mendota, then called " Saint Peter's." Gen. SIBLEY himself says this step was largely owing to H. L. DOUSMAN's solicitation, and to the glowing accounts he gave of Minnesota as a land of game, perhaps knowing Gen. S.'s fondness for field sports.

Mr. SIBLEY arrived at Mendota, November 7, 1834, having rode on horseback from Prairie du Chien, a distance of nearly 300 miles, there being but one human habitation on the way. Then, in all the region now known as Minnesota, there was, excepting the garrison at Fort Snelling, only a handful of white men, mostly fur-traders and Canadian voyageurs. What mighty changes these forty-one years have witnessed. Gen. SIBLEY is now the oldest living settler, save one, in our population of 600,000 people, and it has been his fortune to take a more active and prominent part in the history of that period, than any other living man.

On May 2, 1843, he was united in marriage to Miss SARAH J. STEELE, at Fort Snelling. He had previously, in 1836, erected, at Mendota, the first private dwelling built of stone, in Minnesota, which is still standing. Mrs. SIBLEY died May 21, 1869—being truly one of the pioneer women of our State, and a lady of rare virtues and accomplishments.

Mr. SIBLEY was probably the first civil officer in what is now Minnesota, having been appointed a Justice of the Peace

in 1838, by Gov. JOHN CHAMBERS, of Iowa, which then embraced the territory west of the Mississippi. This is more
fully spoken of elsewhere.

On October 30, 1848, Mr. SIBLEY was elected a Delegate to
Congress from what was then considered as Wisconsin Territory—the residue of the old territory of that name, after carving
the State out of it—with the understanding that he would urge
the organization of Minnesota Territory. It was a trust of
much delicacy and responsibility, for a failure would have been
very discouraging and unfortunate at that juncture, when success was so vital to the interests of the people. He proceeded
to Washington, and, after much effort, was admitted to a seat.
During the session, he was enabled, by hard work and personal
influence, to procure the passage of a bill to organize the Territory of Minnesota. In the fall of 1849, he was again elected
for two years, and re-elected in 1850, serving over four years
in all.

This was a very difficult and trying period for any one to
represent a new Territory like Minnesota, whose needs were
large, and yet with little population, and believed to be, as one
member of Congress declared, "a hyperborean region," unfit
for settlement. Mr. SIBLEY soon exploded that prejudice by
well-written articles for the press, on the climate, advantages
and resources of Minnesota. There were large appropriations
needed for various purposes, and these could be secured only
by persuasive appeals to the members, by tact and vigilance,
and patient urging, so that Mr. SIBLEY was enabled to secure
for the Territory more generous appropriations and liberal
legislation than could have been obtained by any one possessing
less of the esteem and respect of his fellow members, since
nearly everything was secured by personal influence.

In 1855, Mr. SIBLEY was elected a member of the Minnesota
Legislature from Dakota county, and, in 1857, served as a member, and President of the "Democratic wing" of the Constitutional Convention. In the fall of the same year, he was
elected first Governor of the State. Owing to the delay in the
admission of Minnesota, he was not inaugurated until May 24,
1858. His term expired January 1, 1860.

On August 19, 1862, he was appointed by Gov. RAMSEY commander of the military forces sent to quell the· Sioux out- break. He at once took active measures to meet and defeat the Indians, and release the captives, 250 in number, which they held, in both of which designs his tact and intimate knowl- edge of Indian character and mode of warfare, enabled him fully to succeed—also taking about 2,000 Indian prisoners. Over 400 of these were tried by court-martial, and 303 con- demned to death, only 38 of whom, unfortunately, were finally executed on September 29, 1862—President LINCOLN having been persuaded by mistaken humanitarians to interfere in their behalf. Col. SIBLEY was commissioned Brigadier General for gallant services, and, during the winter, remained in command of the military forces in this State. Congress, meanwhile, reduced the number of Brigadiers General, but he was reap- pointed by the President in March, 1863, and accepted, at the request of a large number of leading citizens, who addressed to him a petition to that effect. During the summer, he organ- ized and commanded an expedition to Devil's Lake and the Missouri River, for the purpose of routing and driving off the hostile Sioux hovering on the frontier. The expedition was successful, and defeated them in several battles and skirmishes, returning to Fort Snelling in September. The years 1864 and 1865 were employed in securing the defense of the frontier, and, with the single exception of the GARDNER family, no murders or depredations by Indians took place in the State. On No- vember 29, 1865, Gen. SIBLEY was commissioned as Major General, "for efficient and meritorious services." He was relieved from the command of the District of Minnesota in Au- gust, 1866, and was detailed as a member of the commission to negotiate treaties with the hostile Sioux and other bands on the Upper Missouri River, which was successfully carried out.

In 1871, Gen. SIBLEY served another term in the Legislature, from the 5th Ward, Saint Paul, (of which he became a resi- dent, it might be here noted, in 1862.) He is at present a Regent of the State University, and President of the State Normal Board, and was, for a few months, a member of the Board of Indian Commissioners—which last office he was compelled to resign on account of pressure of business. He has also been, for several years, President of the Gas Company, a Director of the First National Bank, Director of the Sioux City Railroad. &c., besides filling various trusts, such as Park Commissioner, Member of Board of Education, and other bodies. Indeed, it is difficult to see how, in the pressure of so much business, and the exacting demands of society, Gen. SIBLEY finds time to write the interesting papers which may be found in the collections of the Historical Society, on the early history of the State. from which many extracts are made in this volume.

. · The frequent references, necessarily so, on account of Gen. SIBLEY's prominent and active connection with our history for over forty years, and the impossibility of condensing in a few sentences what would require a chapter, renders any further sketch, in this shape, unnecessary. It might simply be added that no one in our State is more widely known and more highly respected and honored than Gen. SIBLEY. His name has been almost "a household word" for one entire generation ; and, with his fine physique and unimpaired powers, it is not too much to hope that even many years of useful and active life may yet await him.

WILLIAM HENRY FORBES

was born on Montreal Island. Canada, November 13, 1815. His father was a Scotchman by birth, and was a member of the Hudson's Bay Company as early as 1785, but, at the time of the birth of the subject of this sketch, he had retired from active business. WM. H. was carefully educated in schools at Montreal, and afterwards apprenticed to the hardware business. ultimately becoming junior partner in the house where he was employed. At that time. Montreal was the chief depot of supplies for the Indian trade of the Northwest, and young FORBES, being constantly placed in contact with the adventurous traders making purchases at his establishment, became interested in their romantic life, and the exciting stories they told about the great Northwest. His love of adventure was finally so aroused, that he resolved to try a career in this region. He consequently withdrew from the hardware business, and accepted a clerkship in the American Fur Company, one of the requisites being that the incumbent could speak and write French, which Mr. FORBES did fluently. He, with his party, came to Minnesota via Superior, and arrived at Mendota in the summer of 1837. H. H. SIBLEY was at that time in charge of the post. Mr. FORBES clerked for him for ten years, and, in 1847, took charge of an establishment for the Company, (called the "Saint Paul Outfit,") at Saint Paul, becoming a resident here, and continuing so until his death. nearly 28 years. In the early days of our city, Maj. FORBES was one of its most active promoters and public spirited men, and was one of the proprietors of the "Town of Saint Paul" when it was first laid out.

When the Territory was organized. Maj. FORBES was elected a member of the first Council from Saint Paul, and afterwards re-elected, serving four sessions as Councillor, and, during his third session, (1852,) was President of the Council. On March 18. 1853, Maj. FORBES was appointed by President PIERCE postmaster at Saint Paul, and held this office for three years. During this year, (1853,) the American Fur Company closed out their business in Saint Paul, and Maj. FORBES formed a partnership with N. W. KITTSON, for the general supplying of the Indian trade. They transacted a very large business for several years. In 1858, Mr. KITTSON retired from the firm, and it was continued until 1862 by Maj. FORBES. The Indian outbreak of that year put a close to the trade, and Maj. FORBES lost considerable at his trading posts, which were plundered by the savages. During the campaign against the Sioux, that year, he served with ability as a member of Gen. SIBLEY's staff, and acted as Provost Marshal at the military trial or court-martial of the 300 Indians who were condemned to death. At the close of this campaign, he was commissioned by President LIN-COLN as a Commissary of Subsistence in the volunteer service, with rank of captain. He was also nominated and elected Auditor of Ramsey county that fall, and served as such during the years 1863 and 1864. During a considerable portion of this time he was absent on military duty, however. In the spring of 1863, he accompanied Gen. SIBLEY's expedition to the Missouri River, as Chief Commissary, and, in the spring of 1864, was ordered to the District of Northern Missouri, as Chief Commissary. He remained there until 1866, and, during the latter part of his term, was engaged, as Chief Quartermaster, in closing up the unsettled affairs of Gen. FREMONT's Department, which he did very satisfactorily to the Government. He was brevetted Major a short time prior to his being mustered out of office in 1866.

He returned to Saint Paul in 1866, quite broken in health, and never recovered his former strength and energy. In 1871, he was appointed Indian Agent at Devil's Lake, a position for which he was admirably fitted, and the duties of which he performed with great success, and with fidelity and honesty. His health continued to decline, however, and, on July 20, 1875, he closed his life, deeply lamented by a large circle of friends. His remains were brought to Saint Paul, and entombed in the Catholic cemetery, on July 25, in the presence of a numerous concourse of friends.

Major FORBES was twice married; first in 1846, to AGNES, daughter of ALEXANDER FARIBAULT, by whom he had one daughter, the wife of Captain J. H. PATTERSON, U. S. A.; and again in 1854, to Miss A. B. CORY, of Cooperstown, New York, by whom he had four children, three of whom are living.

The following very just tribute to Maj. FORBES' character is from the *Pioneer-Press*, which announced his death:

"During his long residence in Saint Paul, he maintained a high character for integrity and honesty, and was honored with many places of honor and trust, in all of which he acquitted himself with a credit which won for him the respect and admiration of all who knew him. No stronger proof of his probity of character could be given than the fact that for many years he has occupied positions of peculiar trust at the hands of the Government—positions such as purchasing and delivering agent in the army, and among the Indian tribes, in which hundreds of thousands of dollars have passed through his hands—and yet neither himself, nor any convenient friend, has ever touched a dollar not legitimately earned. The extremely moderate circumstances with which he was surrounded during his official career, and up to the time of his death, are in striking contrast to those of many others who were similarly situated during the war and since."

CHAPTER V.

THE TREATIES OF 1837.

THE TREATIES OF 1837—THE COUNTRY EAST OF THE MISSISSIPPI THROWN OPEN TO SETTLEMENT—MEMORIAL OF SETTLERS ON THE RESERVATION—THE RESERVATION SURVEYED—SETTLERS OBJECT TO BEING DRIVEN OFF—SOME ACCOUNT OF THOSE SETTLERS, &C.

THE year 1837 was a memorable one in Minnesota history, for during that year occurred the treaties referred to in the preceding chapter—one of the most important events in the career of our State—throwing open, as they did, for the first time, the fine agricultural land of the delta between the Saint Croix and Mississippi Rivers, to the plow of the farmer, and the inexhaustible pineries of the Saint Croix Valley to the axe of the lumberman.

The first of these treaties was made by Gov. HENRY DODGE, of Wisconsin, (for whom our Dodge county was appropriately named,) with the Chippewas, at Fort Snelling, July 29, 1837. By this treaty, the Chippewas ceded to the United States all their pine or agricultural lands on the Saint Croix and its tributaries, both in Wisconsin and Minnesota.

In September, 1837, a delegation of about twenty chiefs and braves, by direction of Gov. DODGE, proceeded to Washington, to make a treaty ceding their lands east of the Mississippi. They were accompanied by Maj. TALIAFERRO, their agent, and SCOTT CAMPBELL, interpreter. The Fur Company was represented by H. H. SIBLEY ; while ALEXIS BAILLY, JO. LA FRAMBOISE, A. ROCQUE, LABATHE, the FARIBAULTS, and others, fur-traders, &c., were present. JOEL R. POINSETT, a special commissioner, represented the United States. On September 29, the terms of the treaty were agreed on, and the articles signed by both the high contracting parties. By this treaty, the Dakotas ceded to the United States all their land

5

east of the Mississippi River, including all the islands in the same. They received therefor $300,000, to be invested in five per cent. stocks, the income of which shall be paid to them annually; $110,000 to be divided among the mixed bloods; and $90,000 to payment of debts owed by the tribe, &c.

This treaty—the extinction of whatever "title" the red men had to the region named—was, as observed above, a very important event for Minnesota. It was the key-note for the settlement of the State. It opened the way for the hardy frontierman with his red shirt, and axe and plow. Hitherto, every foot of what is now Minnesota, except the little reservation around Fort Snelling, had been the property, after a fashion, of a few barbarians—but this obstacle was no longer to exist. Once the white man had gained a foothold on the soil, following the precedent of two centuries, he would soon enlarge his grant, until he had swept out of his way its original tenants. A breach had been made in the barriers that shut out civilization from this territory, through which the forlorn hope pressed their way, with the great army of occupation following eagerly behind.

This treaty, too, led the way for the first settlement of our city, as we shall presently see.

MEMORIAL OF SETTLERS ON THE RESERVATION.

Prior to the treaty, and before its ratification by the Senate, the summer following, there was much anxiety on the part of the settlers on the Reserve, to ascertain in what condition they would be left, after the territory east of the Mississippi was thrown open to squatters. A few families of Red River refugees and others had been allowed by the humane Col. SNELLING to settle on the Reserve temporarily, as being the only place that could be offered them, but latterly there had been quite a hostile feeling against them on the part of the officers of the fort. Col. JOHN H. STEVENS, of Minneapolis, in his address on the "Early History of Hennepin County," before the Minneapolis Lyceum, 1856, says: "At that time, and both before and since, the commanding officers at the fort were the lords of the north. They ruled supreme. The citizens in the neighborhood of the fort were liable at any time to be thrust in the guard-house. While the chief of the fort was the king. the subordinate officers were the princes. and persons have been deprived of their liberty and imprisoned by those tyrants for the most trivial wrong. or some imaginary offense." The offense which was charged against ABRAHAM PERRY. LOUIS MASSIE and others. was that their cattle broke into the enclosures of the fort. and committed other depredations. They had repeatedly been requested and cautioned to leave. but they still hoped that they would not be driven away. On August 16. 1837. they sent to the President of the United States. (MARTIN VAN BUREN.) the following memorial :

  " The undersigned citizens of the settlement near Fort Snelling. beg leave to make known to you the interest they feel in the contemplated purchase of the Sioux lands in this vicinity. In 1804. a treaty was made by General PIKE with the Sioux Indians. under which he purchased a certain portion of their country. extending from the Falls of Saint Anthony to the mouth of Saint Peter's River. and the prevailing opinion has been. until very recently. that this treaty had received the sanction of Government. It was under this impression that the undersigned settled upon the lands they now occupy as part of the public domain. They were permitted to make improvements and retain unmolested possession of them for many years by the commanding officer of the post. and the other officers of the Government employed here. who believed the land belonged to the United States. and that the settlers were only exercising the privileges extended to them by the benign and salutary laws which have peopled the western country with a hardy. industrious and enterprising class of citizens.

  " The undersigned will further state that they have erected houses and cultivated fields at their present places of residence. and several of them have large families of children who have no other homes. All the labor of years is invested in their present habitations. and they therefore appeal to the President and Senate of the United States for protection. If a treaty should be made at Washington. as we have heard suggested. and the lands we now occupy be purchased from the Sioux for a military reservation, we ask that a reasonable and just allowance be made us in the treaty for our improvements," &c.

This memorial was signed by Louis Massie, Abraham Perry, Peter Quinn, Antoine Pepin, Duncan Graham, Jacob Falstrom, Oliver Cratte, Joseph Bisson, Joseph Reasch, Louis Dergulee, and others. Col. Samuel C. Stambaugh, sutler at Fort Snelling, was empowered to present it, and represent the settlers in any negotiations, and reference was made to Gov. Henry Dodge for the truth and justice of the statements.

SURVEY OF THE RESERVATION.

On October 19, Lieut. E. K. Smith, First Infantry, made a survey and map of the Reservation, by command of Maj. J. Plympton, Commander of the Post, who had arrived during that summer. He says, in his report to Maj. P.:

" The white inhabitants in the vicinity of the fort, as near as I could ascertain, are: 82 in Baker's settlement, around old Camp Coldwater, and at Massie's landing. On the opposite side, 25 at the Fur Company's establishment, including Faribault's and Le Clere's, 50. Making a total of 157 souls in no way connected with the military.

" This population possess and keep on the public lands, in the immediate neighborhood, nearly 200 horses and cattle. I am inclined to believe that this estimate will fall short of the actual number."

This map Maj. Plympton returned to the War Department on October 19, accompanied by a letter plainly indicating his intention to eject all settlers on the Reserve. One reason he alleges is the scarcity of timber for fuel on the Reserve: " It now (he says) causes much labor and inconvenience to the garrison to obtain the necessary fuel—and, should this point be required for the next 20 years for military purposes, the difficulty will be very great, and very much increased."

In acknowledging receipt of this communication, November 17, the Secretary of War instructed Maj. Plympton as follows :

" If there be no reservation already made for military purposes, at your post, please mark over what in your opinion will be necessary to be reserved."

A memorandum from the War Department says : "March 26, 1838, Major P. transmitted a map of such a tract *embracing a considerable quantity of land on the east side of the Mississippi River.*"

In endorsing this memorial. Mr. STAMBAUGH says :

" The persons who sign the above memorial reside in the Saint Peter's settlement, about half a mile from the fort. They are the only individuals having houses and improvements on the west side of the Mississippi River, with the exception of Mr. BAKER, whose principal trading establishment is in this settlement. No others can be affected by a purchase of land necessary for a military reserve."

In a subsequent letter to Hon. JOEL R. POINSETT, Secretary of War, dated February 11, 1839, Col. STAMBAUGH says :

" The memorial speaks for itself, and I would not act as the representative of the memorialists if I were not convinced that their claims are founded on justice, and their improvements secured to them by a custom which has grown into common law in all cases of this character. Independently of the legal right, however, I believe that humanity and good policy will secure them a reasonable allowance for the improvements and privileges they are willing to abandon. The memorial is signed by all the settlers on the west side of the Mississippi, with the exception of B. F. BAKER. There are three or four settlements on the east side of the Mississippi River, but, as it was not supposed that an attempt would be made to extend the reservation across the river, the settlers did not join in their memorial."

SOME ACCOUNT OF THE SETTLERS.

As near as I can ascertain, after extensive inquiry, the three or four settlers on the east side were : JOSEPH TURPIN, FRANCIS DESIRE, DONALD McDONALD, "old man" CHORETTE, and, perhaps. SCOTT CAMPBELL, BARTHOLOMEW BALDWIN, and ABNER POWEL.

JOSEPH TURPIN is said to be the first man who built a house

east of the Mississippi. Mr. TURPIN was born at Montreal, Canada, about 1775. He came, sometime about the beginning of the present century, to Prairie du Chien, with his brother AMABLE, of whom a sketch is given elsewhere, and subsequently emigrated to Selkirk's Settlement, where he remained some years. In 1831, as near as I can ascertain, he left Red River with a company of refugees, some of whom settled near Fort Snelling, and, not long after that date, built a house on the east side of the Mississippi. This house he subsequently sold to JOSEPH RONDO, another refugee. He afterwards lived many years at Mendota, where he died in 1865—aged over 90 years.

Of "old man" CHORETTE. I have been able to learn little that is reliable. He was a Canadian, lived at Red River some time, and settled near Fort Snelling the same year as RONDO, TURPIN and others. He has probably been dead some years. I have been informed that he has children living in this vicinity, but have been unable to find them.

FRONCHET, or DESIRE. was a native of France, and, probably, at the time mentioned, was 50 years of age, as he always boasted of having been a soldier of NAPOLEON, and probably was. He had also served in the United States army, at Fort Snelling latterly, and (Mrs. JAMES PATTEN thinks) was discharged there. The explorer and scientist, J. N. NICOLLET, while at Mendota, in 1836, preparing to go toward the Upper Mississippi on his expedition, employed DESIRE, then attached to the garrison, as an attendant. He speaks of him in his work as follows : "Having received good testimonials of his character. I accepted his offer, and have nothing but praise to bestow on his activity, patience, and the cheerfulness which he manifested even in the midst of some trying circumstances to which we were exposed." DESIRE, having spent most of his life in the army, was unfitted, at his age, when he left the army, for any very active pursuits, while his intemperate habits also brought on him repeated troubles. He made a settlement east of the Mississippi, where he led a lonely life for some time, but was, in 1840, expelled from the Reserve with other settlers. In 1842, he came to Saint Paul, and secured employment from Sergt. RICHARD W. MORTIMER, who had just settled there, and J. R. IRVINE and others. DESIRE could not work much, but did such light labor as was necessary, interspersing it with fearful sprees, lasting sometimes two weeks, in which he would roll on the ground anywhere, helpless and insensible. He came near freezing to death several times in these debauches, but was always cared for by his acquaintances, who liked him very much, as he was a kind-hearted, good-humored and vivacious companion. DESIRE lived at Saint Paul some two years, and then went to Elk River, into which he fell during one of his sprees, and was drowned.

DONALD McDONALD was born in Canada, in 1803, of Scotch parents. At the age of 15 years he left Canada, with Captain MILES MONTGOMERY, and went to Hudson's Bay. He was, for some years, in the employ of the American Fur Company, and traveled very extensively over the Northwest. He put up (he says) the third house on the east side of the Mississippi. Subsequently he claimed the land where the Half-Way House now is. This land, he says, he sold to DENOYER, "for a barrel of whisky and two Indian guns." He subsequently went to Crow Wing, where he married a half-breed, and had a numerous family.

CHAPTER VI.

THE FIRST SETTLEMENT OF SAINT PAUL.

PIERRE PARRANT, OR "OLD PIG'S EYE"—SOME ACCOUNT OF THE OLD COON—HE MAKES THE FIRST CLAIM IN SAINT PAUL—ABRAHAM PERRY AND THE GERVAIS BROTHERS FOLLOW—PHELAN AND HAYS, AND SOME ACCOUNT OF THEM—THE INDIANS SHOOT PERRY'S CATTLE—RATIFICATION OF THE TREATY—A MYSTERIOUS CHARACTER—PARRANT MORTGAGES HIS CLAIM.

THE long winter wore to a close, and the spring of 1838 had thawed away its snow and ice. The treaty had been made, and that it would be ratified, there was no reasonable doubt. Why not anticipate the latter form, by making claims in advance? The thought was inspiring. Some of the pine-fringed streams along the Saint Croix, already resounded to the lumberman's axe. At Fort Snelling and Mendota were a number of keen fellows, looking eagerly on, and waiting for a good chance to seize on some of the rich territory so soon to be open to the impatient speculator. Among them was one

PIERRE PARRANT,

a Canadian voyageur, who chanced to be, at the time, hanging around Mendota, waiting for something to turn up. PARRANT had lived some time at Sault Ste. Marie, then at Saint Louis, where he had been in the employ of McKENZIE and CHOUTEAU, and afterwards at Prairie du Chien. He came to Mendota in 1832. It must be related, that he bore not the most enviable character. It was hinted that he left Sault Ste. Marie on account of some irregularities of conduct that were distasteful to the good people there. Maj. TALIAFERRO, the Indian Agent, appeared to estimate his character somewhat low. In one place in his journal, under date of August 23d, 1835, he writes: "Ordered PIERRE PARRANT, a foreigner, prohibited from the trade, not to enter the Indian country in any capacity."

PARRANT seems, in defiance of this order, to have entered the Indian country, for Maj. TALIAFERRO again writes, on October 12th, that it was reported that he had done so—and adds that, if found true, "a military force would be sent after him, and he would be sent to Prairie du Chien." PAR-RANT's personal appearance may have somewhat favored the estimate of his character. He was a coarse, ill-looking, low-browed fellow, with only one eye, and that a sinister-looking one. He spoke execrable English. His habits were intemperate and licentious, and, at the date we speak of, he was past the meridian of life—probably sixty years of age.

Such was the man on whom Fortune, with that blind fatuity that seems to characterize the jade, thrust the honor of being the founder of our good city! Our pride almost revolts at the chronicling of such a humiliation, and leads us to wish that it were on one worthier and nobler that such a distinction had fallen. But history is inexorable, and we must record *facts* as they are.

PARRANT kept his one eye open to the main chance, it would seem, and, after surveying the situation of things with his optic, he concluded not to wait the ratification of the treaty, but to seize on some good spot in advance. For certain reasons, he desired to get as near the fort and to Mendota as possible, while getting just outside the lines of the Reserve, as far as they could be ascertained. These reasons were, that he could sell whisky to the soldiers and Indians undisturbed by the authorities at the fort, who had been greatly annoyed at the surreptitious sale of liquor to those two classes, by some unprincipled traders and hangers-on around Fort Snelling, and were endeavoring to break up the traffic as far as possible. Hence, he selected, as the most eligible spot for such a business, the mouth of the creek which flows out of "Fountain Cave," in upper town. PARRANT wisely judged of the convenience of the place to his customers. It was near the river, where the Indians and others could paddle to his very door, and then, too, he could get his supplies easily, and, if necessary, dilute the article profitably, by a judicious admixture of the unfailing stream flowing out of the cave. Here, in the coolie, a secluded and lonely gorge in the river bank. PARRANT. about the first of June, in the year of our Lord 1838. began erecting his hovel. He. the immortal *parent* of our saintly city, and of the noble army of whisky-sellers who have thriven since that day—it, the first habitation, the first business house, of our Christian metropolis of to-day ! Thus was our city "founded" —by a pig-eyed retailer of whisky. The location of the future Capital of Minnesota was determined, not by the commanding and picturesque bluffs. a noble and inspiring site whereon to build a city—not by the great river flowing so majestically in front of it, suggestive of commerce and trade—but solely as a convenient spot to sell whisky. without the pale of law !

ANOTHER SETTLER—ABRAHAM PERRY.

Almost simultaneously with the advent of PARRANT, came another settler—ABRAHAM PERRY. (or PERRET,) and family, having been compelled to leave the Reserve on the west side. as referred to a few pages back.

ABRAHAM PERRY was born in Switzerland. about the year 1780, and was brought up as a watchmaker. He married in Switzerland, and three children were born to him there. About the year 1820, he, with a considerable number of his fellow countrymen. were induced to emigrate to the Red River Colony, by one of Lord SELKIRK's agents. "Their occupations had been mechanical, (says NEILL.) chiefly that of clock-making, and they were not adapted for the stern work of founding a colony in the interior of North America. From year to year their spirits drooped, and when the Switzers' song of home was sung, they could not keep back their tears." Repeated calamities oppressed the colony—untimely frosts. grass-hoppers and other causes despoiled their harvests, and finally the great flood of 1826 gave the finishing blow to their hopes. A large number of the Swiss determined to emigrate to the United States. It was reported that they would be kindly received at Fort Snelling, and allowed to settle there, and, in 1827, a number of families came to that point. ABRAHAM PERRY among them. The kind-hearted SNELLING allowed such as wished to locate near the fort. PERRY, who had brought with

him a number of cattle, located a mile or two above the fort,
near "Cold Spring," built a cabin, opened a farm, and was
soon prosperously fixed. Two children had been born to him
at Red River, and, during his residence at Fort Snelling, two
more, making six daughters and one son in all. Meantime,
two of his oldest daughters were married. In the spring of
1838, as referred to before, Maj. PLYMPTON drove all the settlers off the west side of the Reserve, PERRY among them.
This was a cruel blow to PERRY, who had just begun to be
comfortably fixed, and was now in the evening of his days,
with quite a family dependent upon him. But, driving his
flocks before him, like ABRAHAM of old, he journeyed across
the river, looking for a new home. Wishing, like PARRANT,
to get just without the bounds of the Reserve—which he was
informed by Maj. PLYMPTON intersected the Mississippi at
Fountain Cave—he made a claim just below that of PARRANT,
on the beautiful stream which flows across the road there, and
erected a habitation about where the City Hospital now stands.
His herd* was soon grazing on the luxuriant meadow grass
about him, giving new hopes that perhaps at last he might pass
the evening of life in peace.

But even this hope was destined to prove delusive ere long,
as we shall see a few pages subsequently. In fact, scarcely
was PERRY's new roof-tree reared, when the Sioux appeared
and threateningly ordered them to leave. It seems that, although the Indians had bartered away their lands, they still
looked with a jealous eye upon them, and were loth to see the
stranger and the pale-face occupy them and prosper. PERRY
gave them no satisfaction, however, and, on June 9, a party of
the Kaposia band, probably headed by *Wa-kin-yan-ton-ka*, or
BIG THUNDER, (LITTLE CROW's father,) went to Fort Snelling, and complained to Maj. TALIAFERRO, Indian Agent,
about PERRY and PARRANT settling on their lands, before the
treaty had been ratified, and they received any consideration.
Nothing was done at that time concerning the alleged intru-

---

* Col. JOHN H. STEVENS, in the address before quoted, says: "PERRY at one time
owned more cattle than all the rest of the inhabitants of what is now Minnesota, if we
except Mr. RENVILLE."

sion, as a steamer arrived just then, on which came a passenger, who reported to have heard that the treaty was ratified. A little premature, however. But at all events, PARRANT was suffered to sell whisky, and PERRY to herd his flocks, undisturbed.

Not undisturbed either, for a few weeks subsequently, viz.: on October 18. Maj. TALIAFERRO writes in his journal, that Mrs. PERRY and CHARLES PERRY, her son, came to the fort and complained that the Indians had killed three of her cattle, and wounded a fourth. This was sometime after the ratification of the treaty, too, and that fact must have been known to them. But I am of the opinion that PARRANT's whisky must have caused this latter outrage, more than any other cause. Perhaps Maj. TALIAFERRO took this view of it, too, for he merely adds in his journal: '' They (the Sioux) will have to pay $200 for the affair out of their next year's annuity.''

THE TREATY RATIFIED.

While these events were progressing, however, the treaty of September 29, 1837, was slowly passing through the Senate. On June 15, a final vote was reached on it, and it was ratified. Just one month later, (news traveled slow those days,) the steamer Palmyra landed at Fort Snelling, with the glad news. It produced some excitement among those who had been waiting so long to make claims, and they at once started off to seize on eligible points, which had already been picked out by covetous eyes.

N. W. KITTSON states that the boat arrived in the evening, and, after dark the same night, he, FRANKLIN STEELE and ANGUS M. ANDERSON, started off to make a claim at Saint Anthony Falls. JOSEPH R. BROWN left at the same time for the Saint Croix, where he drove the stakes of a new town.

THE GERVAIS BROTHERS SETTLE HERE.

On the 13th day of July, 1838, BENJAMIN GERVAIS and PIERRE GERVAIS, made claims near ABRAHAM PERRY, and proceeded to erect habitations. The GERVAIS brothers were Red River refugees.

BENJAMIN GERVAIS was born at Riviere du Loup, Canada. July 15, 1786. About the year 1803, he went to Red River, in company with several Canadian families, who settled there. GERVAIS did not himself settle there that year, but made trading voyages back and forth to Canada until the year 1812, when he took up his residence there, and was in the employ of the Hudson's Bay Company for several years. On September 29, 1823, he was married at Fort Garry, by Bishop PROVENCHER. to Miss GENEVIEVE LARANS, a native of Berthier, Canada. and went to farming at a place called La Pointe, about a mile and a half below Fort Garry. Their story is that of all the · Red River refugees—the floods, grasshoppers, untimely frosts. hard winters, &c., drove them away to a more habitable region, and, in 1827, Mr. GERVAIS, with his wife and three children, proceeded to Fort Snelling, near which they settled.

On being turned away from the Reserve, Mr. GERVAIS proceeded to the neighborhood of Mr. PERRY. and made a claim a little below that settler, running from the river to the bluff. Having one or two stout boys. born during his residence on Red River, he proceeded to make a clearing, and soon had quite a farm in operation.

PIERRE GERVAIS was 17 years younger than his brother. He, too, had lived at Red River several years, and came from there to Mendota in 1826. where he entered the service of the American Fur Company. He made a claim near BENJAMIN GERVAIS, which occupied about what is now known as "Leech's Addition."

ANOTHER PRONUNCIAMENTO FROM MAJOR PLYMPTON.

Though the above settlers thought that they were, beyond any doubt, settling outside the bounds of the Reservation, as far as they were understood at that time, it is possible that the authorities at the fort took a different view of it, and regarded it as an intrusion on the sacred domain of the Government. On July 26, 1838, Maj. PLYMPTON issued an order forbidding "all persons. not attached to the military, from erecting any building or buildings, fence or fences, or cutting timber for any but for public use, within said line, which has been surveyed and forwarded to the War Department, subject to the final decision thereof," &c.

Whether this order was called out by the fact of PERRY, the GERVAIS families and others settling within the imaginary lines of PLYMPTON's Reserve, or not, it is not absolutely known. It is quite probable he did refer to those squatters, however, as in the letter accompanying a copy of the order to the War Department, he says:

"HEADQUARTERS FORT SNELLING, July 30, 1838.

"SIR: I take the liberty to enclose to you herewith a copy of an order which I deemed necessary to publish to protect the land which has been marked out as a military reservation at this post, against encroachments, which were every day forcing themselves upon my notice.

"Without interfering with the property of any individual, I shall strictly enforce my order till the pleasure of the Department shall be known upon the subject, presuming that my duty to the public and the spirit of my instructions call for such a course.

"My order must, as a matter of right, more particularly allude to persons urging themselves within the line at this time, than to those who I found, on my arrival here last summer, settled down near the fort. The authority for these settlements being made, I have to presume, is to be found or is known at the Department, although I have not been successful in finding any record of it in the office of this post.

"The character and extent of these settlements and improvements was given in my communication of the 19th October, 1837.

"I have the honor to be, very respectfully, sir, your obedient servant,

"J. PLYMPTON,

"Major United States Army, Commanding Post.

"ADJUTANT GENERAL U. S. A., Washington, District of Columbia."

About the same date that the news of the ratification of the treaty was received at Fort Snelling, and shortly after, three soldiers were discharged from the Fifth Regiment, named ED-WARD PHELAN, JOHN HAYS and WILLIAM EVANS, all three natives of Ireland. They resolved to make claims in the newly ceded tract, and, finding some settlers along the river below the cave, fixed on this locality as the most likely one for their purpose.

EDWARD PHELAN

was the youngest of the three. He was a man of splendid physique, over six feet in height, muscular and active. He bore not the most enviable character. He is reported to have been immoral, cruel, revengeful and ,unscrupulous. By his own boasting, he had led a lawless and criminal life before entering the army, and was one whom most civil and well-disposed persons avoided as a dangerous person. His future career will show that· this estimate of his character was well founded.

Since the foregoing was written, I have, by the courtesy of the Adjutant General U. S. A., been supplied with the following " descriptive list" of PHELAN, from the records of the War Office :

"WASHINGTON, D. C., Oct. 20, 1875.

" SIR : In reply to your letter of the 7th instant, I respectfully inform you, that, upon an examination of the official records, it appears that *Edward Felyn* enlisted June 8, 1835, at New York City, for three years, and was assigned to Company E, Fifth Infantry, and discharged June 8, 1838, by reason of expiration of service, at Fort Snelling, Wisconsin Territory, a private. He was twenty-four years of age when enlisted, had gray eyes, brown hair, fair complexion, and was six feet two and one-half inches high; born in Londonderry, Ireland, and by occupation a laborer.

" Very respectfully, your obedient servant,

" S. N. BENJAMIN,

" Assistant Adjutant General."

WILLIAM EVANS

was a fellow countryman of PHELAN's, and near the same age. He selected for his claim a spot on Dayton's Bluff, near the Dayton Mansion, and lived there a dozen or more years. He subsequently moved to what is now Washington county, and is said to be a farmer in that locality at present—but I have been unable, after several efforts, to get his address. or to secure any information from him.

SERGEANT JOHN HAYS.

Serving in Company E; Fifth Regiment, was Sergeant JOHN HAYS, also a native of Ireland, who, at the time PHELAN and EVANS made their claims, was expecting his discharge in a few months. and wished to settle near his old comrades. He, therefore, made an arrangement with PHELAN, that the latter

was to make for him (HAYS) a claim alongside his own, and
hold it until his discharge, and agreeing that he would furnish
for PHELAN some money which the latter was to use in erecting a cabin, &c., which they would jointly occupy, when he
came out of the army. HAYS was a man of exactly the opposite characteristics as the ruffianly PHELAN. He was of middle
age at the time we write—his hair somewhat bleached with
two or three terms' service in the army. He was something of
a martinet in discipline, precise and exact in his dress, bearing
and actions, gained by his long military service. His form
was spare but erect, and he had a dignified and respectable
bearing, that impressed everybody who met him. favorably.
Every one of the earliest settlers of Saint Paul who knew JOHN
HAYS, speaks of him with unqualified praise, as an honest,
good, courteous and clever old gentleman. He was unmarried, and, during his service in the army, had saved his pay,
which, at the time of his discharge, amounted to a considerable sum. The records of the War Department give the "descriptive list" of HAYS, when he re-enlisted in 1836, as follows :

"JOHN HAYS, age 37 years, born in Waterford, Ireland; occupation,
a laborer; blue eyes, light hair, light complexion, height five feet
eight and three-fourths inches. Re-enlisted in Company E, Fifth Infantry, April 25, 1836, for three years; discharged at Fort Snelling,
Minnesota, April 25, 1839, by reason of expiration of service, a sergeant."

His age, when discharged, would, if the above figures are
correct, be about forty, but he is spoken of by all who knew
him, as being much older than that, and probably was, as for
good reasons he might have understated his age when mustered in.

PHELAN MAKES A CLAIM.

As remarked above, these three soldiers resolved to make
claims in this vicinity. PHELAN was the first to secure his
discharge, and, after prospecting hereabouts, selected as a claim
a tract of ground fronting on the river, running back to the
bluff, and bounded (approximately) by what is now Eagle and
Third streets on the west, and Saint Peter street on the east.
On the side of the bluff, under Third street—about where the

soap factory now stands—he built a log house, a mere hovel, it is described, to "live" in for the present.

At request of HAYS, as before stated, PHELAN selected for him*, a claim adjoining his own on the east, fronting on the river, and running back to the bluffs, extending probably from what is now Saint Peter street, down to somewhere near the present Minnesota street. He was to hold this claim for HAYS—according to the agreement with H.—until the latter got his discharge, the subsequent spring, and thereafter HAYS was to live with him in the hovel under the hill.

A MYSTERIOUS CHARACTER.

Sometime during the summer or fall of 1838, a stranger "turned up." from no one knew where, and built a cabin on the bank near where Lindeke's mill now is—between that and the gas works. Nothing more was known concerning him than that his name was "JOHNSON." Where he came from, his past life, his object in settling in such an out-of-the-way place, were all wrapped in a profound and embarrassing mystery, that baffled the most curious scrutiny of the suspicious settlers hereabout. A woman was living with him, presumed to be his wife, and she had a young child. What deepened the mystery, in the eyes of the plain, simple inhabitants of that primeval period, was the fact that "JOHNSON" and his wife had evidently moved in society of a kind much superior, in a social, or fashionable point of view, to that which would usually be found in the claim shanties of the frontier at that period. Their manners were elegant and refined, and they dressed in expensive and fashionable clothing. In fact, it was not so much the reserved and secluded manners of JOHNSON that first attracted suspicion against him, as his fine clothes ! We almost shrink from recording the fact that, at one period of our history, to be well dressed was to become an object of suspicion. That is sadly changed now, to an opposite extreme. One needs

---

* VETAL GUERIN, who gave me very minutely his reminiscences of early days, thought that the claims were owned in the opposite way, i. e., that the upper one PHELAN intended for HAYS, and the lower one he meant to be his own. The other settlers, however, give the account of it as I have recorded it above.

only a skillful tailor to enable him to become the pet of quite
a numerous circle of persons who ought to know better, but
who find out. after being repeatedly victimized, that good character and good clothes are not inseparable.   No such nice dis-
tinctions troubled the men and women of 1838. however.   But
when they saw a man threading our springy bogs or thorny
thickets in patent leather gaiters and broadcloth clothes and
silk hat, it must be confessed that there *was* some ground for
being a little shy of him.   The most charitable would have
admitted that he had at least eloped with some other man's
wife, and came to this secluded region to avoid notice.   But
there were others who suspected a still more heinous offense.
He could not, they thought. support all this style without labor,
unless he had robbed some one down below, and fled with the
ill-gotten booty, or else was a counterfeiter.   The last suspicion
gained the most prevalence. and was strengthened by an incident that occurred the following spring, probably.   One cold.
dark, stormy night, when a perfect tempest was raging, one
of the settlers, who had been down the river. to Pig's Eye,
probably, arrived at Johnson's cabin. cold. weary, wet and
hungry, and asked permission to remain all night and get some
food, as he did not feel able to get the rest of his way home in
the storm and darkness.   Strange to say, this request was refused : in fact, he avers that Johnson would not even open the
door for him.   This. taken in connection with the other suspicious circumstances, was, to the settlers hereabouts, proof
strong as words of holy writ that Johnson must be a counterfeiter.   The settlers at last hinted to him their suspicions, and
added a threat that " the authorities at the fort." a class everybody seemed to stand in awe of. were going to arrest him.
Whether Johnson had been guilty of any wrong or not, will
never be known, but this last information seemed to make him
uneasy.   He hastily sold his claim to James R. Clewett,
and decamped down the river.

PARRANT MORTGAGES HIS CLAIM.

But we must not lose sight of old Parrant. located at the
cave.   During all this time he was driving a flourishing trade,

selling whisky to both Indians and whites. Occasionally a party of soldiers, bound on a spree, would come down to his ranch, get soaked with his red-eye and tangle-foot brands, and fail to report next day. Hence a guard would have to hunt them up, and the poor fellows would sojourn in the guard-house, or wear a ball and chain for a period. Two or three times the officers at the fort threatened to tear his shanty down, but never executed the threat at that time. His place was searched once or twice, with the intention of demolishing all liquor found, but the old fox was too sly to be caught that way. He didn't keep much stock in sight. The rest of it was *buried* near by, where no one but himself could find it. Some say he used to hide it in the cave.

But old PARRANT lost his place at last. In the fall of that year—1838—he borrowed from WILLIAM BEAUMETTE, of Mendota, the sum of $90, and, to secure it to the latter person, gave him the following judgment note, the original of which the writer has in his possession :

"SAINT PETER'S, 12th November, 1838.

"On the first day of May next, I promise to pay to GUILLAUME BEAUMETTE, ninety dollars, for the value received, without defalcation.

* his
"PIERRE X PARRANT.
mark.

"Witness :

"A. M. ANDERSON.

"H. H. SIBLEY.

"Know all men by these presents, that I, PIERRE PARRANT, residing near the entry of the Saint Peter's River, and in Wisconsin Territory, do hereby make over, transfer and quit-claim to GUILLAUME BEAUMETTE, of said Saint Peter's, all my right, title, and interest in and to all that tract or portion of land which I, the said PARRANT, now reside upon and occupy, at the cave, so-called, about four miles below Fort Snelling, to have and to hold the same to the said GUILLAUME BEAUMETTE, his heirs and assigns forever.

'Provided always—and it is hereby expressly understood between the parties. that if the said PIERRE PARRANT shall pay or cause to be paid, on or about the first of May next, to the said BEAUMETTE, the sum of ninety dollars, amount of a certain note of hand given by me, the said PARRANT, to the said BEAUMETTE, then this transfer to be null, and of none effect, otherwise to remain in full force and virtue.

his

" PIERRE X PARRANT. ·[L. S.]

mark.

" Signed, sealed and delivered in presence of—

" H. H. SIBLEY.

" A. M. ANDERSON."

The above document is in the handwriting of H. H. SIBLEY, who was then, or at least shortly afterward, a Justice of the Peace of Clayton county, Iowa, with a bailiwick extending from the present Iowa line to the British Possessions.

WILLIAM BEAUMETTE,

to whom the above note was given, was a Canadian by birth, who had emigrated to Red River about 1818 or 1819. He was a stone mason by trade, and, while at Red River, helped to build the present Fort Garry. At the time of the exodus from Selkirk's Settlement to Fort Snelling, BEAUMETTE accompanied the refugees, and proceeded to Mendota, where he lived some years. He did not become an actual resident of Saint Paul until some time after the date of this occurrence. He married a sister of VETAL GUERIN, and lived in Saint Paul for over twenty years. He died here in November, 1870, aged about 70 years.

Here, for the present, we must leave this real estate transaction.

CHAPTER VII.

EVENTS OF THE YEAR 1839.

THE EXCLUSION OF SETTLERS FROM THE RESERVE ARGUED—SURGEON EMERSON ACCUSES THEM OF DEMORALIZING THE SOLDIERS WITH LIQUOR—GEN. WOOL CORROBORATES THIS—THE LIQUOR TRAFFIC WITH INDIANS—PARRANT LOSES HIS CLAIM—ORIGIN OF " PIG'S EYE"—SETTLERS AT THE GRAND MARAIS—FIRST MARRIAGE, BIRTH AND DEATH—THE MURDER OF HAYS—WAS PHELAN GUILTY?—SURVEY OF THE RESERVATION—ORDER FINALLY ISSUED TO EXPEL THE SETTLERS—THE WISCONSIN LEGISLATURE PROTESTS—VETAL GUERIN JUMPS THE HAYS CLAIM.

EARLY in 1839, the exclusion of the settlers on the Reserve again occupied the attention of the authorities at the fort. The ostensible reason was the illicit liquor traffic which some of them carried on, but, from the subjoined letter of Col. SAMUEL C. STAMBAUGH, sutler at Fort Snelling, to the Secretary of War, quoted on page 61, other motives may have been at work. Referring to the lines of the Reserve, as adopted by Major PLYMPTON, he remarks :

A SIGNIFICANT DOCUMENT.

" Nor was it thought by any one that the line would cross the Saint Peter's. There is land enough on the west side of (or between) these rivers, in the Indian country, to make a reservation of any extent, which will not be bounded by western settlers for a long time.

" You will perceive, by an examination of the survey and plat before you, that the line as run is both awkward and unnatural. It commences some distance above the Falls of Saint Anthony on the west side of the Mississippi, but, instead of crossing immediately and traversing the country to strike the angle of the river below the fort, it runs along the west side about three miles below the Falls, where it crosses the river, and thence strikes across the country to Carver's Cave, which is three miles below Fort Snelling by the course of the river.

" The land, embracing the Falls of Saint Anthony, on the east side of the river, has, since its purchase by the United States, been improved by settlements so as to secure a pre-emption, and it is now held in possession by Doctor WRIGHT, FRANKLIN STEELE, and myself, (one-half section,) and one section by Major PLYMPTON, Captain SCOTT, and Doctor EMERSON. These settlements include the best positions immediately above the Reservation, as surveyed. If the military Reservation is made to include Carver's Cave, below Fort Snelling, it will embrace all the steamboat landings on the Mississippi River along a distance of twenty miles below the Falls, as the country is broken and swampy nine miles below the cave, and hence no steamboat landing can be procured by settlers within a distance of twelve miles below Fort Snelling, and the rapids produced by the Falls will prevent boats ascending above the Reservation line. The property, therefore, in which I, with others, claim to have an interest, would be greatly enhanced in value, by a military Reserve, which would place our claim most contiguous to the fort. But I believe the military service cannot be benefited by such a measure, and the adoption of it would produce universal dissatisfaction when the country comes into market, and would now be a great mortification and inconvenience to visitors, who will crowd the Falls of Saint Anthony during the summer months, if houses for their accommodation can be erected in the vicinity of Fort Snelling. The bluffs of the river immediately opposite the fort are very high and difficult of ascent, and the current of the river strong and deep. They are exposed to the eye of the sentinel for more than a mile up and down the river, so that no soldier can cross and enter a house on the opposite side without detection. Whereas, if settlers are forced back into the interior, out of sight and beyond immediate investigation, they will be of an inferior class, and can, if so disposed, bring whisky in kegs into the forest, within a short distance of the fort, with but little risk.

"The same objections exist to the extension of the Reserve beyond the Saint Peter's River. In a year or two, in all probability, the Indian title will be extinguished on that side of the river, so as to secure both sides of the Mississippi, and the citizens of Iowa Territory will extend their settlements to the rich valley of the Saint Peter's. If, therefore, the line is established as surveyed, it will take in all the boat landings near the junction of the Saint Peter's and Mississippi, and the people of Iowa can have no town or depot within from 10 to 15 miles distance, centered by this important point.

"I have taken the liberty of submitting to you these undigested remarks, because I know that the extension of the military Reserve for Fort Snelling, beyond the Mississippi and Saint Peter's, will give great dissatisfaction to the people who go to purchase land and settle in that country. I have heard but one opinion expressed concerning it from all who have visited that place since I have been there. The United States Commissioners, Judge PEASE and General EWING, who were there last summer, after the survey was made, expressed the same opinions here given. If a military force must be kept up, at a heavy expense, to preserve peace between the Indians and our own citizen settlers, the latter should not be thrown out of sight and out of hearing of that protection, but, as is usual, the first settlers should be permitted to locate as near that protection as possible. As the line has been run by the survey now before you, with the Mississippi and a forest of several miles intervening, an Indian force can intercept all communication with the fort, and the inhabitants may be massacred before the military can be apprised of the attack. Whereas, if the settlements would border on the river, they could furnish a shelter for those in the interior, and be covered by a six-pounder from the fort. A friendly intercourse and feeling would thus also be kept up between the military and civil power, which is a matter of the highest importance in times of Indian troubles."

THE ILLICIT SALE OF LIQUOR TO SOLDIERS.

On March 10, Maj. PLYMPTON addressed a long letter to the War Department, mainly in reference to the lines of the Reserve, and the settlers thereon, rehearsing the troubles the settlers had given him by selling liquor to the soldiers, and urging their expulsion. The surgeon of the fort, Dr. EMERSON, also addressed the following letter to the Surgeon General:

"FORT SNELLING, April 23, 1839.

"SIR: As a friend to the soldier and temperance in the army, I am induced to make to you, as head of the department to which I have the honor of belonging, a statement of our situation at this post. Since the middle of winter we have been completely inundated with ardent spirits, and consequently the most beastly scenes of intoxication among the soldiers of this garrison and the Indians in its vicinity, which, no doubt, will add many cases to our sick-list. The whisky is brought here by citizens who are pouring in upon us and settling themselves on the opposite shore of the Mississippi River, in defiance of our worthy commanding officer, Major J. PLYMPTON, whose authority they set at naught. At this moment, there is a citizen, once a soldier in the Fifth Infantry, who was discharged at this post while Col. SNELLING commanded, and who has been since employed by the American Fur Company, actually building on the land marked out by the commanding officer as the Reserve, and within gunshot distance of the fort, a very extensive whisky shop. They are encouraged in their nefarious deeds in consequence of letters received by them, as they say, from Saint Louis and Washington, mentioning that no Reserve would be acknowledged by the proper authority. If such is the fact, (which I doubt very much,) I can only say that the happiness of the officers and soldiers is at an end at Fort Snelling.

"In my humble opinion, the immediate action of the Government is called for, to give us relief in pointing out the military Reserve, which ought not to be less than twenty miles square, or to the mouth of the Saint Croix River, especially as the Indians are allowed by treaty to hunt on it. I am certain, if the honorable Secretary of War knew our situation, not a moment's time would be lost in turning the wretches off of the Reserve, who live by robbing the men of the garrison of health, comfort, and every cent they possess. Pardon me, sir, if I err in writing so, but I feel grieved to witness such scenes of drunkenness and dissipation where I have spent many days of happiness, when we had no ardent spirits among us, and, consequently, sobriety and good conduct among the command. May I presume to ask you to use your influence with the proper authority to mark out the Reserve, and rid us of those harpies or whisky-sellers who destroy the health of the soldiers, and, consequently, their usefulness to their Government and country.

"With great respect, I have the honor to remain your obedient servant,

"J. Emerson,

"Surgeon U. S. A.

"Thomas Lawson,

"Surgeon General U. S. A.

"The immediate action of the Government is called for in this matter.

"E."

This letter was referred by the Surgeon General to the Secretary of War, and, on June 2d, the post at Fort Snelling was visited and inspected by Brig. Gen. John E. Wool, who, in his report to the Secretary of War, strongly endorsed the above views, as follows:

"My object at this time is to call your attention particularly to his peculiar situation in regard to the Indians and white inhabitants who are permitted to occupy the country surrounding his post. The views of Major Plympton on this subject have been on several occasions presented to the War Department, and at length in his communication of the 11th March last, and which, from my own observation, I am confident are correct, and, if not attended to in due season, his predictions in relation to the Indians and whites will be verified.

"The white inhabitants, aware of the large amount of money annually paid by the United States to the Indians residing in that region of country, avail themselves of the means in their power, confident of the protection of the Government, of introducing at all points, and within half a mile of Fort Snelling, intoxicating liquors, which is no less destructive to the discipline of the troops than hazardous of the peace and quiet of the country. Such is the character of the white inhabitants of that country, that, if they cannot be permitted to carry on their nefarious traffic with the Indians, it will sooner or later involve them in a

war with the United States.   If the Government would avoid such a result, it should immediately adopt measures to drive off the public lands
all white intruders within twenty miles of Fort Snelling, and prohibit
intoxicating liquors from being introduced into the Indian country, or
on lands not sold by the United States.

" Again, it is well known that the Sioux and Chippewas have been at
war from time immemorial, and no prospect of its termination or of
peace being established between the two tribes.   The introduction of
whisky, which is as common almost as water, by no means tends to
lessen their national hatred; on the contrary, it prompts collisions and
war, and, consequently, a source of constant and increasing anxiety to
the commanding officer, which no vigilance can guard against.   The
sacrifice of blood and treasure in the late war in Florida ought at least
to admonish us that we ought to be on our guard, and, by timely measures, prevent similar results."

These reports and communications were taken under advisement by the Secretary of War, and soon induced him to take
decisive action in the case. as will appear hereafter.

It may be thought that unnecessary space and prominence
has been given to these documents regarding the lines of the
Reserve, and the conduct of some of the settlers thereon.   But
the reader will soon perceive. if he has not already. that they
are of the greatest historical value and importance, as giving
the reasons and causes which first tended to the settlement of
the locality which afterwards became Saint Paul, and determined the *location* of our city.   Hence, they could not be
omitted from a full and impartial history, and deserve the
careful attention of the reader.

THE LIQUOR TRAFFIC.

Perhaps the inquiry has arisen in the mind of the reader,
was the illicit liquor traffic carried on so extensively as has
been intimated above, and was it productive of the evil consequences mentioned, to the Indians and soldiers?

I think there is abundant testimony from various sources to
prove that it was.   Intemperance among the soldiers, as Surgeon EMERSON says, has always been one of the worst enemies
to their health, good discipline and *morale*.   How to prevent
it always has been, and is now, one of the most difficult problems of the good officer.   Maj. TALIAFERRO, Indian Agent at

the fort, in his journal, before quoted, refers in many instances to the trouble brought on soldiers by the illicit sale of liquor to them.   On June 3d, 1839, he notes that *forty-seven soldiers were confined in the guard-house for drunkenness, in one night*, having been arrested in an uproarious spree in a whisky hovel across the river, kept by a man named MINK, who was, for that offense, sent out of the country.   Mrs. JAMES PATTEN, of Minneapolis, (then living in the fort with her father, RICH-ARD W. MORTIMER, a Commissary Sergeant,) states that, every winter, after settlers began to locate west of the river, and sell liquor clandestinely, soldiers lost their lives by falling down on their way back to the fort, from DONALD McDONALD's, while intoxicated, and freezing to death.   They would scale the walls, and run away, in order to go up to that groggery.   The bodies of some who died thus were eaten by the wolves. Others, less fortunate, lost their hands or feet, and dragged out the rest of their lives, miserable cripples.   The trouble and expense, and strategems soldiers would resort to to obtain liquor, shows the irresistible thirst that overpowers reason and self-command.   A few years before the above date, a Sergeant MANN, one winter night, *gave eighty dollars for a gallon of whisky*, which probably cost the dealer a shilling.

Judge IRA B. BRUNSON, of Prairie du Chien, the Deputy Marshal of Wisconsin Territory, who, in 1840, was charged with dislodging the settlers from the Reserve, says that at that time a considerable part of the soldiers were men of intemper-ate habits before they joined the army, and many of them en-listed while drunk, so that, being habituated to the use of liquor, they would run all sorts of risk to satisfy their cravings.

The effect of the sale on the Indians was even worse. "Under the influence, [says NEILL,] of a vile class of whisky-sellers that infested the neighborhood of what is now the capi-tal of Minnesota, the Dakotas were a nation of drunkards. Men would travel hundreds of miles to *The place where they sell Minne-wakan*, as they designated Saint Paul, to traffic for a keg of whisky."   Rev. GIDEON H. POND, the editor of the *Dakotah Friend*, says, in an article dated September, 1851 :

"Twelve years ago they bade fair soon to die, all together, in one drunken jumble.   They must be drunk—they could hardly live if they were not drunk. Many of them seemed as uneasy when sober as a fish does when on land. At some of the villages they were drunk months together. There was no end to it. They would have whisky. They would give guns, blankets, pork, lard, flour, corn, coffee, sugar, horses, furs, traps, anything for whisky. It was made to drink—it was good—it was *wakan*. They drank it—they bit off each other's noses—broke each other's ribs and heads—they knifed each other. They killed one another with guns, knives, hatchets, clubs, fire-brands—they fell into the fire and water, and were burned to death and drowned—they froze to death, and committed suicide so frequently that, for a time, the death of an Indian, in some of the ways mentioned, was but little thought of by themselves or others. Some of the earlier settlers of Saint Paul and Pig's Eye remember something about these matters. Their eyes saw sights which are not exhibited now-a-days."

WHAT SAINT PAUL OWES TO WHISKY!

Out of what humble circumstances sometimes spring great results. The history of Saint Paul exemplifies it. The illicit sale of liquor by some unscrupulous squatters on the Reserve, led to the expulsion without its lines of all the settlers, whether guilty of that offense or not, and resulted in forming a settlement at another point, which ultimately grew into the Saint Paul of a later day. Thus the very corner-stone of our civic existence was laid in whisky! To some extent the village throve on whisky at an early day, and whisky is yet an element of power in our midst, (especially in politics,) despite the noble crusade of Bishop IRELAND and the temperance societies. In fact, the first steamboat that ever landed at the shores of Saint Paul, the Glaucus, Captain ATCHISON, May 21, 1839, stopped to put off six barrels of whisky for DONALD McDONALD, since known as the "Half-Way House," being afraid to take the liquor any further up the river, for fear it would be seized and destroyed by the authorities at the fort.

It was always a mystery to the writer how such quantities of liquor could have been used by ordinary consumption, those days, unless the early settlers of this locality were "powerful" thirsty fellows, got up on the sponge order. But Gen. R. W. JOHNSON, in his address before the Old Settlers' Society of Hennepin county, gives a charitable construction of it that explains the whole question satisfactorily. He says that the old

pioneers were about to settle in a region of which they had
very little knowledge, and were afraid it might be infested with
rattlesnakes, hence used considerable whisky to guard against
the effects of the poison in case they should be bit.   It must
have been an efficacious remedy, as we believe there is no case
on record of any one ever dying in this locality from a snake-
bite, and, indeed, we never even heard of any one getting bit!
But they were right in being careful.

PARRANT LOSES HIS CLAIM.

But we must not lose sight of that real estate operation between PARRANT and BEAUMETTE, mentioned on page 75.   Before the note became due, BEAUMETTE. probably forced by the
pressure of circumstances, sold the note to JOHN MILLER. of
Mendota.   MILLER was a stone mason by occupation. as was
BEAUMETTE.   He built General SIBLEY's house at Mendota,
the first stone private dwelling house in Minnesota.   About
1844, he was drowned in the river near Grey Cloud Island.

When the first of May came round, PARRANT was unable to
lift the note, so MILLER became a real estate owner of PAR-
RANT's claim, by no expensive process of foreclosure.   He did
not keep it long, but transferred it to one VETAL GUERIN. a
young voyageur, of Mendota, in settlement of a debt of $150,
due the said GUERIN.   The latter never got possession of it at
all, the old adage about ·· many a slip 'twixt the cup and the
lip" being exemplified in this case, for some unscrupulous sin-
ner, whose name history has not recorded, jumped the claim,
and despoiled GUERIN of his property.   Retributive justice
overtook the graceless jumper soon after, as the United States
Marshal tore down his house and drove him off the Reserve,
as will be seen a little further along.

PARRANT MAKES ANOTHER CLAIM.

The ROMULUS of our future city, after losing his mercantile
establishment at the cave, at once made another claim.   He
selected a tract just east of Serg't HAYS' claim, fronting on the
river, extending from Minnesota street to Jackson street, approximately. and thence back to the bluff.   About where the

foot of Robert street now is, he erected on the bank—afterwards known as Bench street, and since cut down—a hovel in which to reside, and carry on his liquor trade. He occupied this claim about a year.

THE ORIGIN OF "PIG'S EYE."

PARRANT, as before remarked, had only one eye that was serviceable. He had another, it is true, but such an eye! Blind, marble-hued, crooked, with a sinister white ring glaring around the pupil, giving a kind of piggish expression to his sodden, low features. ROSWELL P. RUSSELL, now of Minneapolis; who was a sutler's clerk, at Fort Snelling then, and was frequently back and forth through the village during those days, bestowed on PARRANT the suitable and expressive sobriquet. "Pig's Eye," and, after a little while, he was generally known by that appropriate nickname. (The Frenchmen called it *O'eil de Cochon.*) Finally, the name became attached to the locality itself, in the following manner :

One day, in 1839, EDMUND BRISSETT, a young Canadian, who had come to Fort Snelling in 1832. and was doing odd jobs of carpentering for the settlers hereabouts. such as furniture, doors, sash. &c., was stopping at PARRANT's, and wanted to send a letter to JOSEPH R. BROWN, who had a trading post on Grey Cloud Island, 12 miles below, and was a Justice of the Peace. But where should he date the letter at, was the problem ? "I looked up inquiringly at PARRANT, (says BRISSETT, in relating the circumstances,) and, seeing his old crooked eye scowling at me, it suddenly popped into my head to date it at *Pig's Eye,* feeling sure that the place would be recognized, as PARRANT was well known along the river. In a little while an answer was safely received, directed to me at Pig's Eye. I told the joke to some of the boys, and they made lots of fun of PARRANT. He was very mad, and threatened to lick me, but never tried to execute it." Thus the name bestowed on the place in a joke, stuck to it for years, and it is jocosely called by it to this day. After PARRANT removed to the bottom, below Dayton's Bluff, some three or four years subsequently, the name became attached to that locality, and it will probably be known as such, until the end of time.

SETTLERS AT "PIG'S EYE" IN 1839.

During the summer of 1839, quite a number of Canadians settled at the locality now known as Pig's Eye, then called the *Grand Marais.* [PIKE, who was here in 1805, speaks of it by that name in his work.] Among them were: AMABLE TURPIN, MICHEL LECLAIRE, ANTOINE LECLAIRE, FRANCIS GAMMELL, —— LASART, JOSEPH LABISINIER, HENRY BELLAND, —— CHEVALIER, AMABLE MORIN, and CHARLES MOUSSEAU. It is possible, however, that some of these may have located there in the fall of 1838, after the ratification of the treaty was known, but at least the above, with perhaps more now forgotten, were living at Pig's Eye in the year mentioned. They were all in the employ of the Fur Company, as voyageurs, a portion of the year, and, when not needed by the company, cultivated their little farms in quiet.

AMABLE TURPIN was the father of Mrs. LOUIS ROBERT. He was born at Montreal, Canada, about the year 1766, as, when he died, in 1866, he was in his 100th year—a span of life that falls to the lot of but a small percentage of mortals. While a young man, he went to Mackinac, and thence to Green Bay, and finally to Prairie du Chien, where he was in the employ of the American Fur Company for many years. The date of his settlement in Prairie du Chien is not now remembered accurately, but it must have been early during the present century, as when the British captured that place, in 1814, Mr. TURPIN was a citizen of influence and widely known in the Northwest. He had, during his long life, traveled on business for the Fur Company, over every portion of the Northwest, while it was an utter wilderness, only penetrated occasionally by adventurous fur-traders or devoted missionaries. He was generally selected by the Fur Company for any mission or voyage of • more than usual difficulty, danger and hardship. His adventures, during his many perilous journeys among the Indians, and in the forests and lakes of the Northwest, would fill volumes. He possessed a physique of extraordinary power and endurance.   He lived at Pig's Eye several years, and ultimately removed to Saint Paul, where he died May 4, 1866, having almost rounded out a century.   Mrs. TURPIN used to teach the catechism to the half-breed children at the Grand Marais, before the arrival of Father GALTIER—being the first religious teaching in this locality, except the missionary work among the Indians.

MICHEL LeCLAIRE and ANTOINE LeCLAIRE were, I believe, brothers.   They came from Canada—date unascertained by the writer.   ANTOINE LeCLAIRE, I think, had lived at Mendota several years before settling at Pig's Eye.   It is probable that MICHEL LeCLAIRE was the first settler at the Grand Marais, as the locality was known along the river shortly after that time, as "Point LeClaire." [See letter of Rev. L. GALTIER, *post.*]   LeCLAIRE had a dispute, several years subsequent to this date, with PIERRE PARRANT, about the ownership of a claim at the Grand Marais, which is fully narrated a few pages further on.   LeCLAIRE died at Pig's Eye, about the year 1849, leaving quite a numerous family, some of which still live in this vicinity.   He seems to have been a carpenter by trade, as VETAL GUERIN states that he made the doors and windows for his (G.'s) cabin, in 1840.

Of ANTOINE LeCLAIRE, or his subsequent history, I have been unable to learn anything.

FRANCIS GAMMEL'S history will be found more fully narrated in the events of the year 1842, where he plays a somewhat conspicuous part.

JOSEPH LABISINIER came from Canada originally, and lived some time at Red River, where he married a Moutinier woman. He came from Red River to Fort Snelling, in 1836, with the same company in which RONDO *et als.* immigrated to Minnesota.   One or two of his cotemporaries think he settled at Pig's Eye in the fall of 1838—but at least he was living there as early as 1839.   In 1842, he made a new claim, occupying a part of Jackson and Robert street hill, and extending down to about Twelfth street.   He erected a cabin near the head of Jackson street, which was burned down about three years ago. His claim he sold to JAMES R. CLEWETT, in 1843—consideration, a horse—and retired a little further back, toward Lake

Phelan, where he made a new claim. He died at Osseo, Minnesota, several years since, at quite an advanced age, leaving several children. some of whom reside here yet. His widow died about five years ago.

HENRY BELLAND, another resident of the Grand Marais in 1839, subsequently resided in West Saint Paul for many years, and is still a citizen of that locality.   •

AMABLE MORIN now lives at Wheatland, Rice county.

CHARLES MOUSSEAU was in reality more a resident of Saint Paul than of Pig's Eye, since his claim was on Dayton's Bluff, and not in the Marais at all. MOUSSEAU was a native of Canada—born 1807. He came to Minnesota in 1827, as a voyageur of the Fur Company. In 1836, he was married to FANNY PERRY, at Fort Snelling, and in the fall of 1838, or spring of 1839, made a claim as above stated, in what is now Saint Paul. This claim he sold, in 1848, to EB. WELD, and moved to Hennepin county, of which he has been a resident ever since. Mr. MOUSSEAU now resides in Minneapolis, and has had twelve children, nine of them now living.

DENIS CHERRIER came to the Grand Marais in the fall of 1839. He is a native of Prairie du Chien,—born 1816. Late in the fall, he started for Pig's Eye, on a steamer, with a stock of goods, but the river closed with ice at the head of Lake Pepin, so that the boat could not get through, and CHERRIER came on in a canoe. He sold his goods that fall and returned to Prairie du Chien, but came up again the next year, and has been a resident of Saint Paul ever since. He has owned several claims at different times, and, had he held on to any one of them, might be well off, but, like many of our pioneers, he sold them for a mere song, and is still poor. DENNY's violin used to enliven the dances in early days, and some of the girls of thirty years ago—grandmothers now—may remember how they danced all night to his music.

JAMES R. CLEWETT.

During this year, JAMES REUBEN CLEWETT became a resident of the little settlement. Mr. CLEWETT was born in England, in 1810, and came to America in 1829. He lived in

Canada for a couple of years, and, in 1831, was hired by GABRIEL FRANCHERE, an agent of the American Fur Company, to come to Minnesota in the service of that company, as a voyageur, clerk, &c. On arriving at Prairie du Chien, CLEWETT was assigned, by the late HERCULES DOUSMAN, to ROCQUE's Trading Post, below Lake Pepin. At that time he could not speak a word of French, but was soon compelled to learn it, as well as Sioux, because English was not spoken by any one at the post. No one but CLEWETT could read or write, and he kept all the books and accounts of the post. After serving at ROCQUE's two years, in 1834 he was sent to Lake Traverse to "old man" MOOER's Trading Post. He remained in that region until the winter of 1838–9, when he came to Grey Cloud Island, below Saint Paul, with JOSEPH R. BROWN, who latterly had been in charge of the Lake Traverse Post. After remaining there, and at Mendota a short time, he went to live at ABRAHAM PERRY's, on his claim in upper Saint Paul, and in April of 1839, married ROSE PERRY, one of the daughters of the old gentleman, being the first marriage in Saint Paul. Soon after, CLEWETT purchased the claim of "JOHNSON," which subsequently (1843) passed into the possession of Hon. NORMAN W. KITTSON, and was laid out as "Kittson's Addition." He then purchased a small claim of LABISINIER, on Jackson street hill, where he resided until 1851, when he removed to White Bear Lake, and has resided there since that date. Mr. CLEWETT has had 12 children, eight of whom are married, and have considerable families. He has been engaged in steamboating on Red River for two or three seasons past, and is still active and hearty, bidding fair to live for a score of years yet.

THE FIRST MARRIAGE, BIRTH AND DEATH.

The year 1839 witnessed the first marriage, birth and death, which occurred in the little hamlet that subsequently became Saint Paul—the initial of the long series of those "important events" in the life of each one of its future citizens, which will gladden or sadden households, as long as the stream of humanity flows.

7

The first birth of a white child, was in the family of BENJA-MIN GERVAIS. His youngest son, BASIL GERVAIS, was born September 4, 1839, and is now, at the age of 36 years, a respected citizen of Centerville, Anoka county.

In a newspaper sketch, which the writer of this published several years ago, it was stated, (on the authority of the late VETAL GUERIN, then our oldest settler,) that his son, DAVID GUERIN, now deceased, was the first white child born in Saint Paul. Mr. GUERIN supposed this was the case. Subsequent investigation of church registers, however, shows this to be an error. DAVID GUERIN was not born until the fall of 1841. The register of Saint Gabriel's Church, at Prairie du Chien, shows BASIL GERVAIS to have been born September 4, 1839, and baptized by Rev. A. RAVOUX, then at Prairie du Chien, May 10, 1840, while his mother was on a visit to that place. Mr. CLEWETT was long under the impression that his oldest son, ALBERT, was the first white child born here, but it was not until January, 1840, some four months after Mr. GERVAIS was born.

The first marriage, conformable to the laws of the land, which occurred in Saint Paul, was that of J. R. CLEWETT, to ROSE PERRY, in April, of this year. The ceremony was performed by Rev. J. W. POPE, a Methodist missionary at Kaposia.

Of the first death we will now proceed to speak.

THE MURDER OF HAYS.

PHELAN and HAYS, who were partners in the claim business, had been residing in the cabin on PHELAN's claim, since April of this year, 1839. It was in a lonely spot, a mile or more from any other habitation, and but seldom did any one visit the cabin of the two settlers. PHELAN, as before remarked, was regarded by the other settlers, as a bad, unscrupulous, wicked man. HAYS was supposed to have considerable money, received on his discharge from the army, and the two held in common several cattle and other personal property. The two men were as unlike as possible in their disposition, character, &c., and it was known that they did not agree very well. Such was the situation of matters in September, 1839.

About the middle of that month, HAYS mysteriously disappeared. He was missed for several days, and, to inquiries as to his whereabouts, PHELAN gave evasive and unsatisfactory answers. The rumor of his disappearance reached Fort Snelling, where HAYS was well known and liked. TALIAFERRO makes this record in his journal :

" Sunday, 15th September, 1839, a man, by name HAYS, an Irishman, lost. Supposed killed—even reported to have been murdered by the Chief *Wa-kin-yan-ton-ka*, [BIG THUNDER—LITTLE CROW'S father.] No belief rests with me. I incline to the opinion that his neighbor, PHELAN, knows something. HAYS lived with him, and had money."

On September 27, TALIAFERRO made the following entry : ·· *Wabsheedah*, or the DANCER, called at the office to say that his sons had found the body of Mr. HAYS, lost some time ago, in the river near Carver's Cave."

Maj. TALIAFERRO at once sent *Wabsheedah* to Maj. PLYMPTON with the following note :

"AGENCY HOUSE, Saint Peter's, September 27, 1839.
" MAJOR : I have sent the bearer, a good Indian, to go with the gentlemen who are in quest of the identity of Mr. HAYS' body, now in the water near CARVER's old cave. The Indian will conduct them to the spot, being so directed by his chief, if requested so to do.
" Very respectfully, your obedient servant,
" LAW. TALIAFERRO, Indian Agent."

The body of poor HAYS was at once secured. On examination, his head, jaws and nose were found badly mashed by violent blows, unmistakably indicating a desperate murder. PHELAN was at once arrested, by warrant issued by HENRY H. SIBLEY, as Justice of the Peace, and, on the 28th, was examined before that officer as to his knowledge of HAYS' death. The evidence adduced and the other circumstances known, were sufficient to justify his commitment to answer the charge of murder in the first degree, and he was consequently confined in the guard-house at the fort, until the next steamboat arrived, when he was sent to Prairie du Chien, county seat of Crawford county, Wisconsin Territory, in which the crime had been committed, to await trial.

DID PHELAN MURDER HAYS?

It is somewhat a late day, 36 years after the event, to place
PHELAN on trial before the public, as to his guilt in the murder
of his partner, but we propose only to advance such facts as
the lapse of time have left, bearing on the case.

Of PHELAN's guilt no one who was resident in this vicinity
had any doubt. Hon. H. H. SIBLEY, who carefully sifted the
evidence on the examination of PHELAN, says it was such as
to leave no doubt of his guilt. Gen. SIBLEY thinks he preserved a copy of the evidence taken—but has been unable, so
far, to find it in his mass of papers. Mrs. BENJ. GERVAIS and
WILLIAM EVANS were two witnesses who were subpœnaed to
go to Prairie du Chien at the trial, the following spring, and
give evidence against PHELAN. What testimony EVANS may
have been in possession of, I cannot ascertain. Mrs. GER-
VAIS, whose memory is remarkably clear for one so aged, says,
among other things, that, a short time before the murder of
HAYS, she asked PHELAN how he and HAYS got along.
"Very badly," replied PHELAN. "He is a lazy good-for-
nothing. But never mind," (he added, with a wicked look.)
"I'll soon get rid of him." ALPHONSE GERVAIS stated that
he saw blood on PHELAN's clothes, and that, when PHELAN's
cabin was searched, bloody clothes were found beneath the
floor. He states, moreover, that he found the place, near the
cabin, where the act was committed, being led thither by a
very sagacious dog he owned, who smelled the blood, and
plainly traced the route by which the body was dragged to the
river from thence. Others also saw these evidences of a murder. J. R. CLEWETT says he thought, at the time, the Indians
had committed the murder; and that one Indian, a few years
afterward, just before his death, confessed that he was the
murderer of HAYS; also, that some of the Kaposia Indians
used to assert that a brother of LITTLE CROW had committed
the act. But Gen. SIBLEY says this is impossible. That had
any Indian committed the act, he (Gen. S.) would certainly
have found it out. Moreover, there was no particular motive
for the Indians to have murdered HAYS, more than any one

else, while two powerful motives would seem to have influenced PHELAN—revenge and avarice.

There is, then, no alternative left, but to record PHELAN as the murderer of HAYS. He must stand, on the chronicles of our city, as its CAIN—the first who imbrued his hands with the blood of his brother—a crime too often, alas, repeated since that day.

THE SURVEY OF THE RESERVATION.

Maj. TALIAFERRO, in his journal, under date of October 5, 1839, says:

"Lieut. THOMPSON is engaged in making the lines for the military Reservation around Fort Snelling. 'From Mississippi five miles up the Saint Peter's; thence west to Lake Harriet, seven miles; thence along Lake Harriet to the Lake of the Isles; thence to the portage landing, above the falls, one-fourth of a mile; across the Mississippi, five miles.' 'The line,' he says further, 'comes below the cave;' and, in another place, 'that it extends much further east than any survey hitherto.'"

Maj. PLYMPTON, on November 29, transmits this map to the War Department, with the following statement:

"The red lines show the boundaries of the Reservation, and which are conformable to the survey of Lieutenant SMITH, with this slight difference: that, in his survey, the principal lines, from river to river, were necessarily (from the season and weather) left imaginary, which, upon an actual survey, will be found (to embrace the necessary woodland and to preserve the cardinal points) to cross the Mississippi a little further down than that imaginarily indicated on the map of Lieutenant SMITH's survey.

"The limits of the Reservation, as now marked, embrace no more ground, I conceive, than is absolutely necessary to furnish the daily wants of this garrison, and, could they be extended further into the country on the east side of the river, it would, no doubt, add to the quiet of this command."

The limits fixed were entirely arbitrary. They were *not* governed by the "daily wants" of the garrison, for the additional woodland secured was of no value or importance to the post, and was never utilized. The line was extended far beyond the possible intent of the Reservation. JOHN R. IRVINE states, that when he came here, four years after, the east line of the Reservation ran about where the Seven Corners now is, thence northwardly to about where the Park Place Hotel stands.

ORDER FOR THE EXPULSION OF THE SQUATTERS FROM THE RESERVE.

But we must return, to preserve the chronological order of events, to the efforts made by the military authorities, for the expulsion of squatters from the Reserve. Hon. JOEL R. POIN-SETT, Secretary of War, after duly considering the letters of Surgeon EMERSON and Gen. WOOL, given in preceding pages, issued the following order:

"WAR DEPARTMENT, October 21, 1839.

"SIR: The interests of the service, and the proper and effective maintenance of the military post at Fort Snelling, requiring that the intruders on the land recently reserved for military purposes, opposite to that post east of the Mississippi River, be removed therefrom, the President of the United States directs that, when required by the commanding officer of the post, you proceed there, and remove them, under the provisions of the act of March third, 1807, entitled 'An act to prevent settlements being made on lands ceded to the United States, until authorized by law.'

"You will satisfy yourself of the shortest period within which the intruders can make their arrangements for removal, and depart from the Reservation, without serious loss or sacrifice of the property which they may have to take with them; and you will promptly make known to them that it is expected they will not delay beyond that period; as, should they do so, it will become your duty to remove them by military force. It is hoped, however, that a resort to such force for this purpose, which, by the act above mentioned, the President is authorized to employ, will not be necessary; but that they will promptly depart, on being informed of the determination of the executive, not to permit them to remain. Should you, however, be unfortunately obliged to use force in order to accomplish the object, you are authorized to call for such as you may deem necessary, on the commanding officer at Fort Snelling. In this event, you will act with as much forbearance, consideration, and delicacy as may be consistent with the prompt and faithful performance of the duties hereby assigned to you, first fully and mildly explaining the folly of resistance on their part, and your own want of discretion in the matter.

"Very respectfully, your obedient servant,

"J. R. POINSETT.

"EDWARD JAMES, Esq.,

"United States Marshal for the Territory of Wiskonsan, Peru."

It was probably the intention of POINSETT and PLYMPTON to have ejected the squatters that fall.   By an accident, however, the above letter was not received by Mr. JAMES for several months, as his reply below shows :

"MINERAL POINT, WISCONSIN TERRITORY, }
"February 18th, 1840.   }

"SIR : By the evening's mail, I have received your instructions of October 21, 1839, relative to the removal of intruders at Fort Snelling. The delay of their receipt has, doubtless, been occasioned by their being directed to Peru, which is in Iowa Territory.

"I have not as yet received any request from the commanding officer of that fort, but shall promptly attend to the duty whenever required.

"Very respectfully, your obedient servant,
"EDWARD JAMES,
"Marshal of Wisconsin.

"Hon. J. R. POINSETT."

ACTION OF THE WISCONSIN LEGISLATURE.

Probably finding there was no stay of execution to be secured from any other source, the squatters within the lines of Maj. PLYMPTON'S Reserve, seem to have appealed to the Wisconsin Legislature to interfere in their behalf.   That body consequently passed the following concurrent resolutions :

"Whereas, the advantages of steamboat landings are of vast importance to an agricultural district, and particularly necessary to the citizens of this Territory residing near the head of the navigation of the Mississippi river; and whereas, the military Reservation of Fort Snelling, in Iowa Territory, has been so surveyed as to embrace the only convenient steamboat landing east of the Mississippi, for fifteen miles below the head of navigation, and also includes a valuable agricultural district, much of which is under a good state of cultivation, and occupied by an industrious and enterprising people, some of whom have made valuable improvements; and whereas, it appears efforts are being made by the military of said fort to procure a section of the Reserve as lately surveyed, for speculative purposes, and without any regard to the good of the military service: Now be it

"*Resolved, by Council and House of Representatives of the Territory of Wisconsin,* That our delegate in Congress be requested to protest against the extension of the military Reserve of Fort Snelling to the Wisconsin side of the Mississippi.

"*Resolved,* That the Governor be requested to forward one copy of the foregoing preamble and resolutions to the Secretary of War, and one copy to our delegate in Congress.

"Approved December 16, 1839."

On January 12, 1840, Governor J. D. DOTY addressed the Secretary of War as follows:

"WASHINGTON, January 12, 1840.

"SIR: The Legislative Assembly of Wisconsin has, by a resolution, approved by the Governor on the 16th of December, 1839, requested me to protest against the extension of the military Reservation of Fort Snelling to the Wisconsin side of the Mississippi River, with which I have now the honor to comply.

"A question of some importance will arise if the Reservation is made, which I beg leave to state: The United States may reserve any portion of its lands from sale, but can it extend a military jurisdiction over so large a tract of country as is embraced in the limits of this Reservation by the simple declaration that it is necessary for military purposes?

"A Territory is a State under a temporary form of government. It may be doubtful with some whether Congress may exercise exclusive jurisdiction over this Reservation, the purchase having been made without the consent of the Legislature of that State. Against the exercise of that jurisdiction the legislative power of that State now protests.

"The subdivisions of the territory northwest of the Ohio are denominated States in the ordinance of 1787. And in the third section it is ordained that 'the laws to be adopted or made (by the Legislature) *shall have force in all parts of the district.*' It also requires the Governor 'to lay out the parts of the district, in which the Indian titles shall have been extinguished, into counties and townships.' An exclusive military jurisdiction would be incompatible with the exercise of this power by the Territorial Government.

"I am advised that a copy of the resolution of the Assembly of Wisconsin has been forwarded to the War Department, and I beg leave to refer to the reasons therein stated.

"I have the honor to be, sir, with great respect, your obedient servant,

"J. D. DOTY.

"Hon. J. R. POINSETT, Secretary of War."

VETAL GUERIN.

A few pages back, mention was made of one VETAL GUERIN, who purchased PARRANT's original claim, but who never came into possession of it, for reasons there stated.

VETAL GUERIN was born in Saint Remi, Canada, July 17,

1812.   His father was Louis Guerin, a voyageur by occupation, who died in 1865, at the ripe age of 83.   Vetal grew up into the same occupation as his father.   In 1832, when he was 20 years of age, a lithe, sinewy young fellow, Vetal enlisted in the service of the American Fur Company, under

VETAL GUERIN.

Gabriel Franchere, for three years.   He was to join a company bound for the Upper Mississippi, consisting of 134 men, in charge of four barges of goods.   They left Montreal, May 5, 1832, and made the entire journey to Mendota by water, through the lakes, Green Bay, the Fox and Wisconsin Rivers, and up the Mississippi.   The entire season was consumed in this trip, and it was late in the fall when the party reached the company's post at Mendota.

Guerin served the company his stipulated three years, and,

after that term had expired, worked by odd jobs for the company, and for Mr. FARIBAULT and other traders, at Mendota and Traverse de Sioux, for three or four years longer.

GUERIN's first investment in Saint Paul real estate had not proved a paying one, but, nevertheless, he soon after determined to repeat the experiment. Looking about, in the fall of 1839, he found the HAYS claim, which PHELAN still pretended to own, by virtue of his partnership with HAYS, unoccupied, and quite likely to be so as far as either of its former owners was concerned—one being dead, and the other in prison 300 miles away, with a good prospect of stretching hemp. As the claim suited VETAL pretty well, he forthwith squatted on it, and proceeded to erect a cabin. This cabin, so he stated to the writer, was a very unpretending affair, about 16x20 feet, built of oak and elm from the woods surrounding it, with a bark roof and a floor of split and hewed puncheons. The door and sash were made by MICHEL LeCLAIRE, of the Grand Marais, since called Pig's Eye. This cabin stood on the spot now occupied by Ingersoll's Block, and, with some additions and changes, stood there until 1866, when the buildings occupying the site of said block were removed, to make room for it.

Thus, at the close of the year 1839, there were nine cabins within the present limits of the city of Saint Paul. Patience! We shall have a city yet.

CHAPTER VIII.

EVENTS OF THE YEARS 1840 AND 1841.

ORGANIZATION OF SAINT CROIX COUNTY—EXPULSION OF SETTLERS FROM THE
RESERVE—SOME OF THEM COME TO SAINT PAUL—PHELAN RETURNS AND DE-
MANDS HIS CLAIM — GUERIN CHECKMATES HIM — JOSEPH RONDO — VETAL
GUERIN'S SUBSEQUENT HISTORY—PIERRE BOTTINEAU—A CATHOLIC MISSION
FOUNDED HERE—FATHER GALTIER AND FATHER RAVOUX, &C.

CRAWFORD county, Wisconsin Territory, had been created and organized, (as noted on page 39,) in 1819.   For
twenty-two years its boundaries were unchanged.   In January.
1840. through the influence of JOSEPH R. BROWN, a bill was
passed creating '' Saint Croix County."   The boundaries of
the new county included all that part of Crawford county lying
west of a line running northward from the mouth of the Porcupine River on Lake Pepin to Lake Superior.   The county
seat was fixed at BROWN's town-site of '' Dakota," about the
upper end of the present city of Stillwater.   In the fall of this
year, at the election for Representatives, JOSEPH R. BROWN
was elected a member of the Wisconsin Assembly, for two
years.   Henceforth this region commenced to have a voice
in the public affairs of the Territory, to which it had been
hitherto a mere unnoticed back settlement.   But Saint Paul
must have stood for several years to Wisconsin about in the
same relation that Pembina used to, to Minnesota.   Its representatives, from this date until the organization of Minnesota
Territory, are given on page 45.

EXPULSION OF SETTLERS FROM THE RESERVE.

When Marshal EDWARD JAMES, of Wisconsin Territory,
received the order for the expulsion of the settlers on the Reserve, he sent it to his deputy, IRA B. BRUNSON, of Prairie du
Chien, to execute.   As it was now near the end of winter,

and traveling very difficult and insecure. Mr. BRUNSON delayed his journey until the opening of navigation in the spring, when he took the first boat for Fort Snelling, about May 1, and proceeded to execute his unpleasant task.

In an account of the transaction Mr. BRUNSON wrote for me, he says that he gave the settlers several days' notice to remove, but they disregarded the warning, so that he was compelled to call upon Maj. PLYMPTON for a military force to execute the orders *vi et armis.* On the 6th day of May, 1840, the settlers on the Reserve were dishoused and driven off, and every cabin within the lines destroyed.

In a memorial from the expelled settlers to Congress, praying for indemnity for their losses, presented by Delegate H. H. SIBLEY, in 1849, and again in 1852.* the settlers state that the soldiery fell upon them without warning, treated them with unjustifiable rudeness, broke and destroyed furniture wantonly, insulted the women, and, in one or two instances, fired at and killed cattle. Mr. BRUNSON denies, positively, in general and in particular, these statements. He states that the soldiers acted reluctantly in the matter, but civilly, under the command of a Lieutenant, and under his (BRUNSON'S) supervision, and in their presence. As the settlers refused to budge, they had to carry their household goods out, but none was broken intentionally, and no unnecessary force was used.

ABRAHAM PERRY, the GERVAIS brothers, RONDO, and other of the early settlers, of Saint Paul, were among those whose houses were destroyed. To these poor refugees it was a cruel blow. The victims of floods, and frosts, and grasshoppers, in the Red River valley, and once before expelled from the Reserve, (west side,) it seemed that the cup of disaster was charged to the brim for them. Mournfully gathering up their effects and flocks, they set out once more to find a home.

FINDING NEW HOMES.

On being dishoused, the unfortunate settlers retreated beyond

---

* No action was ever taken by Congress on this Memorial, beyond referring it to a committee, which never reported on it.

the line of the Reserve, and there made preparations for beginning life once more.

ABRAHAM PERRY and family sojourned for the present in the house of his son-in-law, JAMES R. CLEWETT. Almost broken down by his repeated misfortunes, and by the severe toil and hardships of the past few years, PERRY seemed never to recover from these buffets of hard fortune. His health gradually declined. For some time his lower limbs were so paralyzed that he could not stand. He still endeavored to engage in agricultural labor, and actually cut down trees while sitting on the ground. He died in May, 1849, aged 73 years. His wife, Mrs. MARY ANN PERRY, died in 1859, at an advanced age, at the residence of CHARLES BAZILLE, her son-in-law.

ABRAHAM PERRY had seven children, the three oldest of whom were born in Switzerland, two at Red River, and the two youngest at Fort Snelling. His only son, CHARLES PERRY, born in Switzerland, now lives at Lake Johanna, Ramsey county. Mr. PERRY's daughters all married in this vicinity, as follows : SOPHIA married PIERRE CREVIER, and lives near Watertown, Minnesota. FANNY married CHARLES MOUSSEAU, 1836 ; residence, Minneapolis. ROSE ANN married J. R. CLEWETT, 1839 ; residence, White Bear. ADELE married VETAL GUERIN, 1841 ; residence, Saint Paul. JOSEPHINE married J. B. CORNOYER, 1843 ; residence, Minneapolis. ANNIE JANE married CHARLES BAZILLE, 1846 ; residence, Saint Paul. Nearly every one of PERRY's children have raised large families, and he had over 75 grandchildren.

GERVAIS BUYS PARRANT'S CLAIM.

BEN. GERVAIS, on losing his home near the creek, in upper town, at once proceeded to PARRANT's claim, before mentioned and purchased of that swine-optical individual, all his right, title and interest to said real estate, together with the hereditaments and appurtenances, and so on. Reader, what do you suppose GERVAIS paid to "Old Pig's Eye" for this property, now in the heart of our city? *Ten dollars!* It is now worth several millions.

PARRANT had an uncompleted cabin on the edge of the bluff,

about where the corner of Robert and Bench streets now is. GERVAIS finished this, and occupied it as a dwelling for several years.

PARRANT at once made a new claim on the lower levee, and erected another hovel, where he continued his whisky business until 1843, when LOUIS ROBERT purchased his claim. But of this hereafter.

PHELAN'S TRIAL.

In the spring of 1840, the case of PHELAN, who for several months past had been lying in the guard-house at Fort Crawford, Prairie du Chien, awaiting trial for HAYS' murder, was taken up by the court of Crawford county. I have been unable to ascertain just what action was had in his case. Hon. IRA B. BRUNSON, now County Judge at Prairie du Chien, at my request, carefully searched the records of the court at that period, and before and after, but can find no reference to the case. The only explanation is, that the case was brought before the grand jury, who failed to find a bill against PHELAN, and he was discharged. Mrs. GERVAIS and WM. EVANS went to Prairie du Chien as witnesses, but their evidence probably failed to convince the grand jury of PHELAN's guilt, and he was allowed to go his way.

PHELAN VS. GUERIN.

When PHELAN made his way back to Saint Paul, which he soon did, he found VETAL GUERIN in possession of the HAYS claim, which he (PHELAN) still pretended to own, by virtue of his partnership with HAYS. He at once proceeded to demand of GUERIN, possession of the claim. The result we give in GUERIN's own words, dictated to the writer in 1866:

"PHELAN called at my cabin, accompanied by JAMES R. CLEWETT as interpreter, as I could then talk no English. He demanded possession of the claim. I replied that I would not give it up, as I believed I was rightfully entitled to it. Some more talk ensued, and, finding that I was not disposed to yield to him, PHELAN told JIM to say that if I was not off by a certain day—say a week from then—he would put me off by force. As PHELAN was a large, powerful man, and I was small and light, he could have easily picked me up and carried me outside the claim lines. After making this threat, PHELAN went away.

"As I knew I could not deal with PHELAN single-handed, I told some of my voyageur companions at Mendota how matters stood, and three or four of them, strong, 'husky' fellows, came down to stay with me. A supply of liquor and some cards made time pass merrily. On the day PHELAN had set to put me off the claim, sure enough, he made his appearance—axe in hand and sleeves rolled up—with CLEWETT as interpreter. Through the latter, PHELAN inquired if I would leave. I replied, no. PHELAN got very mad at this, and said, 'tell the d— little Frenchman I will take him under my arm and throw him off the claim.'

"I then said to my men, who were inside, that I thought it was time for them to interfere. They came out, and, throwing off their coats, told PHELAN that if he did not go way and leave me alone, they would pitch him over the bluff! And, moreover, if he ever molested me, they would lynch him. PHELAN knew they were not fellows whom it would do to trifle with, and, as he had just got out of one bad scrape, didn't want to get into any further trouble, if he could avoid it. He finally left, saying he would take the law of me. He thereupon commenced an action before JOSEPH R. BROWN, Justice of the Peace, at Grey Cloud Island, to recover possession. BROWN examined into the case, and found that PHELAN was absent from his claim more than six months at one time. So he told PHELAN that he had lost all title to it, and that I could not be ejected. I had no further trouble with him, and kept peaceable possession of the claim."

GUERIN GIVES AWAY HALF HIS CLAIM.

When GUERIN had thus quieted title to his claim, he proceeded to do a very generous act for a friend, PIERRE GERVAIS, who had recently been expelled from the Reserve, and was looking for a new home. Feeling lonesome, and, wanting a neighbor, he gave, without any consideration, one-half of his claim—or at least a good share of it—to PIERRE, on condition that the latter would come and live there. GERVAIS accepted the offer, and built a cabin about where Mrs. Dr. MANN's block is now, corner of Third and Saint Peter streets. He lived here about two years, and, in 1842, sold the claim to DENIS CHERRIER for $150, and moved into lower town, where he got another small tract. CHERRIER, in turn, sold the claim, in 1843, to SCOTT CAMPBELL for $300, and, in 1848, CAMPBELL sold out to WM. HARTSHORN and others.

JOSEPH RONDO.

A few pages back, reference was made to JOSEPH RONDO, a refugee from Red River, who was one of the earliest squatters on the Reserve, east of the Mississippi. His house was one which was destroyed by the soldiery on May 6, 1840.

JOSEPH RONDO was born near Montreal, Canada, in 1797. When quite a lad, some 17 or 18 years old, he engaged as a voyageur in the service of the Hudson's Bay Company, and was sent to the Pacific Coast. He passed several years in the laborious work of his calling, on Frazer River, Great Slave Lake, Fort Edmonton, and other posts on the extreme west and north of the Hudson's Bay Company's dominions.

About 1827, he settled in the Red River Colony, near Fort Garry, and, having married JOSEPHINE BOILEAU, a Kootenais mixed blood, established a farm there. The troubles which afflicted the colonists have already been referred to. After enduring them for eight years, Mr. RONDO, in company with the GERVAIS brothers, BEAUMETTE, BRUCE, BLANC, MICHEL DUFENI, LABISINIER, GOODRICH, and others—about 60 in all— left the Red River Colony, and settled near Fort Snelling. RONDO purchased a house on the west side, of JOSEPH TURPIN, from which he was ejected on May 6, 1840, with the other settlers.

Following the example of PERRY, GERVAIS and others, RONDO then came to the lower side of the Reserve, looking for a new claim. PHELAN offered his for sale, including the unfurnished hovel under the hill, the scene of the HAYS tragedy, for $200. RONDO purchased the same, and, finishing up the house, lived in it a season or two, until he could build a more comfortable one.

PHELAN MAKES A NEW CLAIM.

Having now lost or disposed of all his real estate in Saint Paul, PHELAN made a new claim on the creek that now bears his name, and built a cabin about where HAMM'S brewery is. This claim enclosed a fine water-power on the creek, and, in 1844, it was purchased by WILLIAM DUGAS, for a mill-site, as will be found more fully narrated in the events of that year.

SOMETHING MORE ABOUT VETAL GUERIN.

GUERIN lived more than a year alone in his cabin, but such a solitary, bachelor life must have become very distasteful to him. So, he persuaded one of the few young women which the little village then boasted of, Miss ADELE PERRY, to share his lot. On January 26, 1841, Father GALTIER made the twain one flesh, at Mendota. Returning to the settlement, a gay and pleasant party was given to the new couple, at the house of BEN. GERVAIS, during the evening. DENNY CHERRIER says he fiddled that night until he was exhausted.

The domestic outfit of the young couple was not an extravagant one. Furniture was only obtainable those days from Saint Louis. The settlers generally made their own furniture. The bridal bed was a bunk of boards, on which hay and a red blanket, which GUERIN had brought from Mackinac, were spread. Mrs. GUERIN soon afterward traded a shawl to some Indians for feathers, and thus softened the rough edges of life a little. GUERIN's chest, that held all his goods and effects, served for a dining table, until a better one could be procured.

A few rods from GUERIN's cabin, was PARRANT's establishment, and the powerful nature of the *minne-wakan* he sold the Indians there, used to turn them sometimes into red demons. In one of their crazy sprees, the Indians killed GUERIN's cow and pig, and destroyed other property. Indeed, the lives of GUERIN and his bride were oftentimes in danger, and their honeymoon was somewhat a stormy one, take it all in all. These devilish sprees of the Indians occurred occasionally for several years. Once, when Mrs. GUERIN was nursing her first child, about two months old, some nine or ten Indians made an attack on the house, and tried to kill GUERIN. They broke in the window, and attempted to crawl in. Mrs. G. concealed herself under the bed, expecting to be murdered. GUERIN seized an axe, and was about to brain the first pagan whose head appeared through the window. This would have been a very unfortunate affair for GUERIN, had it happened, but, luckily, before any bloodshed occurred, a friendly chief, named "HAWK's BILL," came up, and remonstrated with the

8

drunken brutes, urging them to leave. While they were parleying, Mr. and Mrs. GUERIN, with the child, slipped out of
the door, and fled to Mr. GERVAIS' house. The Indians then
went away, after shooting GUERIN's dog with arrows.

Another time, GUERIN was leaning on the gate-post of his
garden, when some drunken Indians, coming up Bench street
hill, fired at him. A ball struck the post, making a narrow
escape for VETAL. Again, as he opened his door, one morning, an iron-headed arrow whizzed past his head, and stuck
in the door-jamb. Another close call, but GUERIN survived
them all.

At that time, Mendota was the only place where supplies
or necessaries of any kind could be obtained, and these usually
of a simple character. Pork, flour, tea and sugar, were about
all that could be purchased in the way of provisions, but game
was very plenty, and some farming on a small scale had begun.
In the summer after his marriage, GUERIN enclosed a small
field, embracing the land now lying between Saint Peter
and Cedar, Bench and Sixth streets, and plowed it up for a
garden. His oxen were "Red River" cattle. Mrs. GUERIN
used to help him by driving the oxen. GUERIN, one year,
raised considerable grain, but could not sell it, or get it ground
up—so it laid in his granary until it rotted. There was no
grist-mill in this region, for custom use, until LEMUEL BOLLES
established his, on Bolles Creek, in 1845.

It needs but little more space to speak of GUERIN's subsequent life, and, perhaps, it is as fitting here as anywhere. In
his little cabin he kept the even tenor of his way, even when
the whirl of real estate speculation was turning men's brains.
While his neighbors were selling out at what they deemed
fabulous sums, and moving away, GUERIN held on to his
claim—nay, refused tempting offers for it, and was called a
fool for so doing. And it did seem foolish when, in 1843, he
declined $1,000 for his land. Had some dream of a future
splendid city, rising like a palace of enchantment, come to
him, as he slept in his bark-roofed cabin? Verily, one would
think so. But fortune befriended the plain, humble Frenchman. Suddenly his acres leaped into great value. He was a

rich man. His dream had been realized. Yet, with property valued at over $100,000, he was the same plain, unassuming man as he had been in his pioneer cabin. True, he built a finer house, in 1849, corner of Wabasha and Seventh streets, where he resided until his death, but he assumed no parvenu airs, and no foolish pride puffed him up, though ample means compensated him for the hardships and privations of his earlier years. He gave to his children the education of which he had been denied. His generosity was a distinguishing trait. After the town was laid out, in 1847, he gave away property worth now a round quarter million—one block for the court-house, several lots to the church, and for other purposes. During his years of plenty, he was unceasingly beneficent to his poor countrymen, who always found in him a liberal and sympathizing friend. Honest and candid himself, his simple faith and trust in other men's honor, was large and confiding— a trait that continually enabled sharpers to defraud and over-reach him, until his ample fortune melted away by reverses, which, before his death, sent him into the bankrupt court. In his prosperous days, every enterprise for the good of the city, met his generous aid, and yet he, the once owner of millions, the princely donor of estates to the public, died poor, and his family have since felt the pinchings of want. His last illness was long and painful, but patiently borne. He died November 11, 1870, aged 58 years, and his funeral was attended by a large gathering of old settlers and early citizens. The common council properly honored his memory by erecting a monument over his remains, which now repose in Catholic cemetery.

The excellent portrait of him, given elsewhere, was taken from a small card photograph, the only one he ever had made, and which was taken, not long before his death, at the urgent request of the writer.

PIERRE BOTTINEAU.

In 1841, PIERRE BOTTINEAU settled in Saint Paul, with his brother, SEVERE BOTTINEAU, and purchased of BENJ. GER-VAIS, a small tract of land on what was afterwards known as

Baptist hill. PIERRE BOTTINEAU is one of the most notable characters of the Northwest. 'He was born in the Red River settlement, his father being a French Canadian, and his mother a Chippewa woman, and came to Fort Snelling, in 1837, where he was in the employ of General SIBLEY for a while, as guide, interpreter, &c. He was one of the settlers expelled from the Reserve, and came to Saint Paul, as above stated. He lived here six years, when he sold his claim, and made a new one at Saint Anthony Falls, which he subsequently laid out as an addition to the city. He was also the first settler at Maple Grove, or " Bottineau's Prairie." in Hennepin county.

Perhaps no man in the Northwest has passed a life of more romantic adventures, exciting occurrences, hair-breadth escapes, and " accidents by flood and field," than Mr. BOTTINEAU. He has traveled over every foot of the Northwest, and knows the country like a map. He speaks almost every Indian language in this region, and his services as guide and interpreter have always been in great demand. He was guide to Col. NOBLES' wagon road expedition to Frazer River, in 1859, to Captain FISK's Idaho expedition of 1862, and Gen. SIBLEY's expedition to the Missouri River, in 1863, &c. His adventures, could they be faithfully written, would make a volume of surpassing interest. Mr. BOTTINEAU is now about .65 years of age, but is as strong and active as he was thirty years ago.

A CATHOLIC MISSION FOUNDED.

With whisky as an element of traffic, making brutes of the white men and demons of the red men—making Saint Paul— i. e., the little hamlet which was its nucleus—a by-word, even among the savages, there is no knowing what depths of abasement might have awaited it, had not a mighty and powerful moral influence been thrown into the scale against rum—and that was, a Christian church.

In 1839, Bishop LORAS, of Dubuque, had visited Fort Snelling and Mendota, with a view of establishing mission churches in a region, as yet, destitute of them, but which was now beginning to attract notice, and attention, and population, and

bade fair, ultimately, to become of importance.   In a letter to
a relative in Ireland, [published subsequently in the "Annals
of Faith," Dublin, 1840,] he says:

> "DUBUQUE, July, 1839.
>
> "I have just returned from Saint Peter's, [Mendota,] where I made my
> second mission, or episcopal visitation.   Though it lasted only a month,
> it has been crowned with success.   I left Dubuque on the 23d of June,
> on board a large and magnificent steam vessel, and was accompanied by
> the Abbe PELAMOURGUES, and a young man who served us as interpre-
> ter with the Sioux.   After a successful voyage of some days, along the
> superb Mississippi, we reached Saint Peter's.   Our arrival was a cause
> of great joy to the Catholics, who had never before seen a priest or
> bishop in those remote regions; they manifested a great desire to assist
> at divine worship, and to approach the sacraments of the church.   The
> wife of our host was baptized and confirmed; she subsequently received
> the sacrament of matrimony.   The Catholics of Saint Peter's amount to
> 185, fifty-six of whom we baptized, administered confirmation to eight,
> communion to thirty-three adults, and gave the nuptial benediction to
> four couples.
>
> "Arrangements have been made for the construction of a church
> next summer, and a clergyman is to be sent, when he is able to speak
> French, (which is the language of the majority,) English, and the
> Sioux.   To facilitate the study of the latter, we are to have, at Dubuque,
> this winter, two young Sioux, who are to teach one or two of our young
> ecclesiastics."

Bishop LORAS remained thirteen days at Mendota, and then
returned to Dubuque in a canoe.   The next spring, he was
reminded, one day, when an up-bound steamer whistled for the
landing, of his promise to send a priest hither.   He selected
Rev. LUCIAN GALTIER for the work, and, in one hour, that
clergyman was en route to his new field of labor.

REV. LUCIAN GALTIER.

The following extract from a memoir of Father GALTIER,
written by Rev. JOHN IRELAND, for the Historical Society,
gives an account which will be read with interest:

> "LUCIAN GALTIER was born in France, Department of Ardeches, A.
> D. 1811.   From an early age, he looked forward to the priesthood as
> his vocation, and was a student of theology in the seminary of his na-
> tive diocese, when Bishop LORAS, the then newly appointed prelate
> of Dubuque, arrived in Europe, in quest of laborers for the immense

region confided to his spiritual charge.· The missionaries, whom the Bishop persuaded to follow him to the wilds of western America, were Rev. JOSEPH CRETIN, afterwards Bishop of Saint Paul; Rev. JOSEPH PELAMOURGUES, now Vicar General of Dubuque; Rev. A. RAVOUX, now Vicar General of Saint Paul; * * * and Rev. L. GALTIER. The party landed in New York, in the fall of 1838. Messrs. GALTIER and RAVOUX, who had not yet completed their studies, proceeded to Emmitsburg College, Maryland, where they remained about a year. They were ordained in Dubuque, January 5, 1840.

"The diocese, of Dubuque comprised what was then the Territory of Iowa, the present State of Iowa, and as much of Minnesota as lies west of the Mississippi. The east side, though under the direct jurisdiction of the Bishop of Milwaukee, was, however, generally attended to by Dubuque priests, who, geographically, were in closer proximity than those of other dioceses."

Of his arrival at Mendota, and subsequent founding of the church which gave the name to our city, let us copy from an account written by himself, in 1864. at the request of Bishop GRACE :

" On the 26th of April, 1840, a Saint Louis steamboat. the first of the season, arrived at Dubuque, bound for Fort Snelling. Rt. Rev. Dr. LORAS immediately came to me, and told me he desired to send me toward the upper waters of the Mississippi. There was no Saint Paul at the time; there was, on the site of the present city. but a single log house, occupied by a man named PHELAN, and steamboats never stopped there.

" The boat landed at the foot of Fort Snelling, then under command of Major PLYMPTON. The discovery that I soon made—that there were only a few houses on the Saint Peter's side, and but two on the side of the fort, surrounded by a complete wilderness, and without any signs of fields under tillage—gave me to understand that my mission and life must henceforth be a career of privation, hard trials and suffering, and required of me patience, labor and resignation. I had before me a large territory, too, under my charge—but few souls to watch over. * * *

" In that precarious and somewhat difficult condition, I continued for over a year. * * * A circumstance, rather sad in itself, commenced to better my situation, by procuring for me a new station and a variety in my scenes of labor. Some families—most of whom had left the Red River settlement, British America, on account of the flood and the loss of their crops, in the years 1837 and 1838—had located themselves all along the right bank of the Mississippi, opposite the fort. Unfortunately, some soldiers, now and then, crossed the river to the houses of these settlers, and returned intoxicated—sometimes remaining out a day or two, or more, without reporting to their quarters. Consequently, a deputy marshal, from Prairie du Chien, was charged to remove the houses. He went to work, assisted by soldiers, and unroofed, one after another, the cottages, extending about five miles along the river. The settlers were forced to look for new homes; they located themselves about two miles below the cave. Already a few parties had opened farms in this vicinity; added to these, the new accessions formed quite a little settlement. Among the occupants of this ground were RONDO, (who had purchased the only cultivated claim in the place, that of PHE-LAN,) VETAL GUERIN, PIERRE BOTTINEAU, the GERVAIS brothers, &c., &c. I deemed it my duty to visit occasionally those families, and set to work to choose a suitable spot for a church.

SELECTING A SITE FOR THE CHURCH.

"Three different points were offered, one called La Point Basse, or Point LeClaire, (now Pig's Eye)—but I objected, because that locality was the very extreme end of the new settlement, and, in high water, was exposed to inundation. The idea of building a church, which might at any day be swept down the river to Saint Louis, did not please me. Two miles and a half further up on his elevated claim, (now the southern point of Dayton's Bluff,) Mr. CHARLES MOUSSEAU offered me an acre of his ground but the place did not suit my purpose. I was truly looking ahead, thinking of the future as well as of the present. Steamboats could not stop there; the bank was too steep, the place on the summit of the hill too restricted; communication difficult with the other parts of the settlement up and down the river.

"After mature reflection, I resolved to put up the church at the nearest possible point to the cave, because it would be more convenient for me to cross the river there, when coming from Saint Peter's, and because, also, it would be the nearest point to the head of navigation, outside of the Reservation line. Mr. B. GERVAIS and Mr. VETAL GUERIN, two good quiet farmers, had the only spot that appeared likely to answer the purpose. They consented to give me jointly the ground necessary for a church site, a garden and a small graveyard. I accepted the extreme eastern part of Mr. VETAL's claim, and the extreme west of Mr. GERVAIS'. Accordingly, in 1841, in the month of October, logs were prepared and a church erected, so poor that it would well remind one of the stable at Bethlehem. It was destined, however, to be the nucleus of a great city. On the 1st day of November, in the same year, I blessed the new *basilica*; and dedicated it to 'Saint PAUL, the apostle of nations.' I expressed a wish, at the same time, that the settlement would be known by the same name, and my desire was obtained. I had, previously to this time, fixed my residence at Saint Peter's, and as the name of PAUL is generally connected with that of PETER, and the gentiles being well represented in the new place in the persons of the Indians, I called it Saint Paul. The name 'Saint Paul,' applied to a town or city, seemed appropriate. The monosyllable is short, sounds well, and is understood by all denominations of Christians. When Mr. VETAL GUERIN was married, I published the bans as being those of a resident of 'Saint Paul.' A Mr. JACKSON put up a store, and a grocery was opened at the foot of the GERVAIS claim. This soon brought steamboats to land there. Thenceforth the place was known

THE CHAPEL OF SAINT PAUL.

as 'Saint Paul Landing,' and, later on, as 'Saint Paul.' When, sometime ago, an effort was made to change the name,* I did all I could to oppose the project, by writing from Prairie du Chien."

It would seem that Father GALTIER was not a bona fide resident of Saint Paul, at any time, but only came here at regular intervals, to preach and administer sacraments. On the 25th of May, 1844, he left Saint Peter's, and went to Keokuk, Iowa. In 1848, he returned to France, and remained a little time, but soon again was at work in the mission field. He was now placed at Prairie du Chien. In 1853 and 1865, he

*This was while the act creating the Territory was before Congress. Some members objected to the name, and proposed to change it,

REV. LUCIAN GALTIER.

First Catholic Priest in Saint Paul, and who gave that name to our city.

VERY REV. A. RAVOUX, V. G.

visited Saint Paul, and felt a warm pride in its growth. On February 21, 1866, he was called to his reward.

It may here be stated, that, when the little log chapel was taken down, several years later, (about 1856, I believe,) the logs and pieces were all marked and numbered, and laid by, with the intention of sometime rebuilding this truly historical structure.

Thus was the infant city baptized with a Christian name. Pig's Eye no more—"now, by Saint PAUL, the work goes bravely on." "One shudders to think," (said a writer in the *Pioneer*,) "of what the place would have come to if it had not been rebaptized—of the horrible marble squint of a Pig's Eye following it around the world. The head of navigation, with such an eye glaring from its socket were a pestiferous Medusa's head, blasting everything within five miles of it with its stony leer—blasting the rocks, especially. Imagine the effect of a Pig's Eye in a senate committee. Think of a Pig's Eye for a seat of government. Who would have come to live under the bristling lashes of a Pig's Eye? What should we have done for clothes? What Jew would have domiciled in the leering eye of a pig? Or any pen have been held in honor but a pig-pen?"

In the first "New Year's Address" ever printed in Minnesota, written, probably, by GOODHUE, January 1, 1850, the sequel is given :

> "Pig's Eye, converted thou shalt be, like SAUL ;
> Arise, and be, henceforth, SAINT PAUL !"

ARRIVAL OF FATHER RAVOUX.

During the fall of 1841, Rev. AUGUSTIN RAVOUX arrived from below, and has been, ever since that date, a resident of Minnesota, and, most of the time, of Saint Paul. From a sketch of the good father, in the *Northwestern Chronicle*, I copy the following :

"Father A. RAVOUX was born January 11, 1815, at Langeac, in Auvergne, France, about 20 miles from Puy, where he spent three years in the Petit Seminaire, and four years in the Grand Seminaire. Right Rev. M. LORAS, previously Pastor of the Cathedral Church, of Mobile,

Alabama, having been consecrated, in 1837, Bishop of Dubuque, Iowa, before visiting his diocese, went to France, in order to have a few missionaries and some pecuniary means for his poor and new diocese.

"Early in the spring of 1838, he visited the Grand Seminaire of Puy, and delivered before the seminarians an urgent invitation, in order to induce some of them to accompany him to America. Deeply moved by the discourse and tears of the good Bishop of Dubuque, whom he had never seen or heard of before, l'Abbe A. RAVOUX, then a sub-deacon, offered himself to him for the missions of his diocese. In September, 1838, they left France for the United States, and after 45 days' navigation, they reached New York. The Rt. Rev. Bishop was accompanied, also, by his Vicar General, Father CRETIN; by Rev. A. PELAMOUR-GUES, who, in 1858, was appointed Bishop of Saint Paul, (but declined accepting the charge;) by l'Abbe GALTIER, who gave to our city its name, and by two other sub-deacons.

"A few days after, Father RAVOUX was sent to Prairie du Chien, where he exercised the holy ministry till September, 1841, when he received from his Bishop the commission of visiting the Sioux, being in the northern part of the disocese of Dubuque, in order to see if there was any prospect of establishing a mission among them. He left Prairie du Chien, for the Upper Mississippi, spent a few days with his friend, Father GALTIER; was then invited to go, in a canoe, to Traverse des Sioux; accepted the invitation with many thanks, and, after four or five days, arrived at Traverse. He was there the guest of Mr. PROVENCAL, an old and respectable gentleman, who had been a trader with the Indians for about forty-five years. While here, he commenced the study of the Sioux language, in which he soon became quite proficient, meantime preaching to the Indians by interpreters. He soon after proceeded to 'Little Rock,' and, in January, 1842, went to Lac qui Parle. After having passed there two or three months, performing the same duties as at Traverse and Little Rock, he returned, early in the spring, to Mendota, where he spent the greater part of the summer with his friend, Father GALTIER. During that summer, Rev. L. GALTIER visited the Catholics living at Lake Pepin and on the Chippewa River; meanwile, Father RAVOUX attended the mission of Mendota, and Saint Paul, and taught the catechism in Sioux to the Messrs. FRENIERES' families, who were encamped for several weeks near the church at Mendota. At their invitation, he accompanied them to Lake Traverse, being by them informed that he would find there several hundred families of Sioux, who would be glad to see him and hear the good tidings of the Gospel. Unfortunately, when they reached the place, the Indians, four or five families excepted, had already left for their winter expedition. He spent about two weeks near the banks of the lake, baptized many persons belonging to the families of the FRENIERES. and returned to Mendota. He there, at the request of the FARIBAULT family, established a mission at Little Prairie, (now Chaska,) and remained some time. While here, he wrote a catechism and other religious books, in Sioux.

"In the spring of 1843, he went to Dubuque, to see the Right Rev. Bishop LORAS, who gave him some encouragement; then he left Dubuque for Prairie du Chien, where he spent almost two months, and printed, with a small printing press, belonging to Very Rev. J. CRETIN, a book in the Sioux language;* and then returned to his mission.

"In the months of January, February, and March, 1844, 23 Indians and half-breeds received the sacrament of baptism, but, unfortunately for that new mission, Rev. L. GALTIER was, in the spring of the same year, removed from Mendota to Keokuk, and Father RAVOUX had to take his place, until another priest would be sent from Dubuque. Right Rev. Bishop LORAS had promised to send one after a short time, but, though he renewed, again and again, his promise, he could not fulfill it, and so Father RAVOUX had under his charge, Mendota, Saint Paul, Lake Pepin and Saint Croix, till the 2d of July, 1851, when Right Rev. Bishop CRETIN arrived at Saint Paul."

From the time that Father GALTIER left, until about 1849, Father RAVOUX preached alternate Sundays at Mendota and Saint Paul. The latter year, his flock here increased so that he spent two Sundays here, and the third at Mendota, and so on, until Mendota was made a parish by itself, and Saint Paul's church had the exclusive labors of a priest. Father RAVOUX's life has been spared to witness glorious fruits from his early labors. Beloved by a large congregation and revered by all, he is still actively pursuing his holy calling, with the prayers of his flock that his days may yet be many amongst us.

PROGRESS OF SETTLEMENT.

About this period, the agricultural region between the Mississippi and Saint Croix began slowly settling up. During the summer of 1841, a mission was established at Red Rock, by Rev. B. F. KAVENAUGH, superintendent of the Methodist missions among the Sioux and Chippewas. He was accompanied by his family, WILLIAM R. BROWN, (afterwards of Saint Paul,) CHARLES CAVILEER, a Miss JULIA BOSWELL, and Mrs. MARTHA BOARDMAN, the two latter as teachers for the mission. Mr. BROWN erected the buildings for the mission, and subse-

---

*Wakantanka ti Cancu—*Path to the House of God.*

quently he and CAVILEER opened a farm.   In 1842, DANIEL HOPKINS established a store there, and, in 1847, removed it to Saint Paul. Mr. CAVILEER also removed to Saint Paul, shortly after this, (1845,) and, in 1851, went to Pembina, where he has been postmaster almost a quarter of a century.

Soon after, other farmers settled in the Cottage Grove region—HIRAM HASKELL, J. W. FURBER, JAMES S. NORRIS, and others.   JOHN A. FORD and Rev. JOHN HOLTON also settled at Red Rock, and a few families at Point Douglas— DAVID HONE among them.

CHAPTER IX.

EVENTS OF THE YEAR 1842.

Henry Jackson Settles Here—Also, Sergeant Mortimer—Fronchet and "Old Pelon"—Stanislaus Bilanski—The Battle of Kaposia—Strange Scenes.

ON June 9, 1842, there landed in Saint Paul, as we may now call it, a man whose name must always be prominently mentioned in connection with the early history of our city.

HENRY JACKSON

was born in Abingdon, Virginia, February 1, 1811. In early life he acquired but a limited education, though he ultimately, by reading and study, became a good penman and accountant, and acquired a fair amount of scholarly culture. He was shrewd, energetic, and self-reliant, and had a large share of humor and penetration into character. He was of a somewhat roving disposition, however, and, while quite a young man, went to Texas, where he was engaged in the "Patriot War" of 1836-7, with the rank of orderly sergeant. He then made his way back to the States, and lived for a time at Buffalo, New York, where, on May 27, 1838, he was married to Miss Angelina Bivins. He soon after emigrated to Green Bay, Wisconsin, and from there to Galena, Illinois, where he went into business, but failed. He then, (1842,) resolved to remove to Saint Paul, and, gathering his worldly goods together, was landed at our lower levee, on a dark, rainy night, when it required considerable search and trouble to secure a shelter for the night. This was finally accomplished at the Clewett place, where the Perrys were then living. Mr. Jackson and family remained here several days, and then rented of old Parrant a cabin on the levee, where they lived until their own house was ready in the fall.

JACKSON soon purchased of BEN. GERVAIS a small tract of land, about three acres, lying in the block now bounded by Jackson and Robert, and Bench and Third streets. It was then a high bank or "bluff," a part of which still remains, in rear of the Saint Paul Fire and Marine Building. Here, on a point overlooking the lower levee, JACKSON built a log or pole cabin, and opened a small stock of goods suitable for the Indian trade. He soon did a prosperous business, and, in a short time, by his activity, tact and sagacity, became a leading man in the community.

During his residence in Saint Paul, JACKSON held several important offices. In 1843, he was appointed by Gov. DODGE, of Wisconsin, a Justice of the Peace—the first one who ever filled that office in our city. In 1846, he was appointed the first postmaster of Saint Paul; and, in 1847, was elected a member of the Wisconsin Assembly, for two years. He was also a member of the first Territorial Legislature of Minnesota, and a member of the first town council. On April 28, 1853, he removed to Mankato, being almost the first settler in that town, where he died July 31, 1857. Jackson street, in this city, and Jackson county, Minnesota, were named for him.

Mrs. JACKSON subsequently became the wife of JOHN S. HINCKLEY, Esq., of Mankato, and still resides in that city. Mrs. H. has kindly furnished the writer, (who visited her for the purpose,) with many interesting and valuable facts of early days. It has been her fortune to pass her entire life, after marriage, in frontier towns, several of which she has seen grow up from a few cabins to prosperous cities, and endured such privation and hardships as every pioneer woman must necessarily undergo. She has now, in her house, at Mankato, *the first clock* which was ever brought to Saint Paul.

SERGEANT R. W. MORTIMER.

On August 17, 1842, RICHARD W. MORTIMER, usually known as "Sergeant MORTIMER," settled in Saint Paul. MORTIMER was a native of Leeds, England, and was born about the year 1800. His father was a man of some wealth, and young MORTIMER was educated at Eton College. When

19 years of age, in company with a younger brother, he ran away from home, in a foolish, school-boy freak, and went to Canada. His brother soon returned, but RICHARD W. was too proud to do so, and, as a result, was disinherited. He had been splendidly educated, however, and soon turned it to account by procuring an appointment in the Signal Service of the British Army, in which he remained several years. He subsequently emigrated to the United States, and was appointed Commissary and Quartermaster Sergeant, holding both positions for some years. He came to Fort Snelling in 1835, and lived in the fort until 1842, excepting a short time during the Florida war, when he accompanied the troops to that region. During his residence in Canada, he was married to a Miss ELIZABETH MAXWELL, and two children were born there. Three were also born in Fort Snelling.

In the year 1842, Sergeant MORTIMER got tired of army life, and, having saved about $4,000, he concluded to settle in this region. He, therefore, purchased from JOSEPH RONDO, eighty acres of his claim, fronting on the river, and bounded on the east by Saint Peter street, and on the west by Washington street. The exact sum paid for this, I have been unable to ascertain. There was an old house on the claim, at the time, but MORTIMER built, near where ROBINSON's drug store now is, a good hewed log house, with a shingle roof, which his daughter, Mrs. MARIA PATTEN, thinks was the first shingle roof in Saint Paul. MORTIMER made other improvements, and soon opened quite a lot of goods suitable to the trade at that time. He also expended considerable in cattle and horses, and had about 40 acres under cultivation.

Sergeant MORTIMER was really unfitted for the new life in which he had engaged. There were many troubles he had not anticipated. He had expended nearly all the ample sum he had saved in his army life, in his improvements and stock, and realized but little from them at last. The trade was small and the people poor. He was filled with vain regrets that he had ever left the army, and it weighed on his mind so that it affected his health at last. He was a liberal and public-spirited man, and, had he lived, would have been a prominent citizen. The first flag every raised in Saint Paul, was procured by him, at the expense of $35. He had one of his men raise it on a pole, in front of his house, on Christmas, 1842. There seems to have been almost as much rivalry between upper and lower town, those days, as there was subsequently, for the flag had been flying but a little while, when some wicked scamp, from the lower part of the village, cut it down. MORTIMER was terribly enraged when he found it out, and was about to put in force Gov. DIX's famous order—" if any man hauls down the American flag, shoot him on the spot." He went to load a gun, and ordered his horse to pursue the offender. His wife, fearing there would be bloodshed, unloosed the horse, and there was so much delay before he was caught, that MORTIMER's anger cooled down.

Mr. MORTIMER did not live long after his residence in Saint Paul. On January 8th, 1843, he was attacked with hemorrhage, resulting from an injury received a short time before, and died at the age of 43 years. He left a widow and five children—two sons and three daughters. His oldest daughter is now Mrs. J. R. PATTEN, an estimable lady of Minneapolis. His second daughter, FANNY, married AARON FOSTER, an old settler of Saint Paul. Both are now dead. His youngest daughter, LILY, is now Mrs. ROBERT CLINGER, of Philadelphia. His two sons, WILLIAM and GEORGE, served in the late war, the former giving an arm to his country. Mrs. ELIZABETH MORTIMER died at Minneapolis, January 15, 1873.

While Mr. MORTIMER was living in Saint Paul, there worked for him, and for his family after his death, an old soldier named FRONCHET, or DESIRE—as he was generally called— referred to more at length on page 62. FRONCHET was a faithful servant, and highly valued despite his infirmities. He always boasted of his Parisian origin and purity of language, affecting to sneer at the Canadian French, whom he declared he could scarcely understand. Poor FRONCHET! Whisky finally got the better of him, and he came to a sad end.

" OLD PELON."

Shortly after JACKSON opened his trading-house in lower

town, he began to feel the need of an interpreter who could talk Sioux, and assist him in selling and buying with his red customers.   Opportunely, there happened along, at this juncture, from Prairie du Chien, a Canadian ex-voyageur, commonly known as "Old PELON."   What PELON's Christian name was, no one happens now to remember, nor is it of much moment, since, probably, we have sufficiently identified him by the title given.   Old PELON was quite a character in his way— vivacious, polite, good-natured, shrewd, faithful, he proved a valuable aid to Mr. JACKSON, and remained in his service for several years.   GOODHUE, who met PELON at the Indian treaty of Traverse de Sioux, in 1851, relates this incident of the old coon:

PELON used to tend JACKSON's bar, while Saint Paul was only the western suburb of Pig's Eye.   At that time, all sorts of liquors were sold out of the same decanter, and a stranger, coming in once, asked PELON if he had any confectionery? PELON, not knowing the meaning of the word, supposed it was some kind of liquor, passed out the decanter of whisky to his customer, saying: "Oui, Monsieur, here is confecshawn, ver good, superb, magnifique, pretty fair."

PELON afterwards kept a saloon of his own on the lower levee, but, ultimately, age and infirmities overtook him, and he died in 1852, at "old man LARRIVIER's," on Lake Phelan.

STANISLAUS BILANSKI,

who settled in Saint Paul this year, was a Polander by birth, and had lived in Wisconsin prior to coming to Saint Paul.   He purchased a claim and cabin on the point of second table-land between Phelan's Creek, and Trout Brook, near the machine shops of Lake Superior and Mississippi Railroad Company, called then "Oak Point," and lived there several years.   BILANSKI was an uxorious individual, and had a facility for marrying and divorcing wives, that ultimately brought him to an untimely end.   While living with his fourth wife, in 1859, he died, on March 11th of that year, under circumstances that showed he had been poisoned.   The full particulars of the

9

case will be found in the chapter devoted to the events of the year 1859.

THE BATTLE OF KAPOSIA.

In September of this year occurred the famous battle of Kaposia, between the Chippewas and Sioux. References will be found in the previous pages of this history to the savage warfare that had been waged for several years between these two hostile tribes, whose deadly feud must have begun generations ago, and sacrificed a hecatomb of warriors during those years.

Early in the spring of 1841, three Chippewa warriors proceeded to the vicinity of Fort Snelling, and lay concealed in a thicket there, looking for Sioux scalps. Ere long, KAIBOKA, a Dakota chief, accompanied by his son, and another Indian, passed along, when they were at once killed and scalped, and the cowardly assassins escaped. Enraged at this act, a war party from LITTLE CROW's village, at Kaposia, headed by that chief, equipped themselves and started on a campaign of revenge. Three of LITTLE CROW's sons were in the party. Near the Falls of Saint Croix, they fell in with the Chippewas. Two of CROW's sons were shot dead, and the party returned. Another section of the expedition penetrated the Ojibwa country as far as Pokeguma, where there was a village of Indians and a missionary station, at which EDMUND F. ELY, for several years subsequently a resident of this city, was present. The Dakotas attacked this, but inflicted little damage on the enemy, losing two of their own number.

In revenge for this raid, the Chippewas, in 1842, determined to attack the Sioux village, of LITTLE CROW, at Kaposia. A war party of about 40 was formed at Fond du Lac, and, in their downward march, they were joined by recruits from the Mille Lac and Saint Croix bands, until the party numbered about 100. They arrived unnoticed at the bluff back of Pig's Eye, where they halted in Pine Coolie, the ravine just back of the old poor-house, to reconnoiter. This was about 10 o'clock in the forenoon.

Just at this moment, a Red River half-breed, named HENRY

Sinclair,* who was in the employ of the missionaries Kavenaugh, at Red Rock, came along on the trail, riding a pony.
Him they hailed, and inquired, " if there were any Dakotas
about." Sinclair was about to reply, when his pony took
fright, and started off at break-neck speed. He did not try to
check him, but galloped on, and in a few minutes, arrived at
the mission house, where he reported what he had seen.
There were two Sioux at Rev. Mr. Kavenaugh's house, who
at once started off on the run to alarm the men at Kaposia.
Mrs. Thomas Odell, then Miss Elizabeth Williams, a
half-breed girl, was a pupil at the Red Rock mission. She
states that, a moment after the Indians left, the rattle of guns
was heard, showing that the work of death had commenced.
But we must go back a little.

On Pig's Eye bottom, a little distance from Pine Coolie,
where the Chippewas were lying in ambush, was the cabin
and field of Francis Gammel, a French Canadian, who had
come to Minnesota as a voyageur, in 1829, and had lived at
Mendota. He was now married to a Dakota woman, and they
had one child, David Gammel, then an infant. That morning,
an old Indian, named Rattler, a brother of old Bets, well
known to the early residents hereabout, had gone over to Gammel's house, with his two wives, and a son and daughter, infants, in order to help Mr. and Mrs. Gammel hoe their corn.
Gammel and his wife, and one of Rattler's wives, were in
the field at work. The other Mrs. Rattler complained of
being sick, and went into the house, whither old Rattler
followed. The three children were playing near by.

Just at this moment, a squad of Chippewas, who had been
sent out to reconnoiter, sneaked through the bushes outside
the field, and seeing the two Sioux women at work, fired a
volley at them. Mrs. Rattler fell dead, and Mrs. Gammel
was mortally wounded. Gammel picked her up and carried

---

* Sinclair came from Selkirk Settlement, in 1839, piloting a drove of cattle. He
was a simple-hearted, honest fellow. One time he was sick, at Mendota, and Surgeon
Emerson, at the fort, sent, by some one, a box of pills, for him to take a dose from.
N. W. Kittson called on him a little while after this, and found that Sinclair had not
only swallowed all the pills, but was then chewing up the box! S. afterwards went to
Sauk Rapids, or Crow Wing, where he died a few years ago.

her into the house, followed by some of the blood-thirsty Chippewas, who *rushed in and scalped the dying woman in his arms*, and at once retreated, not knowing of the presence of RATTLER and his other wife, in an adjoining room. As they bounded off, giving the scalp-halloo, GAMMEL seized a gun and fired at them, wounding one in the leg, but they did not, at any time, offer to molest him. Just then they observed the little boy of RATTLER, who was endeavoring to hide in the bushes. They seized him and cut off his head. The little son of GAMMEL,* and the daughter of RATTLER, named *Ta-ti,* (HER LODGE,) escaped unnoticed. This affair had all occurred in a moment, and was undoubtedly a military blunder of the attacking party. Their design had been to crawl, unobserved, to the bank of the river, opposite Kaposia, and there, concealed in the dense shrubbery, lie in wait for some unsuspecting party of Sioux, and massacre them. But, seeing the Dakota women in the field, they had rashly attacked them, thus giving the alarm prematurely.

If they had carried out the first named plan, they could not have chosen a more opportune time than that day. The Sioux at the village were in the midst of one of their drunken sprees, and, as is customary at such times, the squaws had hid their guns and other weapons, to prevent them from doing each other any harm. The firing across the river first gave them the alarm that the enemy was near, when great excitement at once prevailed. The men hunted up their concealed weapons, meantime giving their barbaric war-whoop, and yelling like so many demons, in order to scare the enemy, probably. In this vocal exercise they were joined by the squaws and children. As soon as they could arm themselves, the Sioux bravely advanced across the river to attack the enemy. The latter, by this time, had advanced near the bank of the river, about where the quarantine grounds now are, and here the battle mainly

---

*GAMMEL's son, DAVID, grew up to manhood at Mendota, and served in a Minnesota Regiment. Old RATTLER died in 1851, of an overdose of whisky. TA-TI, his daughter, afterwards became the wife of *Wa-kin-yau-ta-wa,* (HIS THUNDER,) sometimes called "CHASKA," who saved GEORGE H. SPENCER's life, in 1862, and was poisoned accidentally the year following. TA-TI now lives at Mendota. FRANCIS GAMMEL died at Mendota, in 1871.

took place.   It raged with great spirit for a couple of hours, during which the firing was incessant.   Some hand-to-hand encounters also took place between the two sides, while the forest and bluffs rang with their incessant yelling.   The firing was plainly heard in Saint Paul.   Every inch of the battle-ground was hotly contested.   Toward noon, the Chippewas began to fall back, and soon retreated on their path, followed by the Sioux, who pursued them over the bluff, and several miles toward Stillwater.   The Chippewas left some nine or ten dead bodies on the field, and may have carried off their wounded.   The Sioux also lost heavily.   Different accounts place their loss at nineteen or twenty, including the mortally wounded, who died subsequently.   The dead Chippewas were at once scalped, while the squaws amused themselves by hacking and mutilating them.   "Old BETS" went around pounding their heads with a huge club.   One of her sons, afterwards called *Ta-opi*, or WOUNDED MAN, was so named because wounded in this fight.

When the Chippewas first made the attack, a messenger was sent to Fort Snelling with the intelligence.   It was the policy of the Government to prevent and punish these inter-tribal carnages, and Major DEARBORN at once dispatched a party of soldiers from Companies D, G and H, First Infantry, who at that time garrisoned the fort, to Kaposia, to stop the conflict.   The party came down below Pickerel Lake in boats, and thence across by land, but did not arrive until after the conflict was over.   THOMAS S. ODELL, now of West Saint Paul, was one of this party.   I am indebted to him and his wife for many of the minor incidents of this strange affair.

CHAPTER X.

EVENTS OF THE YEAR 1843.

NOTICES OF SOME SETTLERS—JOHN R. IRVINE, J. W. SIMPSON, WILLIAM HARTS-
HORN, A. L. LARPENTEUR, SCOTT CAMPBELL, ALEX. R. McLEOD, &C., &C.—
RONDO SELLS HIS CLAIM—AN INDIAN IN PURSUIT OF WHISKY.

DURING the year 1843, there was quite an accession to
the population—among others. JOHN R. IRVINE, C. C.
BLANCHARD, J. W. SIMPSON, ANSEL B. COY, WILLIAM
HARTSHORN, A. L. LARPENTEUR, SCOTT CAMPBELL, AN-
TOINE PEPIN, &c., &c.

JOHN R. IRVINE

was born in Dansville, New York, November 3, 1812. When
a boy, he worked at blacksmithing, but, about the age of 17,
removed to Carlisle, Pennsylvania, where he learned the trade
of plastering, and, in 1831, was married to Miss NANCY GAL-
BRAITH. He afterwards returned to Dansville, and resumed
blacksmithing. In 1837, he emigrated west, living for three
years in Green Bay, and, in 1840, settled in Prairie du Chien,
where he went into the grocery trade. While living in Buffalo,
New York, he had become acquainted with HENRY JACKSON—
indeed, he and JACKSON had come to Green Bay together, the
latter soon removing to Galena, however. About February,
1843, JACKSON was on his way down the river to purchase
goods, and, stopping at Prairie du Chien, there found his old
friend, who was in business with ANSEL B. COY and C. C.
BLANCHARD. JACKSON at once urged him to remove to Saint
Paul, as being a much more promising place for trade, rapid
growth, &c., than Prairie du Chien. So warmly did he set
forth the advantages of Saint Paul, that Mr. IRVINE resolved
at least to visit it and see the land of promise. He accordingly
came up here in the latter part of that winter, in a sleigh, with

a load of groceries and other goods for sale, and, after looking
around over the field, resolved to remove here.   He therefore
purchased of JOSEPH RONDO the balance of the old Phelan
claim (remaining after the sale of about half to Sergeant MOR-
TIMER.)   The price paid for this tract was $300.   RONDO had
at that time a very good log dwelling built on the French plan,

JOHN R. IRVINE.

(i. e., the logs squared and let into grooves—not notched at
the corners.)   It stood about where the northwest corner of
Third and Franklin streets would now be.   With some additions, it made a very comfortable dwelling, and was used by
Mr. IRVINE for several years.   Mr. IRVINE thinks that the
claim he bought of RONDO contained 300 acres.   It extended
back to the marsh on the Lake Como road, which residents of
some 15 or 20 years ago may remember.

After purchasing this property. Mr. IRVINE returned to Prairie du Chien. to remove his family and business hither. He placed his household effects and goods in a large Mackinac boat, and, as soon as navigation opened, hired the steamer Otter, on her first trip up, to tow it to Saint Paul. His partner. ANSEL B. COY, came with the goods. but Mr. BLANCHARD did not come up until a few weeks subsequently. Mr. IRVINE arrived some time in June with his family. The boat was run up the slough between the upper levee and the main land, and moored there. It was then all heavy timber and underbrush in that locality, and, as there was no road—hardly a foot-path from the bluff down to the water—the unloading and carrying of the goods up the bluff was no small job.

A dense forest covered the bottom land near the upper levee. Mr. IRVINE cut immense quantities of wood for steamboats off of that bottom, without apparently making any impression on it. Upper Third street, from the seven-corners to the bluff, was a quagmire, almost without bottom. Cows used to stick there years after this, to the great trouble of their owners. Along the side of the hill, near Pleasant and College avenues. was a morass, with a forest of cedar and tamaracks growing on it. No one at that day could have imagined it would. in so few years, become the valuable property it now is, covered with comfortable residences. For several years, Mr. IRVINE cultivated a considerable part of his land for a farm.

Mr. IRVINE subsequently (about 1845, he thinks) purchased the MORTIMER claim, and, in 1848, entered the land (which had then been surveyed) in the land office at Stillwater. In November, 1848, for $250, he deeded the east half of the north-west quarter of section 6, town 28, to HENRY M. RICE. which afterwards became a part of Rice and Irvine's Addition. But of this anon.

Mr. IRVINE has been one of our most active and useful citizens during his thirty-two years' residence. The ample property, which his foresight and prudence prompted him to secure and hold, is now one of the finest portions of our city. The proceeds of most of it which has been sold, has been reinvested in erecting substantial business blocks, mills, warehouses, and

other buildings, which now stand as a credit to the enterprise
of the owner.   Although 63 years of age, a period when most
men court repose, Mr. Irvine is still actively engaged in business, and is known as one of our most energetic and hard-
working men.   Mr. Irvine has served our county in the
Legislature, and other elective bodies, and perhaps no one of
our pioneer settlers more fully enjoys the esteem of the public
than he, and the wish that the "great reaper" will long delay
his visit.

The amiable wife of Mr. Irvine, is one of the first white
women who settled in Minnesota, and has endured the privations and struggles of pioneer life, with others of that noble
few, who deserve especial mention.   Mr. and Mrs. I. have one
son and six daughters living, most of the latter married to well-
known citizens.

When Irvine bought Rondo's claim, the latter at once
made a new claim in and near the marsh, on the Lake Como
Road.   When the land was entered, in 1848, it was noticed
that the lines overlapped somewhat, but land was so cheap
then, that such things were hardly noticed.   A few acres were
not worth disputing about.

FURTHER ABOUT RONDO.

Mr. Rondo subsequently laid out quite an addition on this
claim, or a part of it, and it has of late years become valuable
property.   The marsh has been so drained and graded that it
can scarcely be found, except by close search.

Rondo has raised a large family, and has a number of grandchildren to bear his name down to posterity.   He lives in a
plain manner, in his brick house, on the street which is called
after him, and, though nearly 80 years old, worked hard in the
harvest field this summer.   His long life has been full of interesting events, and, as one of his ancestors lived to 112, and two
more over a century, Mr. Rondo, now our oldest living settler
resident among us, may live a score of years yet, to see still
more generations of his descendants.

C. C. BLANCHARD.

With Mr. Irvine, came Christopher C. Blanchard, who

had been his partner in business in Prairie du Chien, and continued that relation after arriving here.   Mr. BLANCHARD was not pleased with Saint Paul, however, and soon returned to Prairie 'du Chien, and thence to Saint Louis.   No tidings have been received of him for some twenty years, and he may not now be living.   BLANCHARD was a married man, and his wife's sister, Mrs. MATILDA RUMSEY, lived with him.   When he went back down the river, Mrs. RUMSEY remained here, residing with Mr. IRVINE'S family.

ANSEL B. COY.

who had also been a partner of IRVINE, at Prairie du Chien, as before stated, came to Saint Paul quite early in the spring, in charge of the goods.   He, too, was not suited here, and soon after returned.

ALEXANDER MEGE.

During the season of 1843, a Frenchman named ALEX. MEGE, who had lived at Prairie du Chien, came to Saint Paul, and purchased the interest of COY, when that gentleman left. MEGE and IRVINE dissolved subsequently, and MEGE kept a store in a building on the Mortimer claim.   On June 23, 1845, he was married to Mrs. MATILDA RUMSEY, at Mr. IRVINE'S house, by Rev. Father RAVOUX.   In 1847, Mr. and Mrs. MEGE removed to Montrose, Iowa, where Mrs. MEGE subsequently died.   Mrs. RUMSEY is the lady mentioned elsewhere who taught the first school in Saint Paul.

J. W. SIMPSON.

JAMES W. SIMPSON was born in Virginia, 1818.   We have seen it asserted, that in his younger days he was a clergyman, but do not state this on positive authority.   He came to Minnesota in 1842, and resided about a year at Sandy Lake, where he was connected with the mission in some capacity, and then came to Red Rock, where he resided a short time, settling at Saint Paul in October of 1843.   He bought an acre of BENJ. GERVAIS, where Union block now stands, and opened a store, the second one in the village.   He afterwards sold this, and bought a tract between Baptist hill and the Merchants' Hotel, where he lived until his death. He soon after established a commission business on the levee, which he continued until within a year or two of his death. He was elected county treasurer in 1849, and so scrupulously just and honest was he, that he turned over at the end of his term the identical coin collected by him, having kept it as a fund separate from any other money. About 1868, his health failed, and he was very feeble for some months. Indeed, his death was prematurely reported once or twice. It finally came to his relief on May 30, 1870, in the 52d year of his age. He died respected by all. Mr. SIMPSON was married, in 1846, to a Miss DENOYER, a niece of LOUIS ROBERT.

WILLIAM HARTSHORN

was born at Dedham, Massachusetts, in 1794. He learned the trade of hatter when a boy, and subsequently removed to Springfield, Massachusetts, where he established a store, and continued in the fur and hatting business for several years, part of the time on a large scale, as he once made a sale of furs to JOHN JACOB ASTOR, for $100,000. Adversity came upon him, however, and he sold out his business, removed to Brockport, New York, subsequently to Lewiston, thence to Michigan City, &c., where he was in the hotel and stage business, and, in 1839, settled in Saint Louis, where he engaged again in the fur and peltry trade.

In 1843, he started for the Upper Mississippi, to purchase furs. On the way up, he met HENRY JACKSON on the steamer. JACKSON told him he had some furs to sell, which induced him to stop here. The result of the visit was, that he and JACKSON formed a copartnership, and HARTSHORN, returning to Saint Louis to close up his business there, settled in Saint Paul in September, although he did not bring his family up for some months afterwards. The first deed on the Ramsey county records, is one dated April 23, 1844, in which JACKSON deeds to WILLIAM HARTSHORN, for $1,000, the "half of three acres, it being the place where said JACKSON now lives, lying immediately on the Mississippi River, known as the Saint Paul's Landing."

Mr. HARTSHORN also bought, that year, or early in 1844. a tract of GERVAIS, on his claim. bounded by what (now) would be Sibley and Minnesota streets. and Fourth and Sixth streets. In 1846, when PIERRE BOTTINEAU sold his claim, (Baptist hill,) he describes it as "bounded on the west by HARTSHORN." There was a log house on this tract. about where the Schurmeier block now stands.

The copartnership with JACKSON lasted only about two years. and Mr. HARTSHORN, withdrawing, moved to the old Mortimer claim. and commenced business there on his own account. He also had one or two stores or trading posts in other places. at Saint Croix Falls and on the Minnesota River. He increased his business so at one time, that he had several of these outside stations. D. B. FREEMAN. who had clerked for him in Saint Louis. and AUG. FREEMAN; A. L. LARPENTEUR. ED. WEST, of New York: W. H. MORSE, of Stillwater ; and others, clerked for him, and JOSEPH CAMPBELL, JOSEPH DESMARAIS, ANTOINE and SAM. FINDLEY were employed by him at various times, as interpreters. It was also through him that WILLIAM H. RANDALL, of New York, came to Saint Paul, in 1846.

In the winter of 1847–8, Mr. HARTSHORN disposed of his interest to JOHN and WILLIAM H. RANDALL, the FREEMANS and LARPENTEUR. under the name of "FREEMAN, LARPENTEUR & Co.," and removed to Stillwater. Not liking that place. he soon returned to Saint Paul, and re-embarked in trade. He continued in business until 1864, when disease fastened on him, and he died January 2, 1865. A newspaper sketch says of him : "He was an honest and pure-minded man, with a kindness of heart and absence of guile that made him beloved by all. Ever upright himself, in his simplicity, he perhaps placed too much confidence in others. and hence, though at times well off, he was over-reached to an extent that kept him in reduced circumstances most of his life." Mrs. TYLE HARTSHORN, his venerable widow, who, with him, sustained the privations and hardships of pioneer life, died March 4. 1874.

WILLIAM E. HARTSHORN, his only son, is still a resident of Saint Paul.

AUGUSTE L. LARPENTEUR

was born May 16, 1823, at Baltimore, Maryland. His father was an emigrant from France. In 1840, he went to Saint Louis, to enter into business there with a relative, and, some time after his arrival, got acquainted with WILLIAM HARTSHORN, who had been up to Saint Paul on a fur-buying expedition, and had formed a partnership with HENRY JAČKSON. He engaged LARPENTEUR, in 1843, to go to Saint Paul with him, and gave him charge of an invoice of goods and horses. LARPENTEUR at once started for Saint Paul, on the steamer Otter, Capt. SCRIBE HARRIS, and arrived here September 15, 1843.

HARTSHORN & JACKSON had their trading house in the Jackson building, on the point. LARPENTEUR was in the service of the firm about two years. In 1845, Mr. HARTSHORN dissolved with JACKSON, and moved up to the Mortimer place, where he opened business on his own account, and Mr. LARPENTEUR remained with him, having mainly the charge of the whole business. In 1848, Mr. HARTSHORN retired from the trade, and disposed of his interest in it, with a quantity of real estate, to a new firm, called FREEMAN, LARPENTEUR & Co.— WM. H. RANDALL, of New York, having, also, an interest in it. They completed a warehouse on the levee, which HARTSHORN had commenced, and continued there until the death of DAVID B. FREEMAN, in January, 1850, when the business was wound up and passed over to JOHN & WM. H. RANDALL. In the spring of 1850, Mr. LARPENTEUR built a frame store on Third street, just above Jackson, and started business for himself. In 1847, we should state, he built as a residence for himself, the building on Jackson street, afterwards, for many years, known as the " Wild Hunter Hotel." In 1855, he built the four-story brick block on the corner, and used it several years as a store, carrying on a large business. The hard times of 1858 compelled him to close up, and eventually he lost all his fine property on that street.

In 1845, Mr. LARPENTEUR was married to Miss MARY J.

Presley, sister to Bartlett Presley, and, like most of our early settlers, has had a numerous family.

SCOTT CAMPBELL,

another of the settlers of the year 1843, was a half-breed son of Colin Campbell, (a Scotch trader, well known throughout the west during the early part of this century,) and was born at Prairie du Chien, in 1790. He acted as interpreter at Fort Snelling, for some 25 years, and also was in the employ, at various times, of Frank. Steele. N. W. Kittson, and others. After quitting the Indian agency at the fort, he came to Saint Paul, and bought a small claim of Denis Cherrier, say running from Wabasha to Saint Peter streets, and back two or three blocks. He erected a dwelling, subsequently, about where Zimmerman's art gallery now is. In 1848, he sold this claim to Wm. Hartshorn, for a small sum, and moved to a claim on the Saint Anthony road, just beyond Denoyer's, where he died, in 1850, in destitute circumstances. Campbell is said to have been a man of some ability, but of intemperate habits, which caused him to lead an unhappy life. His wife, Margaret Campbell, was a Menominee half-breed, and always bore the name of an industrious, worthy woman. She is still a resident of Saint Paul.

Campbell had five sons and four daughters. When his sons were young boys hereabouts, they were known as good-natured and well-disposed lads, but some of them afterwards turned out very badly. Baptiste was among the Indians executed at Mankato, in 1862, for murder and other crimes during the massacre. Hypolite, another son, was also engaged in the massacre, and fled to Manitoba, where he now lives. Scott Campbell, Jr., died in the insane asylum, November 17, 1870. He was regarded as a quiet and inoffensive man. Joseph Campbell, the oldest of the sons, was at Yellow Medicine when the outbreak occurred, and was forced by the Indians to accompany them. Mr. Heard says, in his valuable history of the massacre, that Campbell was shown to be innocent of any complicity in the outrages, and, by his kindness and aid to prisoners, deserved praise. He also wrote the letters from LITTLE CROW to Gen. SIBLEY, which led to the negotiations by which the white prisoners were released. JOSEPH CAMPBELL has lived in Saint Paul for several years past, and is well spoken of by persons in whose employ he has been.

JOHN L. CAMPBELL, the youngest of the sons, was a scoundrel, without any redeeming qualities. He was born at Mendota, in 1832, and, after growing up to manhood, led a vicious and abandoned life. He was cruel, revengeful, licentious and intemperate. He is said to have committed, or been concerned in, several murders while a young man. In 1861, he enlisted in Company A, Brackett's Battalion, and served nearly three years with them. His officers had a great deal of trouble with him, and he is charged with several murders, robberies, &c., while in the service. In 1864, while home on veteran furlough, he deserted, and cast his lot with the outlawed Sioux. While engaged in a raid with them, in April, 1865, they murdered the JEWETT family, near Mankato. JOHN CAMPBELL was captured at Mankato, on May 2d, and some of the clothes of the murdered man found on him. He was tried by a lynch court, the following day, and hung to a tree, after confessing his guilt and restoring some money stolen from JEWETT's house. CAMPBELL was a man of more than usual physical beauty—had long, curly, black hair, dark, expressive eyes, and a finely proportioned figure.

ALEX. R. M'LEOD.

ALEXANDER RODERIC MCLEOD was the son of a Scotch Canadian. According to some old settlers, he was a native of Canada, but others assert as positively that he was born in the Hudson's Bay territory, near the Rocky Mountains. JOSEPH RONDO says that MCLEOD's father was a prominent officer of the Hudson's Bay Company, and that MCLEOD (the son) was born at a post in the Rocky Mountains, and that he (RONDO) saw him there, and held him on his lap when he was a small infant. MCLEOD's mother, says RONDO, was a Metis. Others say that MCLEOD was a pure blood white man. MCLEOD's father must have been a man of some influence. There is a

"Fort McLeod," named for him, near Peace River, and a "McLeod River," near Fort Edmonton.

A. R. McLeod came to Saint Paul in 1843. What year he came to Minnesota, I cannot learn with exactness—probably 1838 or 1839. He was employed by the American Fur Company for a short time, and was, also, a clerk for Frank. Steele. McLeod was a man of extraordinary powerful physique, and great endurance. On one occasion, he walked on snow-shoes from Saint Croix Falls to Saint Paul, about sixty miles, in one day, and, arriving late in the evening, found a French ball in progress, and danced the rest of the night, as gay and active as any one. A few pages further on, will be found an account of McLeod killing a man with whom he had a quarrel, by blows of his fist.

A few months after coming to Saint Paul, (September, 1843,) McLeod married a half-breed girl, named Nancy Jeffries, then living at Pig's Eye, daughter of a trader well known in this region at that time. Mrs. McLeod is living in West Saint Paul.

In 1844, McLeod purchased some land of Benj. Gervais, in connection with Louis Robert. McLeod built, on his portion, a square log building, on the site of the recent Central House. It was then only one story high. The next year, he had a frame upper story and attic added to it, and the whole was weather-boarded. A year or two subsequently a wing was added, &c., and thus, little by little, it grew into the Central House of a later day, which was for years a hotel well known to old residents, and was (1849–50–51) used for the Legislature and Territorial officers.

McLeod, after living there a year or two, subsequently (1846) rented the building to other parties, and moved to a claim on Phelan's Creek, near the Stillwater road, which is sometimes called "McLeod's Creek," owing to that fact. He lived here four years, and moved to West Saint Paul, where he lived most of the time until his death. In 1862, he enlisted in Company A, Sixth Minnesota Regiment, and died of disease at Jefferson Barracks, Missouri, November 14, 1864, aged 47 years.

OTHER SETTLERS OF 1843.

ANTOINE PEPIN, ALEXIS CLOUTIER, and JOSEPH GOBIN, who came from Red River together, several years previous, this year settled in the RONDO neighborhood, and made claims near the swamp on the Lake Como road.

ANTOINE PEPIN was a Canadian, and had lived at Red River several years. He must have come from there about 1831 or 1832, as about that time he was appointed by Maj. TALIAFERRO. blacksmith to the Sioux. TALIAFERRO says, in his journal: :" He is a faithful man, hard-working and honest. He is a good blacksmith." He records in another place that PEPIN had worked until his hands were swelled and blistered. making traps for poor Indians. not able to buy any. In 1836, Maj. TALIAFERRO displaced him, in favor of OLIVER CRATTE. because it was necessary to have some one for blacksmith who could repair guns, and PEPIN did not understand that craft. PEPIN then settled near the fort, or at Mendota. and came to Saint Paul, as before mentioned. PEPIN lived about 20 years after settling in Saint Paul, and died about a dozen years ago, in a little house on part of his old claim. He has one or more children still living hereabouts.

Of CLOUTIER and GOBIN, I can get but little information, except that both are now dead. I do not find the names on any of the recent census rolls, and judge that no descendants of either are yet living in this locality.

DAVID THOMAS SLOAN was engaged in trading with the Chippewas—a part of the time for HARTSHORN and JACKSON, and subsequently on his own hook. He afterwards went up to the Chippewa country, where he married a sister of the chief HOLE-IN-THE-DAY. A gentleman, who knew her, says she was one of the best looking Indian women he ever saw. SLOAN died a few years ago, near Crow Wing. A daughter of his was raised by Mrs. TULLIS, wife of Judge AARON W. TULLIS, who was sheriff here in 1859–60, but both Mrs. T. and SLOAN's daughter are now dead.

JOSEPH DESMARAIS was a French and Chippewa half-breed, born in the Red River settlement. He came to Fort Snelling,

10

as guide and interpreter for the party of refugees with which
RONDO and others came. DESMARAIS settled in Saint Paul,
in 1843, and purchased a piece of ground about where the
Merchants' Hotel now stands. as near as I can make out. His
property is frequently mentioned on the early records. and his
name was signed as a town proprietor to the recorded plat.
DESMARAIS was an interpreter for JACKSON for some time. He
had quite a family of children, some of whom live hereabouts
yet. His wife died in 1847, and he went off in the Indian
country, where he still lives, or was, not long ago.

LOUIS LARRIVIER came from Red River. About 1843, he
made a claim near the head of Robert and Wabasha streets.
and including the ground the Capitol now stands on. CHARLES
BAZILLE purchased it of him, not long after. LARRIVIER then
moved to a place near the foot of Phelan's Lake. His wife,
who was a half-breed, died at Little Canada. LARRIVIER subsequently became blind from sun-stroke. and, having no means
of support. was sent to the poor-house, where he died about
two years ago.

XAVIER DELONAIS came from Red River. also. He lived
here for some time. then removed to Little Canada, and thence
to Rice Lake, where he died about two years ago. His wife is
also dead, and a married daughter is living in West Saint Paul.

MINOR INCIDENTS.

A Frenchman, named GEROU. a butcher by occupation, who
lived near the Denoyer place, first established the sale of fresh
meat in the village this year.

The Indians were very troublesome this year, and perpetu-
ally drunk. One day, Mrs. MORTIMER, who was endeavoring
to close out the stock of goods belonging to her late husband,
was in her house, when an Indian stalked in. and, seeing a
camphor bottle standing on a shelf. took a deep swig. supposing it was whisky. As soon as he detected the nauseous
taste, he gave a grunt of rage, and, seizing a measure. turned
some vinegar into it from a barrel. supposing that also was
whisky. He dashed down a heavy draught of it without stopping to taste it. Mrs. MORTIMER saw the storm coming and

fled for safety to Mr. IRVINE's house, pursued, a moment after, by the infuriated Indian, with uplifted tomahawk, but IRVINE disarmed him and sent him off. The Indian had left the vinegar running, however, and the whole of it was gone when Mrs. MORTIMER returned.

This year, among the " real estate sales," N. W. KITTSON purchased CLEWETT's claim, the latter purchasing LABISINIER's claim.

CHAPTER XI.

EVENTS OF THE YEAR 1844.

CHARLES REED FREEZES TO DEATH—CAPTAIN LOUIS ROBERT SETTLES HERE—
CHARLES BAZILLE ALSO ARRIVES—WILLIAM DUGAS BUILDS THE FIRST MILL—
LITTLE CANADA SETTLED—ROBERT BUYS OUT PARRANT—A NOVEL LAND
CASE—THE FINAL CAREER OF PHELAN—THE END OF OLD PARRANT—MARRY-
ING BY BOND—RELIGIOUS ITEMS.

THE winter of 1843-4 was quite a severe one, and the
snow fell unusually deep.

CHARLES REED FREEZES TO DEATH.

. In March, 1844, a young Canadian Englishman, named
CHARLES REED. a carpenter by occupation, who was helping
to build a house for "old GEROU," the butcher, near DENOY-
ER's. came to town to visit, and started back late in the afternoon.   A violent snow storm came on when REED got a mile
or so on his way.   REED did not return to GEROU's at the
time expected, and was missing several days.   One day, a
daughter of Mr. PEPIN's was going near the swamp, on the
Lake Como road, when she noticed a dog, which accompanied
her, gnawing something, and, on examination, was shocked to
find it was a man's head !   The same day, or a day or two
after this, a Canadian, who was hunting partridges in the swamp,
found REED's body, with the head gnawed off. The poor
fellow had evidently got bewildered by the storm, and, wandering in a circle, had fallen down and perished.   REED had
lived at Prairie du Chien before coming to Saint Paul.

This year witnessed several valuable accessions . to our
population, among them Captain LOUIS ROBERT, CHARLES
BAZILLE, &c.

·CAPTAIN LOUIS ROBERT

was one of the most prominent men connected with the early

history of Saint Paul. He was of Canadian parentage, and was born at Carondelet, Missouri, January 21, 1811. His early life was spent in that region, and in the fur trade of the

CAPT. LOUIS ROBERT.

Upper Missouri River. He traversed the whole of the Missouri valley, while a young man, meeting with innumerable hair-breadth escapes. About 1836 or 1837, he went to Prairie du Chien, and, in the fall of 1843, came to Saint Paul with some goods, which he sold. He then determined to remove here, and did so in 1844. Came to what is now Saint Paul, then a place of only three or four cabins. He purchased a part of the claim of BENJ. GERVAIS, and other property, for $300, which ultimately became worth two or three million dollars, and embarked in the Indian trade here—his foresight and energy being of great value to the infant town, to the development of which he gave his whole energy. In 1847, he was one of the original proprietors of the "Town of Saint Paul," when it was laid out. He took a prominent part in the "Stillwater Convention" of 1848, and was largely instrumental, by his influence, in securing the location of the Capital at Saint Paul. In 1849, he was appointed County Commissioner for Ramsey county, and rendered it important service. He was, also, elected a member of the Territorial Board of Building Commissioners. Though without the advantages of education in early life, he had a large fund of information, gained by travel and contact with men, and was gifted with excellent business capacity and judgment. In the early days of our city he took an active part in politics, and wielded a large influence. He was very generous and liberal in aiding any worthy object, for the public good—gave freely of his means, and also donated valuable property to the church. The bells of the Cathedral and French Catholic church were gifts from him. In the way of private charity, his hand was ever open, and he never refused to render a friend any favor that lay in his power. In the year 1853, he engaged in the steamboat business, and, at different times, owned five steamers. He was, also, largely engaged in the Indian trade, and supply contracts, when the Indian massacre occurred, in 1862. He lost quite heavily in that outbreak, and nearly lost his own life, which the Indians seemed determined to take, only escaping by secreting himself for a considerable time, while they were searching for him, by laying in a marsh, with merely his nose out of water! Captain ROBERT was widely known throughout the State, and as widely respected by all the old settlers. He was the true embodiment of the pioneer—generous, brave, energetic, liberal, and "broad guage," as it is termed, in his manners.

Unlike many of his fellow pioneers, who allowed millions to slip through their fingers and died poor, Captain ROBERT saved a fine estate, valued at $400,000. He died, after a painful illness of several months, on May 10, 1874, universally lamented. He was married in 1839, at Prairie du Chien, to Miss MARY TURPIN, who survived him, with two daughters, one the wife of URI L. LAMPREY, Esq.

CHARLES BAZILLE

was born in Nicollet, near Montreal, November 5, 1812, and, while a young man, came west, and settled in Prairie du Chien, Wisconsin. He was a carpenter by occupation. He first met LOUIS ROBERT at Green Bay, and subsequently became more closely acquainted with him at Prairie du Chien. When ROBERT came to Saint Paul with his goods, in the fall of 1843, BAZILLE accompanied him. They returned to Prairie du Chien before winter, but, in the spring of this year, removed to Saint Paul, and became permanent residents.

BAZILLE built, this summer, for Captain ROBERT, what was undoubtedly the first frame house in Saint Paul. It was designed as a sort of warehouse to store goods landed by the boats, and stood on the lower levee, about where the Milwaukee and Saint Paul passenger depot now is. The frame of this building was made of lumber *hewn by hand*, no sawed dimension stuff being obtainable. After the old shell had served its day and generation for a number of years, and the room was needed for a better building, it was removed to near the corner of Fourth and Minnesota streets, where it still stands. [number 58 East Fourth street.] It is beyond doubt the oldest building in the city.

Mr. BAZILLE also commenced to build, this fall—for WILLIAM DUGAS, who came this year—a grist and saw mill at what was called the falls of Phelan's Creek, or McLeod's Creek—the first mill built in what is now Saint Paul. This mill stood on the west bank of Phelan's Creek, a few yards south of where the Stillwater carriage road crosses it. It is referred to more fully elsewhere.

On December 28, 1845, Mr. BAZILLE was married, at Men-

dota, to ANNIE JANE PERRY, the youngest daughter of ABRA-
HAM PERRY.   They have, like all the other pioneer settlers of
our city, been blessed with a numerous progeny.

Mr. BAZILLE purchased, at quite an early day, a claim previously owned by old LARRIVIER (before mentioned.)   This
subsequently was laid out as an addition to Saint Paul, in connection with his brother-in-law, Mr. GUERIN, and became
immensely valuable.   Mr. BAZILLE had, however, disposed of
most of it before it had greatly enhanced in price.   The
square, or block, now owned by the State, known as the "Capitol Square," was a gift from Mr. BAZILLE to the United States,
and, with the generous recklessness common to the early land
owners, he gave away many other lots and blocks, now worth
perhaps $100,000 in all, and yet, in the evening of life, he,
like many other of our pioneers, is in very limited circumstances.   For many years, Mr. BAZILLE carried on the brick
business on the Lake Como road and other places.

WILLIAM DUGAS.

to whom reference was made in the sketch of Mr. BAZILLE,
was a Canadian, and came to Saint Paul in 1844.   In the first
record book in the Ramsey County Register of Deeds Office,
[that commonly called "Saint Croix," because this was in
that county then,] we find a deed from EDWARD PHELAN to
WILLIAM DUGAS, dated September 2, 1844, of "160 acres on
Faylin's Creek and Falls,"—so it was spelled by whoever
drew up the deed—J. W. SIMPSON, probably, as he used to do
most of the *conveyancing* of that period.   This land is now
known as the southwest quarter of section 29, township 29,
range 22.   It is the second deed on the Ramsey county records.
The consideration given was $70.

DUGAS, who was a millwright by occupation, and had undoubtedly purchased the claim for the fine water-power on it,
at once set about erecting a saw and grist-mill.   He employed
Mr. BAZILLE to assist him.   The mill was two stories, about
25x50 feet in size.   It was not completed that fall, but was
finished and got into running order the next year (1845.)   The
saw was worked a short time; but there was such difficulty in

getting logs, and such a small demand for lumber, that the mill was almost a failure from the start. The burrs were never put in at all. Some 18 months after the date of his purchase, (February 28, 1846,) DUGAS sold the claim and all improvements to ALEX. R. McLEOD, for $835.

DUGAS then settled at New Canada, or in that vicinity, as he was elected one of the members from that precinct, to the first Territorial Legislature, in 1849, along with WM. R. MARSHALL, then of Saint Anthony. He subsequently lived in Saint Paul, in 1850 and 1851, and, after that, removed up to the Crow River valley, and now resides there.

FRANCIS M'COY AND JOSEPH HALL

were two other settlers of this year. Both were carpenters, and continued to live here until after the Territory was organized and the town incorporated. HALL died some years ago. Of McCoy's present whereabouts, or whether he is still in the flesh, I can learn no tidings.

LITTLE CANADA SETTLED.

When BENJAMIN GERVAIS sold his claim to LOUIS ROBERT, he at once moved about eight miles northward from Saint Paul, and, on the lake that now bears his name, he and his sons made claims. He was the first settler of the town of New Canada—but this is given more fully in the sketch of New Canada township, in the latter part of this work.

MORE ABOUT PHELAN.

After PHELAN sold his claim at the falls of the creek now named for him, he made another claim on what was known those days as "Prospect hill"—the ridge on the upper side of Phelan's Creek, just north of where the West Wisconsin Railroad crosses it. This claim he did not keep long, but sold it to HENRY JACKSON. W. G. CARTER, a cousin of JACKSON'S, lived on it for some time, and, in 1849, perhaps, Mr. J. sold it to ALEXANDER WILKIN, by whom it was transferred to others, and finally laid out as an addition—called "Arlington Heights."

PHELAN was a sort of pacha of many claims, for he at once made another, (the fifth one he took in what is now Saint Paul.) This was to the east of the others a little, and extended, probably, as far as Trout Brook. This claim he sold, in 1849, to EDMUND RICE, who entered it in the land office, and it subsequently became his addition to the city.

In the spring of 1850, PHELAN was indicted by the first Grand Jury that ever sat in Ramsey county, for perjury. When the sheriff went to apprehend him, it was found that PHELAN had fled his bailiwick, and, in company with EB. WELD, started for California. It was shortly afterwards reported here that PHELAN had come to a violent end, while crossing the plains. The account states that he acted so brutally and overbearingly toward the other men in the same caravan, they were compelled to kill him, in self-defense. The murdered HAYS was avenged! It is a disgrace, that the name of this brutal murderer has been affixed to one of our most beautiful lakes—one that supplies our households with water. Last winter, Senator W. P. MURRAY made an effort to have the name changed to " Goodhue Lake," but it did not succeed, as it should have done.

ROBERT BUYS OUT OLD PARRANT.

In addition to his purchase of GERVAIS' claim, or what remained of it after GERVAIS' sales to various parties, ROBERT also purchased of old PARRANT, his claim on the lower levee, the one he had made after the sale of his cabin and land to GERVAIS. The extent of the bounds of PARRANT'S claim here, I have not been able to get very definitely, but it could not have been a very large piece.

PARRANT then abandoned Saint Paul, much to the sorrow of the good people here, no doubt, and removed to Pig's Eye, or the Grand Marais, where he made another claim, adjoining that of MICHEL LeCLAIRE.

THE CASE OF LE CLAIRE VS. PARRANT.

But unkind fate, although it had thrust on old Pig's Eye the honor of being the ROMULUS of our city, seemed to give him no rest for the sole of his foot, nor permit him to long enjoy an undisturbed habitation. LeClaire and Parrant quarreled about the lines of their respective claims, although neither of them cultivated ten square rods of ground, and all the land in dispute would have been dear at ten shillings. Perhaps they thought that " principle was involved," and so neither would give up. Finally, LeClaire summoned Parrant before Squire Joseph R. Brown, Justice of the Peace at Grey Cloud. There was tall swearing on both sides. In fact, so strong was the testimony that Squire Brown, with all his sagacity and discrimination, could not tell on which side to make the decision. His irresistible love of a joke finally helped him out of the dilemma. He decided that neither of the parties had any valid claim to the land in dispute, as they had not properly staked it out in the presence of witnesses, and defined its boundaries. It would, therefore, be the just property of the first who should do so. The result was, of course, a foot-race back to the claim, to see who should first arrive and plant the stakes.

Both the contestants started off, eager and anxious. A race of eight miles was before them, over bogs and sloughs, and through jungles and forests. Parrant was old and logy, but strong and tough, and avarice nerved up his strength; while LeClaire was younger and more active. Both strained every nerve, and long in doubtful balance hung the scales. But in this contest, fortune favored LeClaire, who soon began to outstrip the panting Parrant, who, nevertheless, toiled steadily along, hoping some lucky chance might yet enable him to win. But he was doomed to disappointment. Le-Claire arrived long enough in advance to drive his stakes in the presence of witnesses, and secure his claim, when the exhausted founder of our city arrived, sick, mad and furious, to find himself the butt of jeers and ridicule.

Parrant was so worked up by this misadventure, that he soon after sold his claim and left the neighborhood. He started for Lake Superior, designing to return to Sault Ste. Marie, but died on the journey, of a disease resulting from his own vices.

MARRYING " BY BOND."

During this year, or possibly the year previous, HENRY JACK-
SON was appointed, by the Governor of Wisconsin Territory,
a Justice of the Peace.   There was some delay in getting the
commission, &c., after his bonds had been sent to Madison, as
the mails in winter were very slow.   One day, a couple came
to his house, very anxious to be married.   JACKSON informed
them that he was not yet authorized to perform that ceremony
legally, and they would have to defer their marriage a few
days.   This was a great disappointment to the loving hearts
that were so anxious to "beat as one," but they could not
think of postponing the happy hour.   JACKSON was equal to
the dilemma.   He proposed to *marry them by bond*—i. e.,
that they should give a bond that, when his commission arrived,
they would appear and be legally married by him, and in the
meantime they could live together.   They gladly consented to
this.   The bond was made out and signed, and the happy
couple went on their way rejoicing, &c.

Any public officer who could bridge over little difficulties
like this, was a handy man to have around.   JACKSON was
justice, postmaster, hotel-keeper, legislator, clerk of court, and
several other functionaries combined in one.   He even used
to naturalize foreigners, "by bond," probably.   But then,
like vaccination, if it didn't take the first time, it could be
renewed.

CHURCH ITEMS.

In May of this year, Father GALTIER left his mission field
here, and was transferred to another field of labor.   Father
RAVOUX then officiated at Saint Paul and Mendota alternately,
for some five or six years longer, until the parish was divided
into two.

In the fall of this year, the first Protestant service was held by
Rev. Mr. HURLBUT, a missionary of the Methodist church,
who remained in this region about a year.   The service was
held at the house of HENRY JACKSON.

CHAPTER XII.

EVENTS OF THE YEAR 1845.

PROBABLE POPULATION AT THIS DATE—A POLYGLOT VILLAGE—SETTLERS OF THIS
YEAR—LEONARD H. LaROCHE—THE FUTURE MERCHANTS' HOTEL—FRANCIS
ROBERT—THE FREEMAN BROTHERS—W. G. CARTER—CHARLES CAVILEER—A
MRS. RUMSEY STARTS THE FIRST SCHOOL—S. COWDEN, JR., ALSO TRIES IT.

AT the beginning of the year 1845, there were probably
about thirty families living in and around what, by that
date, was pretty well known in this region as " Saint Paul."
There were also a few persons—single men—laborers, mechanics, voyageurs, trappers, &c., who composed a sort of
floating population ; so that the village, or settlement, (for it
was so scattered about, from the seven-corners to Phelan's
Lake, that it was hardly even a village,) had begun to be a
point of some considerable promise. LOUIS ROBERT, HENRY
JACKSON, JOHN R. IRVINE. WM. HARTSHORN, J. W. SIMPSON,
and others, were now engaged in trade, and were bending all
their influence and energies to benefit the infant metropolis,
and draw population and traffic hither.

At this time, by far the largest proportion of the inhabitants
were Canadian French, and Red River refugees, and their
descendants. There were only three or four purely American
(white) families in the settlement, while most of the French
were intermarried with the native race, so that not more than
one-half the families in the place, if that many, were white.
In the families of the mixed bloods, the Sioux, Chippewa,
Menominee, Cree, Kootenais, Winnebago, and perhaps other
tongues, were spoken. English was probably not spoken in
more than three or four families.

SETTLERS OF 1845.

Among the new comers this year, were FRANCIS CHENE-

VERT, DAVID BENOIT. LEONARD H. LaROCHE, FRANCIS
ROBERT, AUGUSTUS and DAVID B. FREEMAN, W. G. CARTER,
CHARLES CAVILEER, and others.

LEONARD H. LaROCHE was a Canadian by birth, and, by
occupation, a carpenter. He was engaged in trade for awhile
with DAVID FARIBAULT, in a little store which stood on what
was afterwards called Bench street. On August 13, 1846, LA-
ROCHE purchased from HENRY BELLAND a small tract of
ground, described in the deed as "bounded on the front and
back by HENRY JACKSON's land, and on the sides by McLEOD
and DESMARAIS." The consideration was $165. This is prob-
ably the land on which the Merchants' Hotel of to-day stands,
as, during that year (1846) LaROCHE built a cabin of tamarack
logs, which, with some additions, afterwards became the
"Saint Paul House," of which the Merchants of to-day is the
outgrowth. LaROCHE sold this property to SIMEON P. FOL-
SOM, in 1847, and went to Crow Wing, where he died about
1859 or 1860.

W. G. CARTER, or "GIB." CARTER, as the old settlers better
knew him, was a cousin of HENRY JACKSON. He was a native
of Virginia. When he came here, he lived for two or three
years on the claim which PHELAN sold JACKSON, called then
"Prospect hill." CARTER was, in 1848, a member of the
Stillwater Convention of that year. He subsequently made
a claim, or, at least, owned a piece on the Fort road, and died
there about 1852. His widow still resides in this city.

FRANCIS ROBERT was a younger brother of Capt. LOUIS
ROBERT, and a native of Missouri. After his arrival here,
he was engaged in the fur trade for LOUIS. In 1848, while
descending the rapids of the Saint Croix in a birch-bark canoe,
he was thrown out and badly injured on the rocks, by a blow
on the chest. From this injury he never recovered, and, after
months of suffering, died on September 27, 1849, aged 30
years. Out of respect, the Legislature, which was then in
session, adjourned for one day, to attend his funeral.

FRANCIS CHENEVERT was a clerk of LOUIS ROBERT. He was
born at Prairie du Chien, of Canadian parents. He appears,
from the Register of Deeds' records, to have purchased (in

connection with David Benoit) the claim of Pierre Bottineau, on June 16, 1846. Chenevert was unmarried, and
lived here until 1865, when he died at the residence of a friend
on Robert street.

Of David Benoit I can get little or no information that is
reliable. He probably resided here but a very short time.

Augustus and David B. Freeman had been residents of
Saint Louis. The latter had been employed by Wm. Hartshorn, while in business there, and was engaged by him to
come to Saint Paul, when he established his own store here, in
1845. Augustus Freeman was also employed by Mr. Hartshorn. The Freemans, in connection with A. L. Larpenteur, and possibly with Wm. H. Randall, continued the
business of Hartshorn, when he retired from it, a couple of
years later. David B. Freeman died in January, 1850, under
the following circumstances: He was going over to Stillwater
in a sleigh, which was overturned, and the horses got away.
Freeman pursued them a couple of miles, becoming over-
heated, and then sat down on the snow to rest. In consequence
of this, he caught a violent cold, inflammation of the lungs set in,
and he died after a very short illness. Freeman was an Odd
Fellow, and, although the Odd Fellows' Lodge had not been
instituted then, the members buried him with the honors of the
order. He was interred on what was afterwards Pearl street,
in the First Ward. The remains were dug up in 1863, while
some improvements were going on there, and recognized by
the "three links" on the coffin. This was the first Odd Fellows' funeral in Minnesota. Augustus Freeman subsequently
went to New York and died there.

Charles Cavileer came to Minnesota in 1841, in company
with the missionary, Rev. B. F. Kavenaugh, and Wm. R.
Brown, and settled at Red Rock. He was a saddler by trade,
and, in 1845, located in Saint Paul, which was then becoming
enough of "a place" to carry on that business. He occupied,
for some time, a building on the levee, and in 1847, perhaps,
moved up to what was once called Saint Charles street. In
1848, he and Dr. Dewey engaged in the drug business. Mr.
Cavileer was Territorial Librarian for a few months, and, in

1851, removed to Pembina, where he has been postmaster almost ever since that year.

THE FIRST SCHOOL.

During this spring, or early in the summer. Mrs. MATILDA RUMSEY, who had come to Saint Paul a few months before. with Mr. BLANCHARD and his wife, (the latter her sister,) established a small school for children, in a log building on the bottom, near the upper levee. This was. beyond doubt, the first school in Saint Paul. There were only a handful of scholars, however, and the school was not kept up long. On June 23, Mrs. RUMSEY was married to ALEXANDER MEGE, and the school was abandoned.

A young man, named S. COWDEN, Jr., then attempted to reestablish the school. There is some disagreement among the old settlers, as to whether he did carry on one or not. Some think he did not succeed in opening one, but others are certain that he taught in the fall of that year. COWDEN was a young man, who had worked awhile for HENRY JACKSON. He came from Prairie du Chien, and was married to a Winnebago halfbreed. COWDEN died some years ago. and his wife is living at the Winnebago Agency, in Blue Earth county.

CHAPTER XIII.

EVENTS OF THE YEAR 1846.

INCREASE OF TRADE AND TRAVELING—THE ESTABLISHMENT OF A POST-OFFICE—
MOVEMENT TO ORGANIZE MINNESOTA TERRITORY—SETTLERS OF 1846—WIL-
LIAM H. RANDALL—JAMES "MC" BOAL—THOMAS S. ODELL—HARLEY D. WHITE
AND OTHERS—INDIAN TEMPERANCE MOVEMENT—REV. DR. WILLIAMSON SET-
TLES AT KAPOSIA—AND WRITES EAST AFTER A SCHOOL MA'AM FOR SAINT
PAUL, &C.

SAINT PAUL had now become quite a "point" on the
river.   There were only three or four points on the Upper
Mississippi, above Prairie du Chien, where boats ever touched,
and only one where they landed with any regularity.   Saint
Paul might be classed in the latter list.   Considerable goods
were now received here by the five or six traders who carried on business in the village. and there was some passenger business to and fro.   Strangers, travelers, and tourists.
generally—sometimes an adventurous trader, from below,
seeking for a location—would occasionally land, to "look
around" a little.   There was no tavern to go to, and HENRY
JACKSON, whose hospitality was a distinguishing trait, usually
invited them to his house, where they were entertained free of
charge.

JACKSON was a Justice of the Peace, a merchant, and a sa-
loon-keeper combined.   To accommodate all these branches of
business, he kept on enlarging his hostelrie, until it grew into
quite a caravansary.   JACKSON was a man of a great deal of
force, originality and humor, and " the boys" usually liked to
"loaf round" there, until it became a kind of headquarters for
trade, news, gossip, politics and general exchange.   It soon
became a sort of post-office, too.   Nearly every boat that landed
would have a handful of letters or papers directed to persons
in Saint Paul, and these, by a sort of established custom, were
handed to JACKSON, because there was no one else to receive

11

them, probably. JACKSON used to keep them piled up on a
shelf in his store. When any one asked for mail, the whole
bundle was thrown down on a table or counter, and the party
picked out what he wanted. That was before the days of cheap
postage. A letter from the Eastern States those times, cost 25
cents. A letter from England was 50 cents. Now it is two
cents, i. e., by postal card.

ESTABLISHMENT OF A POST-OFFICE.

It soon became evident that a post-office was a necessity
here, and the proper petition was forwarded to the Post-office
Department at Washington, and favorably considered. The
records of that Department show that the office was established on April 7. 1846, and a commission to HENRY JACKSON,
as postmaster, issued the same day. The business was so
small, however, that it is scarcely probable that the emoluments were worth scrambling for. It is different now.

Having now the rank and emoluments of a post-office, JACK-
SON conceived that some effort should be made, for appearance
sake, at least, to establish post-official regulations and conveniences, and so set about making the first case of boxes, or
pigeon-holes, that the Saint Paul post-office ever possessed or
used. Out of some old packing cases, or odd boards, he constructed a rude case, about two feet square, and containing 16
pigeon-holes. These were labeled with initial letters. The
whole affair was awkwardly constructed, apparently with a
wood-saw. axe and knife, for temporary use, and, after serving
for two or three years, was laid aside. Fortunately, it was not
lost or destroyed, and finally, after Saint Paul became a flourishing city, the widow of Mr. JACKSON, (Mrs. HINCKLEY, of
Mankato,) gave it to the Historical Society, as a relic of early
days. It now graces the cabinet of that institution, and is
about the most decidedly '' historical" relic of their whole col-
lection. showing, as it does, at a glance, the whole story of
the wonderful and rapid growth of our city. The Society
value it above all their other relics, and will not part with it
for any sum. no matter how fabulous, or we should advocate
its purchase and enclosing of it in a glass case for an ornament

to the present post-office, to show the contrast of thirty years—the first and the last, the alpha and omega of Saint Paul post-offices.

Saint Paul was not the first post-office established in this region, as some have supposed. "Lake Saint Croix Post-office," afterwards called Point Douglas, was established on July 18, 1840, and Saint Croix Falls on July 18, 1840. Stillwater was made a post-office January 14, 1846, about four months before Saint Paul.

Saint Anthony Falls, this year, gave promise of being a point of importance. This is why PIERRE BOTTINEAU sold his claim on Baptist hill, on June 16, for $300, and removed to the Falls, where he bought, for $150, a considerable tract, which afterwards became Bottineau's Addition, and built the second house in the place. In his deed of the claim on Baptist hill, (to FRANCIS CHENEVERT and DAVID BENOIT,) he describes it as "bounded east by KITTSON, north by CLEWETT, west by HARTSHORN and JACKSON, and south by LOUIS ROBERT," and "containing 100 acres." This was merely an estimate—there could not have been that much.

TERRITORIAL FORESHADOWINGS.

The people of Wisconsin Territory had, for some months, been making efforts to secure a State government. On August 6, 1846, the act of Congress, to enable Wisconsin Territory to frame a State Constitution, &c., was passed. The Convention met on October 5, and adjourned on December 16. Hon. WILLIAM HOLCOMBE, of Stillwater, represented Saint Croix county. The Constitution, as framed, provided for the western boundary of Wisconsin down the valley of the Saint Croix, thence down the Mississippi, so that the region now known as Minnesota was thus "left out in the cold." A little out of its regular order, I might here say that this Constitution, which was voted on in April, 1847, was rejected by the people of Wisconsin.

On December 23, 1846, after the above Convention had adjourned, and, probably on the presumption that its action would be ratified, Hon. MORGAN L. MARTIN, the Delegate from Wisconsin in Congress, introduced a bill to organize the Territory of Minnesota.* This bill fixed the western boundary of the Territory on the Red and Sioux Wood Rivers. The bill was bandied about for several months, and, on March 3, 1847, put to sleep "on the table." Thus early was a Territorial government for Minnesota foreshadowed.

Among those who settled in Saint Paul this year, were Wm. H. Randall and William Randall, Jr. ; James M. Boal, Thomas S. Odell, John Banfil, Harley D. White, David Faribault. Louis Denoyer, Jo. Monteur. Charles Roleau, &c.

WILLIAM H. RANDALL.

was born in Roxbury, Massachusetts, May 8, 1806. He was in business in New York, in 1845, with his brother John, when Wm. Hartshorn went there to purchase goods. Mr. Randall seemed to feel a great interest in Saint Paul, made many inquires regarding it, and. the following year, accompanied Mr. Hartshorn out. and resolved to settle here. He seemed to have, from the first, a firm faith in the future greatness and prosperity of the place. He soon after, with his brother, and, perhaps, the Freemans and A. L. Larpenteur, succeeded to Mr. Hartshorn's business, and became owner of a large amount of valuable property, in the heart of the city. He was one of the proprietors of the Town of Saint Paul when it was laid out in 1847. This property became immensely valuable, and, just prior to the crash of 1857, "Father Randall," as he was called, was considered a millionaire. In the early days of Saint Paul, he was one of its most prominent and public-spirited citizens. In 1848, he built the stone warehouse now used by the Milwaukee Railroad. It was a great building for that day. He also graded the levee and improved streets at his own expense, and always subscribed liberally to every public enterprise. The panic of 1857 wrecked him, as it did every heavy owner of real estate, and his once ample

---

*Hon. H. M. Rice says that the late H. L. Dousman, of Prairie du Chien, was the first to urge the adoption of the name, "Minnesota," on account of its geographical fitness, and the beauty of the name.

fortune slipped away. In an obituary sketch, the editor of the *Press* said: "Generous to a fault, and singularly indiscriminate in his friendship, he made loans and endorsements to others, that completely wrecked his princely fortune. While he had property, it was freely used, entitling him to the appellation of a public benefactor. Mr. RANDALL was fitted for that era of our social development, when every man knew and trusted his neighbor as a brother—when legal forms and technicalities were not needed or resorted to, to protect one's rights. Alas! that a higher civilization and social advance should bring, with many blessings, so many wrongs and evils unknown to the simpler, ruder forms of society." The *Pioneer,* also, said: "We have never known a more kindly-hearted man. There are many who owe their start and success in life to his generosity. Very many others, strangers, stricken by sickness in a strange land, who owe life itself to his nursing; and in our cemeteries, scores of mounds mark the graves of those who, having no relatives to minister to them in their fatal illness, were soothed and comforted by the tender hand, and open purse, and sympathizing voice of that kind old man, with whom suffering was always a bond of friendship." Even amid the disasters of 1857, he was cheerful and hopeful— and was always the welcome guest of the social circle. On July 30, 1861, he died of heart disease, aged 55 years, and was buried by the Masonic Fraternity and the Old Settlers of Saint Paul. JOHN H. RANDALL, Esq., of the Saint Paul and Pacific Railroad, and E. D. K. RANDALL, merchant, are sons of Mr. RANDALL.

WILLIAM RANDALL, Jr., was the oldest son of WM. H. RANDALL. He was born at Roxbury, Massachusetts, December 19, 1829, and came to Saint Paul with his father. He was an artist of no common ability, and, as a caricaturist, was very skillful. Some political caricatures he made during the early days of the Territory, are spoken of as being brim full of sarcasm. He died in October, 1851, aged 22 years—an untimely end, cutting short, in the very flower of life, a career of promise and hope.

ED. WEST was also an employee of the firm of HARTSHORN,

RANDALL & Co. He came from New York here, but did not reside in Saint Paul long, leaving, as I learn, for the Indian country, and probably is dead.

JAMES M'CLELLAN BOAL,

usually termed "JIMMY *Mc* BOAL" by the old settlers, was one of the curious characters of early days. BOAL was a Pennsylvanian by birth, and had served a term in the army. He was probably discharged at Fort Snelling, shortly prior to his coming to Saint Paul. He was a painter by occupation, and quite an artist also, and was the first who ever pursued that calling in Saint Paul. He was in partnership with MARSHALL SHERMAN, about 1849 or 1850. BOAL was renowned for his good-heartedness and improvidence. He would loan or give away anything he had, without any thought of the morrow. In 1849, BOAL was elected a member of the Territorial Council from Ramsey county, for two years. About 1851, he moved to West Saint Paul, and formed a partnership with THOMAS S. ODELL, in the trading business. While residing here, he was appointed by Gov. RAMSEY as Adjutant General of the Territory, and held that office until a change of administration occurred in 1853. He was also elected a member of the House of Representatives, in 1852, from Dakota county. He removed to Mendota about 1855, and died there, after a long illness, in the year 1862, leaving a family. There is a street in Saint Paul named for him, but is called by his sobriquet, " *Mc* BOAL," instead of by his correct name.

THOMAS S. ODELL

is a native of New York. He came to Fort Snelling in 1841, as a soldier in the First Infantry, and was mustered out of service in 1845. The following year he settled in Saint Paul. He was chainman to the surveyor who laid out the town plat in 1847. In 1850, he moved to West Saint Paul, and built a log house, for a trading post with the Indians, which is still standing on his property. He states that it was the first house built on that side of the river, which was still unceded by the Sioux.

HARLEY D. WHITE

is a native of Connecticut. He came west about 1841 or 1842, and, after DANIEL HOPKINS opened his store at Red Rock, in the latter year, Mr. WHITE was with him, either as a partner or an employee. He came to Saint Paul, in 1846, and was employed by HENRY JACKSON, as a trader among the Sioux. He went to Point Douglas not long after, where he married a Miss TAINTER, in 1849. He then removed to a farm near Red Wing, where he ran for the Legislature in the same fall, against JAMES WELLS, of Wabasha. WELLS got the certificate, and WHITE contested his seat, but failed to oust him. Mrs. WHITE died a few months after this, leaving a daughter, now an estimable lady of this city. Mr. WHITE then returned to Connecticut, and, at last accounts, was living there.

JOEL D. CRUTTENDEN was a native of the District of Columbia, and came to Saint Paul when he was quite a youth— not being of age. He subsequently went to Crow Wing, and was a member of the first State Legislature from that county.

LOUIS DENOYER

was born at Saint Louis, Missouri, and lived there until he became a resident of Saint Paul. He married a sister of LOUIS ROBERT. Mr. DENOYER resided, while in Saint Paul, on a claim on Phelan's Creek. About 1850, he removed to what is now Belle Plaine, then called "Robert's Creek," and has lived there since that date. J. W. SIMPSON married one of his daughters.

DAVID FARIBAULT

was a quarter-breed son of JEAN BAPTISTE FARIBAULT, one of the earliest traders in Minnesota. DAVID opened a trading house on what would now be described as Bench street, between Jackson and Robert. He purchased considerable property here, as early as 1846, since we find on the Registry of Deeds, sales of property by him to HENRY H. SIBLEY, and others, early in 1847. FARIBAULT built, (in 1847,) the New England House, a frame building, which stood about where the gas company's office now is, and which was burned down in 1860.   He now lives on the Sheyenne River, Dakota Territory.

JOHN BANFIL was a native of Vermont, and was born in the year 1810.   He rented the McLeod House, after his arrival in Saint Paul, with the intention, I believe, of opening a hotel, but it was never regularly kept by him as such.   In the spring of 1849, he removed to Manomin, Minnesota, and engaged in the hotel business there, in which he still continues, and also erected a mill.   In 1857, Mr. BANFIL was elected from his county a member of the first State Legislature. (Senate.)

CHARLES ROLEAU and JOSEPH MONTEUR were Canadian Frenchmen.   They are still residents of our city.

THE CART TRADE WITH RED RIVER.

There had grown up, during the last two or three years, quite a large and profitable trade with the Red River Settlement.   The venture of N. W. KITTSON, trading between Mendota and Pembina, is fully given elsewhere.   When the advantages and profits of that trade were demonstrated, Jo. ROLETTE, of Pembina, and his uncle, ALEX. FISHER, organized a cart brigade, and made trading trips to Saint Paul. It succeeded very well, and, in 1847, as many as 125 carts came to Saint Paul, selling furs and bringing goods here. ROLETTE & FISHER came by the Sauk River route.   Mr. KITTSON's carts came via Traverse de Sioux.   He ultimately adopted the other route, and it then became the main road to Pembina, and, in 1859, was improved for a post route by the Minnesota Stage Company—ultimately giving way to the "iron horse."

"JOSEPH ROLETTE

was a son of the late JOSEPH ROLETTE, of Prairie du Chien, who was agent of the American Fur Company for a number of years, and a man of great influence and energy.   JOSEPH, Jr., was born about 1820, and, in his younger days, was noted for daring and activity.   In 1843, he came to Fort Snelling, and, soon after, went to Pembina, where he concluded to settle.   The condition of society there—the free, half-wild manners of the people, untrammelled by the restraints of more refined society, and their generous improvidence and half-nomad life, part hunter, part farmer—just suited Jo. He married in the winter of 1854-5, and had a numerous family.

"Jo. was best known to the early residents of Saint Paul as a member of the Legislature. He was first elected to the Legislature (House) of 1852, and re-elected in 1853, 1854, and 1855. He was, also, elected to the Council of 1856 and 1857, and a member of the Constitutional Convention in 1857. When the State Constitution was adopted, shutting Pembina out of Minnesota, it was supposed we had seen the last of ROLETTE. But, in December, when the Legislature met, here was 'the gentleman from Pembina,' with his credentials, as usual, and, of course, he was admitted. What would a Minnesota Legislature those days be without Jo. ROLETTE? He was a sort of time-honored institution. When the Republicans came into power the next year, however, he was compelled to retire from public life.

"Jo. was just the sort of man to be popular with the boys in those days. His *bonhomie*, his jolly nature, his hearty and good-humored disposition, his generosity, all made him liked, even by those politically opposed to him. He had faults, of course, just as every human being has, but they were the very outgrowth of his free, generous, hearty nature. They were not allied to anything mean, or small, or sordid. If Jo. had one failing more marked than another, it was his generosity and improvidence. He would give away anything or everything to oblige another, without any thought of his own wants. His spendthrift nature, at last, brought want to him, and he died actually poor.

"Jo. was never happy without he was engaged in some practical joke. His spiriting away the Capital-removal bill was a mere joke of his—as he did not care a straw were the Capital went, but he simply saw a chance to have some fun. His hearty and natural laugh, when he got a good joke on anybody, almost seems to echo through the corridors of the Capitol yet. Alas, the old 'International' and 'American'—spots that bring back his well-known figure and face—are gone, too."

AN INDIAN TEETOTAL MOVEMENT.

The unfortunate effects of intemperance among the Indians, has been fully referred to in previous pages. From year to year, they grew worse instead of better. and shameful scenes were to be witnessed in and near the village. Every few days, a band of the savages would come to Saint Paul, and, getting furiously drunk, endanger the lives of the inhabitants. Time and time again, were the latter compelled to flee from the red demons, who, though passably civil when sober, were very devils when maddened with fire-water.

Strange as it may seem, a temperance movement commenced
this year among the Indians themselves. LITTLE CROW—he
who was killed in 1863—while on a spree this year, was shot
and wounded by his own brother. When he got sober, on the
principle of the devil who resolved to turn monk, he determined to put a stop to drinking in his tribe, and make teetotal-
ers out of his followers. He therefore applied to Mr. BRUCE.
the Indian Agent at Fort Snelling, for a missionary to reside
at his village. Willing to encourage such a laudable desire to
reform, Mr. BRUCE wrote to Dr. THOMAS S. WILLIAMSON,
then at Lac qui Parle, who was a devoted missionary, and.
besides, a skillful physician, asking him to establish a school
at Kaposia. Dr. WILLIAMSON consented, and, in November,
1846, removed to that place. He established a school—and
soon had a number of Indian and half-breed scholars—among
the latter, several girls, who afterwards married white citizens.

SAINT PAUL IN 1846–7.

While laboring for the welfare of his red children. Dr.
WILLIAMSON felt that something must also be done for the
white people at Saint Paul, who were without much educational or religious advantages. He accordingly wrote to ex-
Governor Slade, of Vermont, President of the "National Popular Educational Society," asking him to send hither a good
teacher. As his letter contains. probably, the first written
description of Saint Paul, I give it nearly entire :

" My present residence is on the utmost verge of civilization, in
the northwestern part of the United States, within a few miles of the
principal village of white men in the Territory that we suppose will
bear the name of Minnesota, which some would render 'clear water.'
though strictly it signifies slightly turbid or whitish water.

" The village referred to has grown up within a few years, in a
romantic situation, on a high bluff of the Mississippi, and has been
baptized by the Roman Catholics, by the name of Saint Paul. They
have erected in it a small chapel, and constitute much the larger portion of the inhabitants. The Dakotas call it, *Im-ni-ja-ska*, (white rock,)
from the color of the sandstone which forms the bluff on which the
village stands. This village has five stores, as they call them, at all
of which intoxicating drinks constitute a part, and I suppose the principal part, of what they sell. I would suppose the village contains a

dozen or twenty families living near enough to send to school. Since I came to this neighborhood, I have had frequent occasion to visit the village, and have been grieved to see so many children growing up entirely ignorant of GOD, and unable to read His Word, with no one to teach them. Unless your Society can send them a teacher, there seems to be little prospect of their having one for several years. A few days since, I went to the place for the purpose of making inquiries in reference to the prospect of a school. I visited seven families, in which there were twenty-three children of proper age to attend school, and was told of five more in which were thirteen more that it is supposed might attend, making thirty-six in twelve families. I suppose more than half of the parents of these children are unable to read themselves, and care but little about having their children taught. Possibly the priest might deter some from attending, who might otherwise be able and willing.

" I suppose a good female teacher can do more to promote the cause of education and true religion, than a man. The natural politeness of the French, (who constitute more than half the population,) would cause them to be kind and courteous to a female, even though the priest should seek to cause opposition. I suppose she might have twelve or fifteen scholars to begin with, and, if she should have a good talent of winning the affections of children, (and one who has not should not come,) after a few months, she would have as many as she could attend to.

" One woman, [Mrs. IRVINE,] told me she had four children she wished to send to school, and that she would give boarding and a room in her house to a good female teacher, for the tuition of her children.

" A teacher for this place should love the Saviour, and for His sake should be willing to forego, not only many of the privileges and elegances of New England towns, but some of the neatness also. She should be entirely free from prejudice on account of color, for among her scholars she might find not only English, French and Swiss, but Sioux and Chippewas, with some claiming kindred with the African stock.

" A teacher coming should bring books with her sufficient to begin a school, as there is no bookstore within three hundred miles."

Leaving this letter to go on its long, and. (in those days,) slow journey, we close this chapter.

CHAPTER XIV.

EVENTS OF THE YEAR 1847.

THE STATE MOVEMENT IN WISCONSIN—SETTLERS IN 1847—J. W. BASS, BEN. W. BRUNSON, S. P. FOLSOM, W. H. FORBES, DR. J. J. DEWEY, MISS BISHOP, &C.— THE LATTER OPENS A SCHOOL—J. W. BASS ESTABLISHES A HOTEL—ORGANI- ZATION OF A STEAMBOAT LINE—CAPT. RUSSELL BLAKELEY—POLITICALNOTES.

THE Wisconsin State Constitution was voted on, April 6, 1847. For some cause, it was rejected by the people. It had been sufficient, however, together with Mr. MARTIN'S bill, to call considerable attention to Minnesota, and it was deemed certain, that, within a few months, it would be organized into a separate Territory. This fact being known abroad, caused the commencement of quite an immigration to Minnesota, during the year 1847. Stillwater and Saint Anthony grew rapidly, this season, and Saint Paul had considerable accessions to its population. Among other

SETTLERS IN 1847,

were: JACOB W. BASS, BENJ. W. BRUNSON, DANIEL HOP- KINS, AARON FOSTER, SIMEON P. FOLSOM, JOHN BANFIL, C. P. V. LULL, WM. H. FORBES, PARSONS K. JOHNSON, WM. C. RENFRO, Dr. JOHN J. DEWEY, and G. A. FOURNIER. Nor must Miss HARRIET E. BISHOP be omitted from the list of " settlers" this year.

A full sketch of Major WM. H. FORBES is given in Chapter IV, and need not be repeated here.

JACOB W. BASS

was born in Braintree, Vermont, 1815. He emigrated west when a young man, and lived for some time at Plattville, Wis- consin, then at Prairie du Chien, and subsequently at North McGregor, Iowa, where he was owner of the ferry, proprietor of a hotel, and a part of the time in the mercantile business. He married, while at Prairie du Chien, Miss M. D. BRUNSON, a daughter of Rev. ALFRED BRUNSON, one of the pioneers of Wisconsin, and, soon after, with BENJ. W. BRUNSON, engaged in the lumber business at Chippewa Falls.   In 1847, he and BRUNSON sold out their business, and came to Saint Paul. Mr. BASS arrived in August, and, soon after, leased a building on what is now the corner of Third and Jackson streets, which he opened as a hotel, under the name of "Saint Paul House." Mr. BASS was appointed postmaster, on the 5th of July, 1849, and held that office until March 18, 1853.   He continued in the hotel business until 1852, when he sold out, and opened a commission and forwarding warehouse on the levee, which was a prominent business house for some years.   During the past three or four years, Mr. BASS has been largely engaged in farming in Watonwan county.

BENJAMIN W. BRUNSON •

was born in Detroit, May 6, 1823.   He is a son of Rev. ALFRED BRUNSON, of Prairie du Chien, the well-known pioneer preacher and writer.   When thirteen years old, Mr. BRUNSON removed to that city, where he resided until 1844, when, in company with his brother-in-law, JACOB W. BASS, he went into the mill business at Chippewa Falls, Wisconsin.   They continued there until May, 1847, when he removed to Saint Paul, and, in the fall of that year, assisted his brother, IRA B., to survey the town plat.   Mr. BRUNSON secured a considerable tract of land, at an early day, lying east of Trout Brook, which, in June, 1852, he laid out as "Brunson's Addition." In 1861, Mr. BRUNSON enlisted in Company K, Eighth Minnesota Volunteers, and served three years, as Orderly Sergeant and First Lieutenant.   He was one of the charter members of Saint Paul Lodge Number 2, I. O. O. F., and, also, one of the early members of the Masonic order.   Like all our pioneers, he has experienced many reverses of fortune—to-day rich, to-morrow poor.   Mr. BRUNSON, pursuing his profession of surveyor, has surveyed a considerable part of our own city into streets and lots, when it was a "wilderness" still, and has laid out some of what are now the most flourishing towns of Minnesota. Mr. Brunson was elected a member of the first Territorial Legislature, and re-elected to the second session. He was also a Justice of the Peace for several years.

SIMEON P. FOLSOM

was born December 27. 1819, in Lower Canada. near Quebec. His parents were natives of New Hampshire, and returned to that State when he was quite young, subsequently removing to the State of Maine. During 1837. 1838 and 1839, Mr. Folsom was attending academy, teaching school, and engaged in the lumbering business. In the fall of 1839, Mr. Folsom came west, and settled in Prairie du Chien. and not long after engaged as clerk to Henry M. Rice. trader to the Winnebagoes. at Fort Atkinson. In 1841, he returned to Prairie du Chien. and was Deputy Sheriff for two years. In 1843. he was engaged in surveying public lands. and in 1844 and 1845, was County Surveyor of Crawford county. also reading law with Hon. Wiram Knowlton. In 1846, he joined a volunteer company to go to the Mexican War. but the company was sent. instead, to garrison Fort Crawford, where he remained one year. On July 25, 1847, he landed in Saint Paul, and has, most of the time since. been engaged in surveying and the real estate business. He was the first City Surveyor of Saint Paul, in 1854. In 1861, he enlisted as a private in Company H. Seventh Minnesota, and served in that capacity three years. He was a member of the School Board in 1858. 1859 and 1860, and has been, for several years. in the employ of the Saint Paul and Pacific Railroad. I am indebted to Mr. Folsom for valuable assistance in securing items about early days.

WM. C. RENFRO

was a cousin of Henry Jackson. He was a Virginian by birth, and a young man of ability and education, though unfortunately. too convivial in his habits. He had studied for a physician, and, probably, graduated, but never practiced his profession. further than some gratuitous advice to the poor, pulling teeth, or small matters of that kind. Renfro came to an unfortunate end, a few months after his arrival in Saint Paul, as will be found narrated in the next chapter.

DR. J. J. DEWEY.

The first regular practicing physician who settled in Saint Paul, was Dr. JOHN J. DEWEY, who arrived on July 15, of this year. Dr. DEWEY is a native of New York, and is a brother of ex-Governor DEWEY, of Wisconsin. He had, not long before his arrival here, graduated at the Albany Medical College. The want of a good, reliable physician, which Dr. DEWEY was, had been badly felt in the town, and his coming was very grateful to the good people of that day, who, though generally pretty hearty and rugged, were not entirely and always free from the visitations of sickness and accident. Hitherto there had been no medical or surgical aid nearer than Fort Snelling. Dr. DEWEY was a member of the first Territorial Legislature, and established, (in 1848,) the first drug store in Minnesota.

PARSONS K. JOHNSON

was born in Brandon, Vermont, May 8, 1816. His mother was a grand-daughter of JONATHAN CARVER, noticed in previous chapters of this work. During his boyhood days, he was a schoolmate of a lad, who, in after days, became widely known—STEPHEN A. DOUGLAS. Mr. JOHNSON, in early life, learned the tailoring business, and emigrated west—settling in Saint Paul in August,* 1847, and was, beyond doubt, the first person who carried on the tailoring business in Saint Paul. Mr. JOHNSON was elected a member of the first Territorial Legislature. In 1850, he was married to Miss LAURA BIVINS, a sister of Mrs. HENRY JACKSON. He removed to Mankato, in 1852, with JACKSON, at which place he has been postmaster, member of the Legislature, (1855–56,) Justice of the Peace, &c.

---

* Mr. JOHNSON registers the date of his arrival in the Old Settlers' book, as August, but says that he and B. W. BRUNSON assisted Miss BISHOP in organizing the first Sunday school. Miss B. gives the date of that occurrence as July 25, which is, probably, more correct, as she kept a written diary.

DANIEL HOPKINS

was a native of New Hampshire, and was born in the year 1787. Previous to coming to Saint Paul, he had been in business in Green Bay, Prairie du Chien, &c., and at Red Rock, settling at that place in 1842. On August 7, 1847, he purchased of HENRY JACKSON, a lot which would now be on the corner of Third and Jackson streets. The consideration was $200. Mr. HOPKINS erected a store, where he did a general merchandizing business. He also purchased considerable real estate in Saint Paul. In 1852, he went to Saint Louis to purchase goods, and, while on his return home, was seized with sudden illness on the steamer, and died June 13, 1852, aged 65 years.

AARON FOSTER

was a native of Pennsylvania, and was born in 1817. He came to Stillwater in 1846, and the following year to Saint Paul. Soon after his arrival here he was commissioned a Justice of the Peace. Very many of the deeds of that period appear to have been acknowledged before him. His regular occupation, however, was carpenter, and he worked at that several years. He married a Miss FANNY MORTIMER, daughter of Sergeant MORTIMER, a settler of 1842. FOSTER went to Kansas about 1854 or 1855, and in May, 1864, enlisted in the army, but died of disease at the recruiting station, before regularly entering the service. Mrs. FOSTER died in Minneapolis, about September 1, 1875.

CORNELIUS V. P. LULL is a native of New York, and settled in Saint Paul, October, 1847, pursuing his occupation as carpenter. Mr. LULL was appointed Sheriff of Ramsey county, by Governor RAMSEY, in the fall of 1849, and, soon after, elected for a full term. He " still lives" in our city.

FRED. OLIVIER and G. A. FOURNIER, came to Saint Paul as clerks and agents of LOUIS ROBERT. Both are natives of Canada. Mr. OLIVIER resides here still, and Mr. FOURNIER is in the trading business at Yellow Medicine.

GOV. SLADE FINDS A TEACHER.

When Governor SLADE received Dr. WILLIAMSON's letter,

describing the deplorable educational and religious condition of the people of Saint Paul, he referred the letter to Dr. C. E. STOWE, husband of HARRIET BEECHER STOWE, who forwarded it to his sister-in-law, Miss CATHERINE BEECHER, who was then at Albany, New York, instructing and training a class of young ladies for teachers. By her it was placed in the hands of Miss HARRIET E. BISHOP, as being a proper person to accept and fill the proposed post of duty.

Miss BISHOP is a native of Vermont, and was early filled with a wish to become a teacher of youth, and with considerable missionary spirit. She was an ardent member of the Baptist church. She tells us, in her pleasant book of frontier experiences, "Floral Homes," published in 1857, that, when the request to go was put to her, it was the occasion of quite a mental struggle, in which the dangers and trials to which a feeble and timid young lady would be subjected in such a position, and the sacrifice of leaving home, friends, and the comforts of civilization, for a rude habitation in a rough frontier settlement, were weighed against the call of duty, and the opportunity of doing good. The latter sentiments, at length, predominated over her fears, and she decided to go. Journeying by land to Cincinnati, she came thence by river. On July 16, 1847, she was landed at Kaposia by the steamer "Argo," of which our present townsman, Capt. RUSSELL BLAKELEY, was clerk, and remained a short time an inmate of Dr. WILLIAMSON's family. A day or two afterwards, she was taken in a canoe, paddled by two stout young squaws, to Saint Paul. "A cheerless prospect," she adds, greeted her. "A few log huts composed the town—three families, the American population. With one of these, [J. R. IRVINE,] distant from the rest, a home was offered me. Theirs was *the* dwelling—the only one of respectable size, containing three rooms and an attic." After making arrangements to secure a school room, Miss BISHOP returned to Kaposia, until the building could be made ready.

The building selected was a log cabin, which stood on the site of what is now known as Dr. Mann's Block, corner of Third and Saint Peter streets. It had formerly been occupied

by Scott Campbell, as a dwelling, but Scott had built
another house. Though the building was a plain one, it probably answered for a pioneer school. Miss Bishop describes
it : " Some wooden pins had been driven into the logs, across
which rough boards were placed for seats. The luxury of a
chair was accorded to the teacher, and a cross-legged table
occupied the center of the loose floor." The attendance of
scholars was small, at first—Miss Bishop thinks only four or
five, but Mrs. Patten thinks, nine or ten. At least, it increased to this latter number very soon, and, by fall, it was
found necessary to have a larger and better building. This
was secured on Bench street, just west of Jackson's stand,
and was used until a building could be built, the following
year, for the purpose of a school.

FIRST SUNDAY SCHOOL IN SAINT PAUL.

On July 25, 1847, says Miss Bishop, in her work, the first
Sunday school in our city was held. Seven scholars attended,
and there was such a mixture of races among these, that an
interpreter was necessary, who could speak English, French,
and Sioux, before all could be made to understand the instructions given. The school increased to twenty-five scholars, by
the third Sunday, and was continued successfully for several
years, and, finally, became the Sabbath school of the First
Baptist church—so that said society claim to have the oldest
Sunday school in Minnesota.

SURVEY OF THE TOWN-SITE.

The rapid growth of the town this season, and the more
frequent demand for real estate—which was now bringing
prices that must have astonished the old pioneers who were
still living in a plain, easy, slow sort of way in their bark-
roofed cabins—seemed to point to the necessity of having a
portion of the site laid out into lots. Louis Robert and
others favored this project, and it was soon carried into effect.
Ira B. Brunson, of Prairie du Chien, was employed to do
the surveying, in connection with his brother, Benj. W. Ira
arrived in August, and commenced operations. Thomas S.

ODELL, now of West Saint Paul, was chainman. The tract now known on the maps and in the Registry of Deeds as "Saint Paul Proper," was then laid out. We have no comment to make on it, except as to the narrowness of the streets, and the absence of alleys. But, then, the good people of 28 years ago, could hardly have dreamed that we would have 35,000 people in the lifetime of the men who laid out the town! It was a mistake—but one so excusable we haven't it in our heart to blame them.

The tract, as surveyed then, contained only about 90 acres, but included all the principal business part of the town, and the more thickly settled portion. The names of the proprietors, as given on the recorded plat, are: LOUIS ROBERT, DAVID LAMBERT, HENRY JACKSON, BENJ. W. BRUNSON, CHARLES CAVILEER, HENRY H. SIBLEY, J. W. BASS, A. L. LARPENTEUR, WM. H. FORBES, J. W. SIMPSON, HENRY C. RHODES, L. H. LAROCHE, J. B. COTY and VETAL GUERIN. Some of these persons were not residents and land owners in 1847—but secured an interest subsequent to that date. As the land in this locality had not at that time been surveyed by the United States, and could not be entered, neither could the town plat be entered, and was not until April 28, 1849. It was signed on February 28, 1849, by the above gentlemen, three of whom, (DAVID LAMBERT, HENRY C. RHODES, and J. B. COTY,*) were not residents in September, 1847, but settled subsequently.

After the property was surveyed, the lots or blocks were deeded to each owner, so that he would have a title to his own land. B. W. BRUNSON testified in the Saint Charles street case, tried in 1866: "We had meetings about once a week at the time, in regulating proprietors' lines. There was a committee to determine who owned lots, and when the lines were so that parties entering the town could own equitably:

---

* JOHN BAPTISTE COTY was a Canadian by birth, and a carpenter by occupation. He was one of the charter members of Saint Paul Lodge, No. 2, I. O. O. F., but afterwards withdrew from that order, by command of the clergyman who married him. COTY returned to Canada about 1852, or 1853. Though a "proprietor" when the plat was signed, I think he was not a resident when the town was surveyed.

most of those difficulties were settled before the plat was signed."

In vol. 8, p. 491, Supreme Court Reports of Minnesota, will be found a decision on the question as to whether the dedication of the plat was valid.

From the records in the Surveyor General's office of this district, I find that the United States surveys of the land in and around Saint Paul, were made in the fall of 1847. The town lines were run by JAMES M. MARSH, in October, and the subdivisions made by ISAAC N. HIGBEE, the following month.

ESTABLISHMENT OF A HOTEL.

Reference was made to the establishment, by J. W. BASS, of a hotel, during this season. It was in the building spoken of in the last chapter, commenced in 1846, by LEONARD H. LaROCHE, and subsequently completed and enlarged by S. P. FOLSOM, in the summer of 1847, and finally considerably extended and improved by Mr. BASS. The first part built was 20x28 feet, a story and a half high, and was built of tamarack logs, hewed square and laid on a small foundation. When this building was taken down, in 1870, to give way to the Merchants of to-day, the logs were found as sound as when put up, 23 years before. Judge GOODRICH, the enthusiastic Secretary of the "Old Settlers' Association," secured one of the logs, and had a gavel and chest constructed out of it, for the use of the Association.

At that time, the building was situated on quite a bank, and when this was dug down, in 1853-4, to grade Jackson and Third streets, the log structure was left almost one story above ground. So a stone basement was built up under the log structure. Mr. BASS leased the building in August, 1847, at $10 per month. He gave it the name, "Saint Paul House," and made considerable additions to its size, and improvements in its interior and exterior, raising it to two full stories, &c. It was then quite a good-sized building, for those days, and Mr. BASS kept a right smart tavern in it, too, and old settlers say it helped the town considerable, for no one would want to go to a town that had no good hotel.

The Saint Paul House, and its larger successor, played no insignificant part in the history of our city and State. It was here that, on June 1, 1849, the Territory was organized by the Territorial officers. The post-office was held in it a couple of years, and, in one of the additions to the building, a lodge of Sons of Temperance and Free Masons was held.

The subsequent history of this pioneer hotel deserves mention. Mr. BASS retired from it, in 1852, and various persons essayed to "keep" it, until July, 1856, when E. C. BELOTE leased it. He managed it until 1861, when JOHN J. SHAW and WM. E. HUNT leased it. Mr. HUNT soon retired, and Col. SHAW continued it until 1873. During this period, the present fine structure was built. Mr. SHAW gave way to Col. ALVAREN ALLEN, the present proprietor.

ORGANIZATION OF A STEAMBOAT LINE.

Another important event of this year, one which greatly aided the settlement of this region, was the organization of a steamboat company, to run regular packets from Galena to Mendota and Fort Snelling. Hitherto, only stray boats would make trips to this region, whenever they could get loads that would pay. During this season, Messrs. CAMPBELL & SMITH, of Galena, BRISBOIS & RICE, H. L. DOUSMAN, of Prairie du Chien, H. H. SIBLEY, of Mendota, and M. W. LODWICK, of Galena, purchased the steamer "Argo," with the intention of organizing, the next spring, the "Galena Packet Company." The "Argo" was destined to be the pioneer of an important trade. M. W. LODWICK, was commander, and RUSSELL BLAKELEY, of Galena, was clerk. The "Argo" was designed to make trips once a week, and did a pretty fair business that season.* Unfortunately, she struck a snag, near Wabasha, in October, and sank. Capts. LODWICK and BLAKELEY then went to Cincinnati and purchased the "Dr. Franklin," which came out the next year, and was a popular packet for those days: she ran for several seasons.

---

* From a record kept at Fort Snelling, by PHILANDER PRESCOTT, for some years, we find the number of steamboats arriving there about those times, stated as follows: 1844, 41 boats; 1845, 48 do.; 1846, 24 do.; 1847, 47 do.; 1848, 63 do.; 1849, (Saint Paul,) 95 do.

CAPT. RUSSELL BLAKELEY.

one of the pioneer steamboat men of the Upper Mississippi. was born at North Adams, Massachusetts, April 19. 1815. In 1817, his parents removed to Leroy. Genesee county, New York, where he grew up to manhood. From there he went to Peoria, Illinois. in 1836, and to Galena in 1839. In 1844. he went to Wythe county, Virginia, where he remained three years, returning to Galena in 1847.

When the "Argo" was put on the river. in June of that year. Capt. BLAKELEY was engaged as clerk, and, after that boat sank. of the "Dr. Franklin." which succeeded her, running the latter part of the time as captain. Also. in 1853. he ran the "Nominee." and. in 1854, took command of the "Galena," a famous and popular packet in her day, which was burned July 1, 1858, at Red Wing. During this period. thousands, perhaps tens of thousands, of the earlier citizens of our State, have been brought here by Capt. BLAKELEY. on one or the other of the above packets. a fact which made him more widely known. probably, at that time, than almost any other man in this region. If Capt. B. would write a faithful account of steamboating in those days. with his personal reminiscences of men and events, it would make an interesting chapter of our pioneer history.

In 1855, he was appointed agent at Dunleith. of the Packet Company, and soon after bought out the interest of CHARLES T. WHITNEY in the Northwestern Express Company. the firm then becoming J. C. BURBANK & Co. Capt. BLAKELEY came to Saint Paul to reside in 1856. Soon after, the firm became largely interested in mail contracts, stage and transportation lines. &c.. a full account of which is given in a future chapter. Mr. BURBANK retired from the company. in July, 1867. and the business is now continued by Capt. BLAKELEY and C. W. CARPENTER. Esq. Capt. B. is also largely interested in the railroad business, being a director of the Sioux City Railroad. and is a member of several other business organizations, contributing largely. both in capital and time. to promote the prosperity of our city and State. and build up its literary and other institutions.

SAINT·CROIX COUNTY,

which had, up to this time, been included in Crawford county for judicial purposes, was, this year, detached, and reorgan-

CAPT. RUSSELL BLAKELEY.

ized, with Stillwater as the county seat. In June, the first term of any court ever held in what is now Minnesota, was held there, by Judge CHARLES DUNN, of the United States District Court. HARVEY WILSON, of Stillwater, was appointed

Clerk of the Court, and has held that position nearly, if not all, the time since.

POLITICAL NOTES.

The Wisconsin State Constitution, mentioned on page 164, was voted on April 6, 1847, but, for some reason, defeated. A second Convention was held on the 13th of December, 1847. Its results will appear a little further on.

At the election held this fall, for Representative from the District composed of Crawford, Saint Croix, Chippewa and LaPointe counties, to the fifth Legislative Assembly of Wisconsin, HENRY JACKSON was chosen a member. A special session was held October 17–27, 1847, and the regular second session of the fifth Assembly was held February 7, to March 13, 1848.

CHAPTER XV.

EVENTS OF THE YEAR 1848.

DEATH OF WM. C. RENFRO—RAISING FUNDS FOR A SCHOOL HOUSE—RELIGIOUS
AND TEMPERANCE MOVEMENTS—TERRITORIAL MOVEMENT—THE STILLWATER
CONVENTION—H. H. SIBLEY ELECTED DELEGATE—SALE OF THE LAND AT
SAINT PAUL—H. M. RICE BUYS INTO THE TOWN-SITE—MEMOIR OF MR. RICE—
MEMOIRS OF DAVID OLMSTED AND OTHERS—LIST OF PRE-TERRITORIAL SET-
TLERS—GENERAL REMARKS ON THAT PERIOD.

THE year 1848 was a sort of pivotal period in our history.
It was marked, too, with important events—the adoption
of a State government by Wisconsin, leaving Minnesota without a government—the efforts of our citizens to secure a Territorial organization, which were soon after successful—the
purchase from the United States of the site of the city and the
lands surrounding it—the influx of new settlers, some of them
men of capital, education and influence—the increase of trade,
and in the importance of the place, &c. Thus, the year 1848
was a sort of intermediate period, between the era of the wilderness and unorganized society, and that of a government of
law and order, emerging from chaos, as it were, into the dig-
nity of an established commonwealth.

DEATH OF WM. C. RENFRO.

The first event of the year 1848, which we have to record,
was the death of WILLIAM C. RENFRO, by freezing. REN-
FRO, as stated in the sketch of him a few pages back, was a
young man of education and ability, but addicted to the use of
intoxicating drinks. About the first of January, while stopping at his cousin's, W. G. CARTER's, on "Prospect hill,"
near the bend of Phelan's Creek, he arose in the night, while
suffering from *mania a potu*, and wandered toward town.
Being missed, search was made, and, on January 3d, his life-
less body was found under a tree, near the present Saint Mary's
Catholic church. He was clad only in his shirt, drawers, &c.

RAISING FUNDS FOR A SCHOOL HOUSE.

Miss Bishop, in her work before quoted, gives some account of a sewing circle raising funds for a school house :

"The first winter (1847–8) closed in upon us. * * * Books were the companions that enlivened the solitude of our evenings. The social pleasures of the vicinity were merged in a weekly ball for those who enjoyed what, according to the report of the parties, was little else than, in western parlance, a ' whisky hoe-down.' What rational, social pleasure can we devise that shall elevate the moral tone of society? was the theme of discussion, when Joseph R. Bowron,* of Saint Croix, proposed that a ' Ladies' Sewing Society' be instituted, to aid in the erection of the proposed school house, and, for our encouragement, generously pledged $10, for a commencement. Accordingly, the ' Saint Paul Circle of Industry' was formed, with eight members.† We remember, with an allowable pride, that the first payment on the lumber for the first school house, was made with money earned with the needle by the ladies of this circle."

Miss Bishop further hints that they had good success in soliciting subscriptions. and received $50 from officers at the fort. She adds :

" The specified object of the building was the accommodation of the school, church, court, occasional lectures, elections, and, in short, all public gatherings; with the expectation that an expenditure of $300 on a building 25x30 feet. would be all that would be required for at least ten years."

This building was completed sometime in August. 1848. It stood about where Dr. Alley's block now stands, and was used for church services. day-school. lectures, &c.. until as late as 1851, when several denominations had erected chapels of their own. It was burned at the great fire, in 1857, which swept that whole square. The building was erected by Jesse H. Pomeroy. The lot was a gift from Jno. R. Irvine.

RELIGIOUS PROGRESS—TEMPERANCE.

The first Protestant sermon, as before noted, ever preached in Saint Paul, was by Rev. Mr. Hurlbut. a Methodist Episco-

---

* Joseph R. Bowron died at Hudson, Wisconsin, April 10, 1868.

† Miss Bishop, Mrs. Jackson, Mrs. Bass, Miss Harriet Patch, and Mrs. Irvine were among the members.

pal missionary, in 1844. Rev. E. A. GREENLEAF preached the next sermon in June, 1846. Mrs. HINCKLEY thinks Rev. Father GEAR,* Episcopal missionary at the fort, preached the third sermon, in the same year. September 5, 1847, Dr. WIL-LIAMSON preached the fourth Protestant sermon.

After Miss BISHOP's arrival, she kept a diary of events, principally of religious matters, which gives some interesting ideas concerning the progress of religion in Saint Paul during this year. We condense a few notes, as follows:

"January 30. Mr. GEAR preached in afternoon.

"February 20. Mr. GREENLEAF preached.

"March 19. 'Visiting, hunting, wrestling, drinking, gambling, &c., are the pastimes of this holy day.'

"April 2. Mr. PUTNAM preached.

"April 23. VIOLA IRVINE (a little daughter of J. R. IRVINE,) died from a severe burn, by accident.

"June 26. Mr. CAVENDER acts as Superintendent of Sunday school.

"July 10. Preaching by Rev. LEMUEL NOBLES.

"July 17. Prof BENT [a professor in the University at Middlebury, Vermont,] lectured.

"July 24. B. F. HOYT preached.

"October 16. Rev. Mr. COPELAND, of Indiana, preached.

"October 23. Mr. HOYT preached.

"November 6. Mr. HOYT preached.

"December 4. Rev. BENJ. CLOSE, the Methodist preacher of the Saint Paul and Stillwater circuit, preached.

"December 31. Mr. CLOSE preached and organized a class, the first move towards organizing a Protestant church in this city."

During this season, Miss BISHOP says, in her book, the religious element in the village was greatly reinforced by the arrival of Mr. B. F. HOYT and A. H. CAVENDER. "The former occasionally broke the bread of life to the listening few. When the number of disciples had increased to five or six, on November 9, 1848, a weekly prayer meeting was established. Hon. H. M. RICE made the liberal offer of $200 and ten town lots toward the first church edifice, [Market Street Methodist,]

---

*Rev. EZEKIEL G. GEAR was born at Middletown, Connecticut, September 13, 1793. In 1836, he went to Galena, and, in 1837, was appointed Post Chaplain at Fort Snelling. In 1860, he was transferred to Fort Ripley, and, in 1867, placed on the retired list. He died October 13, 1873, aged 80 years. In the early days of Saint Paul he was well-known to our pioneer settlers.

which offer was accepted.   During the same winter, Rev. Mr.
GEAR held monthly, and finally semi-monthly service in Saint
Paul."

It may be interesting to know that the first temperance society in Saint Paul—perhaps in Minnesota—was organized this
summer, by a few young folks—some of them scholars in Miss
BISHOP's school.   The pledge itself was drawn up by JAMES
M. BOAL, who was quite an artist, and decorated it with
drawings and emblematic designs.   Miss BISHOP still has the
paper, the first written temperance pledge, beyond doubt, in
the State.   Shortly after this, the young men of the town organized a temperance society, about thirty of them taking the
pledge.   ALEX. R. McLEOD was elected president—but, Miss
B. adds, regretfully, that he did not keep the pledge very well.

REMARKABLE SCENE IN A JUSTICE'S COURT.

Under the head of the administration of justice in early
days, it occurs to us to chronicle a curious affair which occurred this summer.   HENRY JACKSON was a Justice of the Peace
this year, and was trying some ordinary case in his caravansary
on the point.   The matter had been submitted to the jury, and
they had retired to consider a verdict, being locked up, by the
constable, in a room, where there was only one little outside
window.   Among the six men thus confined, was one skillful
violinist, (CHARLEY MITCHELL, I believe,) who was always
in request for balls and convivial assemblages.   On the day of
the trial, a man had come over from Stillwater, for the purpose
of hiring the violinist, and taking him back to that piney settlement, to fiddle for a ball that was coming off the same evening.   On finding the violinist locked up, with no prospect of
an early release, he became somewhat nervous, lest he should
not be able to return in season with the manipulator of the
bow.   The jury, unluckily, were not able to agree on a verdict,
and spent several hours in a fierce discussion of the case, some
of them getting "fighting mad" on the question.   About this
time, the Stillwater man got desperate, as he saw the afternoon
waning away, and determined to take an opportunity to speak
to the violinist at all hazards.   He, thereupon, got a box or

some other standing place, and climbed up to the window,
where he held a confab with the fiddling juryman. At this
point, one of the disagreeing jurors accused the latter of being
in surreptitious communication with an outsider, and of receiving a bribe! Of course, this brought the dispute to blows at
once, in which the whole jury were busily engaged in less than
a minute. Chairs and tables were broke to splinters, and two
or three jurors were pounded badly. Among the latter was
the violinist, who had a shocking "head put on him," and
suffered a dislocated arm, &c. The constable, justice and
others rushed in to quell the fight, when the jurors who were
able to go, broke out and ran away, and this ended the case.
The Stillwater man returned without his musician, and the
ball was postponed indefinitely.

MORE GOVERNMENTAL PROGRESS.

Wisconsin held a second Constitutional Convention, as before remarked, which convened on December 15, 1847, and
adjourned on February 1, 1848. The Constitution framed by
them, and which was voted on and adopted March 13, 1848,
fixed the State boundaries as they are now seen on the maps.
Congress admitted Wisconsin as a State, on May 29, following.
The question was thus definitely settled, that what is now
Minnesota, was "left out in the cold," with no government,
unless, fortunately, they inherited the abandoned Territorial
government of Wisconsin, and many claimed that this was the
case. The question considerably agitated the people of the
region west of the Saint Croix and Mississippi, and, after considerable "talk," it was resolved by the Saint Paul men to
hold a meeting and canvass the matter. The meeting, which
could not have been a large one, for there were scarcely 20
English-speaking men in Saint Paul at that time, was held at
Jackson's caravansary in July.* This was undoubtedly the
first public meeting on the subject, or perhaps on any subject

---

* A prominent old settler thinks this meeting was held in the street, instead of in a
house, mainly because there was more room out of doors, and logs were plenty, which
could be used as seats, and to make "smudges" with. He says most of the public
meetings those days, were held in the street.   •

of a public nature, and it was strongly urged that measures be taken to secure a Territorial government for the balance of Wisconsin, then unprotected by law.

THE STILLWATER CONVENTION.

On the 5th day of August, a public meeting of the same kind was held at Stillwater, and it was resolved to circulate a call for a general convention of all persons interested, to meet at Stillwater on August 26. The call was made, and, at the time mentioned, the Convention was held. Sixty-one persons appear to have been present, as we find that number of names signed to a memorial adopted during the session. Among those present from Saint Paul, were : LOUIS ROBERT, J. W. SIMPSON, A. L. LARPENTEUR, DAVID LAMBERT, HENRY JACKSON, VETAL GUERIN, DAVID HEBERT, OLIVER ROSSEAU, ANDRE GODFREY, JOSEPH RONDO, JAMES R. CLEWETT, EDWARD PHELAN, WM. G. CARTER, &c.

At this meeting a letter was read from Hon. JOHN CATLIN, Secretary of State of Wisconsin, stating that, in his opinion, if a Delegate were elected, he would be permitted to take his seat—and that the *Territory* of Wisconsin was still in existence.

JOSEPH R. BROWN, H. H. SIBLEY, MORTON S. WILKINSON, HENRY L. MOSS, FRANKLIN STEELE, DAVID LAMBERT, and others, appear, from the proceedings, to have taken a prominent part. A committee was appointed to draft a memorial to Congress, resolutions, &c., and the Convention adjourned to dinner.

While at dinner, (Hon. H. L. Moss states,) there was considerable caucusing as to the location of the Capital for the proposed Territory, and the Saint Paul delegates carried the day—it being generally understood that Saint Paul was to be fixed on as the Capital, but Stillwater was to have the State's prison, and Saint Anthony the university—a parole agreement, which was, by a future Legislature, carried out.

When the Convention reassembled, J. R. BROWN reported the proposed memorial, together with voluminous resolutions, reciting the necessity of having a Territorial government—providing for the appointment of a delegate to visit Washington, and urge an immediate organization of the proposed Territory : also, for the appointment of a committee of six, to collect information and statistics, for the use of said delegate, and a " central committee" of seven, to correspond with and aid said delegate. The resolutions and memorial were adopted, and the latter signed by all the members present.

ELECTION OF A DELEGATE.

The Convention then proceeded to elect a delegate to Washington, and Hon. HENRY H. SIBLEY, of Mendota, was elected, and furnished with proper credentials. It was expected that the delegate so elected was to defray his own expenses. Mr. SIBLEY accepted the proposed mission, however, and promised the Convention to go on, and use his utmost endeavors to accomplish the important trust committed to him.

Shortly after this, Hon. JOHN H. TWEEDY resigned as Delegate to Congress from Wisconsin, and Hon. JOHN CATLIN, claiming to be acting Governor of Wisconsin Territory, if there was now any such thing, came to Stillwater, and issued a proclamation, on October 9, ordering a special election, to fill the vacancy. On October 30, said election was held. Mr. SIBLEY and HENRY M. RICE were the only candidates, and there was little or no effort made by either to secure an election, though some of the friends of each got up a small canvass. In fact, neither of them desired it, as far as any personal motives were concerned, as the condition of things was very dubious, and it seemed very improbable that the Delegate elected would be permitted to take his seat. General SIBLEY was elected, as it turned out, and, in November, proceeded to Washington.

PURCHASE OF THE TOWN-SITE FROM THE UNITED STATES.

Meantime the Government surveys of land in this neighborhood had been progressing, and, on August 14, 1848, the first sale of lands occurred at the land office, at Saint Croix Falls, in pursuance of a proclamation of President POLK. At this sale, 27 whole and fractional townships, or 436,737 acres, were offered for sale—part lying in Wisconsin. but only 3,326 were sold, at $1.25 per acre. At this sale. the town-sites of Saint Paul. Saint Anthony and Stillwater were offered for sale. A gentleman present gives the following account of it:

"The land office for the Chippewa land district was opened by Gen. SAMUEL LEECH, Receiver, and Col. C. S. WHITNEY, Register, at the Falls of Saint Croix, in the first part of August, 1847. The first sale in this District commenced on or about the 15th day of August, 1848, and continued for two weeks. The second sale commenced on or about the 15th day of September, of the same year, and, also, continued for two weeks. At this latter sale, the first lands were disposed of, that are now comprised within the limits of Minnesota, including the towns of Saint Paul, Saint Anthony and Stillwater. At this period, there were very few white settlers within what is now the Territory of Minnesota: and they were principally located within and immediately surrounding the above named towns. For the better accommodation of the people—the conveniences of travel being very poor—the land officers gave timely public notice of the exact day upon which certain townships would be offered for sale; so that at no one time were there more than forty or fifty persons present. There were no 'speculators' in attendance at this sale; which accounts for the fact that there was but one contra bid during the whole sale, and that was between two settlers, who resided somewhere in the neighborhood of Cottage Grove, in Washington county. It seems, that, after having secured their respective claims, they could not agree upon which should have a certain eighty-acre tract, composed of timber land lying adjacent to each. I believe that the successful bidder got it at about ten cents above the minimum price per acre.

"The most exciting time during this sale, at which there were a great number of people present, was on the day and the day before that on which the town-site of Saint Paul was offered for sale. The good people of this vicinity were very fearful that the sale would be infested with a hungry set of speculators, as has too often happened at land sales in the west, ready with their gold, to jump at every chance that presented itself, and bid over the actual settler. To guard against this emergency, it was understood beforehand that the Hon. H. H. SIBLEY, should bid in the town-site of Saint Paul, and the claims of such Canadians as did not understand English sufficiently to do so for themselves; and, to aid and assist him in this mission, a large and well-armed force, composed principally of Canadian Frenchmen, were present at the sale. Their fears, however, were not realized, and they were permitted to purchase their lands without molestation.

"In 1849, after much delay and difficulty, the land office at the Falls of Saint Croix, was removed to Stillwater. A remonstrance against this removal was made by the members of the Wisconsin Legislature; their objections, however, were overcome by the establishment of an additional land district in Wisconsin."

Gen. H. H. SIBLEY, in his " Reminiscences of the Early Days of Minnesota," published by the Historical Society, says of this sale : "I was selected by the actual settlers to bid off portions of the land for them, and, when the hour for business had arrived, my seat was invariably surrounded by a number of men with huge bludgeons. What was meant by the proceedings I could, of course, only surmise, but I would not have envied the fate of the individual who would have ventured to bid against me."

Saint Paul Proper, being owned by various parties, the owners selected H. H. SIBLEY, LOUIS ROBERT and A. L. LARPENTEUR, as trustees, to enter the lands in question, and deed the lots, blocks, and fractions to the parties who were entitled to the same. This was quite a difficult task, and required not a little trouble and patience to sift out the real and equitable owners in some cases. Finally, every piece was conveyed, by the above trustees, to the rightful owner, and their decision acquiesced in. Some of the simple Canadians, who did not understand English very well, or the forms of conveyancing, suffered their title to remain in General SIBLEY's name, in some cases, two or three years, thinking they were secure there, and it required actual persuasion and trouble on the part of Gen. S. to get some of them to receive the deeds and conclude the transfer by registry.

THE WINNEBAGO REMOVAL.

In 1846, the Winnebagoes, then on a reservation in Iowa, ceded their land to the United States, and accepted, instead, a Reservation now in Todd county, Minnesota. But, in 1848, when the time came for their removal, they refused to go, and their removal was only accomplished by much patience and strategy on the part of H. M. RICE, E. A. C. HATCH, DAVID OLMSTED, S. B. LOWRY, JOHN HANEY, Jr., N. MYRICK, GEO. CULVER, RICHARD CHUTE, Lieut. JOHN H. McKENNEY, now

13

of Chatfield, and other agents, soldiers and traders. They were finally located near Long Prairie Agency, about July 1. This movement resulted in securing, as citizens here, either that year or soon after, most of the above gentlemen. Mr. Rice bought property here, and made valuable improvements ; Olmsted and Rhodes established a trading outfit, while E. A. C. Hatch, N. Myrick, and George Culver ere long made Saint Paul their home.

II. M. RICE BUYS A PART OF THE TOWN-SITE.

On November 14, Mr. Rice purchased, of John R. Irvine, the "east half of the northwest quarter, of section 6, town 28, range 22 west," for the sum of $250. This soon became a part of Rice and Irvine's Addition, which was surveyed the same winter, by B. W. Brunson. This was an important acquisition for the town. J. W. Bond says, in "Minnesota and its Resources," that the very *name* of having H. M. Rice interested in the town, gave it a new influence in the estimation of persons abroad. Ex-Governor Marshall, in his address before the Old Settlers of Hennepin county, February 22, 1871, considers that this fact had more to do with turning the scale in favor of Saint Paul, at a critical juncture, than anything else.

HON. HENRY M. RICE

was born in Waitsfield, Vermont, November 29, 1816. He is a lineal descendant of the famous Warren Hastings, one of the most remarkable men connected with the history of England during his time. His grandfather was engaged in the French War of 1755, and was taken prisoner to Canada at one time, and ransomed. He attended academy at Burlington, and studied law about two years with Hon. Wm. P. Briggs, of Richmond, Vermont. In 1835, Mr. Rice emigrated to Detroit, Michigan, with Hon. Elon Farnsworth, then a resident of that Territory. In 1837, he was appointed Assistant Engineer under the State of Michigan, to locate the Sault Ste. Marie Canal and other works.

In 1839, Mr. Rice came to Fort Snelling, Minnesota, where he remained in the sutler department until June, 1840, when

he was appointed sutler at Fort Atkinson, in what is now
Iowa.   He soon after became connected with P. CHOUTEAU,
Jr. & Co., and had charge of the trade with the Winnebagoes
and Chippewas, having a large number of trading posts
throughout the Chippewa country, from Lake Superior to Red
Lake, and thence to the British Possessions.   No man among
the early traders was better acquainted with the Lake Superior
and Northern Minnesota region than Mr. RICE.   He has
traveled over every portion of it, and knew all the old traders,
whose names have now passed into history.

In 1846, a delegation of Winnebagoes visited Washington
to negotiate a treaty with the United States for their Reservation in Iowa.   One of their principal chiefs being taken sick,
Mr. RICE was appointed a delegate in his place, and was in-
strumental in accomplishing a sale of their lands, then needed
for the growing settlements of whites.   On August 2, 1847, at
Fond du Lac, Lake Superior, Mr. RICE and Hon. ISAAC VER-
PLANK, as commissioners on the part of the United States,
purchased from the Chippewas of Lake Superior and the
Mississippi, the country lying on the Mississippi and Long
Prairie Rivers, for a new Reservation for the Winnebagoes.
On the 21st of the same month they also purchased from the
Pillager Indians, at Leech Lake, the country lying between
the Otter Tail, Long Prairie, Crow Wing and Leaf Rivers,
for a Menominee Reservation, but it was never used for that
purpose.   Mr. RICE subsequently, in 1851, 1853, 1854, 1863,
and other dates, was largely instrumental in consummating
treaties with the Chippewas and Sioux, by which the greater
portion of our State was ceded to the whites, and thrown open
to settlement.

When the Winnebagoes were removed, in the summer of
1848, Mr. RICE aided largely in quelling the threatened outbreak by them, and, in order to accomplish it without trouble,
advanced the expense of removal, over $20,000 in gold, on be-
half of his company.   The Indians were finally taken to Long
Prairie in July.

In order to attend to the receipt of the goods required in the
trade, business compelled Mr. RICE to spend a large share of

his time in Saint Paul. The growing importance of the place, then recently " laid out" as a town, and regularly entered—and which was already spoken of as the future Capital of the coming " Territory of Minnesota"—was one cause of his becoming one of the town-site owners, and, not long after the land had been entered, he purchased a tract, which was soon after laid out as an addition. It is now in the heart of the city, and worth millions. Another cause of Mr. Rice's locating here, and making this the depot for his goods, was the fact that it was the head of navigation. Boats then, as now, could not get above Saint Paul in low or moderate water.

Mr. Rice at once bent his whole energies, and employed his capital to the development of the town. He built warehouses, erected hotels and business blocks in his addition, diverted trade and commerce from other points hither, and influenced men of capital and energy to invest here largely. In a short time the impetus thus given to the place lifted it above competition. He also proceeded to Washington, " on his own hook," while the bill organizing Minnesota Territory, with Saint Paul as its Capital, was pending, and labored for it untiringly. His influence with friends in Congress, and other members, aided largely in turning the scale in our favor.

In the early days of Saint Paul, Mr. Rice was one of its most reliable, ready and liberal promoters of every good enterprise. He donated lots to several churches and public institutions, besides considerable sums in money. " Rice Park," our beautiful resort on summer evenings, was one of his gifts to the public. To one of the institutions of Rice county, named in honor of him in 1853, he gave the documentary portion of his valuable private library, worth several thousand dollars.

In 1853, Mr. Rice was elected Delegate to Congress, and re-elected in 1855. This was the period of the most rapid development of Minnesota, and it imposed on our Delegate extraordinary labor. He procured legislation extending the pre-emption system to unsurveyed lands ; also opening certain military reservations to actual settlers. Land offices were to be established, post routes opened, and post-offices created ;

immense tracts to be purchased from the Indians, and thrown
open to settlement; and appropriations to be secured for improvements. Besides, there were the countless requests from
private individuals, for favors to be secured at the departments,
or for special legislation—so that one can form some idea of
the work Mr. RICE accomplished. Indeed, only those who
lived in Minnesota during that period, can know what it really
owes to him for much of its material progress.

In 1857, Mr. RICE procured the passage of the act endow-
ing our land grant roads with the land, which has alone secured their construction, and resulted in the rapid development
of the State. Also, establishing here a Surveyor General's
office, and, more important in some respects than all, was
the Enabling Act, authorizing Minnesota to form a State government. Mr. RICE's term as Delegate closed in 1857, but he
was at once elected Senator, for six years, by the first State
Legislature. During this term, the rebellion broke out, and
considerable numbers of Minnesota troops were stationed near
Washington. Mr. RICE's kindness and liberality to our soldiers will long be remembered. His house in Washington
was always open, as well as his purse, to the sick and destitute
soldier. During this term, he served on several very important committees, among others, on finance, on military, on
post roads, on public lands, and the special committee to report some mode of averting the threatened rupture between
the North and South.

On March 29, 1849, Mr. RICE was married to Miss MATIL-
DA WHITALL, at Richmond, Virginia. Mr. RICE was, also,
the founder of Bayfield, Wisconsin, in 1856, and the beauty
of the place, and the security of its harbor, vindicates the wisdom of his choice of the location of what must be one of the
most important places on Lake Superior.

Mr. RICE is truly a pioneer. He resided in Michigan,
Iowa, Wisconsin and Minnesota, while each passed from a
Territorial to a State government, and has borne his share of
the hardships, and dangers, and vicissitudes of frontier life.
No candid history of Minnesota can be written which does
not do full credit to his labors for the welfare of our State, and

his name, wherever mentioned by its people, is spoken only with the respect and esteem which his public acts and private virtues deserve.

Sketches of some of the other settlers of 1848 are here given, as fully as space will permit.

DAVID OLMSTED

was born in Fairfax, Franklin county, Vermont, May 5, 1822. At the age of 16 years, he left home to seek his fortune in the west. He finally located in the mineral region of Wisconsin, where he mined some time. In July, 1840, with his brother, PAGE, he moved over to northern Iowa, then unsettled by white men, and made a claim near the Winnebago Reservation, at a place now called Monona. Here they lived several years. In the fall of 1844, Mr. OLMSTED sold his claim and embarked in the Indian trade near Fort Atkinson, Iowa, as clerk for W. G. and G. W. EWING, licensed Winnebago traders. In the fall of 1845, he was elected from the district in which he lived (Clayton county) to the Convention to frame a Constitution for Iowa. He was then only 24 years old. In the fall of 1847, Mr. OLMSTED, in company with H. C. RHODES, purchased the interest of the EWINGS in the Winnebago trade, and, in the summer of 1848, when the Indians were removed to Long Prairie, Minnesota, he accompanied them, opening a trading house at that point, and also in Saint Paul. On August 7, 1849, Mr. OLMSTED was elected a member of the first Territorial Council of Minnesota, and, on its assembling, was chosen President. Mr. O.'s term extended also to the second session (1851) in which he took an active part.

In 1853, he abandoned the Indian trade, and removed to Saint Paul, where he had lived at intervals for several years, and, on June 29, purchased of Col. D. A. ROBERTSON, the *Minnesota Democrat* office. He edited that journal with much ability until September, 1854, when he sold it out. In the spring of 1854, Mr. OLMSTED was elected first Mayor of Saint Paul, the city having just been incorporated. In 1855, he removed to the village of Winona. During the summer of that year he was nominated by a portion of his party, for Delegate to Congress, but failed to secure an election.   Soon after his health began to decline, and he spent a winter in Cuba in hopes of restoring it. but without avail.   He continued to grow feebler until his death, February 2. 1861. which occurred at his mother's house. in Franklin county. Vermont.   During his residence in Minnesota he was one of the most popular men in public life.   The flourishing county of Olmsted was named in honor of him.

WILLIAM D. PHILLIPS.

or " BILLY" PHILLIPS. as he was generally called, was one of the oddest of the many odd characters who favored Saint Paul with their presence in early days.   He was a Marylander by birth. and came to Saint Paul in 1848. to practice as an attorney.   His knowledge of law is said ·not to have been very profound. but he practiced diligently at " the bar." nevertheless.   Oratory was the great hobby and weakness of BILLY D. He imagined he was a second ROSCIUS. and was always ready to speak at any time. on any subject. or in any place.   He never used to see several persons together without itching for a chance to address them on some subject, even from the head of a barrel. or a dry goods box.   His lecture on KOSSUTH. in 1852. a sort of half-drunken rhapsody, will always be remembered, with amusement. by the old settlers who heard it. or, rather, the introduction to it. for he did not reach the body of the discourse when the meeting broke up.   GOODHUE. out of joke, printed about half a column of the balderdash. and then added—" The balance of the lecture is all as good as the above !"

In 1849. Hon. H. M. RICE *gave.* (without consideration.) to BILLY D., several lots. one on upper Third street, about a square below the American House.   Mr. RICE told him to make out the deed, and he would sign it, which was done. But be it recorded, as an instance of mean ingratitude, that BILLY, subsequently. brought a claim against Mr. RICE. of $5. *for making out the deed.* and Mr. R. paid it !   One lot BILLY sold, in 1852, for $600..

That year, BILLY D., who had set high hopes, for a long time, on the nomination of CASS for the Presidency, and frequently declared that CASS, (who, he claimed, was an intimate friend of his,) would make him Governor, at least—finding his fond hopes dashed to the dust, by PIERCE's nomination, left the scene of his ambition and glory, and went to Washington. In 1856, he was appointed to a clerkship in the General Land Office. A year or two later, he was prosecuted for forging the franks of Senator DOUGLAS, and selling them to a patent medicine vender, to mail circulars in. He was acquitted on this charge, and then disappeared from public sight. One old settler saw him, about 1858, looking very much decayed, but, since that date, no tidings have been received from him, and he has, probably, gone to his reward.

HENRY C. RHODES

came from Logansport, Indiana. His nativity and age I have not been able to get satisfactorily, but Mr. R. CHUTE, of Minneapolis, thinks he was born about the year 1820. He was in business at Logansport for W. G. & G. W. EWING, and probably represented that firm at Fort Atkinson, Iowa, in the Winnebago trade. After the removal of the Winnebagoes, he went to Long Prairie, and soon after, in connection with DAVID OLMSTED, established an agency here. He purchased some property about where AUERBACH, FINCH & SCHEFFER's store now is, and had a store and dwelling house there. In 1849, he and OLMSTED dissolved partnership, and Mr. RHODES returned to Logansport, with his wife and child. He soon after went to California, where he died, about three years ago. His family remained in Indiana.

EDWIN A. C. HATCH

was born in New York, March 23, 1825. He emigrated to Wisconsin in 1840, and was engaged in the Sioux trade. He first came to what is now Minnesota, in 1843. He was, also, engaged in the Winnebago trade, at Fort Atkinson, Iowa, and after the removal, settled in Saint Paul. Mr. HATCH has been largely engaged in the Indian trade and other enterprises

growing out of it, since his residence here, and perhaps no
man in Minnesota is more accurately informed concerning the
various Indian nations in the Northwest than he.   In 1856,
President PIERCE asked H. M. RICE to name some one whom
he could appoint Agent of the Blackfeet Indians—adding that,
whoever accepted the post did so at the risk of his life.   Mr.
RICE suggested Mr. HATCH, and he was appointed.   In carrying out his duties, Mr. H.'s life was in danger innumerable
times, but he is a stranger to fear, and always escaped harm
by his coolness and daring.   Once, in Wisconsin, he refused
to let some insolent Sioux have goods they demanded, and
they threatened to help themselves.   Mr. HATCH opened a
keg of powder, lit his pipe, and told them to go on with their
threatened raid.   The Sioux slid out as fast as possible.   In
June, 1863, Mr. HATCH was commissioned a Major in the
volunteer service, with instructions to recruit an Independent
Cavalry Battalion of six companies, for frontier service and
defense.   Maj. HATCH soon had his battalion in the field, and
commanded it a year, when he resigned.   While stationed at
Pembina, he was enabled, by strategy, to secure the capture
of SHAKOPEE and MEDICINE BOTTLE, who were hung at Fort
Snelling in 1865.

BUSHROD W. LOTT

was born at Pemberton, New Jersey, May 1, 1826.   His
father removed to Saint Louis in 1837, and at the Saint Louis
University, a Catholic college, Mr. LOTT received his education.   After leaving college, he went to Quincy, Illinois,
where he studied law, and was admitted to practice in 1847.
In 1848, he accompanied Gen. SAMUEL LEECH, who had just
been appointed Receiver of the land office at Saint Croix Falls,
to that place, and acted as clerk of the first land sales in this
region.

   In the fall of that year, he settled in Saint Paul, and commenced the practice of law, and land agency, which he continued some years.   Mr. LOTT has been elected by his party,
the Democratic, to several official positions.   He was Chief
Clerk of the House of Representatives in 1851, and a member

in 1853 and 1856. In the former session he was a candidate for Speaker, and was beaten by Dr. DAVID DAY, the Whig candidate, after 22 days' balloting, by one vote.

He was president of the town council for two years, and city clerk (1866–7) for a year and a half.

In 1862, he was appointed by President LINCOLN, United States Consul to Tehuantepec, Mexico, and held that office until 1865. Mr. LOTT was a charter member of Saint Paul Lodge, I. O. O. F., and one of the earliest members of the Christ church (Episcopal.)

WILLIAM H. NOBLES

was born in New York, in 1816, and was a machinist by trade. He came to Saint Croix Falls, in 1841, and assisted in putting up the first mill there. He subsequently removed to Willow River, since called Hudson, where he built the first frame house in the place. He also lived at Stillwater several years, (1843–48.) and came to Saint Paul in 1848. He opened the first wagonmaker's shop in this city, and made the first wagon ever made in Minnesota. A part of the shops used by Col. NOBLES is still standing, now used by the firm of QUINBY & HALLOWELL. In 1856, he was elected a representative in the Legislature from Ramsey county. In 1857, Col. NOBLES, under appointment from the Government, laid out a wagon road to the Pacific, through the southwestern part of Minnesota, and, in recognition of this service, Nobles county was named for him. He discovered one of the best passes through the Rocky Mountains, now known as "Nobles' Pass." In 1862, he was elected by the "Seventy-Ninth New York Volunteers," known as the "Highlanders," as Lieut. Colonel, and served with them in South Carolina, afterwards resigning his commission, on account of disagreement with the other officers of the regiment. He was then cotton collector for the Government some time, United States revenue officer, master of transportation of troops at Mobile, and held other positions. After the war, his health became seriously impaired, which induced him to remove to the Waukesha Springs, in Wisconsin, and, subsequently, to the Hot Springs, Colorado, where he

now is, in very feeble health.   Col. Nobles has a remarkable
inventive genius, and has patented several valuable inventions,
but, as usual in such cases, others have borne off all the profits.

NATHAN MYRICK

was born in Westford, Essex county, New York, July 7, 1822.
At the age of 18, he came to LaCrosse, Wisconsin, and was

NATHAN MYRICK.

the founder of that town, in which he stills owns an interest,
and which he laid out in 1842.   From 1841 to 1848, Mr.
Myrick was engaged in lumbering on Black River.   During
the latter year he settled in Saint Paul, and has been a resident
of this place ever since, except once or twice, when business
compelled his removal for a short time.   He is in the Indian
supply business, an occupation which has made him thoroughly
acquainted with the frontier.

ABRAM H. CAVENDER

was born in Hancock, Hillsborough county, New Hampshire,
1815. He attended school for two years, and then went into
a machine shop and cotton factory, where he had charge of a
weaving loom for eleven years—most of the time in Nashua,
New Hampshire. Married, in 1840, a daughter of DANIEL
HOPKINS, mentioned in the preceding chapter, and, in 1843,
removed to Ohio, where he lived five years. In May, 1848,
he settled in Saint Paul. In December, 1849, he commenced
blacksmithing and wagonmaking on Robert street, the business having expanded into the large carriage establishment of
QUINBY & HALLOWELL.

BENJ. F. HOYT

was born at Norwalk, Connecticut, June 8, 1800. When a
young man, he settled in western New York, and after a few
years removed to Ohio, where he secured a tract of land
deeded by the Government to some of his ancestors for services
in the revolution. Here he married, and resided until 1834,
when he removed to Illinois, in which State he resided until
he came to Saint Paul, in the summer of 1848. He purchased
for $300 that property now bounded by Jackson and Broadway,
and Eighth street and the bluff. This was laid out as an addition the next spring. Mr. HOYT dealt largely in real estate
during his residence here, and has at various times owned
property now worth millions. Mr. HOYT was an ardent
Methodist. When he came here, finding no society, he accepted the appointment of local preacher, and exercised its
duties for sometime very acceptably. He always objected to
the use of the word, "Rev." to his name, saying he was not
regularly in the ministry. As a lay-member he was a valuable
worker for his church, giving liberally and taking an active
part in every movement. To his exertions is mainly due the
first church built by his sect on Market street, while Oakland
cemetery was projected by him and secured mainly by his
effort. Hamline University also owes much to his active work
and his always open purse. To the poor he was unceasingly
generous—not only giving freely, but taking an active interest

in enabling them to help themselves. In his later years, he spent considerable of his time in this way. So much was he respected and loved, he was generally known as "Father Hoyt." In person he was tall and dignified, with a mien of kindness and benevolence, yet always unobtrusive and retiring. The sincerity of his religious professions was best shown by his exemplary walk. Mr. Hoyt died on September 3, 1875, without much illness, but from the final decay of strength, at the ripe age of 75.

WILLIAM FREEBORN

was a native of Ohio—born 1816. He arrived in Saint Paul May 25, 1848. He owned, at one time, considerable property in the city and county, and was quite a prominent citizen, being a member of our town council one term. In 1853, he removed to Red Wing, and was one of the first settlers there. He was elected, from that district, (then called Wabasha county,) a member of the Council of 1854–55, 1856–57. In 1855, the Legislature named a county for him. During the gold excitement of 1862, Mr. Freeborn emigrated to the Rocky Mountains, and now resides in San Luis Obispo, California.

DAVID LAMBERT

was a native, if I mistake not, of Connecticut, at least, he graduated at Trinity College, Hartford. He studied law, and soon after emigrated to the west, settling first in Little Rock, Arkansas, and then in Wisconsin. In 1843, he became editor and publisher of the *Madison Enquirer*, and showed marked ability as a journalist. He subsequently sold out the paper to his brother, Henry A. Lambert, and, in 1848, settled in Saint Paul. He took a prominent part in the Stillwater Convention, this year, and was regarded as a young man of brilliant ability and promise. Some domestic unpleasantness, at times, rendered him misanthropic and reckless, and, to forget care, he resorted to the bowl. On November 2d, 1849, while returning from Galena, on a steamboat, he leaped from the roof of the steamer, during a paroxysm of nervous excitement, and was drowned. He was only about thirty years of age.

OTHER SETTLERS.

W. C. MORRISON was born in Whitehall. New York. January 20. 1815. He resided, while young, at Cleveland. Detroit, Chicago. Galena. Dubuque, and other places, and. in 1848. came to Saint Paul. He says there were then only 15 families here. Mr. MORRISON has been actively engaged in trade since his arrival, and is widely known in business circles.

LOT MOFFET. a gentleman well-known in Saint Paul in early days. was a native of Montgomery county. New York. where he was born in 1803. He was, for some years, proprietor of the ·· Temperance House." on Jackson street. sometimes called by old settlers, ·· Moffet's Castle." on account of its unfinished condition for some time. Mr. MOFFET was a scrupulously honest man. and very benevolent. Many will recollect his venerable appearance. as he usually wore a patriarchal beard. He died December 28. 1870.

WM. B. BROWN came from the ·· lead region." in Wisconsin. He purchased. at an early day. the corner on which the Warner Block now stands. He died some years ago.

PRE-TERRITORIAL SETTLERS.

The following is believed to be a complete and accurate list of all the pre-territorial settlers and residents in Saint Paul. with the years in which they came :

1838.
Pierre Parrant.
Abraham Perry.
Edward Phelan.
William Evans.
———— Johnson.
Benjamin Gervais.
Pierre Gervais.

1839.
John Hays.
James R. Clewett.
Vetal Guerin.
Denis Cherrier.
Charles Mousseau.
Wm. Beaumette.

1840.
Joseph Rondo.
Rev. Lucian Galtier.
Rev. A. Ravoux.

1841.
Pierre Bottineau.
Severe Bottineau.

1842.

Henry Jackson.
Richard W. Mortimer.
———— Pelon.

Joseph Labisinier.
Francis Desire.
Stanislaus Bilanski.

1843.

John R. Irvine.
Ansel B. Coy.
James W. Simpson.
William Hartshorn.
A. L. Larpenteur.
Alex. R. McLeod.
Christopher C. Blanchard.
Scott Campbell.
Alexis Cloutier.
Francis Moret.

Antoine Pepin.
Alex. Mege.
David Thomas Sloan.
Jo. Desmarais.
S. Cowden, Jr. [or Carden.]
Charles Reed.
Louis Larrivier.
Xavier Delonais.
Joseph Gobin.

1844.

Louis Robert.
Charles Bazille.
William Dugas.

Thomas McCoy.
Joseph Hall.

1845.

Leonard H. LaRoche.
Francis Chenevert.
David Benoit.
Francis Robert.
Wm. H. Morse,
Antoine Findlay.

Charles Cavileer.
Wm. G. Carter.
Augustus Freeman.
David B. Freeman.
Jesse H. Pomeroy.
———— Gerou.

1846.

James M. Boal.
Wm. H. Randall.
William Randall, Jr.
Ed. West.
David Faribault.
Charles Rouleau.

Thomas S. Odell.
Harley D. White.
Joel D. Cruttenden.
Louis Denoyer.
Joseph Monteur.

1847.

Wm. Henry Forbes.
J. W. Bass.
Benj. W. Brunson.
Daniel Hopkins, Sr.
Miss Harriet E. Bishop.
Aaron Foster.

John Banfil.
Fred. Olivier.
Wm. C. Renfro.
Parsons K. Johnson.
C. P. V. Lull.
G. A. Fournier.

1848.

Henry M. Rice.	Wm. B. Brown.
A. H. Cavender.	Hugh McCann.
Benj. F. Hoyt.	B. W. Lott.
Wm. H. Nobles.	H. C. Rhodes.
David Lambert.	David Olmsted.
Wm. D. Phillips.	Hugh Glenn.
W. C. Morrison.	Nels. Robert.
Nathan Myrick.	Andre Godfrey.
E. A. C. Hatch.	Dav. Hebert.
Richard Freeborn.	Oliver Rosseau.
William Freeborn.	Wm. H. Kelton.
Alden Bryant.	Andy L. Shearer.
Lot Moffet.	E. B. Weld.
A. R. French.	Albert Titlow.

Date unknown. ——— Archambault and Marcil Coutourier.

GENERAL REMARKS ON THE PRE-TERRITORIAL PERIOD.

The labor of collecting the names of the above settlers, and of determining, with any exactness, the year of their settlement, and of securing the occurrences, events and incidents of the period from 1838 to 1849, was a task that almost discouraged me from pursuing the work, more than once. The time occupied—the physical labor of running back and forth, and the nerve-wear—spent on this little list, no one can get much idea of, except, perhaps, a few of the old pioneers, to whom I made repeated visits, with a catechism of what may have seemed to them very trifling questions. Yet it was only by these little incidents, ascertained by such questioning, much like a detective would work up a trace, that I was enabled to compile the list above, and fix the right names to the right years. So that, on the period from 1838 to 1849, I expended more time, labor and patience, than on all the rest of the 37 years of our history. It should be remembered, that this was before there were any newspapers, any census lists, any public records, or any written records of any kind. So that I had to depend alone on the memory of residents of that period, some of whom could not tell the year in which they themselves came !

It was deemed more important to chronicle this period carefully, because it is the portion of our history most needing preservation. In ten years more, it would have been impossible to collect the facts given above. The memories of those not dead would have then become so weak from age as to be totally unavailable.

It may be objected by some that too much space has been used in collecting these "simple annals of the poor," and recording the career of men known as obscure and humble. But the descendants of these "rude forefathers of the hamlet," whom better opportunities may raise above the lives of toil *they* spent, will in future years read these pages, and feel with some pride that history, like the photographic camera, depicts even the minutest details, which, while they may be scarcely noticed in the general effect, have their value in making up the perfect picture.

The period from 1840 to 1849, may be called the arcadian days of Minnesota. The primitive, easy-going simplicity of the people, isolated as they were, from the fashions, vices, and artificial life of the bustling world, was in strange contrast with the jostling throng of immigration that poured in a few months later, changing their steady-going habits and plain manners into a maddening, avaricious race for gold. Up to this time they were contented and unambitious, and pursued the "even tenor of their way" along the "cool, sequestered vale of life," unagitated by the exciting events that stirred other communities. Their worldly means was small and their income limited, it is true, but their wants were few and simple. They were honest, forbearing, generous and charitable. Crime was unknown. "Why," said an old settler, speaking of those happy days, "board of the best kind was only $3 per week." But the influx of immigrants, many of them greedy for speculation, selfish and unscrupulous in many cases, soon changed the character of the times. Their quiet, dreamy, slow, and sober-going primitive simplicity was gone. Even the price of the necessaries of life was inflated. "You new comers," said one of the pioneers, more in sorrow than anger, "have raised the prices of things so that what we used to get for ten cents now costs a quarter."

14

THE MEN OF 1848.

In the *Pioneer* of June 14, 1849, GOODHUE thus does honor to the pre-territorial settlers :

" It is proper for those who are flocking into our Territory, to know who those men are who were here, struggling with privations before Minnesota had a name in the world.   They are the men who, by their voluntary exertion, sustained our Delegate on his mission to Washington, for the accomplishment of what, few believed, *could* then be accomplished—the recognition of our rights as a Territory distinct from Wisconsin.   Every Territory, in its earlier days, has its times that try men's souls.   The inception of a State, whether settled by the peaceful pioneer, or baptized by the blood of a border warfare, has its trials and troubles.   How darkly hung the cloud of doubt over this region of the Northwest, one year ago.   How like the glorious sunlight, did the first intelligence from our Delegate to Washington last spring, burst through that cloud of doubt.   There were men here, who, from the beginning, saw the end.   We respect, we reverence those men.   Let the men and the women of those days be remembered."

THE YEAR 1848 CLOSED

with anxiety to the settlers in the little village.*   Delegate SIBLEY had gone on to Washington to fight a hard battle there against heavy odds.   Everybody was nervous with expectation—and with the next chapter the curtain rises on a new and exciting act in the drama.

---

*It was but a village, after all.   One cold day, about the beginning of winter, Miss BISHOP records in her diary, J. R. CLEWETT came into Mr. IRVINE's house and said—"My! how this town is growing.   I counted the smoke of 18 chimneys this morning!"

CHAPTER XVI.

EVENTS OF THE YEAR 1849.

CREATION OF MINNESOTA TERRITORY—SAINT PAUL MADE THE CAPITAL—HOW THE
NEWS WAS RECEIVED—ESTABLISHMENT OF THE "PIONEER"—DESCRIPTION OF
SAINT PAUL IN 1849—RAPID GROWTH—EVENTS OF THE DAY—MEMOIRS OF
GOVERNOR RAMSEY, JUDGE GOODRICH, &C.

WE now enter on a period of our history crowded with
the most important events. In fact, this chapter opens
upon a new era in the career of our city and State. Minnesota was on the eve of her political birth. And Saint Paul—
"the little hamlet of bark-roofed cabins"—was just trembling
with eagerness to make a long spring forward.

A "WINTER OF DISCONTENT"

was that of 1848–9. It commenced with unusual severity—unusually early. Snow fell on November 1. To the inhabitants
of the little burg. 200 miles from the nearest settlement and
mail supply. (Prairie du Chien.) hemmed in by snow and ice.
and cut off. almost, from communication with the world, it
must have passed wearily enough. The mails, carried over
the vast reaches of snow on a dog-sledge, or a *train du glace*.
came "only once in a coon's age," as an old settler expresses
it, and a hat-full merely then. but its arrival was an event for
the village, and eager was the rush for letters and papers to
JACKSON's. It was not until January that news of Gen. TAYLOR's election was received, and also advices from Delegate
SIBLEY, who is working hard at Washington to organize a
Territory. but not much encouraged at the prospects of success.

HOW SAINT PAUL BECAME THE CAPITAL.

Indeed. our good city came within an ace of not being the
Capital of Minnesota at all. When Gen. SIBLEY arrived in

Washington, his credentials were presented at the opening of
the session, by Hon. JAMES WILSON, of New Hampshire, and
referred to the Committee on Elections.   This committee held
several meetings on the matter, and were addressed by Gen.
SIBLEY, in favor of his recognition, and by Hon. Mr. BOYDEN,
of North Carolina, and others, adversely.   The committee did
not report, finally, until January 15, 1849, when a majority,
(5,) reported in favor of Gen. SIBLEY's admission, and a minority, (4,) against it.   The majority report was adopted,
however, and he was admitted.

His first work was to secure the organization of Minnesota
Territory, as determined on by the Stillwater Convention.
Upon consultation, it was deemed best that the bill should be
introduced from the Committee on Territories in the Senate.
It was prepared by Hon. STEPHEN A. DOUGLAS, chairman,
by whom the draft was sent to Gen. SIBLEY, for his perusal.
He noticed that Mendota had been designated as the Capital,
whereas, it had been the wish of the people generally, es-
pecially of those participating in the Convention, to have Saint
Paul fixed as the seat of government.

Gen. SIBLEY, without delay, called on Senator DOUGLAS,
and urged him to make that change.   A meeting of the committee was at once called, and the matter taken up.   Gen.
SIBLEY argued that most of the inhabitants of the proposed
Territory resided east of the Mississippi, and there was an
unanimous wish to have the Capital on that side.   Saint Paul
was one of the most prominent places in the region, well located for the seat of government, and was a regularly platted
town, and the land had been entered, so that good titles to
property could be had, &c.   Senator DOUGLAS opposed the
change.   He said he had been at Mendota, not long before,
and was so much pleased with the geographical position of
Mendota, at the confluence of two important rivers, he had
then fixed on it as a good site for the future Capital of this region.   Moreover, the bulk of area, and, ere long, of population, would be west of the Mississippi, and the Capital should
be on the west bank.   He thought the top of Pilot Knob, at
Mendota, would be a grand place for the State House, as it

afforded such a beautiful and extensive view of the valleys of the two rivers.*

Gen. Sibley persisted in the change, and Senator Douglas, after some solicitation, conceded it, and Saint Paul was fixed on as the seat of the Capital, instead of Mendota, after the two places had hung wavering in the balance for some days. Then some member objected to the name, and said there were "too many Saints" in this locality—and this stupid objector had to be argued with, &c.

The bill, so amended, was introduced in the Senate, but its passage met with considerable opposition, as it did also, in the House. Gen. Sibley worked night and day for it, and made personal appeals to all the members he could influence. Hon. H. M. Rice arrived in Washington, about this time, on private business, and threw his earnest efforts and personal influence in the scale also, being personally acquainted with a number of members. The issue was doubtful for some days, but our tutelar saint kindly turned the current in our favor, and the bill finally passed, being approved March 3, 1849.

RECEPTION OF THE NEWS AT SAINT PAUL.

In the slow movements of mails in those days, especially during the season known as the breaking up of winter, it took five weeks for the news to reach Saint Paul. The snow had commenced to melt about March 1, and the dog mail-sledge was suspended. The only way was to wait for a boat, and the news from Lake Pepin was, that the ice was firm and hard. Our last mail had arrived about the first of March, with news

---

* In connection with this statement of Gen. Sibley's successful efforts to locate the Capital at Saint Paul, it might be mentioned, that, in 1853, while Gen. S. was running as a candidate for re-election as Delegate, the charge was made against him, by some partisan journals, of hostility to the interests of Saint Paul, as he was at that time living at Mendota, and some of his property was there. The paragraphs came under the eye of Senator Douglas, and, without solicitation or suggestion, he wrote a statement of the course of Gen. S. in regard to the location of the Capital, and stated that it was unjust that he should be accused of unfriendliness to Saint Paul interests, since he had secured the location of the Capital here, in obedience to the wishes of his constituents, when, to have allowed it to be located at Mendota, would have been of great pecuniary advantage to him. It might be remarked, too, that, when Senator Douglas was here, in 1857, he freely admitted that Gen. S. was right in his conviction that Saint Paul was a much better point for the Capital than Mendota.

two months old. It was now the second week in April, and expectation and anxiety was strained to the utmost tension. A communication in the first number of the *Pioneer* signed D. L., (DAVID LAMBERT,) graphically describes the reception of the news of the organization of the Territory, under the caption, " The Breaking up of a Hard Winter."

"The last has been the severest winter known in the Northwest for many years. During five months the communication between this part of the country and our brethren in the United States has been difficult and unfrequent. A mail now and then from Prairie du Chien, brought up on the ice in a 'train' drawn sometimes by horses and sometimes by dogs, contained news so old that the country below had forgotten all about it. When the milder weather commenced, and the ice became unsafe, we were completely shut out from all communication for several weeks. Sometime in January, we learned that Gen. ZACHARY TAYLOR was elected President of the United States. We had to wait for the arrival of the first boat to learn whether our Territory was organized, and who were its Federal officers. How anxiously was that boat expected! The ice still held its iron grasp on Lake Pepin. For a week the arrival of a boat had been looked for every hour. Expectation was on tiptoe.

" Monday, the ninth of April, had been a pleasant day. Toward evening the clouds gathered, and about dark commenced a violent storm of wind, rain, and loud peals of thunder. The darkness was only dissipated by vivid flashes of lightning. On a sudden, in a momentary lull of the wind, the silence was broken by the groan of an engine. In another moment, the shrill whistle of a steamboat thrilled through the air. Another moment, and a bright flash of lightning revealed the welcome shape of a steamboat just rounding the bluff, less than a mile below Saint Paul. In an instant the welcome news flashed like electricity throughout the town, and, regardless of the pelting rain, the raging wind, and the pealing thunder, almost the entire male population rushed to the landing—as the fine steamboat, ' Dr. Franklin, No. 2,' dashed gallantly up to the landing. Before she was made fast to the moorings, she was boarded by the excited throng. The good captain and clerk [Capt. BLAKELEY] were the great men of the hour. Gen. TAYLOR cannot be assailed with greater importunity for the ' loaves and fishes' than they were for news and newspapers. At length the news was known, and one glad shout resounding through the boat, taken up on shore, and echoed from our beetling bluffs and rolling hills, proclaimed that *the bill for the organization of Minnesota Territory* had become a law!"

The long agony was over.   Minnesota was a Territory, and Saint Paul was its Capital.   Henceforth, we had a future! But let us look at the

CONDITION OF THE TERRITORY

at that time.   It was but little more than a wilderness.   Its entire white population could not have been more than 1,000 persons.   When the census was taken, four months later, after many hundred immigrants had arrived, there were only 4,680 enrolled—and 317 of these were connected with the army, and of the 637 at Pembina, but few were white.

The portion of the Territory west of the Mississippi was still unceded by the Indians.   From the southern line of the State to Saint Paul, there were not more than two or three white men's habitations along the river, now gemmed with flourishing and handsome cities, and the steamers ascending the river had no regular landing places, except to "wood up."   Indeed, such a *terra incognita* as existed at that time, over the now well settled State of Minnesota, seems more the condition of a century ago than of twenty-six years.

But, with this feeble array, the people were big with expectation.   The "elements of empire here, were plastic yet and warm," and needed only the right men to mould them into a prosperous State.   Fortunately, we had the men.   Minnesota may well be proud of her pioneers.   The people of to-day and coming years owe them gratitude and honor, and, in view of the success and prosperity of our State, it may well be said, "they builded better than they knew."   California was just then offering its stores of gold to any one lucky enough to reach there, and it seemed as if all the country was on the move to the El Dorado.   Minnesota, almost unknown, lying in a latitude deemed to be semi-arctic in its character, and inhabited by savages, could scarcely expect to draw immigration. Especially Saint Paul—what would be its condition under the new order of events?   And, presuming that people came here, what resources were there to furnish them business and employment?   The Indian trade, supplying the frontier forts, the lumber business and its supplies, a little fur trade, etc., was

about all.   On this. the 150 or 200 people in Saint Paul were
supported.   If more came. what would these last do?   For it
was still but a village.   GOODHUE stated that when he came,
in April, there *were only thirty buildings in Saint Paul.*

But the problem was soon solved.   Come they did.   It was
not—as WHITTIER wrote—

> " The first low wash of waves, where soon   ·
> Should roll a human sea."

It was the sea itself.   Boat after boat landed at the levee. bringing crowds of new comers. until it became a serious question
where they should lodge. and on what should they subsist.

ESTABLISHMENT OF A NEWSPAPER.

But what would an ambitious western town be without a
newspaper. to herald its importance to the world?   And especially the Capital of a Territory.   Who would know it
existed?   Who would wish to live in such a desolate place—
one too poor to boast of a paper?   But Saint Paul was too
promising a field for the journalist. to long suffer from the
need. and it was right soon supplied.

The first steps to commence the publication of a newspaper in
Minnesota. were taken in August. 1848. by Dr. A. RANDALL.
then an *attache* of Dr. OWEN's Geological Corps. engaged in
a survey of this region by order of Government.   The project
grew out of the celebrated ·· Stillwater Convention" of that
year.   It was this political event which first suggested to the
mind of Dr. RANDALL. that. if there was to be a Territorial
organization here. whether it be a *new* Territory. or the rightful inheritor of the abandoned Territorial government of that
State—it would be necessary to have a newspaper.   Having
the capacity and means necessary to undertake the enterprise.
he set about it. and was promised ample aid by leading men
of the Territory.

RANDALL soon after proceeded to Cincinnati. which was at
that time his home. to purchase his press and material. designing to return that fall.   Winter set in unusually early that year.
however. and he found navigation would be closed before he

could do so.   Meantime he concluded to await the issue of the bill to organize the Territory. which had been introduced into Congress. but did not finally pass until the last day of the session.   By this time, RANDALL, annoyed at the delays, concluded to set up his press in Cincinnati. and get out a number or two of his paper there.   While in Cincinnati, he formed the acquaintance of JOHN P. OWENS,* a young man engaged in the printing business, who had already imbibed the Minnesota fever by reading the debates in Congress on the Organic Act. and a partnership between them was the result.   They at once set to work to get out a number of their paper. which was to be called. the *Minnesota Register*.   It was *dated* ·· Saint Paul. April 27, 1849," but was really printed about two weeks earlier than that date. so as to reach Saint Paul by the day named for publication.   Messrs. H. H. SIBLEY and H. M. RICE had passed through Cincinnati. on their way home from Washington. and contributed valuable articles on Minnesota to the *Register*.   These, added to Mr. RANDALL'S extensive knowledge of the country. gave the paper a very interesting *local* character.   It was the first *Minnesota* newspaper ever printed. and dates just one day in advance of the *Pioneer*. although the latter must be recorded as the first paper printed *in* Minnesota.

Mr. RANDALL, being a man of unsettled purpose and roving disposition. caught the California fever just at this juncture. and sold out his interest in the newspaper to Major NATHANIEL McLEAN. of Lebanon. Ohio. who had determined to emigrate

---

JOHN PHILLIPS OWENS was born near Dayton, Ohio, January 6, 1818. His father, who was a native of Wales, died when the subject of this sketch was seven years old, and during his younger years he worked on a farm, with occasional schooling, until the age of 15.   He then attended Woodward College, at Cincinnati, some two years, when he concluded to learn the printing business, which he did. His embarking in journalism and removal to Saint Paul is given elsewhere. Mr. OWENS continued in the newspaper business in Saint Paul for some 12 or 13 years, being seven years editor of the *Minnesotian*, a leading journal of the Territory. As a political writer he always wielded a large influence. In 1862, he was commissioned Quartermaster of the Ninth Minnesota, and served faithfully with that Regiment until discharged, in 1865, having been brevetted Colonel in the meantime. In 1869, Col. OWENS was appointed Register of the land office at Taylor's Falls, which position he still holds. He is about to publish a ·· Political History of Minnesota," a work for which he has peculiar fitness, and which will comprise his interesting reminiscences of men and events in the early days of Minnesota.

hither, and resume the business of printing, to which he had
been bred, but had not followed for some years prior. The
publishers and editors, under this arrangement, became " Mc-
Lean & Owens." But of this anon.

GOODHUE FOUNDS THE PIONEER.

Among the many men of energy and enterprise, all over the
Union, whose attention had been directed to Minnesota by the
debates in Congress and the passage of the act, was James M.
Goodhue, of Lancaster, Wisconsin, who had been bred a
lawyer, but was, at that time, engaged in a more congenial
pursuit as editor of the *Wisconsin Herald.* When the news
of the organization of the Territory was received, he at once
resolved to remove here and establish a paper. He immediately purchased a press and type, and, as soon as navigation
opened, shipped them to Saint Paul, meantime issuing a
prospectus for a journal, which he proposed to call *The
Epistle of Saint Paul,* but which name he changed, (at the
advice of some friends who objected to its irreligious tone,) before the first issue of his paper, to *The Minnesota Pioneer.*

Of his arrival in Saint Paul, and the issue of his first paper,
Mr. Goodhue, in a subsequent article, gives the following interesting account :

"The 18th day of April, 1849, was a raw, cloudy day. The steamboat ' Senator,' Capt. Smith, landed at Randall's warehouse, lower
landing, the only building then there, except Robert's old store. Of
the people on shore, we recognized but one person as an acquaintance,
Henry Jackson. Took our press, types, printing apparatus all ashore.
Went, with our men, to the house of Mr. Bass, corner of Third and
Jackson streets. * * * C. P. V. Lull, and his partner, Gilbert,
furnished us gratuitously, the lower story of their building, for an office—
the only vacant room in town. * * * The weather was cold and
stormy; and our office was as open as a corn-rick; however, we picked
our types up, and made ready for the issue of the first paper ever printed
in Minnesota, or within many hundreds of miles of it; but, upon search,
we found our news chase was left behind. Wm. Nobles, blacksmith,
made us a very good one, after a delay of two or three days. * * We
determined to call our paper the *Minnesota Pioneer.* One hindrance
after another delayed our first issue to the 28th of April. * * We
were at length prepared for our first number. We had no subscribers;

for then there were but a handful of people in the whole Territory; and the majority of those were Canadians and half-breeds. Not a Territorial officer had yet arrived. * * The people wanted no politics, and we gave them none; they wanted information of all sorts about Minnesota, and that is what we furnished them with. We advocated Minnesota, morality, and religion from the beginning."

In his first issue, he speaks of the *Pioneer* establishment of that day:

"We print and issue this number of the *Pioneer*, in a building through which out-of-doors is visible by more than five hundred apertures; and as for our type, it is not safe from being *pied* on the galleys by the wind."

This building was afterwards used for several years, by THOMAS H. CALDER, now deceased, as a saloon and restaurant, and was burned down in the spring of 1860.

SAINT PAUL IN APRIL, 1849.

In the first number of the *Pioneer*, we find some interesting sketches of what Saint Paul was, in April, 1849. In his leading editorial, the editor says:

"This town, which was but yesterday unknown, for the reason that it had then no existence, is situated on the east bank of the Mississippi River, about five miles south of latitude 45 degrees. A more beautiful site for a town cannot be imagined. It must be added, that bilious fevers and the fever and ague are strangers to Saint Paul. A description of the village now would not answer for a month hence—such is the rapidity of building, and the miraculous resurrection of every description of domiciles. Piles of lumber and building materials lie scattered everywhere in admirable confusion. The whole town is on the stir—stores, hotels, houses, are projected and built in a few days. California is forgotten, and the whole town is rife with the exciting spirit of advancement.

"Saint Paul, at the head of river communication, must necessarily supply the trade of all the vast regions north of it to the rich plains of the Selkirk Settlement, and west to the Rocky Mountains, and east to the basin of the great Lakes, and is destined to be the focus of an immense business, rapidly increasing with the growth and settlement of the new regions lying within the natural circumference of its trade. That extensive region of beautiful land bordering on the Saint Peter's River, as well as all the other tributaries of the Mississippi north of us, will soon be settled, and *must* obtain their supplies through Saint Paul.

Is it strange, then, that Saint Paul is beginning to be regarded as the Saint Louis of the North?"

From the first number of the *Pioneer,* we extract a few items of interest:

"To IMMIGRANTS.—We advise settlers who are swarming into Saint Paul in such multitudes, *to bring along tents and bedding,* to provide for their comfort until they can build houses, *as it is utterly impossible* to hire a building in any part of the village, although builders are at work in every direction, completing houses."

"Rev. Mr. NEILL,* a member of the Presbytery of Galena, is about removing to Saint Paul. Mr. NEILL is expected to preach at the school

---

*Rev. EDWARD DUFFIELD NEILL, mentioned in the foregoing extract, was the first Protestant clergyman who settled in Saint Paul. He was born at Philadelphia, August 9, 1823, and was educated at the University of Pennsylvania, and Amherst College, Massachusetts, graduating there in 1842. He was ordained a clergyman in the Presbyterian church in 1848, but prior to that—in 1847—went to the neighborhood of Galena, where he performed missionary labor in the rough mining region. From there he was transferred to Saint Paul, in the spring of 1849, arriving at this place April 23, and at once commenced his labors in organizing a church. He erected the first Protestant church in Minnesota, on Washington street, near Fourth, in July, 1849, and in November organized the First Presbyterian church. In May, 1850, the first church was burned, and rebuilt at once, corner of Third and Saint Peter streets. Mr. NEILL also organized, in 1855, the "House of Hope," and was its pastor several years. During this period he gave great attention to educational and literary matters. He was appointed Territorial Superintendent of Instruction in 1851, and held that office two years. In 1853, he organized and secured the erection and endowment of Baldwin School. In 1855, he secured the building of the College of Saint Paul, which was for several years a classical academy for young men. He was Secretary of the Board of Education, and, ex-officio Superintendent of Schools, for several years, and Chancellor of the State University, 1858 to 1860. He was also State Superintendent of Public Instruction from 1858 to 1861, and Secretary of the Historical Society from 1851 to 1861.

On June 23, 1861, he was appointed Chaplain of the First Minnesota Volunteers, and served as such over two years. He was then United States Hospital Chaplain until January, 1864, when he became one of President LINCOLN'S private secretaries, and after the death of Mr. LINCOLN, he continued in the same relation to President JOHNSON. In April, 1869, he was appointed by President GRANT, Consul to Dublin, and resided there in that capacity for about two years. He then returned to Minnesota, and became President of the Baldwin School and College of Saint Paul, which were consolidated by the Legislature under the name of "Macalester College."

In January, 1874, Mr. NEILL withdrew from the Presbyterian church and entered the Reformed Episcopal Church. He has written and published several valuable historical works, his "History of Minnesota" being frequently quoted in these pages. He is truly a pioneer clergyman. He performed the first marriage recorded in the records of Ramsey county, and is now marrying the second generation (of persons born in Saint Paul) in the same families. He built the first brick dwelling house in Minnesota—laid the foundations of half a dozen of our best institutions, and has labored hard for a lifetime in the cause of religion, education and human progress, with much success, but to his own loss in estate. His name can never be mentioned by the future people of Minnesota, but with respect.

house, on Bench street, next Sunday, (to-morrow,) at 11 o'clock in the morning."

"The Galena *Advertiser* says there is a prospect of a heavy immigration to Minnesota the present season. We learn that whole colonies are on the move to Minnesota, from the Middle and Eastern States, and from Canada."

"While we are writing, a Sioux Indian has dropped into our office,

REV. EDWARD D. NEILL.

to look at the printing press. He expresses a great deal of curiosity and surprise."

"Mr. RICE, a gentleman equally distinguished for his liberality and enterprise, returned to Saint Paul on the steamboat 'Senator,' last Tuesday. Mr. RICE received a most cordial welcome. He is very much identified with the growth and prosperity of Saint Paul."

RAPID GROWTH OF THE TOWN.

Immigration poured in very rapidly for a few months,

Every boat brought crowds of immigrants, many of whom were unable to find proper accommodations. E. S. SEYMOUR, author of a very entertaining work, " Sketches of Minnesota, the New England of the West," landed here on May 17. Referring to his first view of the town, at Kaposia, he says :

" Its new frame buildings, glistening with the reflection of the rising sun, imparted to it an air of neatness and prosperity. On arriving at the wharf, a numerous throng of citizens and strangers came rushing down the hill to welcome our arrival. I grasped the hand of many an acquaintance, whom I unexpectedly found here. Everything here appeared to be on the *high pressure* principle. A dwelling house for a family could not be rented. The only hotel was small, and full to overflowing. Several boarding houses were very much thronged. Many families were living in shanties, made of rough boards, fastened to posts driven in the ground, such as two men could construct in one day. It was said that about 80 men lodged in a barn belonging to RICE's new hotel, which was not yet completed. Two families occupied tents while I was there. While traveling in Minnesota, I made my headquarters at Saint Paul, where I occasionally tarried a day or two at a boarding house, consisting of one room, about 16 feet square, in which 16 persons, including men, women and children, contrived to lodge. The remaining boarders—a half-dozen or more—found lodgings in a neighbor's garret; this tenement rented for $12 per month. The roof was so leaky that, during the frequent rains that prevailed at that time, one would often wake up in the night and find the water pouring down in a stream on his face, or some part of his person. * * *

" We are now near the dividing line of civilized and savage life. We can look across the river and see Indians on their own soil. Their canoes are seen gliding across the Mississippi, to and fro between savage and civilized territory. They are met hourly in the streets. * * Here comes a female in civilized costume; her complexion is tinged with a light shade of bronze, and her features bear a strong resemblance to those of the Indian. She is a descendant of French and Indian parents—a half-breed from Red River. There goes a French Canadian, who can converse only in the language of his mother tongue. He is an old settler; see his prattling children sporting about yonder shanty, which was constructed of rough boards, with about one day's labor. There he lives—obliging fellow ! exposed to the sun and rain, and rents his adjoining log cabin at $12 per month. Let us pass on to that group that converse daily in front of yonder hotel. They appear to be principally professional men, politicians, office-seekers, speculators and travelers, discussing the various topics growing out of the organization of the new Territory—such as the distribution of the loaves and fishes, the price of lots, the rise of real estate, the opportunity now afforded for the acquisition of wealth or political fame.

" The town-site is a pretty one, affording ample room for stores or dwellings, to any extent desirable.   I could not but regret, however, that where land is so cheap and abundant, some of the streets are narrow, and that the land on the edge of the high bluff, in the centre of the town, was not left open to the public, instead of being cut up into small lots.   It would have made a pleasant place for promenading, affording a fine view of the river, which is now liable to be intercepted by buildings erected on those lots."   *   *   *

MASONIC AND SONS OF TEMPERANCE LODGES.

Early in the growth of the town, the usual secret orders were founded.   The *Pioneer*, of May 19th, says:

" A Division of the Sons of Temperance has been fully organized in Saint Paul, under the title of ' Saint Paul Division, No. 1,' Sons of Temperance.   This is the first Division of that order in this Territory. The Division meets every Tuesday night.   The officers are—LOT MOFFET, W. P.; BENJ. L. SELLERS, W. A.; S. GILBERT, P. W. P.; W. C. MORRISON, R. S.; B. F. IRVINE, A. R. S.; A. H. CAVENDER, F. S.; A. R. FRENCH, T.; C. P. V. LULL, G. C.; B. F. HOYT, A. C.; W. PATCH. I. S.; C. DAVIS, O. S."

" Members of the Masonic Fraternity, in and near Saint Paul, intend to meet together in the room over the *Pioneer* office, on Thursday evening next, [May 31,] at 6 o'clock."—[Ib. May 26.]

The Sons of Temperance soon became quite a powerful organization, and at one time owned a lot and built a building thereon for a hall.   They subsequently lost the property by mortgage, and (oh! profanation) the building was used for a saloon!

EVENTS OF THE DAY.

Early in May, two more printing presses and material for newspapers arrived.   One was the *Register*, before noted— the other was the *Minnesota Chronicle*, which was issued on June 1, by Col. JAMES HUGHES, formerly of Jackson, Ohio.

One or two cases of cholera occurred this season.   On May 3d, L. B. LARPENTEUR, father of E. N. and grandfather of A. L. LARPENTEUR, arrived in the city, and on the 7th died of cholera, aged 71 years.   He had, unfortunately, contracted the disease on his journey up the river.

From the *Pioneer* of May 26, we extract some interesting items :

" ' Scratch up, scrabble up, tumble up, any way to get up,' seems to be illustrated in the sudden growth of building in Saint Paul. Logs which were in the boom at the Falls last week, are now inflated into balloon frames at Saint Paul, ready for a coat of fresh paint. Lots which were the other day considered quite remote, are now 'right in town.' More than seventy buildings, it is said, have been erected here during the past three weeks; and the town is so changed in its appearance, and has so multiplied its inhabitants, that a person absent for three weeks, on returning, almost fancies that he has been taking a Rip Van Winkle slumber."

" There is not a lock of hay to be bought from Galena to Saint Paul."

" Ex-Governor SLADE, of Vermont, General Agent of National Popular Education, arrived on the steamboat ' Senator,' last Thursday, with three young ladies,* who will engage in the responsible and arduous labor of teaching in Minnesota."

" Carpenters in Saint Paul are now fully employed. Mr. BRAWLEY is making a supply of brick, near the upper end of town."

ARRIVAL OF TERRITORIAL OFFICERS.

On May 27, Hon. ALEX. RAMSEY, of Pennsylvania, who had a short time previously been appointed Governor of the Territory, arrived, with his wife, but, being unable to secure proper accommodations at Saint Paul, went, by invitation of Hon. H. H. SIBLEY, to the mansion of that gentleman, at Mendota, where he remained a few days. Several other of the Territorial officers arrived during this month, and we close this chapter with some personal sketches of them.

HON. ALEX. RAMSEY.

From " Barnes' History of the Fortieth Congress," the following sketch is condensed :

"ALEX. RAMSEY was born near Harrisburg, Pennsylvania, September 8, 1815. His paternal ancestry were Scotch—the family of his mother was of German descent. Left an orphan at the age of ten, he was

---

* " In the spring of 1849, Miss MARY A. SCOFIELD joined our feeble band of teachers, and was, for a year, associated with the writer at Saint Paul. A second school house was built, and ample means provided for the instruction of one hundred and fifty pupils."—[Miss BISHOP's " Floral Homes."]

assisted by a relative to obtain an education, and engage in business. He was employed as clerk in a store at Harrisburg for a time, and, about the year 1828, was engaged in the office of Register of Deeds of Dauphin county. He afterwards learned the trade, or at least worked for some time, as carpenter, but, having a strong love for reading and study, he determined to adopt the profession of law. With this in view, he became a student of Lafayette College, at Easton, Pennsylvania, and in 1837, entered the office of HAMILTON ALRICH, Esq., at Harrisburg. He also studied in the law-school of Hon. JOHN REED, at Carlisle, and was admitted to practice in 1839, being engaged a portion of the time in teaching.

"During the celebrated Harrison campaign of 1840, Mr. RAMSEY took a prominent part, and was that fall chosen Secretary of the Electoral College of the State. In 1841, he was elected Chief Clerk of the House of Representatives of Pennsylvania. In 1843, he was nominated for Congress from the district composed of Dauphin, Lebanon and Schuylkill counties, and served in the Twenty-eighth Congress (1843-4.) He was re-elected in 1844, a member of the Twenty-ninth Congress, his term ending March 4, 1847. During these years, Mr. RAMSEY became well-known, not only in his own State, but widely among public men of the country, as evincing those qualities of sagacity and firmness, which have been so marked during his whole career. As chairman of the Whig State committee in 1848, he contributed largely to the election of Gen. ZACH. TAYLOR to the presidency.

"When that brave old soldier was inaugurated, it became his duty to appoint the officers of Minnesota Territory, and he at once tendered the Governorship to Mr. RAMSEY, which was accepted. His commission is dated April 2, 1849, and he immediately proceeded to remove, with his family, to his new home. And here, it should be remarked, that Gov. RAMSEY was married, in 1845, to Miss ANNA E. JENKS, of Newtown, Pennsylvania.

" Gov. RAMSEY arrived at the scene of his official duties on May 27, and four days afterwards, with the other Territorial officers who had arrived, issued a proclamation declaring the Territory organized, and the machinery of law in operation. Other proclamations, dividing the Territory into districts, ordering elections, &c., soon followed, and, with the labor of organizing the machinery of government, securing officers, managing Indian affairs, and administering various trusts, the Governor's chair was no sinecure. When the first Legislature met, in September, it bestowed on one of the first counties created, and, at that time, the most populous and wealthy, the name of our first Governor, a deserved and just compliment.

" Gov. RAMSEY took early measures to procure the extinguishment of Indian titles, by treaty, &c., and by the negotiations made at Mendota and Traverse de Sioux, in 1851, the valuable lands near Lake

Pepin, and 40,000,000 acres in what now constitutes Southern Minnesota, were thrown open to the settler. In the fall of the same year, he visited the Red River Colony and made, at Pembina, a treaty with the northern Chippewas, for the cession by them of 30 miles on each side of the Red River. This treaty was not ratified by the Senate, but in 1863, Gov. RAMSEY, then Senator, made another treaty, accomplishing the intended results, and the Red River valley is now rapidly settling up.

"Various events of Gov. RAMSEY'S term are narrated elsewhere quite fully, and need not be referred to in this sketch. Some of the extracts from his messages, predicting the future growth of the Territory, seem almost prophetic. He evinced his own faith in its future success by large and judicious investments in real estate, which ultimately became of great value, and are the bulk of a comfortable fortune.

"In 1853, Gov. RAMSEY'S term closed, and, in 1855, he was elected Mayor of Saint Paul, for a term of one year. In 1857, when the Republican Convention met, he was nominated for first State Governor, but his party was not successful in that contest. Two years later, he was again nominated, and this time elected by a majority of 3,752 in a vote of 38,918. He was inaugurated January 2, 1860. At that time the State was considerably in debt, taxes difficult to collect, and many other troubles were to be met, but his administration was a very successful one. The following year the rebellion broke out, and this laid new duties and responsibilities on the Governor. One was the proper officering of the regiments from our State, but the very fact that a large proportion of Colonels appointed by him were ultimately promoted to Brigaders, and several to Majors General, while every officer, with exceptions too few to notice, made a good record, is proof enough that the selections were wisely made, of men who have done honor to our State on the field.

"In 1861, Gov. RAMSEY was re-elected. During his second term the Sioux outbreak occurred, adding still further to the responsibilities of the position, but ultimately peace and security was restored to the frontier. In January, 1863, Gov. RAMSEY was elected United States Senator for six years, and re-elected in 1869, serving twelve years in all. During this period, he served on several important standing committees, post-offices and post roads among them. Postal reform occupied much of his attention. He first introduced the bill for the repeal of the franking abuse, and visited France in 1869, to urge cheap international postage, which has since been accomplished. He has also aided, as far as possible, the construction of our Northern Pacific and other railroads.

"This hasty summary," says Mr. BARNES, in concluding his sketch, "will sufficiently indicate the prominent position of Senator RAMSEY. Few of his colleagues have exhibited more tact in establishing and sustaining personal influence. He has proved himself a vigilant guardian of the interests of Minnesota. Of a frank, hearty bearing, his figure, countenance and voice concur to make him a favorite with his associates and with all observers."

Senator RAMSEY, at home, has been prominent in every public enterprise. He has, since the first days of our city, aided liberally every good work, and our churches and other institutions have been recipients of gifts of both real estate and money. He has, also, been an active member of the Historical Society and Old Settlers' Association. At one of the reunions of the latter, as is elsewhere remarked, he kindly volunteered to be the " last man"—a hope his friends indulge in, and, indeed, from his fine, almost rugged health and evenly poised system, there is no reason why their wish should not, be realized.

HON. AARON GOODRICH

was born in Sempronius, New York, July 6, 1807. While a young man, he settled in Tennessee, where he was admitted to the bar of that State, and successfully practiced for several years. He was elected, (though a Whig,) from a Democratic district, a member of the House for the years 1847 and 1848, and, during the latter year, was elected a Presidential Elector on the Whig ticket. On March 19, 1849, he was appointed, by President TAYLOR. Chief Justice of Minnesota, and took up his residence in Saint Paul. He held the first term of court in Ramsey and other counties, and was one of the corporate members of the Historical Society in 1849, and a charter member of the first Masonic Lodge, and a corporate member of the Grand Lodge of Minnesota. His term on the Supreme Bench closed in the fall of 1851, when he resumed the practice of law. In the early days of the Republican party, he was one of its most ready and effective campaign speakers, and drew up the first Republican platform adopted in Minnesota. In 1858, he was a member of the commission to prepare a Code of Pleadings and Practice, and submitted a report of marked ability. In 1860, he was a member of the Republican National Convention at Chicago, and labored to secure the nom-

ination of Wm. H. Seward, for President. Through the
friendship of that statesman, he was next spring appointed
Secretary of Legation at Brussels, which position he filled for
eight years. In 1869, he returned to Saint Paul, and devoted

his leisure to the writing of a work for which he had gathered
materials during his sojourn in Europe, entitled, "A History
of the Character and Achievements of the so-called Christopher Columbus," in which he opposes the claim of Columbus as discoverer of America. The work was published in

1874, by D. APPLETON & COMPANY, New York.   It is original and bold in its conception and handling, and has attracted much notice from scholars.   In 1872, he was a member of the Convention at Cincinnati, which nominated HORACE GREELEY, although he himself constantly voted for Judge DAVIS, of Illinois.   Judge GOODRICH was a prominent mover in the organization of the "Old Settlers' Association of Minnesota," in 1858, and has been its Secretary nearly ever since, devoting much time and labor to its objects.

CHARLES KILGORE SMITH.

Secretary of State, was born in Cincinnati, Ohio, February 15, 1799.   His father was a prominent man in Ohio in early days.   C. K. SMITH was educated at Oxford, Ohio, and, prior to his coming to Minnesota, had held several important offices, and was admitted to practice as a lawyer.   On coming to Saint Paul as a Territorial officer, he became prominent in many useful works.   He was active in establishing a system of common schools in this city.   He was a charter member of the first Masonic, and the first Odd Fellows' Lodge and Encampment in the city, and also one of the first to organize and found the Minnesota Historical Society, of which he was Secretary for two years, and labored faithfully.   He was a man of incisive and determined character, and made many political and personal enemies in Saint Paul.   GOODHUE, of the *Pioneer*, used to attack him without mercy, during his whole career, even accusing him of fraud and malfeasance in office.   Mr. SMITH, at one time, owned considerable property in Saint Paul.   He resigned in November, 1851, and returned to Hamilton, Ohio, where he died September 28, 1866.

COL. ALEX. M. MITCHELL.

Marshal of the Territory, vice TAYLOR declined, was also appointed from Ohio.   He was born in North Carolina ; graduated at West Point in 1835 ; served with distinction during the Florida War ; was then transferred to the Engineer Department, in which he served some time, and resigning, studied law at Yale College, and settled in Cincinnati, where he practiced until the breaking out of the Mexican War, in which he promptly enlisted, and was commissioned Colonel of the First Ohio Volunteers. He was severely wounded at Monterey. On his return to Cincinnati, a splendid sword was presented to him by the citizens, and the bar gave him a dinner. Col. MITCHELL held the office of Marshal until September, 1851. In the fall of 1850, he was nominated for Congress, against H. H. SIBLEY, but was unsuccessful. He left Minnesota about 1853, and afterwards became a resident of Saint Joseph, Missouri, where he died February 26, 1861, aged 52 years. A newspaper obituary said of him : " His last years were clouded with the vice of intemperance."

HENRY L. MOSS

was born in Oneida county, New York, March 23, 1819. He graduated from Union College, in 1840, and commenced the study of law, being admitted to practice in 1842, in the Supreme Court of Ohio, where he was then residing. In 1845, he removed to Plattville, Wisconsin, and, after residing there three years, moved to Stillwater, on April 29, 1848. He was appointed United States District Attorney in March, 1849, and held said office for four years. In 1851, he removed to Saint Paul, and has resided in this city ever since. In October, 1863, he was again appointed United States District Attorney, and held that position until 1868. For some years he has also been largely interested in the insurance business. Mr. Moss was in Washington when our land grant bills were pending, and gave valuable assistance to our delegation in Congress, in lobbying for their passage.

The machinery of government was now ready. In our next chapter we shall see it set in motion.

CHAPTER XVII.

EVENTS OF THE YEAR 1849.—Continued.

THE ORGANIZATION OF THE TERRITORY—FIRST OF JUNE PROCLAMATION—RAPID
GROWTH OF THE TOWN—GEN. JOHNSON'S INTERVIEW WITH GOODHUE—FIRST
FOURTH OF JULY CELEBRATION—THE CENSUS—POST-OFFICE MATTERS—FIRST
ELECTION—FIRST COURTS—ASSEMBLING OF THE LEGISLATURE—LOCATION OF
THE CAPITAL—WM. R. MARSHALL—INCORPORATION OF THE TOWN—ELECTION
OF COUNTY OFFICERS—SCHOOLS ESTABLISHED—FIRST BUSINESS DIRECTORY.

ON June 1, Governor RAMSEY and Chief Justice GOODRICH,
with H. L. Moss, United States District Attorney, and
Judge DAVID COOPER, Associate Justice, seated on beds or
trunks, in a little room, about eight by ten, in the Saint Paul
House, drew up the "First of June Proclamation," as it is
called, announcing the Territorial government organized, and
that "law and order reigned in Warsaw," (as a jocose old
settler used to express it.)   It was written on a washstand, the
only table that could be procured, which Judge G. has preserved as a relic of the event.

To commemorate this event—the formal birth of Minnesota—
the "Old Settlers' Association of Minnesota" hold their annual
meetings on June 1 of each year, and their annual banquets at
the Merchants' Hotel, the successor of the historic Saint Paul
House, the corner-stone of whose new structure was laid by the
Association on June 1, 1870.

ANOTHER HOTEL.

As a specimen of rapid building, the *Pioneer* of June 14,
says:

"That very large house, the Rice House, near the upper landing,
one of the largest hotels north of Saint Louis, was completed, so far
as the carpenter and joiner work is concerned, in ten weeks from its
commencement."

This hotel was afterwards called the "American House," and was a famous point in its day. It was opened to the public on June 28, by Mrs. RODNEY PARKER, formerly of Charlestown, Massachusetts. The hotel burned down on December 20, 1863.

SKETCH OF THE TOWN, JUNE, 1849.

The clever work of Mr. SEYMOUR, before quoted, gives a very readable picture of Saint Paul, about the middle of June:

"On the 13th of June, I counted all the buildings in the place, the number of which, including shanties and those in every state of progress, from the foundation wall to completion, was *one hundred and forty-two.* Of the above, all, except about a dozen, were probably less than six months old. They included three hotels, one of which is very large, and is now open for the accommodation of travelers; a State house, four warehouses, ten stores, several groceries, three boarding houses, two printing offices, two drug stores, one fruit and tobacco store, one or two blacksmith's shops, one wagon shop, one tin shop, one or two baker's shops, one furniture room, a billiard and bowling saloon, one school house, in which a school of about forty children is kept by a young lady, and where divine services are performed every Sabbath by a minister of the Episcopalian, Methodist, Presbyterian, or Baptist persuasion. There is, also, a Catholic church, where meetings are held every alternate Sabbath. At the time mentioned above, there were twelve attorneys at law, six of whom were practicing; five physicians, and a large number of mechanics, of various kinds. *There was not a brick or stone building in the place.* There are, however, good stone quarries in the vicinity, and clay near the town, where persons were employed in making brick."

The rush of immigration to the Territory about this date, seemed to have set in quite briskly. The *Pioneer,* of June 28, says:

"On Wednesday of last week, three steamboats arrived at our landing. They were all heavily laden with merchandize for this point."

ITEMS.

On June 25, Gov. RAMSEY and lady came from Mendota in a birch-bark canoe, and commenced house-keeping in a neat white frame cottage which stood on Third street, about where BEAUMONT's store now is. The Governor's office was kept in the same building,   It was afterwards called the "New England House," and burned down in the spring of 1860.

"An adjourned meeting, for the purpose of consulting upon the expediency of erecting a town house suitable for the accommodation of secular and religious meetings, societies, &c., will be holden at FREE-MAN, LARPENTEUR & Co.'s store, on Saturday, July 7, at 7 p. m.   A. II. CAVENDER, Secretary."—[*Pioneer*, June 28.]

"THE PUMP.—Within the past week the citizens of Saint Paul have erected in the lower square, a pump.   Of course, nothing could be more desirable, or to the city more appropriate.   For what is a town without a town pump?   It is a church without a bishop.   How will a stranger know when he arrives in our steepless city unless it has the centre marked with a pump.   A town pump is useful on numerous accounts. It is the centre exchange, where merchants and financiers do the fiats of commerce.   It is the place for placards of advertisement—a reference for details of information upon all doubtful questions—as when we say—'inquire of the town pump.'   It might do for the stand of a tem-perance lecturer.   It might answer as a whipping-post for rogues of low degree, and might perhaps subserve a patriotic purpose as a ducking engine with which to quench the heat of over-zealous office-seekers."—[Ib.]

"STOP THAT ROOTING UNDER OUR FLOOR!—We are no Jew, but a gentile, or the rooting nation under our editorial sanctum, instead of a respectful notice with our pen, would get punched with a sharp stick. Not that we would find fault with the pigs, for it is all owing to their bringing up.   But really, our equanimity is somewhat ruffled, if our chair is not jostled, by the movements of their hard backs under our loose floor."—[Ib.]

Speaking of the pigs rooting under the *Pioneer* editor's floor, makes apropos an anecdote related by Gen. R. W. JOHNSON,* (in his Old Settlers' address,) who came to Fort Snelling in 1849, as a Lieutenant in the army :   "The boat had

---

*Gen. RICHARD W. JOHNSON was born in Livingston county, Kentucky, February 7, 1827.   He was educated at West Point, graduating in the class of 1849, and was appointed to a command at Fort Snelling, with rank of Second Lieutenant.   He came here that season, and resided in this State several years.   On October 30, 1850, he was married, at Mendota, to Miss RACHEL E. STEELE.   When the rebellion broke out he served in many important battles and campaigns, and was severely wounded near Atlanta, Georgia, in 1864.   For this cause he was ultimately placed on the retired list, having then attained by successive promotions, the rank of Major General, and com-manded the District of Tennessee, &c.   He soon returned to Minnesota, which he had always considered his home while in the army.   Served as Military Professor at the State University 1868-9, and then removed to Saint Paul.   Gen. J. is now President of the Chamber of Commerce, and a leading promoter of all our civic interests.

tied up at the levee.   Taking advantage of the delay, I wended my way to the *Pioneer* office, and was kindly received

GEN. RICHARD W. JOHNSON.

by Mr. GOODHUE.   During the conversation, I observed a hen on her nest under the table, and I ventured to ask him if he designed raising his own poultry."   He replied, "that he had eaten all her eggs, and the old fool is *setting on a couple of brickbats*, and, if she hatches out a brick yard, you may bet your last dollar that hen is not for sale !"

FOURTH OF JULY CELEBRATION.

The Fourth of July was celebrated by the patriotic Saint Paulites in a very spirited and becoming manner. Early in the forenoon a procession, composed of the Territorial officers, civic societies, (what there was,) and a few "invited guests," with our own citizens, making about 500 persons in all, headed by a military band from Fort Snelling, formed in front of the Saint Paul House, and, according to a programme in the *Pioneer*, marched through " a number of the principal streets," (as our newspaper reporters would say,) although said streets were then a jungle of hazel brush and scrub oaks, to a grove on the site of the present Rice Park. Here Governor RAMSEY presided, with Messrs. SIBLEY and RICE as vice presidents. Rev. E. G. GEAR, Chaplain at Fort Snelling, read an appropriate service with prayers. The Declaration of Independence was read by BILLY PHILLIPS, in his most pompous, and rhetorical style, and Judge B. B. MEEKER delivered the oration, filling six columns in the *Pioneer*. The procession then re-formed, and marched to the American House, where a dinner was partaken of, followed by numerous toasts and speeches. The day wound up with a grand ball at the American House, and fireworks. FRANKLIN STEELE acted as chief marshal of the day, with A. L. LARPENTEUR and WM. H. NOBLES as aids. And thus ended the first Fourth of July celebration in Saint Paul.

Gen. SIBLEY, in his address on the early history of Minnesota, relates, that one of our prominent French citizens, on being asked how he liked the proceedings, said—" 'Fore GOD, dat speech of PHILLIPS was ze best speech made to-day." And it is said that " speech" secured BILLY D. the appointment of Prosecuting Attorney by the County Board soon after.

THE CAPITOL AND TERRITORIAL OFFICERS.

The *Pioneer* of July 5, notices the arrival of the Secretary

of the Territory, Hon. CHARLES K. SMITH, of Ohio. Mr.
SMITH at once set about securing apartments, or a building,
for the use of the Territorial officers and Legislature, &c., but
found it almost impossible to do so, as the town was so crowded,
and buildings in demand.   Finally, he secured rooms in the
·· Central House," a weatherboarded log structure on Bench
street, which was then kept as a hotel by ROBERT KENNEDY,
and (having been afterwards more than doubled in size) was
the Central House of more recent days, though since almost
destroyed by fire.   A flag-staff was erected on the bank of the
river, and the national banner run up, to mark the headquarters of government, and here, in these narrow quarters, its
business was carried on.   •

TERRITORIAL CENSUS—APPORTIONMENT.

Pursuant to a provision in the Organic Act, JOHN MORGAN,
Sheriff of Saint Croix county, had been engaged for several
weeks prior to this date, in taking a census of the Territory.
EDMUND BRISSETT took the districts on the Missouri River, and
WM. DAHL the Pembina region.*   The census of Saint Paul
appeared as follows :

Males—540. Females—300. Total—840.

The total of the whole Territory was :

Males—3,067. Females—1,713. Total—4,780.

Of these, over 700 lived in what is now Dakota Territory,
and 367 were not inhabitants at all, legally, being soldiers in
the forts.   The rapid growth of Saint Paul during the summer of 1849, may be inferred from these figures.

On July 7, Governor RAMSEY issued a proclamation dividing
the Territory into seven Council districts, based on the census
just taken, and providing for an election of nine Councillors
and eighteen Representatives, on August 1.   The Territory,
not having been divided into counties, the districts were ar-

---

* DAHL was a genius in the line of censuses. He would be a valuable man for any
ambitious town that wished to get credit for more population than it had. How the
handful of people on Red River swelled, in his hands, to 700, was one of the mysteries
that, as Lord DUNDREARY would say, " no fellah could find out."

ranged by " precincts." The election of a Delegate to Congress was also ordered at the same time, and the assembling of the Legislature fixed for Monday, September 3.

Under this apportionment, what was called the " Saint Paul Precinct," embracing the town of Saint Paul, constituted the Third District, and was entitled to two Councillors and four Representatives. Nominations were soon after made, generally on personal grounds, as party lines had not then been drawn. Indeed, some of our old settlers declare that, in early days, they used to have to *force* office on men—that such a thing as " office-seeking" was unknown in those poor but honest times. There are many who would gladly hail a return of such an era of primitive simplicity.

THE " MINNESOTA REGISTER."

I gave on page 208, an account of the issue of the *Register* at Cincinnati. As soon as the river opened, the press and material of the office were shipped to Saint Paul. J. P. OWENS accompanied it, arriving in May, Maj. McLEAN* being detained by illness at Cincinnati, did not arrive until August. In the meantime, Col. OWENS went to work to get the paper out, and on July 14, issued No. 2. Capt. E. Y. SHELLEY, the veteran typo of Saint Paul, was foreman. The paper was printed in a small office on upper Third street. Some five or six numbers of the *Register* were issued, when it became evident that there were too many newspapers in Saint Paul, and, on the arrival of Maj. McLEAN in August, a consolida-

---

*NATHANIEL McLEAN was born in Morris county, New Jersey, May 16, 1787. He was brother of Hon. JOHN McLEAN, of the Supreme Court of the United States. His father removed to Ohio in 1789, settling in Warren county. NATHANIEL McLEAN learned the printing business at Cincinnati, and, as early as 1807, published a paper at Lebanon. In 1810, he was elected a member of the Ohio Legislature, serving two or three sessions. He was also an officer in the War of 1812. In the spring of 1849, he determined to remove to Saint Paul and embark in the newspaper business. He was then 60 years of age, but remarkably strong and active. On November 3, 1849, he was appointed by President TAYLOR, Sioux Agent at Fort Snelling, which office he held until the spring of 1853. In the fall of 1855, he was elected one of the Commissioners of Ramsey county. This was the last public office he held. He retained his physical powers almost unimpaired until a short time before his death, when he was attacked with cancer, and suffered greatly before his end came, April 11, 1871, aged 84 years. He was an honest and good man. The township of McLean, in this county, was named in honor of him.

tion was effected with the *Chronicle*, as before stated. Col. HUGHES sold out and retired, and went to Hudson, Wisconsin, where he died a couple of years ago. His foreman, S. A. QUAY, took an interest with McLEAN & OWENS in the *Chronicle* and *Register*. The first number of this paper was issued on August 25, from the *Chronicle* office, a well-printed seven column sheet. Mr. QUAY withdrew after a few weeks, and left the Territory. The paper became the Whig organ, and soon had a good patronage from that party.

FORESHADOWINGS OF OUR BRIDGE.

The *Pioneer*, of July 26, contained the following rather prophetic note :

"That the position of Saint Paul on the east side of the river will soon require our town to be connected by a bridge with the west side, as early as possible, at least after the extinguishment of the Sioux title on the west side, is quite obvious. * * * That a bridge can be built from the bluff, near the middle of Saint Paul, many feet above the reach of the tallest steamboats, at no very great expense, by supporting it in the centre by a pier on the island, we have no doubt."

CHURCHES AND RELIGIOUS ITEMS.

The *Register*, of July 21, contains the following :

"Mr. PARSONS [Baptist] will preach at the school house to-morrow morning, at half past ten, and the Rev. Mr. NEILL, [the Presbyterian clergyman,] on the following Sabbath, at the same hour. These gentlemen will continue to officiate alternately, thus affording the citizens an opportunity of attending divine service every Sabbath morning. The means of grace are about being further facilitated in Saint Paul by the erection of two churches, one under the direction of Rev. Mr. HOYT, of the Methodist church, the other to be occupied by Mr. NEILL's congregation."

The *Plattville* (Wisconsin) *Argus* of the same week speaks of the session of the " Wisconsin Annual Conference," in that city. Up to this time, and, we believe, for several years afterwards, Minnesota was included in this conference. Rev. CHAUNCY HOBART was stationed at Saint Paul.

At this time (as noted before) Rev. Mr. NEILL was engaged in building a small frame chapel on Washington street, facing

Rice Park, on a lot contributed by H. M. RICE. His brick dwelling, the first erected in Minnesota, was on the same block facing on Fourth street. The chapel was completed for use in August, being the first Protestant church built in Minnesota. The funds for its erection had been contributed by some relatives and personal friends of Mr. NEILL, in Philadelphia.

POST-OFFICE MATTERS.

On page 154 was given some notes of the establishment of the post-office in Saint Paul, and its equipment of furniture. JACKSON held the post-office three years and three months. During the three years of that time, we incline to the belief that it hardly paid for the trouble of conducting it. But meantime a change came over the hamlet. With the rush of population and business, came also a very great increase of mail matter, and it soon became necessary to lay aside the little case of pigeon-holes, and procure more expanded facilities for serving the public. The *Register*, of July 28, says:

"OUR NEW POST-OFFICE.—Our postmaster, Mr. H. JACKSON, has fitted up his new post-office building on Third street, with great taste and convenience. Every citizen, whose business requires it, can now have a box to himself."

The "new post-office" referred to, was a frame building about where No. 105 East Third street now is. There were only about 200 "glass boxes" in his new equipment, a number considered sufficient for present needs and future, too.

But alas! for the fallacy of human hopes in this world. JACKSON's head (officially) was already in the basket, even while he was planning and building in expectation of profits to come. On July 5, he was decapitated by the new Whig dynasty, and JACOB W. BASS commissioned in his place. The news of political appointments was slower getting circulated those times than in these days of telegraphic journalism, or JACKSON might have saved his time and money. For instance, the *Pioneer* of that week growls in this wise:

"Would any one believe that, in the nineteenth century, our Government would limit Minnesota, situated here in the very heart of the Republic, to one mail a week? We ought to have mails at least tri-weekly during the summer."

As soon as Mr. Bass could make preparations for accommodating the office he took possession of the same. He at once erected a small frame addition, or lean-to, alongside of the Jackson street front of the Saint Paul House, (since called the Merchants) and removed thither the glass boxes or pigeonholes, with the other equipments necessary. The whole room was only about as big as a sheet of paper, but no doubt accommodated the business of that day. Mr. WALLACE B. WHITE. acted as Mr. BASS' deputy during the most of his term. Mr. WHITE was subsequently Territorial Librarian, and now lives in Washington.

THE ELECTION ·

for Councillors, Representatives and .Delegate came off on August 2d. The vote in the Saint Paul precinct stood as follows :

Councillors.

Wm. H. Forbes	187	David Lambert	91
James M. Boal	98		

Representatives.

B. W. Brunson	168	Joseph R. Brown	84
P. K. Johnson	104	A. G. Fuller	24
Henry Jackson	165	Eb. Weld	2
Dr. J. J. Dewey	178		

Those in *italics* elected.

The election developed considerable "life" among the *boys* of those days. The *Pioneer* said it had "gone off" as quietly as could be expected." The *Register*. however, speaking of the rejoicings over the election, reported more :

"FORBES, McBOAL, BRUNSON, DEWEY, JACKSON and JOHNSON, were successively placed in a small-sized 'go-cart,' and hauled through the streets by the enthusiastic crowd, at a speed rather prejudicial to whole necks. The vehicle finally broke down, but the 'boys' were not to be stopped in their rejoicings. So they *carried* their successful friends to the hotel, where such cheering took place, as we scarcely ever heard before. The crowd then dispersed in good order."

Hon. H. H. SIBLEY was elected to Congress without opposition.

BRIEF NOTES.

"The number of retail liquor establishments in Saint Paul and other towns of the Territory, is a LEETLE too great for a sound and healthy state of public morals. It is the subject of remark by strangers, and gives us a bad name at home and abroad, to say nothing of its evil effects upon society."—[*Register*, Aug. 4.]

"SHAMEFUL.—Last Monday night, some person in Saint Paul furnished a band of Winnebago Indians with liquor. Of course, they got drunk and were patroling our streets at night, singing their terrific war songs, and filled with bitter malignity. These things must not be tolerated."—[*Pioneer*, Aug. 9.]

"It is with pleasure that we learn that another school, for the smaller children, will soon be started in the lower town of Saint Paul. In the rush of business, it is pleasant to find the training of the infant minds of the rising generation not neglected."—[*Chronicle*, Aug. 10.]

"Messrs. FREEMAN, LARPENTEUR & Co., with some aid from their neighbors, have erected a staircase from the lower landing to the summit of Jackson's point. It renders the passage up and down the bluff a diversified and pleasant promenade."—[*Pioneer*, Aug. 16.]

These stairs remained there and were used for several years.

"There will be a school meeting at FREEMAN & LARPENTEUR'S on Saturday evening next, at 7 o'clock."—[Ib.]

"We called on friend BRAWLEY the other day, at his brick yard. He is now in a most successful state of operations. He employs two mills, ten men, and has now on hand some 400,000 brick. The quality is better than can be shown north of Saint Louis. If we are really going to build a city we must use brick."—[*Pioneer*, Aug. 30.]

This was the first kiln of brick ever burned in Minnesota. The yard was near the present residence of D. W. INGERSOLL. E. D. NEILL had a dwelling built from this kiln, and the Market Street Methodist Episcopal church was also built from it.

SOCIAL STATISTICS.

Some one in the east having written a letter making inquiry about the Territory, among other things, inquires whether "there are any Odd Fellows' Lodges in the Territory?" Mr. GOODHUE replies: [August 16.]

"As to the Order of Odd Fellows, we have not heard of any, but there are a great many smart bachelors, who will have to continue *odd*, if their other halves do not come along with you immigrants."

16

Mr. GOODHUE was right about the preponderance of the male element of population. The census, taken a few months later, disclosed only 860 females to balance 1,337 lords of creation, a disproportion always found in all new western communities. Thus, 477 of the young bachelors of Saint Paul must have remained unmated, unless, as the jocose editor suggested in another case, they "take up" with some of the "Wenonas of the Sioux nation, who could have been bought any day then for a few dollars each," and, indeed, were continually hanging around, waiting to be bought, at any sum.

In the next issue of the *Pioneer*, however, one of the "brethren of the three links" throws some light on the question of Odd Fellow's Lodges. One, he says, was instituted at Stillwater, on August 15, and "the brethren of Saint Paul have made application for a charter to institute a Lodge in this place."

EARLY COURTS OF THE TERRITORY.

The first court held in Saint Croix county after the Territory was organized, was on August 12. Chief Justice GOODRICH presided, and Judge COOPER assisted. GOODHUE says: "The roll of attorneys is large for a new country. About 20, of the lankest and hungriest description, were in attendance." The term lasted six days. "The proceedings," says the *Chronicle and Register,* "were for the first two or three days somewhat crude, owing to the assembling of a bar composed of persons from nearly every State. But, by the urbanity, conciliatory firmness, and harmonious course taken by the Court, matters were in a great measure systematized." At this session, it was said only one man on the jury wore boots! All the rest had moccasins.

The court of the Second District, Judge MEEKER presiding, "met at the house of Mr. BEAN, on the west bank of the Mississippi, opposite the Falls of Saint Anthony," the same week. The grand jury room was the old government saw mill !

The court of the Third District was held at Mendota in the latter part of August, Judge COOPER presiding. Gen. SIBLEY was foreman of the grand jury. Judge COOPER read the jury an elaborate charge, which, Gen. S. says, only three out of the twenty odd members understood, the rest being French. Maj. FORBES acted as interpreter during the term.

ORGANIZATION OF A MASONIC LODGE.

Reference was made a few pages back to a meeting for the purpose of organizing a Masonic Lodge. The movers in the work applied to the Grand Lodge of Ohio for a Dispensation, which was granted on August 8, 1849. On September 8, the Lodge was organized in the office of C. K. SMITH, who had been designated in the warrant as first Master. Soon after, the officers and members were announced as follows: W. M., C. K. SMITH; S. W., JAMES HUGHES; J. W., DANIEL F. BRAWLEY; Treas., J. C. RAMSEY; Sec., J. A. AITKENSIDE; S. D., LOT MOFFET; J. D., TAYLOR DUDLEY; Tyler, W. C. WRIGHT. Members—AARON GOODRICH, JOHN CONDON, ALBERT TITLOW, JOHN HOLLAND, LEVI SLOAN, C. P. V. LULL, GEORGE EGBERT, SAMUEL H. DENT, D. B. LOOMIS, M. S. WILKINSON, JOHN LUMLEY, H. N. SETZER, JAMES M. BOAL, CHAS. P. SCOTT, O. H. KELLEY, CHAS. M. BERG, WILLIAM H. RANDALL, HUGH TYLER, LUTHER B. BRUIN, A. M. MITCHELL.

The Lodge met for sometime in a room in the Merchants' Hotel building. C. P. SCOTT is said to be the first Mason made in Saint Paul.

ASSEMBLING OF THE LEGISLATURE.

On Monday, September 3, the first session of the Legislature assembled at the Capitol, (i. e., Central House.) the hotel business not being impeded by the law-making branch whatever. On the first floor was Secretary SMITH's office and the "Representative Chamber." Up-stairs was the *library* and the "Council Chamber." As the Council had only nine members, and the House eighteen, it did not require a large room to accommodate either, and no formalities stood in the way of their business.

"Both Houses," said a subsequent writer in the *Pioneer*, "met in the dining hall, where Rev. E. D. NEILL prays for us all, and Governor RAMSEY delivers a message full of hope and far-sighted prophecy, to comfort us withal; and then leaves the poor devils sitting on rough board benches and chairs, after dinner, to work out as they may this old problem of self-government through the appalling labyrinth of parliamentary rules and tactics that perplex their souls. Yet no Legislature which ever sat in Minnesota was made of better stuff than that which assembled to lay the corner-stone of the political edifice."

HOMICIDE.

On the 12th of September, a lad, named ISAIAH McMILLAN, accidentally or carelessly shot another lad, named HEMAN SNOW, near the corner of Third and Franklin streets, with a gun loaded with shot. The charge entered the head of the unfortunate boy, and he soon after died. McMILLAN was tried for homicide, at the February term of the first District Court, held by Judge COOPER, in Stillwater. There not having been proved any malice aforethought in the act, the jury returned a verdict of manslaughter, with a recommendation to mercy. The boy was sentenced to one year's imprisonment, but, as there was no county jail. he was sent to Fort Snelling for confinement, where he was kept as a prisoner for a year, though not closely confined. He appeared to be half-witted, or partially idiotic. This was the first trial for murder in Minnesota, whose soil has so often since been stained with human blood by the crime of CAIN.

BIRTH OF DEMOCRACY IN MINNESOTA.

Hitherto, the party lines had not been drawn very strictly in the new Territory. At the election noticed *ante*, no political questions had entered into the canvass. The first erection of party standards took place at a "Democratic Mass Convention," which met pursuant to call, at the American House, on October 20, 1849. Suitable resolutions were reported and adopted, the *Pioneer* was declared the organ of the party, and from this time dates the bitterness of party strife.

FERRY CHARTERS.

We noticed, a few pages back, an article by Mr. Goodhue, on the necessity of a bridge across the river to West Saint Paul. This must necessarily be, however, a work for the future. To supply something better for travel and commerce to cross the river than a dug-out, a bill was introduced by Hon. Henry Jackson, " to grant a charter to Isaac N. Goodhue to keep and maintain a ferry across the Mississippi River opposite the lower landing, in Saint Paul." The bill did not pass at that session, however, but a notice was soon after placed in the *Pioneer* that James M. & Isaac N. Goodhue would apply to the Commissioners of Ramsey county for a ferry charter across the Mississippi, at the lower landing. The license was granted on January 7, 1850, and, at the same meeting, a ferry privilege was also granted to John R. Irvine, to run one from the upper levee. These ferries plied regularly until the Saint Paul bridge was completed in 1858.

LOCATION OF THE CAPITAL.

The question of the location of the Capital came up during the session, on the consideration of a part of Gov. Ramsey's message referring to that subject. The Committee on Territorial Affairs, to whom it had been referred, reported that :

"They are constrained to give it as their opinion, that Saint Paul should continue to be the seat of government of the Territory until otherwise determined by a vote of the people. Apart from the fact that Saint Paul is the most central point, so far as the present population of the Territory is concerned, the fact that it is the head of navigation on the east of the Mississippi, and accessible to steamboats, is another strong point in its favor. Your committee believe that it is the wish of a majority of the inhabitants of Minnesota, that the location of the Capital should not be changed. With good roads diverging from every point, Saint Paul is easily reached at all seasons of the year."

Considerable discussion ensued during the session on this subject, as to whether the Territory had a right to expend the $20,000 appropriated in the Organic Act, for a Capitol building. The question having been submitted to Hon. W. M. Meredith, Secretary of the Treasury, he replied that the " Department cannot doubt that the public buildings in question can only be erected at the *permanent* seat of government, located as described. Of course, the reply to your inquiry must be, that nothing can be expended from this appropriation until after the location shall be duly made."

So the permanent location was not definitely settled this session, however, but, at the close of the Legislature, it was a drawn battle. Saint Paul remained the temporary seat of government, and the Governor was authorized to rent buildings to carry on the public business meantime.

Ex-Gov. MARSHALL, in his address before the Old Settlers of Hennepin county, February 22, 1871, says, regarding the contest for the seat of government:

"The original act made Saint Paul the *temporary* Capital, but provided that the Legislature might determine the *permanent* Capital. A bill was introduced by the Saint Paul delegation to fix the permanent Capital there. I opposed it,* endeavoring to have Saint Anthony made the seat of government. We succeeded in defeating the bill which sought to make Saint Paul the permanent Capital, but we could not get through the bill fixing it at Saint Anthony. So the question remained open in regard to the permanent Capital until the next session, in 1851, when a compromise was effected, by which the Capital was to be at Saint Paul, the State University at Saint Anthony, and the Penitentiary at Stillwater.

"At that early day, as well as now, caricatures and burlesques were in vogue. Young WM. RANDALL, of Saint Paul, now deceased, who had some talent in the graphic line, drew a picture of the efforts at Capital-removal. It was a building on wheels, with ropes attached, at which I was pictured tugging, while BRUNSON, JACKSON, and the other Saint Paul members were holding and checking the wheels to prevent my moving it, with humorous and appropriate speeches proceeding from the mouths of the parties to the contest. The caricature was quite a good one, and served to amuse the people of Saint Paul for some days. When this question was before me, as Governor, if it had been the old question of removal to Saint Anthony—a very different thing from removal to a point more than a hundred miles from the centre of population, and quite as far from the geographical centre of the State— I do not believe I should have been so ready to veto it."

This was the first struggle on the Capital question. The sessions of 1851, 1857, 1869 and 1872, saw it repeated, as will be noted under those dates.

---

* Gov. MARSHALL then represented Saint Anthony, at which place he lived.

WILLIAM R. MARSHALL.

was born in Boone county, Missouri, October 17, 1825. His father, JOSEPH MARSHALL, was a native of Kentucky, and his mother, ABBY SHAW, of Pennsylvania. In his younger days, Mr. MARSHALL followed

WILLIAM R. MARSHALL.

the business of mining, surveying, &c., and spent several years in the lead region of Wisconsin. In 1847, he came to Saint Croix Falls, and settled there for a few months. During September of that year, he first visited Saint Anthony Falls, on foot. His account of this visit, in his address before mentioned, is worthy of a record here: "When with weary feet, I stood at last, in the afternoon of that day, on the brink of the Falls, I saw them in all their beauty and grandeur, unmarred by the hand of man,—in such beauty of nature as no one has seen them in the past 22 years. As the light of the fast-declining sun of that autumn day bathed the tops of the trees and the summits of the gentle hills, and left the shadows of the wooded islands darkling the waters, and as the plunging, seething, deafening Falls sent up the mist and set its rainbow arching the scene, I was filled with a sense of the awe-inspiring in nature, such as I have rarely since experienced." At that time a claim shanty or two were the only habitations there.

Gov. MARSHALL, on that visit, staked out a claim, and cut logs for a cabin, but could not get a team to haul them. So he left it for the present, and returned in 1849, and perfected his claim, which has since become an addition to the city.

In the fall of 1848, he was elected to the Legislature of Wisconsin, from Saint Croix county, but his seat was contested by JOSEPH BOWRON, of Hudson, on the grounds that MARSHALL lived out of the limits of the State, which had just been admitted.

After settling at Saint Anthony, in 1849, he was elected a member of the first Legislature from that district. He was then engaged in the iron and heavy hardware business. The following summer, he endeavored to get the steamers to deliver his heavy freights at the foot of the Falls, but, as they would not or could not do so, he was compelled to remove his business to Saint Paul, which he did in 1851. He had, in the meantime, it may be remarked, surveyed "Leech's Addition," and other portions of our city. On removing to Saint Paul, he established the first iron store in this city, the same business now continued by NICOLS & DEAN. In 1852, he was elected County Surveyor. In 1853, with his brother, JOSEPH M. MARSHALL, (now of Colorado,) and N. P. LANGFORD, he established a banking house, which was very successful until 1857, when the crash prostrated everything. In 1855, he was the candidate of the Republican party for Delegate to Congress, but the party were not successful in the contest, H. M. RICE being elected; though 10 years later the tables were turned, Mr. MARSHALL beating Mr. RICE for Governor. After withdrawing from the banking business, he engaged in stock-raising and dairy-farming for several years, importing some of the finest cattle ever brought to our State.

In December, 1860, he purchased the *Saint Paul Daily Times,* and, on January 1, 1861, issued it as the *Daily Press,* in connection with NEWTON BRADLEY, Esq., as business manager, and JOSEPH A. WHEELOCK, as assistant editor. The *Press* was very successful, soon absorbing the *Minnesotian,* and has been ever since, until its mergement into another paper, a leading journal of the State.

In August, 1862, Gov. MARSHALL enlisted in the Seventh Regiment,

of which he was appointed Lieut. Colonel. During the Sioux outbreak, he was constantly in active service, and, in several engagements,
led his men with a fearless bravery which has always been a character-
istic. He was also in the expedition of 1863. In November of that
year he was commissioned Colonel. The Regiment went south that
fall, and was soon after assigned to the Sixteenth Army Corps. It had
its full share of battles and campaigns, until the end of the war, Col.
MARSHALL being, in the meantime, brevetted a Brigadier. Shortly after the discharge of the Regiment, in August, 1865, he was elected
Governor of Minnesota, and, in 1867, re-elected for another term. On
the conclusion of his term, January, 1870, he again engaged in banking, being Vice President of the Marine National Bank, and President
of the Minnesota Savings Bank. In 1874, he was appointed a member
of the Board of Railroad Commissioners, and, in November, 1875, was
re-elected Commissioner for two years.

Gov. MARSHALL has been prominent in a number of our public institutions, and in measures and enterprises to benefit the city—such as
the Saint Paul bridge, &c., and in educational matters. He has been
active in organizing the Swedenborgian church in this city, and has
liberally aided other societies. Like most of our pioneers, he rejoices
in sound health and a good constitution, and his active participation in
events may extend over another generation yet.

SAINT PAUL INCORPORATED AS A TOWN.

The Legislature continued in session for 60 days, adjourning
on November 3, 1849. It passed many acts which had a bearing on the material prosperity of the Territory. Nine counties were created, among them one named in honor of the
Governor of the Territory—RAMSEY. Saint Paul was declared
to be the county seat of the same, and, on the first day of November, 1849, a bill was approved, incorporating the " Town
of Saint Paul." It begins as follows :

" *Be it enacted, &c.* That so much of the Town of Saint Paul as is
contained in the original plat of said town, made by IRA BRUNSON, together with Irvine and Rice's Addition, be and the same is hereby
created a town corporate, by the name of the Town of Saint Paul."

Then follows a provision for the election, on the 6th of May
following, "and annually thereafter," of one President, one
Recorder, and five Trustees, each for the term of one year,
the same to constitute a Town Council. They were empowered to appoint a Treasurer and Marshal, and other subordinate

officers.   The President was also to be a Justice of the Peace.
ex-officio, in all matters, civil or criminal.

APPOINTMENTS OF OFFICERS.

On the adjournment of the Legislature, the following appointments by the Governor were announced, for Ramsey
county :

Register of Deeds.—DAVID DAY.*
Sheriff.—C. P. V. LULL.
Commissioners.—LOUIS ROBERT and ANDRE GODFREY.
Judge of Probate.—HENRY A. LAMBERT.

THE FIRST "BANK" IN SAINT PAUL.

The *Pioneer,* of November 15, aired up quite a neat swin-
dle, as follows :

"Some time in September last, there came to Saint Paul a burly-
looking, middle-aged man, of medium stature, dressed in a drab suit,
and wearing a drab-colored fur hat, who called himself ISAAC YOUNG,
and represented that he had formerly been a saddler in Ohio. This
man closeted himself with a Mr. SAWYER, who was then in Saint Paul,
and got him to sign a large number of handsomely engraved pieces of
paper, on which were engraved the words, "*Bank of Saint Croix,
Saint Paul, Minnesota,*" or something of that purport. Mr. YOUNG

---

* DAVID DAY was born in Burke's Garden, Virginia, September 19, 1825, and his
boyhood was passed in the same place.   In 1846, he removed to the lead region of Wisconsin, where he followed mining for three years, studying medicine at night and
other leisure times, and attending the Medical Department of the University of Pennsylvania in winter. He graduated from that Institute in 1849. He came to Saint Paul
in the spring of that year, and commenced the practice of medicine, which he pursued
with much success for several years. In 1854, he entered the drug business, and withdrew from the practice of medicine. During this period he also held one or two important public positions. In 1849, he was appointed Register of Deeds, and the same fall
elected for two years more. He was also a member of the Legislatures of 1852 and 1853,
from Benton county, in which he was temporarily residing, the latter year being elected
Speaker. He retired from the drug business in 1866, being at that time the oldest house
in the State. In 1871, he was appointed State Prison Inspector. In 1874, he was appointed one of the Commissioners of State Fisheries, and also " Seed Wheat Commissioner," to provide the sufferers from the grasshopper raid with seed—both honorary
appointments, without any compensation. On June 1, 1875, he was appointed Postmaster of Saint Paul. Dr. DAY has been a close observer and diligent student of questions
and problems in social science, philosophy and political economy, and at the same time
has been one of our most successful, sagacious and enterprising business men. With
an even temperament, and well-preserved physique, one might almost expect him to be
the " last man" of the old settlers.

disappeared from Saint Paul. The next we hear of Mr. YOUNG, he is in Saint Louis, buying printing paper, and negotiating for goods to send to Saint Paul. Notes of the " Bank of Saint Croix, at Saint Paul," are quoted in the Eastern bank note lists at one per cent. discount, the quotation being furnished by some accomplice in the fraud, living in Wall street, New York. Mr. YOUNG has not reappeared in

DAVID DAY.

Saint Paul, and probably never will. Mr. SAWYER, we learn, was duped in this affair."

ITEMS.

The rush of immigration continued late that fall. The *Pioneer*, of November 15. says : " Steamboats continue to arrive at our wharves, laden with merchandize and passengers."

The *Chronicle*, of September 29, states that 2.135 barrels of cranberries had been shipped below up to that date. The cranberry trade, for several years, was quite a large one. They were mostly gathered by squaws, who traded them for goods and other merchandize at the stores.

Pig's Eye was stated at this time to have a population of forty families.

THE ELECTION FOR COUNTY OFFICERS,

under the new laws passed by the Legislature, took place on November 26. Ramsey county at that time extended up the Mississippi River to its source almost, including, of course, Saint Anthony. The vote stood as follows:

		St. Anthony.	St. Paul.	Total.
Register	*Dr. D. Day*	39	172	211
"	W. D. Phillips	30	·69	99
Sheriff	*C. P. V. Lull*	17	172	189
"	J. R. Irvine	33	60	93
"	Ed. Brissett	19	2	21
Treasurer	*J. W. Simpson*	69	240	309
Commissioners	*L. Robert*	57	202	259
"	A. Godfrey	19	123	142
"	*B. Gervais*	31	167	198
"	John Banfil	37	70	107
"	*R. P. Russell*	54	108	162
Judge of Probate	*H. A. Lambert*	34	·149	183
"	B. W. Lott	33	93	126

Those in *italics* elected.

ORGANIZATION OF PUBLIC SCHOOLS.

An adjourned school meeting of the citizens took place at "the school house," on December 1. Hon. C. K. SMITH, from the committee previously appointed, after reviewing the provisions of the Minnesota Statute on public schools, and that of Wisconsin, still in force, reported, recommending: "That two persons be appointed by this meeting to call on the County Commissioners, and request them to divide the town into a suitable number of school districts, after which an organization of the districts shall be brought about. agreeably to the requirements of the law." Also, that a committee be appointed to procure from JNO. R. IRVINE, a deed to the lot on which the school house then stood, provided the amount still

due for its erection ($80) was paid; and to secure from Mr.
RANDALL a deed for the lot which he had proposed to donate
for school purposes on Jackson street.   Three schools were
recommended to be opened;* one on the RANDALL lot, to be
put up immediately; one in the basement of the Methodist
church, and one in "Mr. NEILL's lecture room."   As teachers
Miss H. E. BISHOP, Miss SCOFIELD, and Rev. C. HOBART,
were recommended; the committees (of two each) who
were to be appointed as above, to be the school trustees until
the town shall be districted, and others elected.

The report was adopted, and the following gentlemen
appointed as the trustees: WM. H. FORBES, JOHN SNOW,
EDMUND RICE, Rev. E. D. NEILL, Rev. B. F. HOYT, J.
PARSONS, and B. W. BRUNSON.

REVIEW OF THE TRADE OF 1849.

The river remained open and navigable this year 242 days,
during which there were 95 arrivals.

The whole mercantile business of Saint Paul for the year
1849, was ascertained at the close of the season to be $131,000.
Of this, $60,000 was computed to be groceries alone.   There
were scarcely any stores devoted exclusively to one branch of
business.   Each had "a little of everything"—groceries, hardware, dry goods, clothing, boots and shoes, &c.   In a short
time, however, this changed, and nearly every merchant devoted himself to one line of merchandize.   The McCLOUD
BROS. established the first exclusively hardware store in Minnesota, during this year.

FIRST BUSINESS DIRECTORY, JANUARY 1, 1850.

In the New Year's Address of the *Pioneer*, mentioned more
fully hereafter, the following business directory is given:

Clergymen.—Rev. Messrs. Ravoux, Neill, Hobart, Hoyt, Parsons.
Lawyers.—Ed. Rice, H. A. Lambert, W. D. Phillips, P. P. Bishop,

---

*The *Chronicle and Register* of January 6, 1850, says that, "our three schools recently
established, are now in full blast, affording by their capacity and location, ample means
for the education of all the children in town."   One of these was the old frame building situated on the west side of Jackson street, below Sixth.   It is now used as a
second-hand store.

Geo. L. Becker, H. F. Masterson, O. Simons, J. A. Wakefield, S. H. Dent, W. B. White, B. W. Lott, James M. Goodhue, L. A. Babcock, C. K. Smith.

Land Agents.—A. V. Fryer, Isaac N. Goodhue.

Physicians.—J. J. Dewey, David Day, Thos. R. Potts, N. Barbour.

Merchants.—Elfelt & Bro., Fuller & Bro., L. Sloan, Fullerton & Curtis, W. H. Forbes, Douglas & Slosson, John Randall & Co., Louis Robert, H. W. Tracy & Co., Daniel Hopkins, Sergeant & Bowen, J. W. Simpson, Bart. Presley & Co., Dewey & Cavileer, N. Barbour, J. C. Ramsey.

Tailors.—Johnson & Brown, W. H. Tinker, J. N. Slosson.

Shoemaker.—Hugh McCann.

Hotels.—American House, by R. Parker; Tremont House, by J. A. Wakefield; Central House, by R. Kennedy; Saint Paul House, by J. W. Bass; DeRocher's House, by DeRocher; Miller's Boarding House, by B. Miller.

Painters.—J. M. Boal, Burrill & Inman.

Blacksmiths.—Wm. H. Nobles & Co., Leverich & Co.

Plasterers.—J. R. Irvine, D. DeWebber, —— Starkfielder, C. P. Scott,

Masons.— —— Barnes, B. Bowles, Wm. Beaumette, —— Hanley, J. Kirkpatrick.

Carpenters.—C. P. V. Lull, Wm. Bryant, A. Foster, W. Woodbury, W. C. Morrison, J. B. Coty, Chas. Bazille, T. Lareau, —— Coit, H. Willey, Eaton & Bro., —— Chase, B. F. Irvine, J. B. Lumbeek, Joseph Brinsmade, H. Glass, J. Frost.

Silversmith.—Nathan Spicer.

Gunsmith —— —— McGuire.

Bakers.—Berry & Bro., K. Stewart, Humphrey & Brinkman.

Wheelwrights.—Nobles & Morrison, Hiram Cawood.

Saddle and Harness Maker.—A. R. French.

Tinner.—C. D. Bevans.

CHAPTER XVIII.

EVENTS OF THE YEAR 1850.

Celebration of New Year's Day—Curious New Year's Address—Balls—
Roads and Mail Service—Sketch of "Old Bets"—A Homicide—Sketch
of Hon. E. Rice—First Term of Court—First Town Election—Daring
Indian Conflict.

THE year 1850 opened auspiciously. The practice of
"making calls" was then inaugurated by the gentlemen
of the city. The day was clear and fine, and all enjoyed it
greatly. The *Pioneer* says:

" The festivities and hilarity of our town on New Year's confirm the
truth that cold weather can never freeze warm hearts. Saint Paul was,
yesterday, swarming with animated fashion. The sideboards of many
of our citizens were provided with free entertainments, which would do
credit to the wealthy burghers of Gotham. At 11 o'clock a. m., our
people assembled at the Methodist church, to attend the exercises of
the Minnesota Historical Society. * * * In the evening, there was
a rush to the ball at the Central House, there being nearly or quite one
hundred gentlemen, with their ladies, present."

THE "PIONEER'S" NEW YEAR'S ADDRESS.

The *Pioneer* issued, on January 1, a New Year's Address,
which created considerable amusement. A few extracts will
show its tone:

" The cities on this river must be three,
Two that *are* built, and one that is to be.
One is the mart of all the tropics yield;
The cane, the orange, and the cotton-field;
And sends her ships abroad and boasts
Her trade extended to a thousand coasts;
The *other*, central for the temperate zone,
Garners the stores that on the plains are grown;
A place where steamboats from all quarters range,
To meet and speculate, as 'twere, on 'change.

The *third will be,* where rivers confluent flow
From the wide-spreading north through plains of snow:
The mart of all that boundless forests give
To make mankind more comfortably live;
The land of manufacturing industry,
The workshop of the nation it shall be.
Propelled by this wide stream, you'll see
A thousand factories at Saint Anthony:
And the Saint Croix a hundred mills shall drive,
And all its smiling villages shall thrive;
But then *my* town—remember that high bench
With cabins scattered over it, of French?
A man named HENRY JACKSON's living there,
Also a man—why, every one knows L. ROBAIR;
Below Fort Snelling, seven miles or so,
And three above the village of OLD CROW?
Pig's Eye? Yes; Pig's Eye! That's the spot!
A very funny name; is't not?
Pig's Eye's the spot, to plant my city on,
To be remembered by, when I am gone.
Pig's Eye, converted thou shalt be, like SAUL:
Thy name henceforth shall be Saint Paul.
When the Wisconsin's wedded to the Fox
By a canal and solid steamboat locks;
When freighted steamboats leave Saint Paul one day,
And reach, the next but one, Green Bay;
When locomotives regularly draw,
Their freighted trains from distant Pembina,
And o'er the bridge rush, thundering, at Saint Paul;
And, at Dubuque, to breathe, scarce make a call;
But hurry onward to the hot Balize,
By flying farms, plantations, houses, trees,—
When from the Cave to Pig's Eye shall extend
A levee lined with steamboats to each end;
When one great city covers all
The ground from Pig's Eye to the Falls,
I then will claim Saint Paul for mine,
The child of 1849."

Some of these visions of the future, though then a mere freak of wild fancy, have been so closely fulfilled since, or are about to be, the doggerel will repay a careful perusal.

BALLS AND SOCIAL BEHAVIOR.

A ball was held on January 17, at the Central House. The

Pioneer criticises it in a humorous way, that would lead one to suppose that society was not as starchy and high-toned those days as we have it at our *bon ton* soirees now-a-days.   It advises gentlemen to wear neither moccasins or heavy boots at balls!   The *Pioneer* also thought it "vulgar for a lady to make up a bundle of cake, nuts and candies at the table to carry home! She might as well pocket the sugar-bowl and teaspoons."

Balls and sociable dancing parties appear to have been about the only amusements in winter-time then, and, without them, the long winter months would have probably been intolerably tedious.   The 22d of February this year was celebrated by a ball at the American House, 80 or more persons being present. The band of the Sixth Regiment generally furnished music for those soirees.   Their leader, Mr. JACKSON, was a famous bugler, and many of our old citizens remember the soul-stirring notes of his favorite instrument.

Another famous ball musician of early days was a colored man, named WM. TAYLOR.   He had a very musical voice, and has "called figures" for hundreds of balls and dances, almost. He was killed by the Indians at Yellow Medicine, in 1862.

ROADS AND MAIL SERVICE.

The *Pioneer* complains, and justly, too, that the mail service during the winter of 1849–50, was execrable.   "*It takes* (groaned the editor) *a month* to get a letter from Washington." The proposals advertised for, a short time previous, called for a weekly eastern mail, during winter.   The contract for this service was let to Hon. H. M. RICE, as will be further noted in a subsequent chapter.   One reason for the poor service, probably, was the absence of good roads.   Prior to this winter, the only road from Saint Paul to Prairie du Chien was on the ice of the river, after it froze—a route of much danger. In November and December, 1849, however, WIRAM KNOWLTON, of Willow River, (Hudson) Wisconsin, laid out a road from Prairie du Chien to that place, via Black River Falls. It was "blazed and marked," he says, in a letter to the *Pioneer*, "the whole way,"—distance, 223 miles.   Some

17

streams were bridged. "and a span of good horses can now haul 1,800 or 2,000 pounds through the whole distance." "Stopping places" could be found a part of the way, but the rest of the route, the traveler must "camp out" in the snow. This road was used as the winter route east by Saint Paul travelers, for several years. WILLOUGHBY and POWERS' stage line ran on it several seasons, and Mr. RICE's mail contract was served on it, at least a part of that time.

At this date, the only mail routes in Minnesota, besides the one above referred to, were from Saint Paul to Fort Snelling and back, weekly; from Saint Paul to Falls of Saint Croix, via Stillwater and Marine Mills, and back, weekly, with one additional trip per week to Stillwater and back. There were, in 1850, only sixteen post-offices in what is now Minnesota.

ORGANIZATION OF CHURCHES.

On December 29, 1849, a Baptist church had been organized, with 12 members, and was "recognized" by a Council the day following. This was the first Baptist church in Minnesota. The *Pioneer,* of January 9, 1850, has the following:

"The First Presbyterian church, of Saint Paul, was organized last Sunday, in the Rev. Mr. NEILL's chapel. Bros, SELBY and TINKER, who had been before chosen elders, were ordained by the laying on of hands, &c. Rev. Dr. WILLIAMSON, of the Little Crow Mission, was present, with several of the native Sioux."

Hon. GEO. L. BECKER* was one of the original members of this church, and is still a member of it.

---

* Hon. GEORGE L. BECKER was born in Locke, Cayuga county, New York, February 4, 1829. In 1841, his father removed to Ann Arbor, Michigan, where he entered the Freshman class of the University of Michigan, in 1842, and graduated in 1846, his class being the second one graduated at that institution. Immediately after graduating he studied law with GEORGE SEDGWICK, Esq., of Ann Arbor, and remained with him until October, 1849, when he emigrated to Saint Paul, arriving here on the 29th of that month. He at once commenced the practice of law, and soon after formed a copartnership with EDMUND RICE and ELLIS G. WHITALL, under the firm name of "RICE, WHITALL & BECKER." About a year afterwards, Mr. WHITALL withdrew, and WM. HOLLINSHEAD, one of the best lawyers who ever lived in the State, joined the firm, which then became "RICE, HOLLINSHEAD & BECKER," one of the most successful and widely-known law firms in the Territorial days of Minnesota, continuing to transact a large and important business until its dissolution in 1856. Mr. RICE, retired during that year, and Messrs. BECKER and HOLLINSHEAD continued the business for another year, when Mr. BECKER withdrew and soon after ceased the active practice of law.

During the last thirteen years, Mr. BECKER has been actively engaged in the important work of forwarding the railroad interests of the State. In 1862, he was chosen Land Commissioner of the Saint Paul and Pacific Railroad. Upon the organization of the First Division of the Saint Paul and Pacific Railroad, (6th of February, 1864,) he was elected President of the same, which position he has held ever since. Under his able management, and, largely by his efforts and influence, 317 miles of road have been con-

GEORGE L. BECKER.

structed. Foreign capital has been enlisted to the extent of millions, thus proving a source of wealth to our State, opening up a vast region hitherto a wilderness, now filled with prosperous towns and fertile farms. In the discharge of his duties, Mr. BECKER has performed an immense amount of physical and mental labor, making frequent journeys east and to Europe, besides carrying on his large office business at home, and filling responsible public offices at the same time.

Mr. BECKER has filled a number of important offices in our State. In 1854, at the

The *Pioneer*, of February 27th, says : "Our Baptist friends are making active preparations for erecting a house of public worship in Saint Paul."

used to flourish about those days, as she did for many years subsequently. No history of Saint Paul can be complete which omits mention of this curious character, so well known to all the old residents. The papers about this date contain numerous references to her—some not very complimentary, perhaps, but they show that "Old Bets" was a sort of favorite, at least, which she certainly was.

Old Bets was a full-blood Sioux woman, of the M'dewakontonwan tribe. She came of a family which was somewhat distinguished in its way. Her Sioux name was *Aza-ya-man-ka-wan*, or Berry-picker. She was born near Mendota, in 1788, and was at the time of her death only 75 years old, though she was generally supposed to be 100. She was "married," after the Indian fashion, to *Ma-za-sa-gia*, or "Iron Sword," who died a few years subsequently at Mendota. She had several children. One daughter was living not long ago in Saint Paul. A son, named *Ta-opi*, or "Wounded Man," born at Mendota, became somewhat noted as a convert to Christianity, and, after his death at Faribault, in 1869, Bishop Whipple published a fine volume of his biography, with an engraved portrait. A town in southern Minnesota has been named for him. One of her brothers was *Ile-in-da-koo*, a famous warrior, prophet and medicine man, who was killed by the Chippewas, some years ago. 'One-legged Jim' was another brother of Old Bets. He had lost a leg in some skirmish, and used to peg

first municipal election, under our city charter, he was elected an Alderman, and, in 1856, chosen Mayor of the city. In 1857, he was elected from Ramsey county one of the members of the Constitutional Convention, and soon after elected one of the three members of Congress to which it was supposed our State (when admitted) would be entitled. During the delay which attended its admission, it became certain that only two members could be received, and Mr. Becker at once resigned. The following year (1859) he was unanimously nominated, at a Convention of his party, for Governor, but the opposite side gained the day. In 1867, he was elected a member of the State Senate from Ramsey county, and re-elected in 1869, serving four sessions in all. Such was the confidence reposed in him by both parties, that, at his last election, no nomination was made against him on the opposite ticket, and he was unanimously chosen. In 1872, Mr. Becker was again nominated for Congress, but his party was not successful in the contest.

Mr. Becker has generously aided all the benevolent, literary and educational institutions of Saint Paul, and is known as one of our foremost citizens in every good enterprise.

around on a wooden stump.   He was well known to most of the early
settlers, and was never backward about begging.

Old BETS lived all her life in this locality.   Miss BISHOP mentions
her frequently in her work, " Floral Homes," and gives a good portrait
of her.   She has been photographed many times, and her pictures,
purchased by tourists, may be found in albums in all parts of the civilized world.   Thousands of them have been sold.   She was always very
proud of this distinction, and of the notice paid her by travelers,
never failing to levy a small tax on them.   MUNGER BROS. once pub-

"OLD BETS."

lished a piece of music (words by J. H. HANSON) based on the supposed
fact that she was 100 years old, and some artist made a very good bust
of her.   So she had become quite an institution in our midst.   She
subsisted by begging for many years.   She was always welcome at the
kitchen doors of the old settlers, and never failed to bear off a wallet of
food.   She was a privileged character in many ways, and no old settler
[she knew them all] would refuse her request for *kosh-poppy* (money.)
She always greeted her acquaintances on the street with a broad grin
of her huge mouth, and a cheerful "ho-ho."   During the Sioux War,
she was very kind to white prisoners, and possessed other good traits.
She was converted to Christianity shortly before her death, by Father

RAVOUX. When her last illness was known, the Chamber of Commerce subscribed a sum of money for her comfort, and she had a Christian burial. She died about May 1, 1873, at Mendota. The portrait herewith is an excellent likeness.

MISCELLANEOUS.

"Some journeyman preacher would make a profitable trip up the Mississippi River, with a supply of blank marriage licenses, there being no person north of Saint Paul, who is authorized, by law, to tie the nuptial knot. Many couples are represented to be in an awful state of suspense. The laws of Minnesota do not anywhere authorize Justices of the Peace to solemnize marriages."—[*Pioneer*, Jan. 30.]

"Many of the people go unshaved, although the village is supplied with three barbers—such is the scarcity of soap."—[Ib.]

"Wood is selling in Saint Paul at about $1.50 per cord."—[Ib.]

"The foundation of a brewery is laid at the upper end of Saint Paul."—[Ib.]

"'GREAT CRY AND LITTLE WOOL.'—Four of the lawyers of Saint Paul were engaged all day last Wednesday, in trying the right of property in a little, old sow."—[Ib., Feb. 27.]

"We would advise each immigrant to Saint Paul this season, as we did last season, to come prepared to build a cheap house immediately, without depending upon hiring a house."—[Ib.]

The *Pioneer* notices the market bare of cured meats: "only fresh meats," it says, "and mallards 20c. a pair." It adds:

"One year ago there were three stores in Saint Paul, sold out at that, so that the place was absolutely bare of goods and provisions. There are now fifteen stores, in one or the other of which almost every article of necessity can be found."

ANOTHER HOMICIDE.

On Friday, February 22, 1850, another homicide occurred. Two men, named ALEX. R. McLEOD and WM. B. GORDON, got into an affray, where the Stillwater road forded Phelan's Creek, about a mile east of town, on or near McLEOD's claim, mentioned on page 136. GORDON was so severely injured that he died next day. McLEOD was arrested and examined before Justice WAKEFIELD. The evidence showed that both men were in liquor, but that GORDON first assaulted McLEOD, striking him with a whip-stock, while McLEOD used nothing but his fist.   He was held to bail in the sum of $200, but, on trial before the next term of court, was acquitted on grounds

EDMUND RICE.

of self-defense. McLeod was defended by Hon. EDMUND RICE.*

* Hon. EDMUND RICE was born in Waitsfield, Vermont, February 14, 1819. He removed to Kalamazoo, Michigan, in 1838; studied law, and was admitted to practice in 1842; was Master in Chancery, Register of the Court of Chancery for the Third Circuit, and Clerk of the Supreme Court of the State. He served in the Mexican War, in

GRAND COUNCIL WITH THE WINNEBAGOES.

On March 14, a deputation of the principal chiefs of the Winnebagoes, who were dissatisfied with their Reservation, waited on Gov. RAMSEY. A grand council was held in the trading house of OLMSTED & RHODES, on Third street, between Jackson and Robert streets. Among the famous chiefs present were ONE-EYED DEKORA, (who took BLACK HAWK a prisoner in 1832,) WINNESHIEK, BIG CANOE, GOOD THUN-DER, LITTLE DEKORA, CARIMONA, LITTLE HILL, and others, more or less prominently known in the history of the North-west, and a number of Sioux also attended. Gen. J. E. FLETCHER, Winnebago Agent, was present, and WM. H. FORBES and JOHN HANEY, Jr., acted as interpreters. They stated their grievances to Gov. RAMSEY, and had a long talk. They were finally persuaded to return to their Reservation and remain there peaceably.

It was at this council that Gov. RAMSEY made his famous temperance speech to the Indians. He admonished them of the dangers of intemperance, and urged them to quit drinking. " The white men," he said, " have quit drinking"—[the inter-preter translated this, but the Indians looked a little astonished and incredulous—so the Governor qualifiedly added,] " *in a great measure!*" The interpreter rendered this literally, to mean a *large-sized vessel!* Old DEKORA, at this, exclaimed, " perhaps they had, but most of them still use a small measure !"

ROADS AND MAILS.

The continual complaint at poor mail facilities has been

1847 and 1848, with the commission of First Lieutenant of the First Michigan Volunteers. In July, 1849, he settled in Saint Paul, and soon became a member of the law firm of RICE, HOLLINSHEAD & BECKER, which, for several years, was a leading law firm in Minnesota. He practiced until 1855. In 1857, he became President of the Minnesota and Pacific Railroad Company, and also President of its successors, the Saint Paul and Pacific, and the Saint Paul and Chicago Railway Companies, till 1872, performing a large amount of service in the organization and starting of our railway system.

Mr. RICE was a member of the Territorial Legislature, in 1851, of the State Senate in 1864 and 1865, House in 1867, and the Senate again, in 1873 and 1874—an instance of popularity extending, in the same direction, over a longer period than any other we have chronicled. Mr. RICE's valuable services to his county and city, not only in the Legislature, but as a pioneer in works of internal improvement—the highways of com-merce—have won for him their lasting gratitude and regard.

before noted. The breaking up of the winter of 1849–50, rendered the ice on the river, which was at that time the public road, very insecure, and many accidents happened, several persons being drowned. On March 29, a mail was received, the first for 20 days, says the *Pioneer*—a deprivation that must have been sorely felt, in the isolated condition of the community then. The *Pioneer*, of February 27, adds:

" The number of letters passing through the post-office at Saint Paul averages nearly 700 per week. The mail to Saint Anthony alone is larger than the whole mail of the Territory was one year ago."

THE MORALS OF SAINT PAUL.

The editor of the *Pioneer* denies reports that had been circulated abroad, that Saint Paul was a disorderly and immoral place. He said, despite the temporary character of many homes, and the floating population—men without families, &c.—and the fact that the town government had not yet organized, the town was orderly and moral. Religious services held in five churches, and well attended—Sunday observed—drunkenness and gambling not openly carried on — good schools, and a good moral tone in community. No violent disorders or crimes.

If whisky was sold, it must have been as villainous " forty-rod" stuff as is now vended. An old Indian, named RATTLER, who had a camp across the river, managed to get a drink in town, one night, and was found dead in his teepee next morning. Whisky that could kill a Sioux Indian that quick, must have been a mighty mean article.

SCRAPS.

About this time, a contest for the cathedral of this bishopric is noted. PIERRE BOTTINEAU and others made profuse offers of lots at Saint Anthony, but some eligible lots were finally secured here, the same on which it now stands, as is narrated elsewhere.

Reference is made to Sergeant E. K. THOMAS, of Fort Snelling, an artist of some skill, who used to paint portraits of Indian celebrities quite skillfully.

FIRST TERM OF COURT—FIRST GRAND JURY.

The first term of court in Ramsey county, was held on Monday, April 8, 1850, with 49 cases on the calendar. Chief Justice GOODRICH presided. Thirteen indictments were found, mostly against gambling-house keepers. McLEOD, for homicide, was acquitted.

There was no jail then. Prisoners were generally sent to Fort Snelling for safe-keeping. The *Pioneer,* of April 16, says:

"JACOB R. SHIPLER, indicted for assaulting his wife with intent to kill, and convicted and sentenced to imprisonment in penitentiary for one year, slipped away from the sheriff and escaped."

The Saint Paul people must have been a very litigious community then, as it is now. The *Pioneer* says: "We have now 25 lawyers in Saint Paul!" What sins could this young and feeble population have committed, that such a punishment was sent on them?

From the records of this term, I find the names of the first grand jury ever drawn for Ramsey county, as follows:

WILLIAM H. NOBLES, WYMAN BAKER, C. D. BEVANS, AND. GODFREY, R. CUMMINGS, FRED. OLIVIER, A. TITLOW, H. R. GIBBS, D. L. FULLER, JNO. FORD, J. M. MARSHALL, JAMES HINTON, JOHN CARLTON, ED. PATCH, LOREN JONES, EBEN WELD, HENRY H. ANGEL, LOUIS PARKER, REUBEN BEAN, S. K. LANE, FRANCIS CHENEVERT, JOHN B. COTY, A. L. LARPENTEUR.

The record adds: "*Some* of the above reported for duty." A part of these lived at Saint Anthony, then in Ramsey county.

THE FLOOD OF 1850.

In the spring and early summer of this year, a great freshet occurred, mainly caused by extreme heavy snows on the Upper Mississippi, and long-continued warm rains early in the spring. The water commenced rising about April 1, and continued most of the month. The floor of the Constans warehouse, still standing, was submerged several inches—higher water, if we mistake not, than has been known since, and, the *Pioneer* of that date said, " unprecedented for many years." The water subsided somewhat when the regular "June fresh" came on, which again carried it up, and it remained high for several weeks. The "Anthony Wayne," a steamer well known in those days, went up to the Falls of Saint Anthony on the flood, and likewise made a trip up the Minnesota River, as did also the "Yankee" a little later.

When the river first rose at Saint Paul, the ice was still firm, and swept down in huge cakes. The *Pioneer*, of April 10, says: "Last evening in Saint Paul, we could hear the noise of masses of ice tumbling over the Falls of Saint Anthony, eight miles distant." The roaring of the Falls used to be heard here several years afterwards, but the improvements there, changing their character, gradually stopped this.

OPENING OF NAVIGATION, 1850.

The *Pioneer*, of April 25, says:

"On Friday morning, the 19th, (arrival of 'Highland Mary,') at 6 o'clock, the smoke of a steamboat was visible at Saint Paul, and the very heart of the town leaped for joy. * * * As she came up in front of RANDALL's warehouse, the multitude on shore raised a deafening shout of welcome," &c.

She brought 500 passengers, not an uncommon load for those days.

"Such has been the anxiety here," continued the *Pioneer*, "for the arrival of steamboats, that nothing else was talked of. Saint Paul seemed likely to go to seed."

An editorial of the same date says: "At length the flood of immigration has burst through the barriers of Lake Pepin. The boats that have already arrived have brought hundreds of strangers amongst us. * * * Let us do everything in our power to welcome, encourage, and build up those who have come to unite their fortunes with ours"—and further recommends that, as the hotels are overcrowded, citizens entertain the strangers at their houses until they can build tenements.

Some idea can be formed, from the above paragraph, of the joy with which the arrival of the first boat was hailed, in early days—opening communication with the rest of the world, after months of isolation.   It was generally a signal for a jollification, at which all rules of restraint were thrown aside.   At one of our Old Settler reunions, a graphic description was given of the president of a temperance society leaning up against CONSTANS' warehouse, two or three hours after the first boat arrived, entirely overcome by his feelings, and retching in an agony of surfeit.   Perhaps, like RIP VAN WINKLE, he thought " that time *didn't count*."   Of late years, the opening of navigation has ceased to be of any importance or interest.   Our railroads have changed all that.

A VISION OF OUR NORTHERN PACIFIC.

In an editorial which now, that over twenty-five years have elapsed, reads with prophetic interest, the editor calls attention to " a short route to Oregon and California."   He thinks, " there is some probability that a railroad will be made from Saint Louis westward, to San Francisco, at no very remote period."   *   *   *   " We wish now," (he adds,) " to turn your attention to another overland route, in the north, which we believe is far easier and safer," and proceeds to argue that Saint Paul is much nearer the Pacific in a direct line, than Saint Louis; also, " that there is a route or trail from the Red River to the Columbia River, over which mails are regularly transported, by the Hudson's Bay Company, with safety and ease."   It must be remembered that the northern route for a railroad was then hardly thought of.   Even the central route was looked on as an impossible scheme, and but few then, even young men, ever expected to see it in their lifetime.

FIRST TOWN ELECTION.

On May 6, pursuant to the terms of the town charter, the first municipal election took place.   There was no contest worth mentioning, and the following officers were chosen :
President.—Dr. THOMAS R. POTTS.*.

---

* Dr. THOMAS R. POTTS was born in the city of Philadelphia, February 10, 1810.   He graduated at the Medical Department of the University of Pennsylvania, in 1831, and settled at Natchez, Mississippi, where he lived 10 years.   In 1841, he removed to Galena, Illinois, and, in 1849, to Saint Paul, where he practiced medicine for 26 years,

Recorder.—EDMUND RICE.

Trustees.—W. H. FORBES. B. F. HOYT. WM. H. RAN-
DALL, HENRY JACKSON, and A. L. LARPENTEUR.

The records of the Board are lost, and the only note of their
proceedings are what appear from time to time in the papers.

A DARING MURDER BY HOLE-IN-THE-DAY.

The *Pioneer,* of May 16, graphically describes a daring act

HOLE-IN-THE-DAY.

of HOLE-IN-THE-DAY, the Chippewa chieftain, who used to be
so well known in Saint Paul :

" On Wednesday, the 15th, at about 1 p. m., there was a great excitement in Saint Paul—Indians yelling at each other across the river, and
running up and down the shores, canoes crossing the river, and everything betokening the utmost exasperation. It seems news has reached

---

being, at the time of his death, the senior practicing physician of our city. He was,
for several years of this time, contract surgeon at Fort Snelling, and also physician to
the Sioux, and Medical Purveyor of this district, Pension Surgeon, &c. He was elected
first President of the Town Board, in 1850, an office equivalent to Mayor. He was,
also, elected City Physician in 1866, and health officer of Saint Paul in 1873. He died
suddenly, while holding that office, on October 6, 1874. He was married at Fort Snelling, in 1847, to Miss ABBY STEELE.

them that a party of Sioux were overtaken, a short distance out of Saint Paul, and two murdered and three taken prisoners. At this moment, a company of the Sioux have started northward through town, stripped of their blankets, in pursuit of the dastardly murderers. This is the first blow (if the story is true) struck by the Chippewas in revenge of the 14 of their tribe, murdered the other day in a sugar camp, by the Sioux.

"P. S. About sunset, on Wednesday, the Sioux returned, with the corpse of one man, (who seems to be the only one murdered,) whom they had in a canoe, nailed up in a box, covered with a red pall. Just at dark, they left the lower landing in sadness, with their canoes, for their village, four miles down the river."

The murder, which was a most daring feat, was committed by HOLE-IN-THE-DAY. He secreted his canoe in the mouth of the creek that runs from " Fountain Cave," and, with one or two other warriors, crossed the river, attacked several Sioux, and killed and scalped one, and got off with the scalp before quite a body of the Sioux, who were near by, could get the alarm. It was a most audacious act. The *Pioneer*, of May 23, says :

"A gentleman, just down from Fort Gaines, says that, on his way down, he met the Chippewa chief, HOLE-IN-THE-DAY, with the scalp of the young Sioux Indian, which that brave took last week in this neighborhood, divided into quarters. He was in fine feather. At night he and his followers had a scalp-dance. In his descent on the Sioux, in the short space of 24 hours, he marched 80 miles, committed the murder, and started for home again."

In order to put a stop, if possible, to these butcheries by the Indians, Governor RAMSEY summoned the chiefs of both tribes, their agents and interpreters, to a council at Fort Snelling, which was held on June 11 or 12. After tedious palaver, a sort of treaty of peace was patched up between the redskins, for about the fiftieth time.

THE CHOLERA

was quite bad this season, and several very sudden deaths occurred. It was quite bad at towns down the river also, and passengers arriving per steamer constituted quite a proportion of the cases. The *Pioneer* declared that not a case had originated here—but that all had been brought from below. Some occurred subsequent to that, at all events.

BRIEF ITEMS.

On May 3, a Lodge of Odd Fellows was instituted, under the title of " Saint Paul Lodge, No. 2," by JOHN G. POTTS.* of Galena. The charter members were, BENJ. W. BRUNSON. JUSTUS C. RAMSEY, COMFORT BARNES. B. W. LOTT. JOHN DUNSHEE, C. K. SMITH, JOHN CONDON, J. B. COTY, and WM. C. HUGGINS.

The *Pioneer*, of May 16. says: " This morning about 10 o'clock, Rev. Mr. NEILL's commodious chapel, in Saint Paul, took fire, by some shavings. and was burned to ashes." This was the first fire which ever occurred in Saint Paul. Mr. NEILL. at once started east to collect funds for a new church. in which he succeeded. In the meantime. he used to preach in an unfinished warehouse, which then stood where Warner's Block now does. At the same time, Dr. WILLIAMSON would occasionally preach in a log building then occupied by JOSEPH R. BROWN, on the site of the present Ingersoll Block. He. several times. preached there to the Sioux, in their language.

A little of the speculative fever. which raged so intensely four or five years later, must have shown itself then. On June 27, 1850. the *Pioneer* remarks: " The cash price of town lots in Saint Paul is too high. It is industry, it is labor, it is actual production. not gambling and speculation. which produces wealth. We want to see more industry and production. and less gambling and speculation." But what would GOODHUE and his compeers have said if they could have foreseen prices 20 years later? They would have kept mum on " gambling and speculation," and bought themselves poor.

On June 19, a young mechanic. named JOHN LUMLEY, died very suddenly of cholera, one of the few fatal cases that occurred this season. He was an Odd Fellow, and had been

---

* JOHN G. POTTS died at Galena, February 13, 1874. At his death he was one of the oldest Odd Fellows in the United States.

initiated only four days previous. The Fraternity turned out at his funeral, the first they had been called on to conduct. Referring to their new white regalia, GOODHUE, who could not resist a joke, even at a funeral, writes that " he had not seen such a display of clean linen since the Territory was formed."

If the mourners went about the streets, there was occasionally festivities and rejoicings likewise, and the bells did not always toll. The census-taker reported 25 marriages in Ramsey county for the year ending June 1, 1850.

CHAPTER XIX.

EVENTS OF THE YEAR 1850.—CONTINUED.

NAVIGATION OF THE MINNESOTA RIVER—THE CENSUS OF 1850—LIST OF RESIDENTS—
ETHNOLOGICAL NOTES—ABORIGINAL ITEMS—THE INDIANS AND THEIR HABITS—
POLITICAL—FREDRIKA BREMER VISITS SAINT PAUL—THE COURT-HOUSE AND
JAIL—BIOGRAPHIES OF OLD SETTLERS, &c.

ONE of the most noticeable events of the year 1850, was the navigation of the Minnesota River. Three boats, the "Anthony Wayne," "Nominee" and "Yankee," made excursions with large pleasure parties of Saint Paulites, each trying to ascend further than the other. The water was very favorable for such experiments, and the "Yankee" ascended 300 miles, thus demonstrating that the Minnesota was navigable.

On July 18, the *Pioneer* says: "The water is now higher than in the spring freshet—higher than it has been for 28 years." The Red River valley was also inundated, and the settlers compelled to flee to the hills.

ITEMS.

"The heavy rains have made the roads from Saint Paul to Saint Anthony in some places impassable. The necessity for a railroad to the Falls is becoming every day more and more obvious.—[*Pioneer*. July 18.]

The conveniences of a city are gradually increasing in Saint Paul. The confectioner, the ice-cart, the milk-man, are among the new conveniences here, and last. but not least, a regular market for fresh beef.—[Ib.]

The "Order of 1001's" flourished in those days. Frequent notices are made of the meetings. and most of the prominent citizens were "roped in" just as they were a few years later into the Sons of Malta. JAMES M. GOODHUE was one of the high officers of the order. A lecture which he once wrote on the "emblems" of the order, illustrated with toys bought

18

in a store, is said to have been a masterpiece of wit, excelling even ALF. BURNETT's great lecture on the menagerie.

CENSUS OF 1850.

Meantime the Federal census of 1850 had been taken, and the result in the county was as follows :

> Males, 1,337; females, 860; total, 2,197.
> No. of dwellings, 384; No. of acres improved, 458.
> Population of Saint Paul, 1,294; No. of families, 257.

Ramsey county at that time, it should be remembered, included Saint Anthony, and, in fact, all of Minnesota on the east side of the Mississippi, except the Saint Croix valley. The census of Ramsey county was taken by CHARLES F. TRACY, who was a resident here from 1849 to 1855.

RESIDENTS OF 1850.

I have, with considerable labor, compiled from the census rolls, the following important and valuable list of residents of 1850. It may be justly termed the '' Battle Abbey Roll" of Saint Paul. Where it was defective or erroneous, I have added to it a number of names gathered from the roll books of societies, poll lists, advertisements, and other sources, so that it is probably quite correct. (It includes only adult male residents :)

Quartus B. Abbott,	B. Allen,	Wm.Armstrong,(col'd,)
Elliot Adams,	Geo. W. Alvord,	Louis Augee.
Peter Allard,	Michael E. Ames,	
J. W. Babcock,	George Bemis,	J. R. Brewster,
Lorenzo A. Babcock,	Lyman L. Benson,	J. W. Brinsmade.
Abram Baker,	Corydon D. Bevans,	O. B. Bromley,
Daniel A. J. Baker,	Henry L. Bevans,	Joseph R. Brown.
John Banfil,	Stanislaus Bilanski.	Oris Brown,
Dr. Nehemi'h Barbour,	P. P. Bishop,	S. F. Brown,
V. B. Barnum,	W. J. Blake,	William Brown.
Comfort Barnes,	James M. Boal,	Luther B. Bruin.
Thomas Barton.	Cyril Boisvert,	Louis Brunel.
F. J. Bartlett.	Elijah Booth,	B. W. Brunson.
Louis Bartlett,	Joseph Boudrette,	Alden Bryant.
Jacob W. Bass.	Charles W. Borup.	William Bryan.

Joseph Bastin,
William Battleford,
Charles Bazille.
Reuben Bean,
J. B. Beauchernier.
Geo. L. Becker.
W. H. Belknap.

Joseph Boudreau,
Joseph Bourcier.
William Bowen,
David Bradley.
Patrick Brady,
D. F. Brawley,
Rev. J. Lloyd Breck.

Louis W. Bryson,
William Buchanan,
Willard Bunnell,
Patrick Burke,
Geo. W. Burkholder.
Alex. Burnett,
Henry C. Butler.

Anthony Caifil,
John B. Callis,
Scott Campbell,
Peter Cardinal,
John J. Carlton,
William G. Carter.
John M. Castner,
John B. Coty,
Charles S. Cave,
A. H. Cavender,
Charles Cavileer.
Hiram Cawood.
Firman Cazeau,
William Chambers.

Peter. Chapdelin,
Warren H. Chapman,
Gabriel Chesefield,
Bruno Chenevert,
Anthony Chosee,
James R. Clewett,
Solomon T. Close.
Francis Cloutier,
Charles Colter,
William Colter.
John Condon,
Alex. Connolly.
Chas. R. Conway.
Philip Constans.

Wm. Constans,
David Cooper.
Wm. F. Corbet.
John B. Cornoyer.
George Cornoyer.
Joseph Cornoyer,
Oliver Courtemanche.
Marcil Coutourier,
F. Couture,
Peter Crevier.
Charles Creek,
J. W. Crosby.
George Culver.
John Cyphers.

Maxime Damas,
Severe Desmarais,
Xavier Desmarais.
George Daniels,
Joseph Daniels,
Dr. David Day.
James Day,
Lyman Dayton.
J. W. DeCamp,

Louis Denoyer,
Narcisse Denoyer.
Sam'l H. Dent,
Wm. DeRocher.
Isaiah DeWebber,
Dr. Jno. J. Dewey,
Rev. L. Dickens,
Dyer Divine,
Henry Doolittle.

Hiram Doty.
Geo. Douglas,
Carter H. Drew,
Taylor Dudley,
D. W. C. Dunwell,
Edward G. Dunford.
Michael Dunning,
Oliver Duprey,
Wm. M. Dwinnels.

Alonzo Eaton.
Benjamin Eaton.
David Ebert,
George Egbert.

Abram S. Elfelt.
Chas. D. Elfelt.
Edwin Elfelt,

Samuel Ells,
Evan Evans,
William Evans.

J. H. Farnham,
Geo. W. Farrington.
John Farrington,
George Farquhar.
Martin Fetcot,
Stark Fielder,
Thos. M. Finch.

S. P. Folsom,
James E. Forbes,
Obed Foote,
Wm. H. Forbes,
B. B. Ford,
Aaron Foster,
Dr. Thomas Foster.

Aug. J. Freeman.
Cyrus Freeman,
Alpheus R. French.
J. Frick,
A. V. Fryer,
Jonathan Frost.
A. G. Fuller,

A. Findley,
Charles Fisher,
Edwin Folsom.

G. A. Fournier,
Richard Freeborn,
William Freeborn,

David L. Fuller,
J. E. Fullerton.
Luther Furnell.

Louis Gabott,
W. B. Gardner,
Leander Garniot,
Napoleon Gautier,
J. Gehon,
R. B. Gibson,
Nathan Gilpatrick,
Francis Gingras,

Joseph Gingras,
Harlow Glass,
Hugh Glenn,
John Glenn,
Joseph Gabin,
Emanuel Goode.
George Goodhue,
Isaac N. Goodhue,

James M. Goodhue.
Aaron Goodrich,
Aaron Gould,
Baptiste Gravelin,
Joseph B. Gravelin, (?)
Edward Greenwood,
Vetal Guerin,
Matthew Groff.

John T. Halsted.
Eberle Handley,
John J. Haney,   •
Frederic Hardy,
George Harris,
E. A. C. Hatch.
Jacob Haus,
Nathan Hawley.
John Haycock.
Edward Hays.   .

John H. Henderson,
John Henley,
Charles J. Henniss,
J. S. Hinckley,
W. W. Hickox,
Rev. Chauncy Hobart,
Samuel C. Hoffman,
John Holland,
David Hopkins,
Peter Hopkins,

B. F. Hoyt,
Lorenzo Hoyt,
William Huggins.
James Hughes,
Richard M. Hughes.
George Humphrey.
James M. Humphrey,
C. S. Hurtick.
B. E. Hutchinson.

B. F. Irvine,

Jno. R. Irvine.

Henry Jackson,
Louis Jacques,
Noel Jaillard.

Dr. Wm. H. Jarvis.
William Jebb,
John W. Johnson,

Parsons K. Johnson,
D. H. Jones.
P. Jones.

S. F. Kauffman.
C. Keller,
Egidus Keller,

Isaac M. Kelley,
M. N. Kellogg,
Robert Kennedy.   .

Philip Kessler,
James Kirkpatrick.
R. C. Knox.

Isaac La Bonissier,
Joseph Labisinier,
John B. LaChappel,
Jacques Lafaire,
Joseph Lafond,
Henry A. Lambert,
Henry F. Lander,
Charles Landres,
Henry Lansing.
Hyele Lapierre,
Peter Lapointe.

Timothy Lareau,
A. L. Larpenteur,
E. N. Larpenteur,
Leonard H. LaRoche.
Louis Larrivier,
William Lauver.
Daniel Lavalle,
Xavier Lavalle.
Andrew Lavier,
W. G. LeDuc,
Michael Lemay.

John Leslie.
Sylvester Leveridge.
John Lewis.
James Lock.
B. W. Lott,
S. B. Lowell,
Jesse Lowe,
S. B. Lowry,
C. P. V. Lull.
John Lumley.

Asa Mallory,
James Marley,
J. Cole Martin,
Henry F. Masterson,
Ira Mathews,
Lewis Mathews,
Thornton Mathews,
Hugh McCann,
Charles McCarron,
V. B. McCulloch,
Nathaniel McLean,
John McCloud, Jr.,
R. West McCloud,

John P. McGregor,
George McGuire,
John McKee,
Edward McLagan,
R. McLagan,
Alex. R. McLeod,
Patrick Meagher,
Rev. J. A. Merrick,
Abraham Michier,
John P. Miller,
Amadis Mini,
A. M. Mitchell,
Lot Moffet,

Joseph Monteur,
Ferdinand Monti,
George W. Moore,
Amable Morin,
Wilson C. Morrison,
Joseph Mosher,
Peter Mullin, .
Alfred Murphy,
Luke Murphy,
D. C. Murray,
Elijah Murray.
Wm. P. Murray,
Nathan Myrick.

Rev. E. D. Neill,
R. R. Nelson,
P. S. Newell,

Geo. C. Nichols,
Jacob J. Noah,
Wm. H. Nobles,

William Noot,
Anson Northrup.

Charles H. Oakes,
David Oakes,
Thomas Odell,

Fred. Olivier,
Louis M. Olivier,
Louis M. Olivier,

David Olmsted,
John P. Owens.

Stephen Palmer,
Antoine Papin,
J. P. Parsons,
Rodney Parker,
Edward Patch,
David Patnande.
Peter Patoille,

E. M. Patridge,
Louis Paul,
Charles Peltier,
Olivier Peltier.
James Phillips,
Wm. D. Phillips,
Allen Pierce,

Jesse H. Pomeroy,
Columbus J. Post,
Calvin Potter,
Dr. T. R. Potts.
Simon Powers,
A. C. Prentiss,
Bart. Presley.

Patrick Quinn,

William Quinn,

Wm. L. Quinn.

Alex. Ramsey,
Justus C. Ramsey,
John Randall,
Wm. Randall,
Wm. H. Randall,
S. R. Randolph,
George Rath(?)
J. W. Reed,
Thomas P. Reed,

Edmund Rice,
Henry M. Rice,
Orrin W. Rice,
David Richardson,
Wm. Roach,
Louis Robert,
Nelson Robert,
A. B. Robinson,
Flavien Roberge,

Barnard Rogers,
John Rogers,
Daniel Rohrer,
Joseph Rondo,
O. H. Root,
Isaac Rose,
Charles Rouleau,
Peter Rougard,
Wm. Russell.

Henry Sage,
Edward J. Sanford,
M. St. Cyr,
Hyacinthe St. Cyr,

Marshall Sherman,
Hile Sikwalen, (?)
George Simon,
Orlando Simons,

Charles Sperry;
Nathan Spicer,
Daniel Steele,
W. M. Stees,

Oliver St. Martin,
Nicholas Schidalin.
Ellis Scofield.
C. P. Scott,
J. W. Selby,
B. L. Sellers,
W. H. Semmes.
Samuel H. Sergeant,
Damas Semper,
C. E. Shaffer,
Nelson Shattuck,
George Shaver,
Geo. W. Shaw.
A. L. Shearer,
Erwin Y. Shelley,

J. W. Simpson,
Edward Sloan,
Levi Sloan.
J. N. Slosson,
Chas. K. Smith,
J. W. C. Smith.
George H. Snider,
John Snow,
J. C. Somerville.
J. R. Spangler,
Jackson Spears.
George Spence.
John B. Spencer,
R. M. Spencer,
Spier Spencer.

Arthur Stephens,
James Steward,
Wm. H. Stiles,
Daniel Stinchfield,
Kennedy Stuart,
David Stockbarger,
Edway Stoughton,
Daniel Strickland,
Sandford Strickland.
Peter Sturgeon,
Andrew Swartz.
Edward Sweeny,
Dr. W. W. Sweney.
Charles Symonds.

William Talkin,
John Tanner,
D. C. Taylor.
Wm. Taylor, (col'd,)
John F. Tehan.
Benj. S. Terry,
John C. Terry.
Robert Terry.
Francis Thibeault.
Benj. Thompson.
G. W. Thompson,

Jas. Thompson, (col'd,)
Joseph Thompson.
Rinaldo Thompson.
Socrates Thompson.
James H. Thoms,
Jeremiah Tibbets.
Albert Titlow,
Henry L. Tilden,
Wm. H. Tinker.
C. S. Todd.
W. M. Torbet,

Geo. Townsend,
C. F. Tracy,
H. W. Tracy,
Fred. W. Travers,
John Trower,
Matthew Troy,
Balthasar Tschudi.
John Tschudi,
E. Inman Turner.
Amable Turpin,
Hugh Tyler.

Pierre Vadnais,
Hugh I. Vance,

Mamime Vanace,
Robert Van Holmes.

Joseph Villaume.

L. B. Wait,
W. S. Wait,
John A. Wakefield.
George Welles,
Henry Wellington.
Martin Wells,
E. G. Wentall,

J. A. Wheelock,
Wallace B. White,
Joel E. Whitney,
Rev. T. Wilcoxson.
Alex. Wilkin,
Amherst Willoughby,

Morton S. Wilkinson.
Samuel Williams,
George Wisgarver,
Simeon Woodbury,
Warren Woodbury,
I. P. Wright.

Anthon Yeorg.

Peter Yoss.

Benjamin Zanger.

SOME ETHNOLOGICAL NOTES.

To one curious enough to study the nationalities which form

our diverse population, the above list is suggestive. For instance, the absence of German names is singular. There are scarcely half a dozen German names on the list. It would appear that the Germans are not a pioneering people, as the Yankees are, or the French. But very shortly after this date the German population increased very rapidly. Look at the census of 1857, given under its proper date. A very large proportion of the names there are German, and are recognized as among our most "solid" and well-to-do citizens, owners of fine business blocks, and comfortable residences, and gratifying bank accounts. Many of them came here, too, poor emigrant boys. By the census of 1860, fully one-third of the foreign-born population were Germans, and the proportion must have increased since then.

Another thing that will strike the observer, is the large percentage of French names on the census of 1850. The Canadian and Swiss French at one time composed the bulk of the population here, and their descendants are still a numerous class. They formed, during the first six or eight years of the city's history, an important element in our midst. Goodhue mentions in 1849, or 1850, that a knowledge of the French language was indispensable to a trader, just as German or Scandinavian salesmen are considered necessary now. The stores then bore the sign, "ici on parle Francaise," just as they do now, "Norske Handels," or "Deutsche Handlung," to attract those classes. Indeed, such a large infusion of French blood in our population, left its impress upon it unmistakably—and a valuable ingredient it was, too.

"WAIT TILL AFTER THE PAYMENT."

The *Pioneer*, of August 1, says: "One would suppose, by the promises about town, that the Indian payment would square every debt in Minnesota, but the 'debt of nature.' Every reply to a dun is, '*after the payment*.'" This used to be the great word among slow payers, for years, showing how much the early business and prosperity of Minnesota depended on the Indian trade, and how the money disbursed unloosed things generally. Afterwards this was changed to, "wait until the logs come down," showing that the lumber business had become the disbursing patron of society. Now-a-days the phrase is, " wait 'till after harvest," an evidence that agriculture is now our main hold.

The *Pioneer*, of August, contains the following : " Rev. Mr. BRECK respectfully invites the attendance of the citizens of Saint Paul at the house of H. A. LAMBERT, Esq.,* on Friday, the 2d day of August, to take into consideration the erecting of an Episcopal church in Saint Paul."

The result of this conference was that a society was organized, and the corner-stone of " Christ church," on Cedar street, laid on September 5, following.

The Town Council, or Board of Trustees, was urged by the *Pioneer* to have the *stumps pulled out of Third street!*

" Brick at the kiln sell at $6 per thousand. We noticed that several good brick buildings are about being erected near the upper landing."— [*Pioneer*, July 4.]

" The people in Saint Paul seem to express a general wish that no building should be erected on the margin of the bluff, or the south side of Bench street. That street when built up, will be unsurpassed for beauty. There ought to be a row of elm shade trees planted on that side; thus Bench street may soon become one of the pleasantest promenades in the world."—[*Pioneer*.]

The *Pioneer*, of August 22, says : " The roar of Saint Anthony Falls was more distinctly audible at Saint Paul than we ever heard it. The 9 o'clock reveille of Fort Snelling came rolling down the channel of the Mississippi as though it were meant for some stray soldiers." How quiet the village must have been those summer evenings. The roar and noise of a great city makes a marked contrast now.

The town about these days, and indeed for several years

---

* HENRY A. LAMBERT was a brother of DAVID LAMBERT, before noticed. He was Judge of Probate for several years, and died in 1863. Though an active supporter of the Episcopal church at the time noticed, he afterwards embraced Catholicism.

later, used to be thronged with Indians, both Chippewas and Dakotas, some buying goods, others begging, stealing, selling peltries, etc. That their presence in such numbers was a nuisance, any early resident can testify. Occasionally some curious scenes were witnessed, the "begging-dance," the "war-dance," and other orgies being frequently performed on the streets, in expectation of some reward from bystanders. On July 9, sixteen chiefs and head men of the Yanktons, in full feather, "sang a wild song," says the *Pioneer*, in front of Gov. RAMSEY's house, to an audience of villagers. Some of the red-skins were accomplished thieves, vide the following from the *Pioneer*:

"SUBSTITUTION OF A THIEF.—The other day, an Indian came into the jeweler shop of Mr. SPICER, on Robert street, and, while there, stole a watch. Mr. SPICER followed him up street, to Mr. FULLER's store, and collared him, and, seeing no one to assist, left the Indian standing by the side of Mr. FULLER's store, while he went inside to get some one to help him search the body of the Indian. Returning in two or three minutes, he found an Indian standing in the same spot, in the same attitude he had left the thief in, his blanket philosophically folded around him, but he was *another Indian*, who had taken the place of the thief during SPICER's absence—while the thief himself slipped around the house and fled."

While the buck Indians were loafing about, smoking, drinking fire-water (if they could get it) and begging money, the squaws did all the labor. The *Pioneer* records, at various times, items explaining scenes familiar to all the old-timers:

"Quite a novel team, consisting of four squaws dragging a train with a load of provisions on it, made its appearance in Saint Paul, on Thursday last."

"The Sioux women are certainly very industrious, and do a great deal of hard labor. It would no doubt be a novel sight to most of the eastern people to see women paddling their log canoes across the Mississippi, heavy laden with wood or fence-posts, and then cording it on the bank, or carrying large posts up a steep bluff for a number of rods, with a child a year or two old on their shoulders. Yet these things are of daily occurrence at Saint Paul, Sunday *not* excepted."

"Many of the children carried about by the Sioux women on their shoulders, look remarkably pale. Like many other phenomena, it is more easy to observe than explain, as the children appear to be in perfect health."

Miss BREMER, the Swedish novelist, when in Saint Paul, gave much attention and considerable space in her book, to the social condition of the Indian females. She says, among other things:

> "'What estimate may be given of the morals and character of the Indian women in this neighborhood?' inquired I, of a lady in Saint Paul, who had resided a considerable time at this place.
>
> "'Many are immoral, and cannot be much commended; but others again there are who are as virtuous and blameless as any of us.'"

Few will be disposed to blame the poor " pagans." who read the following picture of their destitution, from the *Pioneer*, of November 21. 1850:

> "The other evening, near the upper landing, we saw a revolting spectacle—a Sioux squaw, evidently famished, gnawing the head of a dog she had found dead! Judge of the sufferings of these poor wretches. thus gloating over offal and refuse."

It would have been better, of course, for the morals and health of the town, if these creatures, with scarcely any distinction between right and wrong, had not been always hanging around. ready and anxious to earn money by almost any means. but that evil seemed inseparable from the condition of society then.

In the earlier days of our city, the Indians helped to make quite a trade in one way and another. They used to supply the local market with fish, wild fowls, venison, bear meat, cranberries. and other wild fruit, furs and products of the forest generally : besides moccasins, bead-work. and trinkets of that class. They would always demand gold and silver for their products, which they would reinvest in ammunition, blankets. flour, cutlery, or anything they fancied. They were pretty sharp at a bargain, too, be it known, and scarcely ever got overreached. Most of the earlier merchants of our town learned a few Sioux words sufficient to trade with, and some acquired quite a knowledge of the tongue. After the Indians came to know and have confidence in any one, they would trade with him and take his word unhesitatingly. hence became good customers. Those who could not talk Sioux, resorted to signs. The hand held up meant one dollar. A finger out-

stretched signified ten cents.   The finger bent was five cents, and
so on.   Yet the Indians were nearly all sly thieves, and would
pilfer at every chance.   They were inveterate beggars, too.
Give one of them any food, money, or other gratuity, and next
day he would probably return to ask the same favor, and bring
a dozen of his companions with him.   They had any amount
of impudence, too.   They would bolt into a person's kitchen
without knocking, perhaps several " bucks" at once, and beg
or help themselves in a very free manner.   Ladies recently
from the east, not knowing their habits, would thus be fright-
ened into hysterics almost, and the visitors would enjoy the
fright hugely.   Those who understood their habits better,
would tell them " puck-a-chee." [be gone.] in a severe tone,
when they would leave.

There were several of the older stores in our city, which
were the recognized headquarters of these red men, and were
known far and wide among the tribes as such.   LARPENTEUR'S
was one of such places.   Here, at various times, the writer
has seen most of the principal Sioux chieftains of all the bands,
(except, possibly, the Missouri River bands,) and most of the
principal warriors.   At any hour of the day when one might
call there, during any of the early years, several of the plumed
and painted lords of the forest could have been seen.   They
were, apparently, always taciturn and reserved, but any one
in their confidence could have drawn them out in conversation
quite freely.   Had the writer at that time had an opportunity
to collect from these prominent chieftains some account of
their adventures in war and the chase, of their ancestors, and
the traditions of the race, it would have been more interesting
than a romance.   It will ever be regretted that no one did
this, since it is now, perhaps, too late to do so.

Both the Sioux and Chippewas used to frequent our streets
in those days, (the former the most numerous,) yet, although
the two tribes had a mortal hatred for each other, no collision
ever occurred, except the one noted in the events of 1853.
The faces of LITTLE CROW and HOLE-IN-THE-DAY, the two
renowned chieftains of those nations, were very familiar to all
our old residents.   Excellent portraits of each are given in

this volume, and an interesting chapter might be written on each, could the space be spared.

Some of these Indians had very curious names. It is known that, frequently, they name children from some incident, or some physical peculiarity. Two of the Indians who used to be regular frequenters of LARPENTEUR'S, in early days, and were well known to old settlers, had names whose translation would be shocking to ears polite.

LITTLE CROW.

The Indians unacquainted with English, used to greet their acquaintances with the exclamation, "*how*," or "*ho*." Finally, this was taken up by the boys, and became a regular pass-word with them. When raising glasses to take a nip, they would always say, "ho," as a preliminary—a custom that obtained for years, was carried by them into the army, and produced many amusing incidents. One day, an English tourist, who was stopping at the Fuller House, quizzing everything through his eye-glasses, observed this custom, and inquired of a friend, "What makes 'em say 'o when they go to drink? Does it 'urt 'em?"

POLITICAL MATTERS.

The month of August, 1850, was characterized by a strife for Delegate to Congress. No *party* nominations were made. but the election of candidates for Delegate by the different conventions was solely based on personal preferences. Hon. H. H. SIBLEY, Col. A. M. MITCHELL, DAVID OLMSTED, and N. G. WILCOX, were severally put up by their friends. The two latter gentlemen declined, and left the contest to Messrs. SIBLEY and MITCHELL. The campaign was short. the election occurring on September 2.

Of the bitterness of the contest. Gov. MARSHALL, in his annual address before the Old Settlers of Hennepin county, February 22, 1871, said:

"There were no party issues; it was more a contest of rival Indian trading interests. Messrs. SIBLEY and RICE had been partners with the great house of PIERRE CHOUTEAU & Co. A quarrel arose, and, in the fall of 1849, Mr. RICE left the firm. Gen. SIBLEY was then Delegate in Congress. As the election approached, in 1850, Mr. RICE's friends put forward Col. MITCHELL, and supported him with all their great influence. The fears and jealousies of the people were aroused against Mr. SIBLEY on account of his connection with the Fur Company. The cry was *Anti-Monopoly!* I wish those who deprecate party dissensions now-a-days, could know something of the bitterness and personal abuse of that contest in 1850, in which party lines were not drawn. They would not think that well defined party contests were so great an evil."

THE VOTE IN SAINT PAUL.

The election was held "at the house of ROBERT KENNEDY"— afterwards known as the Central House.

The vote was as follows:

Delegate to Congress.

Henry H. Sibley............151	Col. A. M. Mitchell........ 153

Representatives.

P. K. Johnson.............. 126	*H. L. Tilden* 191
Benj. W. Brunson 150	*Edmund Rice*.............. 157
Justus C. Ramsey.......... 204	J. J. Dewey 142
Wm. P. Murray............. 121	Henry Jackson............. 100

Commissioner.

And. Godfrey.............. 130 | R. P. Russell.............. 165

Assessors.

Sam. J. Findley............ 148		Thos. P. Reed.............. 103
George C. Nichols......... 135		I. I. Lewis................. 154
Albert H. Dorr 135		S. H. Sergeant............. 143

County Treasurer.

J. W. Simpson was elected without opposition.
  Those in *italics* elected.

The following minor officers were also elected, mainly without opposition :

Supervisors of Roads.—Lot Moffet, Alpheus R. French, and Pierre Bottineau.

Constables.—Warren Chapman and Warren Woodbury.

School Trustees, Dist. No. 1.—B. F. Hoyt, A. R. French and Rev. J. P. Parsons.

School Trustees, Dist. No. 2.—J. R. Brown, E. D. Neill, Vetal Guerin.

The vote in the Territory on Delegate was: SIBLEY, 649 : MITCHELL, 559.

FREDRIKA BREMER VISITS SAINT PAUL.

In October of this year, the distinguished Swedish authoress, Miss FREDRIKA BREMER, visited Saint Paul. In her entertaining book, "Homes of the New World," about 40 pages are devoted to her visit. A few extracts must suffice :

"Scarcely had we touched the shore, when the Governor of Minnesota and his pretty young wife came on board and invited me to take up my quarters at their house. And there I am now, happy with these kind people, and with them I make excursions into the neighborhood. The town is one of the youngest infants of the Great West, scarcely eighteen months old; and yet it has in a short time increased to a population of 2,000 persons, and in a very few years it will certainly be possessed of 22,000; for its situation is as remarkable for its beauty and healthiness, as it is advantageous for trade.

"As yet, however, the town is but in its infancy, and people manage with such dwellings as they can get. The drawing-room at Governor RAMSEY'S house is also his office, and Indians and workpeople, and ladies and gentlemen, are all alike admitted. In the meantime, Mr.

RAMSEY is building a handsome, spacious house upon a hill, *a little out of the city*, [quite *in* the city now, madame,] with beautiful trees around it, and commanding a grand view of the river. If I were to live on the Mississippi, I would live here. It is a hilly region, and on all sides extend beautiful and varying landscapes.

"The city is thronged with Indians. The men, for the most part, go about grandly ornamented, with naked hatchets, the shafts of which serve them as pipes. They paint themselves so utterly without any taste, that it is incredible."

CHURCH ITEMS, AGAIN.

"The Episcopal church was raised on Tuesday last. There are now in the course of construction three churches, the Presbyterian, Baptist, and the Episcopal. These, with the Methodist and the Catholic, will make five churches in Saint Paul."—[*Pioneer*, October 10.]

In a few days from this time, the First Presbyterian church, rebuilt on its late site, (corner Third and Saint Peter streets,) was finished so as to be used for worship. A bell—the first church bell in Minnesota—was hung in its belfry late one Saturday evening, just in time for the opening services of the new chapel the next morning. Impatient to test its tones, the bell was rung even at that late hour, a source of satisfaction to the Christian people, and of wonder to the pagans, who heard the solemn tones of the church-going bell, pulsating over the "valleys and rocks," for the first time. Only two days subsequently, another bell arrived on a steamboat, an unexpected present from a gentleman in Ohio, and the first one was sold to the Market Street Methodist Episcopal church, in whose belfry it long did good service.

BUILDING OF A COURT-HOUSE AND JAIL.

VETAL GUERIN, the liberal donor of so many lots and blocks for public and church purposes, having deeded to the county a square of land for the purpose of a court-house and jail, on January 16, the County Commissioners advertised for plans for the same. Dr. DAVID DAY, Register of Deeds, and Clerk of the Board, produced the most acceptable plan for a court-house, and was paid $10 for the same. In order to raise the money for the erection of these buildings, the County

Board ordered the issue of some county bonds. When they were put on the market, they were known as the "*Cross Bonds*"—but this is a pretty tough story, and we will not give it unless it is substantiated by the affidavit of at least three disinterested and reliable witnesses.

THE COURT-HOUSE.

The court-house was commenced some time in November, 1850, and completed for use in the following year. FREEMAN & DANIELS were the contractors. It was, for those days, a fine building. It has now been used a quarter of a century, and has played an important part in the history of this generation, not only in law, but the numerous political conventions, public meetings, and even religious services. Three years ago a commission appointed by the city and county, procured plans for a new building, a joint city hall and courthouse, which will probably be built in due time, and the old " historic" court-house removed. In view of this fact, the County Board procured the engraving of the old building herewith, to preserve its familiar " face" in our annals.

The building of the jail was not, however, commenced for

several months after this date. It was a small log building,
weather-boarded, and about as secure as if made of paste-
board. This jail, which was the first prison erected in Minnesota, stood there until 1857, when the present one was built.
Before it was torn down, JOSEPH W. PRINCE, then Deputy

THE OLD JAIL.

Sheriff, got an architect to make the drawing and plan of it,
which now hangs in the County Auditor's office, and which
he gave to the county. The County Board very kindly ordered
an engraving to be made of it, which is given herewith.

MINOR TOPICS.

The *Pioneer* speaks of a restaurant being started, as one
of the "new improvements of the city."

"Last Wednesday, the 14th day of November, Mr. DODD first got
Capt. DANA's steam saw mill in operation, at our lower landing, and
sawed some maple plank, which are to be used in constructing a table to
be placed in the Territorial library; they being the first boards ever
sawed by steam power in Minnesota.—[*Pioneer*, November 28.]

On November 4, a special election was held for a Justice of
19

the Peace, vice JOHN A. WAKEFIELD, resigned. ORLANDO SIMONS* received 192 votes, electing him over LOT MOFFET, who received 39 votes.

Mr. WAKEFIELD had been a member of the Illinois Legislature, in early years, and was author of a "History of the Black Hawk War." He removed, after the resignation noticed above, to Iowa, and, finally, to Kansas, where he died, in 1872. During his residence in Saint Paul, he was proprietor of the Tremont House, and frequently lectured on temperance.

"School District No. 3, was organized on the evening of the 18th inst. P. K. JOHNSON was elected Clerk. The trustees were instructed to employ HENRY DOOLITTLE as a teacher, at $40 per month. A tax of $300 was voted to defray the cost of the school house, and the expenses of the school."—[*Pioneer*, November 28.]

"It is thought advisable by some of our villagers, that we have this winter a series of practical instructive lectures, and that a small admission fee be charged—the proceeds to be applied for the purchase of a fire engine in Saint Paul.—[*Pioneer*, December 12.]

The last steamboat departed this fall on November 18, making a season of 239 days, during which 102 boats arrived, or an average of one boat in two and one-third days.

December 26, 1850, was proclaimed by Governor RAMSEY, as a day of public thanksgiving, the first ever observed in Minnesota. But there were no turkeys to be had those days!

JOURNALISTIC.

On November 25, the *Pioneer* issued a prospectus for a daily, which was not issued in fact until May, 1854, though

---

* ORLANDO SIMONS was born January 18, 1824, at Lyons, Wayne county, New York, and removed to Elmira when young, where he was educated, at the Elmira Academy, Chester Academy, in Chemung county, &c., and afterwards read law. In 1849, Judge SIMONS, in company with another young lawyer of that locality, (HENRY F. MASTERSON, Esq.,) removed to Saint Paul, arriving on June 20. The law firm of "MASTERSON & SIMONS" was then formed, which continued until a few months ago, full quarter of a century, being the oldest law firm in the State. In 1850, Judge SIMONS was elected Justice of the Peace, and, in 1854, elected first City Justice, holding that office six years, during which time his firm administration of its duties was a wholesome promoter of law and order. In the spring of 1875, he was appointed Associate Judge of the Common Pleas Court of Ramsey county, and, in November, 1875, elected for seven years more.

the rapid growth of the Territory and the liberal support given to newspapers seemed to warrant it when first proposed.

On December 10, appeared the first number of the *Minnesota Democrat,* established by Col. D. A. ROBERTSON.[*]

About the same date, the *Chronicle and Register,* the union of the two journals of that name, after several real or ostensible changes in ownership and editorial management, passed into the editorial control of CHARLES J. HENNISS, a young man of talent, but dissipated and unscrupulous. He was a native of Ireland, but had latterly lived in Philadelphia. He died in 1856.

---

[*] Col. DANIEL A. ROBERTSON was born in Philadelphia, Pennsylvania, May 13, 1813. He was descended from Highland Scotch ancestry. At the age of 18, he went to New York, where he studied law, and was admitted to practice in 1839. In the meantime he removed to Ohio, where he engaged in journalism, being editor of the *Cincinnati Enquirer, Mount Vernon Banner,* &c. In 1844, he was appointed United States Marshal for the State of Ohio, which office he held four years. He was a member of the Constitutional Convention of Ohio from Lancaster county, and resigned, after holding the office three months, to come to Minnesota, which he did in the fall of 1850. He soon after established the *Minnesota Democrat,* which became one of the leading journals of the Territory, and was subsequently merged in the *Pioneer.* Col. ROBERTSON at one time owned a large amount of real estate, but after the panic of 1857, its value was seriously reduced. During the period of "good times," Col. R. used his means in accumulating one of the finest private libraries ever brought into Minnesota, consisting of several thousand volumes in different languages, which he afterwards sold to the State University. He also visited Europe in 1856-7, and devoted his leisure in studying various scientific and historical subjects in which he is interested. He was elected a member of the House of Representatives in 1859-60, Mayor of Saint Paul in 1860, and Sheriff in 1863, serving in this office two terms. He was also a member of the Board of Education several years, and performed much valuable labor for our public schools. The Historical Society and Academy of Natural Sciences are also largely indebted to him for their success. He also organized the first Grange of Patrons of Husbandry in the United States, presenting to it a valuable library of books. Col. ROBERTSON has always been a close student of history, political and social science, and other subjects, on some of which he has lectured with much success.

CHAPTER XX.

EVENTS OF THE YEAR 1851.

THE GOODHUE-COOPER RENCONTRE—STRUGGLE OVER THE LOCATION OF THE CAPI-
TAL—SAINT PAUL WINS—A CASE OF INDIAN JUSTICE—LOCATING THE CAPITOL
BUILDING—VIEW IN SAINT PAUL IN 1851—THE RED RIVER CARAVANS—THE
FUR TRADE, &C.—THE EARLY STAGE, MAIL AND EXPRESS BUSINESS, &C., &C.

THE second Territorial Legislature met on January 2. in
the three-story brick building, just completed. of RICE
& BANFIL. which stood where the Third street entrance of
the Metropolitan Hotel now is. and was burned down in the
winter of 1856–7. Saint Paul was represented this year by
WM. H. FORBES and J. McC. BOAL. in the Council. and
JUSTUS C. RAMSEY. BEN. W. BRUNSON. H. L. TILDEN. and
EDMUND RICE in the House—a gallant delegation it was, too.
and a brave fight they made to keep the Philistines from moving the Capital from Saint Paul.

SCRAPS.

"There was a warm election last Monday, for Justice of the Peace.
n Saint Paul. JOHN F. TEHAN had 119 votes, and BUSHROD W. LOTT
had 182 votes, and is elected."—[*Pioneer*, January 2.]

"Our exchange papers perversely spell Saint Paul, *Saint Pauls*,
and Minnesota, *Minesota*. Half the paragraphists in the United States
have scarcely sense and intelligence enough to pick up chips in the
door-yard!"—[Ib.]

HOLE-IN-THE-DAY. the Chippewa chief. addressed the Legislature and citizens. on January 10. at the First Presbyterian
church. His object was to represent the starving condition of
his tribe. and solicit relief for them. His speech is described
as eloquent and pathetic. A committee was appointed to secure the aid desired. and some donations were obtained.
There is no doubt but that the Chippewas were suffering from
starvation. that winter. Many died. and cases of cannibalism
were reported by the papers.

THE GOODHUE-COOPER RENCONTRE.

On January 16, GOODHUE printed a savage and bitter article on "Absentee Office Holders," in which he inveighed, with all the ferocity of his pen, against Col. MITCHELL and Judge COOPER, for absenteeism, &c. On the latter, he was particularly severe, using such terms as, "a sot," "a brute," "an ass," a "profligate vagabond," &c. The article closed as follows :

"Feeling some resentment for the wrongs our Territory has so long suffered by these men, pressing upon us like a dispensation of wrath— a judgment—a curse—a plague—unequalled since the hour when Egypt went lousy, we sat down to write this article with some bitterness, but our very gall is honey to what they deserve."

Of course, such an article as this could not fail to produce a personal collision between GOODHUE and the friends of COOPER, (he himself was absent,) and scarcely had the paper been distributed through the town, ere it bore its natural fruits in a rencontre on the street. Eye-witnesses give a minute account of it, in affidavits afterwards published, but it can only be briefly recited here. GOODHUE had been in the Legislature, and started down street, in company with a friend. After leaving the building a few steps, they met JOSEPH COOPER, a brother of Judge C., who at once advanced and struck at GOODHUE. Both then drew pistols. "Col. GOODHUE (one account says) having a single-barrel pistol, and COOPER a revolver." Some parleying ensued, when Mr. COOPER declared, "I'll blow your G—d d— brains out." Sheriff LULL here ran up, and, commanding the peace, disarmed the parties, but it seems COOPER still retained a knife, and GOODHUE another pistol, with which they renewed hostilities. Some one endeavored to hold GOODHUE, which gave COOPER an opportunity to stab him in the abdomen slightly. GOODHUE then broke away, and shot COOPER, inflicting quite a serious wound on him. COOPER again rushed on GOODHUE, and stabbed him in the back, on the left side. Both parties were then led away, and their wounds dressed, neither being fatally injured. Col. GOODHUE seems to have acted on the defensive during the whole rencontre. In subsequent issues of his journal, he charges that it was a "conspiracy on the part of his enemies to murder him for political revenge, and that COOPER was a mere tool, spurred on by others," &c.

The affair produced great excitement throughout the city, and was angrily discussed, pro and con, by the friends of each. A public meeting was held and resolutions passed, a plan that always acts as a sedative on excited communities, and peace once more reigned.

The Legislative session of 1851 was a stormy one, and several exciting questions tended to divide the members. One of these was

THE LOCATION OF THE CAPITOL,

and other public buildings. Twenty thousand dollars had been appropriated by Congress the summer previous for a Territorial prison, and, by the same act, authority was given the Governor and Legislature to expend the appropriation of $20,000 provided for in the Organic Act, for Capitol buildings. The vexed question was, where should the Capitol be built? Several places competed for it, and the struggle was close and hard contested. Finally, by the vigorous efforts of some of our leading men, a compromise was effected. The Capitol was to be erected at a central point in the town of Saint Paul, the penitentiary at Stillwater, and the University, (incorporated that session,) at Saint Anthony Falls. Thus each were satisfied for the present, and all went merry as a marriage bell for six years, when a rival Saint got jealous of our city, and aspired to Capitolean honors. Gov. MARSHALL, in his address before quoted, says Saint Anthony got the best of this tripartite agreement.

Another question that stirred up strife was the apportionment, and several members bolted their seats, barely leaving a quorum for the rest of the session.

Another subject of controversy was the election of State printer. J. M. GOODHUE, of the *Pioneer*, was the regular Democratic candidate, but Col. ROBERTSON, of the *Democrat*, and HENNISS & VINCENT, of the *Chronicle and Register*, expected to gain votes enough between them to secure the

printing. When the ballot was taken. however. Mr. Goodhue's side proved the strongest. This proved a death-blow
to the moribund *Chronicle and Register.* It soon gave up
the ghost. and a new Whig organ was projected. a sort of
joint stock journal, which, however. was not finally got into
operation until September following.

The session seemed to have been a turbulent one throughout.
Col. Jno. P. Owens afterwards wrote of it:

" The session finally closed on the night of March 31, which was a
day and night of excitement, such as we have never seen since in Saint
Paul, and never desire to. Hundreds of citizens were about the streets
and public places, armed to the teeth, and ready, upon the slightest
provocation, to shoot down their fellow-citizens, who opposed them.
Feelings of enmity. bitterness and hatred were engendered between
citizens during that session of the Legislature, and particularly during
its last days, which extended even into family relations. and were not
eradicated for months, and even years subsequent."

LEGISLATION AFFECTING SAINT PAUL.

Excepting the location of the Capital at Saint Paul, there
was not much legislation this session, affecting the town. Its
corporate limits were extended. however. so as to " include
the additions" recently filed by Bazille & Guerin. Robert
& Randall. Hoyt, and Whitney & Smith. " Saint Paul
Lodge. No. 2. I. O. O. F.," was incorporated. and " Saint
Paul Division. No. 1, Sons of Temperance." This was, to
enable these societies to purchase property, which they soon
after did.

The act providing for the erection of the Capitol in Saint
Paul. enacted that the work should be done under the super-
vision of a board of three commissioners, who should receive
$3 per day. etc. The election for these officers took place on
April 17, resulting in the choice of D. F. Brawley and
Louis Robert. of Ramsey county: E. A. C. Hatch. of
Benton county: and J. McKusick. of Washington county.
The Governor was ex-officio a member and chairman of the
board. The board organized on May 19. Charles F.
Tracy was elected clerk.

CURRENT ITEMS.

Navigation opened quite early in the spring of 1851. The "Nominee" arrived on April 4, and soon business and immigration were quite brisk.

The *Pioneer* refers in one or two places to "*Monk Hall.*" This was a sort of bachelors' retreat, kept in a building corner of Fort and Eagle streets, and was a sort of free and easy club house and political headquarters for the stags of those days. Some poetical genius about that time wrote a few verses for the *Pioneer,* under the heading, "The Last Night at Monk Hall," one or two extracts from which give perhaps a fair view of the inside proceedings:

"Come, pass round the bowl—we'll drink while we stay—
Although from the Hall, ere the dawning of day,
Our order forever wide scattered will be,
No more to *unite* in our wild revelry.

*　　*　　*　　*　　*　　*　　*　　*

Bright spirits of heaven, and spirits of hell,
With their thin airy forms and sulphurous smell,
Flit wildly around us and join in our glee,
Sing to our dancing and bend with us the knee."

Monk Hall was moved across Fort street, and is still standing—the same building used for many years as a store by LUTHER H. EDDY.

A CASE OF INDIAN JUSTICE.

If I have not related already too many stories about Indians, there is one curious incident, almost romantic in its character, that should be chronicled here. One day this spring (April 4) some boys came into town, and reported to Judge GOODRICH that a dead Indian was lying in the bushes back of the brick yard, about where Alderman GATES A. JOHNSON's residence now is. Sheriff LULL, being notified, summoned the Coroner and one or two other officials, and proceeded to the spot. Sure enough, there was a dead Winnebago Indian, who was well known about here those days, by the name of "Dr. Johnson," and examination showed that he had died from a stab. As he had been seen a day or two before with some other Winnebagoes, the probability was that they had given him his quietus, and, as there was an encampment of those Indians not far off, a file of soldiers was sent to the spot, to arrest the murderer, if he could be found. They proceeded to the encampment, and found some of the red-skins quietly cooking their evening meal. The officer in charge of the squad asked one of them, *Che-en-u-wzhce-kaw*, or STANDING LODGE, if he knew anything of how their brother "Lo" had met his end, when STANDING LODGE very coolly and unconcernedly replied, " I killed him !" On further questioning him, he stated that the dead Indian had committed some crime or offense, which, according to the Indian code, merited death, and that he, the speaker, had been selected to give him his quietus, which he did.

There seemed no other way than to apprehend the self-confessed murderer, and ascertain whether the statutes in such case made and provided would not cover his crime, as equally as if one white man had killed another. So the officer told STANDING LODGE to come along. The Indian made no objection, but very quietly followed the officers to town. That night he slept in Sheriff LULL's carpenter shop, the jail not being tenable yet, and made no efforts to escape. Next day, a sort of preliminary examination was held. STANDING LODGE never denied his guilt, but always said, "I did it," when asked. Some urged to let him go, as it would only expose the county to considerable cost to imprison and try him, and it was scarcely worth while to take note of all the quarrels and murders among the Indians, as they were occurring every few days, and but few cared much how many Indians were killed. Others thought it ought not to be passed thus. Finally it was agreed to lay the case over until the grand jury met, about the middle of the month, and meantime, to avoid boarding Mr. Lo at public expense, to dismiss him on his own recognizance. This was explained to STANDING LODGE, and he promised to be on hand when court met. He asked how many days it was, and, on ascertaining, took some sticks and cut notches in them, one for each day, and depositing them in his pouch. started off to join his band. who were hunting muskrats.

Scarcely any one ever expected to see STANDING LODGE again.   But. sure enough. on the first day of court. there he was. sitting on the steps. awaiting his fate. whatever it might be.   BILLY PHILLIPS. the Prosecuting Attorney, was unable to attend to business all that week. so the grand jury did nothing.   Yet the Indian was in attendance promptly every day. and slept at night on the shavings in LULL's shop.   Had he run away. no one would have objected. but he said he had given his word to be there. and must do so.   He even complained. finally. that he was not tried.

Finally the case was called by the grand jury. and. though opposed by some. an indictment was found and returned. The case was never brought to trial.   It was shoved over to the September term. STANDING LODGE meantime being out at large. on his own recognizance. with his bundle of notched sticks as an almanac showing him what day to return.   When the September term began. he was again on hand. but Judge GOODRICH. finding there was no intention to prosecute him. ordered the case to be dismissed.   STANDING LODGE was informed he could go his way.   He shook hands with the officers as unconcernedly and stolidly as ever. folded his blanket around him. and marched off. an imperturbable stoic.   There was really something noble about the fellow. a poor pagan and murderer. though he was. and the incident serves to illustrate one of the curious phases of our early days.

WHITE BEAR LAKE NOTICED.

"A company of young men from Saint Paul, went out to see the country around White Bear Lake, one day last week.   The lake is about 10 miles from Saint Paul, and is six miles long by two or three miles wide.   They represent it as a fine country, the land good and much timber.   They saw many deer, and killed ducks and pheasants.   It is on the east side of the river, and is subject to entry."—[*Pioneer*, April 10.]

GEORGE W. MOORE. the venerable abbot of the Custom House. was one of this party.

LOCATION OF THE CAPITOL BUILDING.

The board of building commissioners did not find a site for the Capitol very easily. Several blocks were offered to them, but defective title, or other considerations, induced their refusal, until June 27, when CHARLES BAZILLE offered block six, Bazille and Guerin's Addition, which was accepted. A warranty deed, consideration $1, was given for the property. It does *not* revert to the giver, as has been reported, if the seat of government is moved.

A plan made by N. C. PRENTISS was chosen. It certainly does credit to his talent. The contract for the building was let for $33,000, but it cost in the end over $40,000.

THE CHARTER ELECTION

occurred on May 6. Party lines were not closely drawn, like our city elections at present—personal issues holding the scales mostly. The following is the vote:

President.....R. Kennedy 146	A. L. Larpenteur....138
	Egidus Keller..........148	*J. E. Fullerton*......143
Members	*Firman Cazeau*........145	J. R. Irvine..........126
of	*Wm. Freeborn* 148	L. H. LaRoche........124
Council.	*R. C. Knox*............154	Chas. S. Cave........122
	Wm. H. Randall........142	G. W. Farrington....130
Recorder.....Henry A. Lambert......140	Wm. D. Phillips.....135

Those in *italics* elected.

SCRAPS.

The *Democrat,* of May 27, has the following items:

"The Council has elected JOHN F. TEHAN, Esq., to the office of Town Marshal. Mr. T. will make a good officer."

"Our citizens are beginning to think of the importance of providing sidewalks for the streets most traveled. As a temporary and cheap pavement, two-inch plank answer."

"About 40 Sioux squaws, with canoes, have been at work on the Mississippi for some days past, driving logs. They receive for their services about a dollar a day each. They are very expert canoe paddlers."

"Our citizens were visited on Tuesday last by a company of 20 or

CORNER OF THIRD AND ROBERT STREETS, IN 1851.

more juvenile Sioux, from LITTLE CROW's band, who danced the ·beggar-dance' in different parts of town. The young red-skins, from 5 to 18 years of age, presented a grotesque appearance. They were naked and painted."

The *Pioneer*, of this date. refers to a Mr. CLUTE. who was in town endeavoring to procure subscriptions enough to build a telegraph from Galena to Saint Paul, $27,000 being required. The amount could not be raised, and the line was not built until 1860.

The District Court of Ramsey county (Judge GOODRICH) was held that spring in Mazurka Hall. The roof was fire-proof. but not water-proof. a heavy rain deluging the·court while in session, and rendering umbrellas necessary.

The rapid influx of strangers and growth of the town. caused unprecedented activity in real estate, property doubling sometimes in one week, says the *Pioneer*. and cautions every-body against the speculative mania and too much inflation.

The first Minnesota paper published outside of Saint Paul. the *Saint Anthony Express*. appeared during the latter part of May.

A HISTORICAL PICTURE.

A short time ago, Dr. J. J. DEWEY presented to the Histor-ical Society. a daguerreotype view of the corner of Third and Robert streets, taken in the spring of 1851. It was enlarged by the photographer. C. A. ZIMMERMAN. and the Ramsey County Pioneer Association ordered it to be engraved for this work.

This is certainly a historical picture. The white frame building on the left. is the same one, I believe, that is now used as a saloon by Voss—the old Haggenmiller place. then occupied by WM. DUGAS. The log cabin on the right was the law office for several years, of L. A. BABCOCK. and others. FINCH, AUERBACH & SCHEFFER's store now occupies that spot. The cabin next to it. was occupied at the date mentioned. as a cigar store and confectionery, by BARTLETT PRESLEY.* and the wing in the rear was his dwelling. The

---

* · BARTLETT PRESLEY is a native of Offerberg, Germany, and came to the United States when eight years of age, settling in Saint Louis. He entered mercantile life very

frame beyond this (about where NOYES BROS. & CUTLER's wholesale drug store now is) was JOHN M. CASTNER's boarding house, and the small building next to that, was a meat shop. WILLOUGHBY & POWERS livery stable appears in its

BARTLETT PRESLEY.

old place. The large building on the extreme right was OLMSTED & RHODES' old store. The house seen between these

---

young, ultimately engaging in the grocery and fruit business, in which he has remained over thirty years. In 1843, he removed to Quincy, Illinois, and was there married. At a subsequent date, he removed to Galena, and, in 1849, to Saint Paul. He here commenced business in an humble way, and, by industry and application, in a few years built up a very extensive business, and acquired a fine competence. Mr. PRESLEY was an Alderman from 1870 to 1874, and Chief Engineer of the Fire Department for six years. To his zealous labors in that office is largely owing the efficiency of our present department. Mr. PRESLEY is now, undoubtedly, the oldest merchant in Minnesota, having been continuously in business here since 1849. He enjoys the esteem and confidence of a wide circle of friends.

buildings, in the distance. was J. C. BURBANK's residence.
and the church on the hill. was the First Baptist church, then
just built.   What could better show the growth of our city
than this picture?

There was quite a flood in the river again this summer.   On
June 26. it reached its highest altitude, being only six inches
lower than the great flood of 1850.

It made steamboating brisk.   The *Pioneer*, of July 3. speaks
exultingly of " eight steamboats having arrived in one week."

About the middle of May, a war-party of Sioux, who were
sneaking about in the Chippewa region, near Swan River.
discovered a Chippewa who had a keg of whisky.   He escaped, leaving his keg behind.   The captors drank the contents, got gloriously drunk, and, in this condition, attacked
some teamsters, who were wagoning goods from Saint Paul
to Fort Ripley.   They killed one, Mr. ANDREW SWARTZ, of
this city—a very worthy man—and went off, leaving his body
in the road, not molesting any of the goods.   A force of soldiers from Fort Ripley pursued the murderers, but did not
overtake them.   The Sioux, subsequently, delivered up five
of the guilty ones, and, while they were being taken to Fort
Ripley for trial, the guard fell asleep, and they escaped.

THE EARLY STAGE, MAIL AND EXPRESS BUSINESS.

The papers, in July, speak of an express line being established between Saint Paul and Galena, by J. C. BURBANK.
As the stage, express and transportation business is so allied.
we will endeavor to briefly sketch their rise and growth at this
time.

The first stage ever run in Minnesota Territory, was by AM-
HERST WILLOUGHBY and SIMON POWERS.   Mr. WILLOUGHBY.
who is a Vermonter by birth, was an old stage driver and
manager—went to Chicago in 1828, and drove in that region
for 20 years.   In the fall of 1848. he came to Saint Paul
·· prospecting." and soon determined to embark in the stage
business here.   He went back to Galena, and in the spring
returned with his partner, SIME POWERS.   They had a nice
span of horses, and a two-seated open wagon, but not much

else. They commenced running this from Saint Paul to Saint Anthony, daily, and sometimes made two trips daily. They ran until September, when their business increased so that they put on a four-horse open spring wagon, that would carry 14 passengers. They ran this conveyance until winter set in. They then ran a line from Saint Paul to Prairie du Chien, over the new road mentioned on page 249, via Stillwater, Hudson, Menominee, Black River Falls, Sparta, &c. They ran this route in the winter season for four winters. The first winter the traveling was very rough. There were no regular stations to stop at, and at night they would sometimes encamp on the snow.

When the spring of 1850 set in, they resumed their four-horse wagon to Saint Anthony, and continued all that season. This year, ROBERT KENNEDY ran a line to Stillwater, and, afterwards, WILLOUGHBY & POWERS put on a line to that place.

In the summer of 1851, WILLOUGHBY & POWERS brought to Saint Paul and put on their line, the first Concord coach ever ran in Minnesota. It is still in use in the Minnesota Stage Company's stock somewhere. Up to the close of this season, they had had no opposition in their business, but, during the fall of 1851, LYMAN L. BENSON and a Mr. PATTISON, came from Kalamazoo, Michigan, where they had been in the livery business, bringing a large outfit. In the spring of 1852, they put on an opposition line to Saint Anthony, called the " Yellow Line." WILLOUGHBY & POWERS' coaches were red, and it was generally termed the " Red Line." A furious opposition sprang up. WILLOUGHBY & POWERS, who had hitherto charged seventy-five cents for fare, reduced their price to a quarter, and, finally, to ten cents, as did also the yellow line, and the latter soon put on an opposition coach to Stillwater also. The war between the red and yellow lines was one of the curious phases of that day. Perhaps some of our readers may remember, when they landed at the levee, how the wordy contest was waged between the rivals. Bishop WILLOUGHBY says the other line had more money than he, but he " always beat them at sassing."

This rivalry, with varying success, continued two seasons or more. In the meantime, WILLOUGHBY & POWERS had increased their rolling stock to eight Concord coaches, and had built up a large livery business besides, at their well-known old stand, corner of Fourth and Robert streets. In 1854, they made a compromise with PATTISON & BENSON, the latter buying off their Saint Anthony line. WILLOUGHBY & POWERS had also, in the meantime, opened, and still ran a line to Shakopee, &c., and also ran the Stillwater branch.

WILLOUGHBY & POWERS soon after (1855) divided their business. W. retaining the livery part, and P. taking the stage lines, which he carried on about two years longer, and then sold out to ROBERT GIBBENS, who was killed at Birch Coolie in 1862.

In the meantime (about 1856) PATTISON, BENSON & WARD, as the firm now was, sold out their business to ALVAREN ALLEN and CHARLES L. CHASE, of Saint Anthony. ALLEN & CHASE extended the lines to the Upper Mississippi, got several mail contracts, and ran them about three years, when they consolidated with J. C. BURBANK and Capt. RUSSELL BLAKELEY's line, the whole forming a copartnership called the "Minnesota Stage Company," of which J. C. BURBANK was the general manager, and Mr. ALLEN superintendent of stock and running arrangements. C. L. CHASE, not long after, sold out his interest to JOHN L. MERRIAM. Col. ALLEN remained a couple of years, when he also withdrew.

The "winter route" down the east side, was run for two or three winters by WILLOUGHBY & POWERS, when, in 1853, M. O. WALKER & Co., of Chicago, got the winter mail service contract, and put on a line down through Minnesota and Iowa, to Dubuque. WILLOUGHBY & POWERS then discontinued their line. The manner in which WALKER ran his line is given in newspaper comments hereafter. WALKER ran his line until 1858–9, when J. C. BURBANK & Co. got the winter mail contract.

In the winter of 1855, J. J. BRACKETT ran an opposition line to Dubuque, via Lakeville, Owatonna and Austin.

In 1854–5, WM. NETTLETON established a line of stages to

20

Superior, which, about 1857, was carried on by C. DOBLE, and soon after was bought out by the Minnesota Stage Company.

At the mail letting in 1850, Hon. H. M. RICE was awarded the contract for the mail from Saint Paul to Prairie du Chien, twice a week during the summer, and once a week during the winter. The compensation was $800 a year. In 1852, this contract was assigned to J. C. BURBANK. A Mr. ORMSBY, of Prairie du Chien, also had, at the same time, a mail contract from that place to Black River Falls. This was also assigned or sublet soon after to Mr. BURBANK.

The history of the Minnesota Stage Company and that of the Northwestern Express Company, are so closely identified, to write the one is almost to give both.

ORIGIN OF THE EXPRESS BUSINESS.

A few paragraphs back, mention was made of the establishment, by J. C. BURBANK,[*] of an express business from Saint Paul to Galena, in connection with the American Express Company, which was running to the latter point as its western terminus. Mr. BURBANK was himself the pioneer messenger of his express. During the summer he ran on the steamer "Nominee," and the next winter made the first trip in that

---

[*] JAMES C. BURBANK was born in Ludlow, Windsor county, Vermont, 1822, and removed to New York in 1831. During his boyhood he worked on a farm, picking up such schooling as he was able, from winter to winter, and, more or less, earning his own living and educating himself. Whatever success he has achieved in life, has been owing to his own efforts and energy.

Mr. BURBANK came to Saint Paul in 1850, and, after trying the lumbering business without success, started the express business, as given fully in this chapter. The growth of the immense business first inaugurated by him, occupied his time and capital until 1867, since which year he has devoted himself to the insurance, banking, railroad and other business. He was one of the early members and warmest promoters of the Chamber of Commerce, which has done so much for our city, and was its president from 1869 to 1871. He has also embarked largely of his capital in the construction of the Saint Paul and Sioux City Railroad, of which he has been a director for several years. He was an active organizer of the Saint Paul Fire and Marine Insurance Company, in 1866, and has been its president and financial manager since its organization, and its remarkable success has been largely owing to his sagacity and foresight. In 1873, Mr. BURBANK led the way in the construction of the street railway, and was president of the same for some time. In fact, there is scarcely a worthy enterprise in our city which he has not aided with capital and personal effort. His career presents a striking instance of what energy and integrity will accomplish—starting in life a poor boy, and at present one of the wealthiest and most honored men in our State.

business from Saint Paul overland. He started from Saint
Paul on the 24th of November, after the close of navigation.

and traveled the Knowlton road, before mentioned, to Prairie du Chien, etc., and thence to Galena. He also had the sub-mail contract on that route, from ORMSBY, of Prairie du Chien, as related before—his mail consisting of one bag. The amount of express matter entrusted to him, on his first trip, he carried in his pocket. He continued these trips through the winter. The whole receipts for express carried that winter—although they were made regularly—would not have paid one messenger's board.

In the summer also he, ran alone, doing the whole agency and messenger business himself, making weekly trips between Saint Paul and Galena on the old steamer "Nominee."

• Saint Paul was then a small village of hardly 2,500 or 3,000 inhabitants, and there were but few settlements on the river, but, with a firm faith in the future, Mr. BURBANK diligently set himself to work to sow the seeds and foster the germs of an express business in what he foresaw was to be a great and populous State. Much of his business at first consisted in filling orders at Galena for merchants in Saint Paul and on the river. In 1852, he formed a partnership with W. L. FAWCETT, who, however, found it too hard work for too poor pay, and he retired from the business in about six months. Then ED. HOLCOMBE, a steamboatman, went in with him, taking the end of the route between Galena and Prairie du Chien, which he ran for the winter of 1852–3, when he got discouraged. But BURBANK still pressed on, running the route himself, and gathering about him a large and increasing business. To eke out the express business, however, he took CHAS. T. WHIT-NEY, since deceased, into partnership, and went, in 1853, into the forwarding business at the upper levee in STEELE's old wharf-boat. Indeed, the business was so large, that when, in 1854, the wharf-boat was moved from the upper to the lower levee, it seriously affected the *business* of upper town, which at that date was even ahead of lower town.

In 1854, the express business had reached such dimensions as to justify the employment of regular messengers and officers at all the principal towns, and, therefore, the Northwestern Express Company, (BURBANK & WHITNEY,) was first duly organized, and the business grew apace, in both its branches, forwarding and express. In 1856, Mr. WHITNEY, whose health was failing, sold out his interest in the firm to Capt. RUSSELL BLAKELEY, who had been connected with the old Galena Packet Company. This was a decided acquisition to the business, and, with two such enterprising and go-ahead, determined men, it took a new start. An office was opened in Saint Paul, in LeDUC & ROHRER's old stand, (where Ingersoll's Block now is.) In May, 1855, C. W. CARPENTER entered the service of the company, as local agent. In 1857, E. F. WARNER was engaged in the Saint Paul office, and has remained in that business ever since, being now local agent of the American Express Company.

An event soon after occurred, which led the firm to engage in the stage business. Previously to 1856, Mr. BURBANK had depended, for the winter conveyance of his express matter, on the famous, or rather in-famous, Walker line. But, in January, 1857, disgusted with his wretched service, and, in one case, his utter refusal to adhere to the terms of his contract, BURBANK & COMPANY determined to do their own carriage, and put on a line of stages between Dubuque and Saint Paul by the interior route, via Decorah, Iowa. Although they originally intended only to carry express matter, they soon put on passenger coaches, and, though they had no mail contracts at that time, ultimately pushed WALKER's slow coaches off the road, as passenger vehicles on this route.

The passenger business having largely increased on this and other routes, Mr. BURBANK made a bold strike for the mail contracts in Minnesota, which had been generally monopolized by WALKER, and, at the general letting in April, 1858, was fortunate enough to be the successful bidder for the down-river mail. In the fall of that year, the company stocked up jointly with ALLEN & CHASE, on the route to LaCrosse, which latter had now become the nearest railroad terminus, and, in the spring of 1859, the Minnesota Stage Company was formed by consolidation with ALLEN & CHASE, and the Minnesota Stage Company's coaches were put on the route from Saint Paul to Saint Anthony, and from Saint Anthony to Crow Wing,

&c., securing the mail contracts owned by the ALLEN & CHASE line. In the summer of 1859, they also bought out the Still-water route from GIBBENS, and the Superior route from C. DOBLE, and the chief stage business of the State became cen-tralized in the new company. In the spring of 1860, Col. JOHN L. MERRIAM,* who was a partner of Mr. BURBANK in the forwarding business, bought out the interest of ALLEN & CHASE in the stage company, and, for more than seven years, Messrs. BURBANK, BLAKELEY & MERRIAM constituted the firm, and carried on the express and stage business as joint partners. At the next Government letting, soon after, this company got all the mail contracts on stage routes in Min-nesota, amounting in the aggregate to about 1,300 miles of staging, besides some 300 miles more of pony routes. The stage business now had grown to such proportions on their hands, that the express business had become a minor consider-ation, and, in 1863, they sold out to the American Express Company all the express territory south of Saint Paul, retain-ing for themselves all north of that point. The large propor-tions to which the staging business had grown may be inferred from the fact, that, in the winter of 1865, they worked over 700 horses, and employed over 200 men.

It is due to these three gentlemen—and especially to the senior partner, Mr. BURBANK, from whose early struggles and tenacity of purpose all the subsequent large business of the firm sprang—to say that their entire business management, as public carriers, from first to last, was distinguished by a lib-

---

* JOHN L. MERRIAM was born at Essex, Essex county, New York, in 1828. While a very young man, he exhibited those pushing, energetic, business qualities, which have since made him so successful. He engaged in the iron trade when a mere boy, and was elected Treasurer of Essex county in 1857. He carried on a large business of various kinds, until his removal to Minnesota in 1861, which he did in order to become a partner of J. C. BURBANK and Capt. R. BLAKELEY in the stage and express busi-ness. He also then, or soon after, engaged in the banking, railroad, manufacturing, transportation and other enterprises, all of which, by his sagacity and good manage-ment, have been highly successful. In 1870, Mr. MERRIAM was elected, (in a district politically against him,) a member of the Legislature, and re-elected in 1871. Both these sessions he was Speaker of the House, and rendered signal service to his constitu-ents. Col. MERRIAM is known as one of our most enterprising and valuable citizens—one whose unblemished character and social qualities have gained the esteem of all.

erality, fairness and justice in all their dealings, which have
been rarely, if ever, paralleled, and that the people of Minnesota are more indebted to them than to any other agency for
pushing out our network of mail communications all over
the State and frontier. They chalked out more new roads,
and built more bridges, than any other hundred or thousand
men in the State.

THE TRANSPORTATION BUSINESS

growing out of these connections, was another feature of the
trade which sprang from such humble beginnings. The firm
of J. C. BURBANK & Co. had done, up to this time, a very
heavy forwarding business, but Capt. B. transferred all his
interest in that branch to J. C. & H. C. BURBANK & Co., who
were largely engaged in the grocery and commission trade also.
In the winter of 1858-9, Capt. B. was in Washington, when
RAMSAY CROOKS, (father of our Col. CROOKS,) agent of Hudson's Bay Company in New York, asked Senator RICE how he
could arrange for the transportation of their goods to Hudson's
Bay, via Minnesota? Mr. RICE told him that Capt. BLAKELEY
was then in the city. An interview was secured, and Mr.
CROOKS appointed J. C. & H. C. BURBANK & Co. his agents.
Capt. BLAKELEY went up to the Red River, that winter, and
examined it, and thought it could be navigated. The next
season, the "Ans. Northrup" was taken out and got to running. Capt. EDWIN BELL, of this city, ran her in 1859, and
first built wing-dams on that river. The boat was not a very
good one, but the firm purchased it, and entered into a contract with Sir GEORGE SIMPSON, Governor of the Hudson's
Bay Company, to transport their goods for the Red River
Settlement, (now the Province of Manitoba,) from Montreal
or New York, through the States, making Saint Paul the
headquarters, which had previously been done via York Factory, in Hudson's Bay. This contract covered a yearly ton-
nage of four to six hundred tons, and was by this firm continued
four years, during which they built the steamer "International," being the first steamer successfully navigated on the
Red River of the North. The business thus inaugurated has

been of untold advantage to the State. It now employs seven steamers, 15 barges, and a large number of men. During the season of 1875. 74,000,000 pounds of freight was carried.

THE RED RIVER TRADE.

The *Democrat,* of July 19, 1851, notices the arrival of the annual caravan of Red River carts, 102 in number. This was always an important event for our merchants in early days. Indeed, the rise and growth of the Red River trade forms a chapter of our pioneer history, which is too important to omit. and may well be given here.

Beginning of the Trade.—Prior to the year 1844, the import of goods, and export of furs, of the flourishing Red River Colony, was through the circuitous and difficult Hudson's Bay route, navigable only two months in the year, and beset with many dangers. In that year, NORMAN W. KITTSON, our well-known pioneer. established a post at Pembina, in connection with the outfit of the American Fur Company at Mendota. and invested some $2,000 in furs, which were transported to the latter point in six " Pembina carts." the latter returning loaded with goods. This venture did not prove remunerative—in fact. occasioned a loss of some $600. The next two years' operations involved a similar, or greater loss. but the trade increased, and, notwithstanding the opposition and even the persecution of the Hudson's Bay Company. which was enraged at seeing its monopoly interfered with. Mr. KITTSON's venture was promising of great results. In 1850, the trade had increased so as to involve a consumption of goods to the extent of $10,000, and a possible proceeds of furs of some $15,000. Five years later, the Pembina Outfit engaged an expenditure of $24,000, with a return of furs of nearly $40,000, and the firm of FORBES & KITTSON was this year (1851) organized (" The Saint Paul Outfit") to carry on the supply business. When Saint Paul sprang into being. in 1849. the terminus and supply depot was shifted here, and in early days was an important source of gain to our city.

The Pembina Carts.—The shipments of furs from that region were. for some 20 years. made in the curious vehicle

known as a " Red River cart," or Pembina cart. This was
a two-wheeled concern, of somewhat rude workmanship, constructed of wood and leather, without a particle of iron, and
would carry 600 or 700 pounds. They generally cost about
$15. In this cart was fastened an ox or pony, geared with
broad bands of buffalo hide. One driver would manage several of these carts, simply guiding the head ox or pony, the
rest being tied to the tail of the preceding cart. The axles
were innocent of grease, and their creaking was horrid ; a
caravan in motion could be heard for miles, almost, in still
weather. The drivers of these carts were also a study. Nearly
all of them were swarthy, half or quarter-breeds, or *Bois
Brules*, as they were termed, and dressed in a costume, a
curious commingling of civilized garments and barbaric
adornments. They were usually clad in coarse, blue cloth,
with a profusion of brass buttons, and a red sash girt around
their waists. Add to this a bead-worked cap, and an Indian's
moccasins, and you have a fair picture of the Red River half-
breed. They presented, also, a curious commingling of races,
the old Scotch, English and French settlers having married
with the Crees and Chippewas, and crossed and recrossed until
every shade of complexion, and a babel of tongues, was the
result.

The distance between Pembina and Saint Paul, by the nearest traveled route those days, was 448 miles.* The caravan
would generally start early in June, as soon there was sufficient pasturage for the cattle, and the down trip would generally consume from 30 to 40 days, arriving here early in July.
An average day's travel was 15 miles. At night the caravan
would encamp at some spot where wood and water was convenient, and draw up the carts so as to form a " corral." Sentinels were always on watch at night, to guard against attacks
from hostile Indians, or horse-stealing raids. The men subsisted, during their journeys, on game, and *pemmican*. The
latter is a preparation of buffalo meat. It is dried, pounded
into shreds, and stuffed into a bag made of buffalo hide, into

---

* This was via **Otter Tail** and **Sauk Rapids**. During some of the earlier trips, the
trail was via **Big Stone Lake** and **Traverse de Sioux**.

which melted tallow is poured, forming one solid mass. This will keep a long time. and, though tasting somewhat *fragrant*, to one unused to it, is a great favorite with Red River men, and half-breeds generally.   It used to be kept for sale in Saint Paul, in early days.

While the caravan was in the city, disposing of furs and making purchases. which generally consumed some days, the carts were usually encamped on the prairie above the city. (toward the trotting park.) and their bivouac was a scene worth visiting, for its novelty and picturesqueness.   For some days the streets of our city would be filled with these strings of carts, constituting, to the stranger. or to one who had never before seen them, a curious sight.   Accompanying the caravans were generally a number of horsemen, the skilled buffalo hunters of Red River, mounted on their tough, shaggy ponies.

In 1844, as noted above. the number of carts on the route between Mendota and Pembina, was only six.   The number increased each year, until. in 1851, it was given at 102.   In 1857. about 500 came to Saint Paul.   In 1858, 600.   In 1859, 1860. and 1861, the number somewhat decreased. as a steamer was running on Red River, which drew off part of the freighting trade. and decreased the land transportation to 216 miles. J. C. & H. C. BURBANK & Co. having established a line of freight teams connecting with the steamer.   In 1863. owing to the Indian troubles. only 275 carts came through.   It was not until about 1867. when the Saint Paul and Pacific Railroad was running to Saint Cloud. that the caravans of carts ceased making their annual pilgrimages to Saint Paul.   Saint Cloud was then for a year or two their terminus. but the increase of freight lines and, in a short time more, the completion of the Northern Pacific Railroad to Red River, quite drove these primitive prairie carts from their old route. and thus caused the decline and fall of one of the most singular features of our transit from the rude traffic of the wilderness to a well-organized commercial community.

The Fur Trade.—Closely connected with this subject is the fur trade. one of the most valuable auxiliaries to our prosperity in early days.   The importation from Red River

by the cart line, was very large, and formed the main supply
of the fur marketed at Saint Paul. Indeed, four-fifths of the
furs and all the robes came from this region. The amounts
handled during the earlier years were reported as follows:

1844	$ 1,400	1858	$161,022
1845	3,000	1859	150,000
1846	5,000	1860	186,000
1850	15,000	1861	198,000
1855	40,000	1862	202,000
1856	97,253	1863	250,000
1857	182,491		

During 1858, 1859 and 1860, the quantity of furs marketed
did not decrease, as the figures apparently show, but the price
declined largely during the "hard times." Then, too, the
prices of furs fluctuated greatly. Mink sold in, 1857, for 15
and 20 cents. In 1863, it rose to $5 and $7.

Being the natural depot for such a large region, at one time
well stocked with fur-bearing animals, Saint Paul was for
some years one of the largest fur markets in America—perhaps second only to Saint Louis, and the trade of the latter
was mostly in robes, a distinct branch of the traffic. The fur
catch of all of Minnesota, a part of Dakota, and northern
Wisconsin, was tributary to this point. In early days, the Indians and a few professional trappers were about all who
caught furs. As the country became more settled, every squatter eked out his living by trapping and shooting, and the larger
game, bear, deer, elk, wolf, &c., soon became quite scarce.
In fact, every farmer's boy, with cheap patent traps, soon entered the war of extermination against the fur-bearing animals.
Every stream, copse and marsh was trapped, and the result is
that the fur "catch" is yearly becoming less, though still
large. The supply of robes from Red River is annually growing smaller, as the bison is now driven further and further from
the settlements each year.

Value of the Red River Trade.—All of the money received for the sale of these furs would be generally spent in
merchandize in our city, and large sums in addition. Thus
the value of the Red River trade to our city in early days can

be estimated.   Staple groceries, liquors, dry goods, blankets, &c., hardware and tools, household utensils, ammunition and guns, clothing, boots and shoes, glass, sash, farm implements, even threshers and mowers, (in parts,) and, latterly, sewing machines.   In 1863, one house sold $4,000 worth of tobacco alone.   The Red River men, it might be noted, sold and bought for coin only.   They never used currency in dealing.

The Freight Trade with Red River.—The rude Pembina cart line was the pioneer of a very valuable freight and transportation movement between Saint Paul and the Red River settlements, and the very large and profitable trade which our city now transacts with the Red River valley, both this side and beyond the British line, but this is more fully narrated a few pages back.

SMALL SCRAPS.

The *Democrat*, of July 22, has the following items:

"The Masonic Lodge has been removed to Rice and Banfil's Block—the Odd Fellows occupying the adjoining room."

"A picnic party of 14 or 15 ladies and gentlemen went out last week to White Bear Lake, 10 miles north, and spent a day very delightfully at fishing and hunting."

[This is probably the first picnic to White Bear Lake that ever occurred.]

"Yesterday a number of workmen commenced excavating for the foundation of the Capitol."

"Hitherto the people of Selkirk have had but two or three mails a year.   They have now (since July) a monthly mail from Saint Paul."

CHAPTER XXI.

EVENTS OF THE YEAR 1851.—Continued.

THE TREATY WITH THE SIOUX—REJOICINGS OVER THE EVENT—HOW THE INDIANS SPENT THEIR MONEY—CREATION OF A BISHOPRIC—RIGHT REV. JOSEPH CRETIN ARRIVES—PURCHASE OF LOTS FOR A CATHEDRAL—COL. ALEX. WILKIN—MOVEMENT FOR A FIRE DEPARTMENT.

THE great event of the year was the treaty with the Dakotas, at Traverse de Sioux, authorized by Congress last year, by which that nation gave up its title to all the land west of the Mississippi, excepting a small reservation—a domain exceeding 21,000,000 acres! The treaty commenced at Traverse de Sioux, on July 2. All the officials, dignitaries, big men, traders and editors of Minnesota were present, and all the chiefs of the Dakotas. The papers were crowded for weeks with their sayings and doings, to the exclusion of almost everything else. Gov. RAMSEY and Hon. LUKE LEA, Commissioner of Indian Affairs, represented the United States.

THE GREAT EVENT CONSUMMATED.

On July 23, the preliminaries of the treaty were all concluded, and the Indians signed the instrument by which they sold, conveyed and transferred to the pale faces, one of the most glorious domains that nature ever created—signed away their heritage and birthright, and were thenceforth strangers and intruders on their own "ancestral acres."* But sentiment is out of place in this day of progress. The resistless march of empire was doomed to sweep away the red man—it had been so for two centuries on American soil, and the treaty of Traverse de Sioux, another chapter of the mournful epic, called forth, not sadness, but rejoicing.

---

*This may be considered merely the poetical view of the subject. Sometimes, when we have an unusually hard winter, our citizens scout the idea that the Indians were cheated in the sale, and wish they hadn't sold their lands at all!

The news of the treaty was received in Saint Paul, with demonstrations of joy. GOODHUE, with his strong gift of prophesy, broke forth in a strain as exultant as the song of Miriam and the Jewish maidens on the shore of the Red Sea. It thrilled through his pen as follows:

"The news of the treaty exhilarates our town, and it looks fresh, and lively and blooming! It is the greatest event by far, in the history of the Territory, since it was organized. It is the pillar of fire that lights us into a broad Canaan of fertile lands. We behold now, clearly, in no remote perspective, like an exhibition of dissolving views, the red savages, with their teepees, their horses, and their famished dogs, fading, vanishing, dissolving away: and in their places a thousand farms, with their fences and white cottages, and waving wheat fields, and vast jungles of rustling maize, and villages and cities crowned with spires, and railroads with trains of cars rumbling afar off—and now nearer and nearer, the train comes thundering across the bridge into Saint Paul, fifteen hours from Saint Louis, on the way to Lake Superior. Is this a dream? What but a dream, then, is the history of the Northwest for the last twenty years?"—[*Pioneer*, July 31.]

IMMEDIATE RESULTS.

More immediate gain resulted from the treaty, viz.: the circulation of many thousand dollars into the pockets of Saint Paul. The *Pioneer*, of August 14, says:

"Last Thursday was a lively day in Saint Paul. Indians all over town with double-eagles, and Third street, especially, was converted into a temporary horse bazaar. Dogs are also in demand. On Friday every Indian who had a horse was anxious to try his speed. Various contests were witnessed between old wheezing cart-horses, running quarter-races at the north end of Jackson street, in sand ankle-deep. A large multitude turned out to see the races."

GROWTH OF CHURCHES.

Nearly all denominations and sects represented in the town, made rapid advancement this year.

The Wisconsin Methodist Conference of that season, which adjourned on July 3, made the following appointments for Minnesota: CHAUNCY HOBART. P. E.; Saint Paul District. T. M. FULLERTON; Saint Anthony Falls. C. A. NEWCOMB; Point Douglas, to be supplied; Stillwater. G. W. RICHARDSON.

This spring. Christ's church. (Episcopal.) on Cedar street. was completed. and was dedicated by Bishop JACKSON KEMPER. on April 12.   Rev. J. LLOYD BRECK was first rector. followed by the Rev. T. WILCOXSON and Rev. J. V. VAN INGEN. &c.

CREATION OF A BISHOPRIC—CONSECRATION OF RT. REV. JOSEPH CRETIN.

The year 1851 was also a season of great encouragement to

RIGHT REV. JOSEPH CRETIN, D. D.

the Catholics. owing to the creation of a bishopric here. and the arrival of Right Rev. JOSEPH CRETIN.   Since the withdrawal of Father GALTIER. in 1844. as before mentioned. Rev. AUGUSTIN RAVOUX had been in charge of the mission at this place and Mendota.   In 1848 or 1849. the congregation here increased very rapidly.   The little chapel had been enlarged in 1847. and was still too small.   Members came from Saint Anthony, Little Canada, Pig's Eye, and other places, to attend services, which were now held every other Sabbath, in French and English, and finally, Father RAVOUX spent two Sundays here consecutively, going to Mendota on the third. It now became evident that more clerical help must be secured. He urged Bishop HENNI, of Milwaukee, to send this, but that ecclesiastic was unable to do so. It led, however, to the erection here of a bishopric, and the appointment of Rev. JOSEPH CRETIN to the charge. The latter was then in Dubuque, and left at once for Europe, to be consecrated.

"After his departure for France, [says Father RAVOUX, in a sketch in the *Northwestern Chronicle,*] aware of the necessity of securing some lots for the cathedral and other purposes, I bought of Mr. VETAL GUERIN twenty-one (21) lots for $800, and for $100 the lot on which now stands the cathedral. This last I bought of another person, who had already some lumber on the ground for a building. He had bought the same on credit of Mr. VETAL GUERIN for $60. He deeded me that lot for forty dollars ($40) profit. I considered the purchase of the twenty-two lots a very good bargain for the church, as also a good one for Mr. VETAL GUERIN, because it was understood that the cathedral and other buildings would be erected on block seven, and such improvements would increase the value of Mr. VETAL GUERIN's property. The event proved that I was not deceived in my expectation. The Right Rev. Bishop after his return from France, paid the money for the 22 lots and received the deed; I had but a bond for the security of our bargain."

Speaking of Rev. J. CRETIN's struggle to make up his mind whether to accept the bishopric, or not, Father RAVOUX further writes that he did so at the advice of the Bishop of Belley :

"He then gave his consent and was consecrated on the 26th of January, 1851. 'Omnia omnibus factus sum,' was the motto engraved on his seal, and in fact the first Bishop of Saint Paul, like the Apostle of nations, was 'all to all.' All those who have been well acquainted with him are convinced that he constantly walked in the footsteps of Saint PAUL, by zeal, piety, charity, humility, incessant labor and patience in sufferings; not only after his consecration, but also when a priest, when in the seminaire, and in the colleges.

"The Right Rev. Bishop spent yet three or four months in Europe after his consecration, in order to procure some laborers for the extensive vineyard intrusted to his care, and many things necessary for the establishment of a new diocese. On the day of the feast of the Visita-

tion of the Blessed Virgin MARY, the 2d of July, 1851, I had the so long
expected and desired visit of the Right Rev. Bishop, who arrived at
Saint Paul, accompanied by two priests* and three seminarians. To
describe the pleasure I felt at their arrival would be a difficult task.

"The Rt. Rev. Bishop was not much surprised at the poverty of the
Catholic church in Saint Paul, for he had been informed of everything.
From the first, he saw hard labor before him, and, full of confidence in
GOD, was not discouraged.

"He put immediately his hand to the plow, and, faithful to the advice
of our SAVIOUR, did not look behind. He knew for whom he worked,
and, however difficult the task might be, supported by Divine grace, he
was always cheerful. Before the lapse of five months after his arrival
in Saint Paul, he had erected on block 7, in Saint Paul Proper, a brick
building, 84 feet long by 44 wide, three stories and a half high, including the basement. That building became immediately the second
cathedral of Saint Paul, and also the second residence of the Rt. Rev.
Bishop, of his priests and seminarians; and, in a few months after, some
apartments of the basement were used as school-rooms for boys. The
young girls were also to be provided with Catholic schools, and, in
1852, the Sisters of Saint Joseph devoted themselves in Saint Paul to
the holy work of their institute, and they opened their schools on the
property of the church, on Third street. * * * * * *

"The Rt. Rev. Bishop died on the 22d of February, 1857. His illness had been very long and painful, but he always continued to be the
good and faithful servant of GOD, bearing with the greatest patience
all his sufferings. When no more able to leave his room, he almost
constantly had his mind occupied about the flock intrusted to his care;
he would often speak to me on that subject, and write letters to his
friends in order to provide for the diverse wants of his diocese. The
last of these letters, which was addressed to a French Bishop, and left
unfinished, was dated February the 21st, 1857. More than once, when
his sufferings were most intense. I heard him exclaim, 'It is good for
me to suffer for my sins! * * As I cannot work, I, at least, ought
to offer my pains to GOD for the faithful and for all!'

"Were I asked what epitaph ought to be written on his tomb, my
answer would be, let these words be engraved upon it: O GOD! 'the
zeal of Thy house hath eaten me up!'"

FIRST THEATRE IN SAINT PAUL.

During the month of August the drama was inaugurated in
Saint Paul. A portion of the troupe of "Placide's Varieties."

---

* I think one of them was the Rev. JAMES MORAN, who officiated here for a year or
more about that time.

21

of New Orleans, then closed as usual during the summer, wandered to Saint Paul, partly for pleasure, partly for gain, and opened a theatre in Mazurka Hall. GEORGE HOLLAND was manager. One of the papers of the day says: " They performed to full houses for two weeks." Among the plays advertised were, " The Day after the Fair," " Swiss Cottage," " Betsey Baker," " Slasher & Crasher," &c. No very " heavy" pieces seem to have been put on the boards.

AN ENGINEERING BLUNDER.

GOODHUE frequently, in those days, urged measures of local importance, that, with criminal indifference, the public and some of its components, disregarded. Had his advice been followed, we would have had a boulevard along the river bluff, for one thing. The streets of additions would have corresponded with those of Saint Paul Proper, instead of presenting the confused maze of angles and crooks our city map now shows—a perpetual misery inflicted on posterity. Speaking of a quagmire on Third street, between Wabasha and Cedar, he advocated cutting the soil off of all the streets running over the limestone rock, thus making a hard, smooth, dry pavement, unequalled in every desirable quality. Strange to say, this simple proposition, for a cheap improvement, was not acted on. The grade was raised so that the streets *had to be filled in*, at great expense, and thus we have quagmires instead of smooth, rock pavements. At this day, it is hard to say what engineer is responsible for this fossilized stupidity; but, as capital punishment has been practically abolished, even if convicted, no adequate punishment exists.

POLITICS.

Political excitement ran pretty high in the fall of 1851, though perhaps a shade less bitter than the year previous. The *Pioneer* launched its thunderbolts at H. M. RICE and his friends, and C. K. SMITH, Secretary of State. The *Democrat* inveighed bitterly against the Whig office-holders. The *Minnesotian* (just established) fired double-shotted guns at Democratic nominees. Both parties, it seems, were split up

into factions, warring against each other. The Federal office-
holders were at swords'-points, and undermining each other.
The war soon terminated in a batch of resignations and
removals.   Judge JEROME FULLER, of New York, succeeded
Chief Justice AARON GOODRICH.   Capt. ALEX. WILKIN* was
appointed Secretary of State, decapitating C. K. SMITH.   Jo-

ALEXANDER WILKIN.

SEPH W. FURBER received a commission as Marshal, vice
TILDEN, &c.

---

* ALEXANDER WILKIN was born in Orange county, New York, December, 1820. He
was the eldest son of Judge SAMUEL J. WILKIN, who had been a member of Congress,
and was otherwise prominent in his State. ALEXANDER studied law with his father,
and practiced for a while at Goshen.   In February, 1847, he enlisted in the Tenth New
York Regiment for the Mexican War, and was commissioned as Captain. He served
under ZACH. TAYLOR during a part of the war, when ill-health compelled him to return
home, and, meantime, peace was declared, and the army disbanded.   In the spring of
1849, he removed to Saint Paul, arriving here on June 20, and practiced his profession
for some months.   On October 23, 1851, he was appointed United States Marshal, and

WAIFS.

The *Weekly Minnesotian* appeared on September 17. as a Whig organ. JOHN P. OWENS' name appeared as editor, and that of JOHN C. TERRY, as publisher. Its very first number created a sensation. Some severe strictures on Capt. WM. B. DODD, provoked the ire of that gentleman, and a rencontre between him and Col. OWENS on the street, was the result. The *Minnesotian* flourished for nearly 10 years, as a leading and influential journal. It gave up the ghost in 1861.

"We need a jail far more than we do a court-house. The criminal law is almost a dead letter for want of a jail to lock up rogues in."—[*Pioneer*.]

GEO. C. NICHOLS, surveyor, has made a splendid and accurate map of the city of Saint Paul, with its additions, which are 15 in number."—[*Democrat*, Sept. 30.]

[This map was the first map of Saint Paul published. Mr. NICHOLS died April 8, 1853, at Madison, Wisconsin, aged 26 years.]

"Never was a city laid out so badly as Saint Paul. The plat looks as if some accident had knocked all the streets into *pi*. Measures should be taken immediately to straighten them."—[Ib.]

"Last week there were 400 Indians out at Rice Lake, gathering cranberries. They gathered about 250 barrels."—[Ib.]

"The country is full of bears. A band of Sioux Indians killed, in two days, in the neighborhood of Rice Lake, 25 bears. Two were seen within a mile of our office, on Saturday."—[Ib.]

---

served until the PIERCE administration commenced, in 1853. He was an unsuccessful candidate for Delegate that fall, and, in 1860, espoused the cause of STEPHEN A. DOUGLAS. During the Crimean War, Capt. WILKIN visited the allied armies, and studied the art of war before Sebastopol. The experience that he then gained was destined soon to be of great value to him. When the rebellion broke out, he recruited the first company of the First Regiment. He acted with conspicuous bravery at Bull Run, and soon after was commissioned in the regular army. On September 10, he was commissioned as Major of the Second Minnesota, and, on March 21, 1862, its Lieut. Colonel. On August 24, 1862, he was commissioned Colonel of the Ninth Minnesota. After serving on our frontier several months, the Ninth was sent to Tennessee, where it took part in the expedition against FORREST. In the battle of Tupelo, Mississippi, on July 14, 1864, Col. WILKIN was shot through the heart, and died instantly. He was a successful and skillful officer, and one of the most fearless and courageous men that ever lived, although of small and slight physique. The Legislature, in 1868, bestowed his name on one of our western counties.

—Judge WESTCOTT WILKIN, brother of Col. W., is one of the oldest and most esteemed members of the Ramsey county bar. He was elected Judge of the District Court in 1864, and re-elected, in 1871, for seven years.

THE ELECTION

was held on October 14. The result in Ramsey county, (which then included Saint Anthony,) was as follows:

	Old Line.		People's Ticket.	
Councillors....	R. R. Nelson	241	*Wm. H. Forbes*	270
	Wm. Freeborn	248	G. W. Farrington	293
Representatives	Robert Kennedy	247	W. P. Murray	272
	Geo. Burns	217	*J. W. Selby*	293
	Hugh McCann	259	C. S. Cave	273
	Egidus Keller	224	*J. E. Fullerton*	306
	Louis Bartlett	220	Sam. J. Findley	279
Sheriff	Geo. F. Brott	312	Anson Northrup	271
	C. P. V. Lull. (Ind.,) 207.			
Register of Deeds.	L. B. Wait	376	*M. S. Wilkinson*	427
Treasurer	Lot Moffet	362	*Sam. H. Sergeant*	401
Attorney	John W. North	371	*Wm. D. Phillips*	414
County Surveyor.	Geo. C. Nichols	380	*S. P. Folsom*	407
Judge of Probate..	H. Fletcher	361	*Ira B. Kingsley*	424
Co. Com'issioner.	J. Locke	377	*Jo. LaBonne*	419
	Warren Chapman	367	*T. P. Reed*	429
Justices of Peace	Charles Creek	211	*Jacob J. Noah*	236
	Orlando Simons	244	John P. Owens	234

Those in *italics* elected.

TOWN GOSSIP.

The *Pioneer*, of October 30, announces the removal of Secretary C. K. SMITH, and the issue of November 20, records his departure from the Territory, in a terribly denunciatory article. When GOODHUE wanted to "go for" any one, he never beat around the bush, but spoke right out.

"There is a large new bell, a very fine one, just received and hung up in the rear of the Catholic seminary, a present from LOUIS ROBERT. There are now four good bells in Saint Paul, and another coming, for the Baptist church."—[*Pioneer*, November 6.]

" NON-RESIDENT LANDHOLDERS.—Avarice and speculation can overlay an infant town—nay, they oppress larger places, like a nightmare. A non-resident may buy up half-a-dozen lots on Third street, and keep them unimproved. The result is ruinous, perhaps, to the business of the whole street. We want to see these gentry used up in every possible way. * * We wish that no man out of Minnesota could own a foot of land in it."—[Ib.]

The *Pioneer*, of October 16, speaks of a contract for the erection of a four-story hotel on the site of Monk Hall. This was the Winslow House, a building which played an important part in our history, and was burned down in 1862.

" Rev. Mr. RIHELDAFFER, a missionary of the Old School General Assembly, has taken up his residence at Saint Paul, with a view of gathering a second Presbyterian congregation."—[*Democrat*, November 4.]

This was the origin of the Central Presbyterian church, which was organized by Mr. RIHELDAFFER, February 21, 1852, at his residence, eight persons participating—Mr. and Mrs. RIHELDAFFER, Mr. and Mrs. R. MARVIN, Mr. and Mrs. G. W. FARRINGTON, J. D. POLLOCK and JONAS GISE. The church was completed in the summer of 1854. Rev. Mr. RIHELDAFFER resigned in 1864, and was succeeded by Rev. F. T. BROWN, in 1867, and Rev. WM. McKIBBIN, in June, 1874.

" Saint Paul is entirely destitute of means for extinguishing fire. Measures should be taken to form a hook and ladder company, immediately. Should a fire occur, let every citizen repair to it with a bucket of water."—[*Democrat*, November 18.]

" Four Sisters of Charity have arrived from Saint Louis, and will shortly commence teaching a ladies' seminary, in the old chapel."—[Ib.]

" The workmen are putting on the roof of the new court-house. It makes a fine appearance."—[Ib.]

Navigation closed this year on the 20th of November. The whole number of steamboat arrivals was 119.

Rev. J. P. PARSONS, pastor of the new Baptist church, died on November 13, while on his way up the river on a steamer, returning from a visit east, to raise means to finish his church. Mr. PARSONS was a native of Onondaga, New York. He came west about 1837, and settled in Saint Paul, May, 1849, as a missionary of the Baptist Home Mission Society. He was forty-nine years of age.

CHARLES SYMONDS, the first ice dealer in Saint Paul, commenced cutting ice this month. He continued the ice business a number of years, and died in 1873.

" Rev. E. D. NEILL has been appointed by the Governor, Superintendent of common schools for the Territory. An excellent appointment."—[*Democrat*, December 2.]

" Plenty of delightful weather, plenty to eat, plenty to drink, but not a word of news from the States for two weeks past."—[*Democrat*, December 24.]

" The grading of Fourth street and the building of the culvert across Jackson street are so far advanced, that the street will be ready for travel in three or four weeks."—[Ib.]

" A friend informs us that there are about 299 applicants for the few offices in the gift of the Legislature."—[Ib.]

" There appears to be considerable activity in buying and selling town lots. Prices are gradually rising."—[Ib.]

" We have a hard-working, judicious and able town council. They work for nothing, and find themselves."—[Ib.]

" A market house is very much needed in Saint Paul."—[Ib.]

MOVEMENT TOWARD A FIRE DEPARTMENT.

The need of some organized association for extinguishing fires, has several times been noticed. The *Democrat*, of December 24, says :

"Mr. R. C. KNOX is making efforts to get up a hook and ladder company. Let everybody help. * * * A meeting will be held at the upper school house on Saturday evening next, for the purpose of forming a fire company."

Probably this movement of Mr. KNOX and others was the little germ which afterwards gave birth to our Fire Department. Prior to this time, and for three or four years afterwards, indeed, the mode of extinguishing fires was somewhat primitive. Whenever an alarm was given, the whole able-bodied population would rush to the rescue, armed with pails, basins, dippers, tubs or any other utensil that came handy. Generally a raid was made on some grocery, and a few nests of pails confiscated. With these a line would be formed, between the fire and some pond, cistern or stream, and the pails then passed from hand to hand. The writer has seen a line two blocks long thus. The original subscription paper carried around by Mr. KNOX is still in existence. Enough was raised to purchase several ladders. They were somewhat heavy, and, as the "boys" had no ladder wagon, but carried them to fires on their shoulders, they could not have made very fast time, and probably had their patience and zeal thoroughly tried. An amusing incident would occur once in a while, however, that lightened their burdens.   On one occasion, the boys got their ladders out from an alley on Third street, near Wabasha, where they used to store them, and started on the run for a fire on Eagle street.   After making good time for two or three squares, they concluded to seize on any team that happened along.   Just then a countryman drove by with a lumber wagon. R. C. Knox rushed up to him, and, in tones that could have been heard at Pig's Eye, almost, ordered the man to "get down and give up that team !"   Knox, we will state for those who don't know him, is about as large as two ordinary men. The countryman gazed at his huge figure a moment, and, either mistaking him for a ghost or a highwayman, actually leaped out of the wagon and ran for dear life !   Bursting with laughter, the boys seized the team, threw off the wagon-box, and soon had their ladders at the fire.

As but little could be generally accomplished in this way, however, the ladders soon fell into disuse.   They were stored away, and for a time served the free use of painters and carpenters.   After the Pioneer Hook and Ladder Company was organized in 1855, three of them were recovered and became the property of that company, and were used for over 13 years.

In the absence of engines or other apparatus, every imaginable means was resorted to to extinguish fires.   A small house once caught fire about that time, when the ground was covered with damp snow.   Some one gave the word, " snow-ball it out," and it was so deluged with snow-balls by the crowd in attendance, that the fire was put out and most of the house saved.

CHAPTER XXII.

EVENTS OF THE YEAR 1852.

THE TEMPERANCE MOVEMENT—PASSAGE OF A PROHIBITORY LAW—TRAVELING ON DOG-SLEDGES—OUTCOME OF THE MAINE LIQUOR LAW—RATIFICATION OF THE SIOUX TREATY—BRUTAL WIFE MURDER—DEATH OF J. M. GOODHUE—MURDERS BY WHITES—MURDERS BY INDIANS, &C.

ON January 1, a Temperance Convention was held. pursuant to a published call. which was largely attended by delegates. An earnest feeling prevailed. The newspapers contain no report of the proceedings, and only indirect allusions to it. Participants say, however, that strong ground was taken for a Maine prohibitory law, and threats to form a temperance party of the prohibitory element did not receive due consideration.

THIRD LEGISLATIVE ASSEMBLY.

The third Legislature met on January 7, in "Goodrich's Block." on Third street, below the Merchants. The Ramsey county members this year were: *Council.*—Geo. W. FARRINGTON, L. A. BABCOCK, and WM. H. FORBES, the latter being President. *House.*—CHARLES S. CAVE, WM. P. MURRAY, SAM. D. FINDLEY, JEREMIAH W. SELBY, and J. E. FULLERTON. Four of our present citizens represented other localities that year—N. W. KITTSON, Pembina; JNO. D. LUDDEN, Marine; Dr. J. H. MURPHY, Saint Anthony; and Dr. DAVID DAY, Long Prairie.

On January 19, Hon. H. L. TILDEN, Secretary of the Council, died. Mr. TILDEN was a native of Ohio, and came to Minnesota in 1849. He was a member of the House in 1851, and had been appointed Marshal of the Territory that year. He was a lawyer by profession, and a gentleman of fine ability. He was buried by the Odd Fellows, of which he was a member, and the two houses attended his funeral in a body.

Gov. RAMSEY read his annual message to the joint convention of both houses, and the citizens, in the Baptist church, "on the hill," then recently finished.

TRAVELING ON A DOG-SLEDGE.

The *Pioneer*, of February 19, says:

"Dr. RAE arrived in Saint Paul on the 14th instant, having performed the journey from Pembina to Sauk Rapids, some 500 miles, in ten days. It was the continuation of a journey from a station on McKenzie's River, about 2,500 miles beyond Pembina. Both journeys were performed on snow-shoes. He was sent last spring to the Arctic coast in search of FRANKLIN, by the Hudson's Bay Company."

The "dog-sledge" used by Dr. RAE, in his long journey over the snow, was presented by him to the Historical Society, as a memento, and may still be seen at their rooms. This was the only mode of winter traveling between Saint Paul and Pembina, until 1859, when BURBANK & BLAKELEY'S line of stages commenced to run to Fort Abercrombie.

A Sauk Rapids correspondent of the *Pioneer*, January 8, says:

"The honorable members elected to the House and Council, from Pembina, viz.: Messrs. KITTSON, ROLETTE and GINGRAS, arrived at Crow Wing on Christmas eve, in 16 days from home, stopping two days at Red Lake by the way. Each had his cariole, drawn by three fine dogs, harnessed tastily, with jingling bells, and driven tandem fashion, at 2:40 at least, when put to their speed. They usually traveled from 30 or 40 miles per day, and averaged about 35 miles. They fed the dogs but once a day, on the trip, and that at night, a pound of pemmican each. On this, they draw a man and baggage as fast as a good horse would travel, and, on long journeys, they tire horses out."

LEGISLATION AFFECTING SAINT PAUL.

The legislation of the third Assembly, affecting Saint Paul, may be summarized as follows:

DANIEL F. BRAWLEY was granted a charter to run a ferry for ten years, from the upper levee to West Saint Paul. (This ferry ran until the completion of the bridge, 1858.)

An act to incorporate the Ramsey County Agricultural Society.

An act granting to JAMES M. GOODHUE and ISAAC N. GOODHUE, the right to run a ferry across the Mississippi River.

TEMPERANCE LEGISLATION.

The prohibitory legislation demanded by the Temperance Convention, and the efforts made by them in the shape of " personal pressure" on the Assembly, resulted in success. A very stringent "Maine Liquor Law" was enacted by the Legislature. The manufacture, sale, or possession of liquor was made a penal offense, to be severely punished. Liquor dealers were prohibited from sitting as jurymen. All liquor found in the Territory was to be destroyed, &c. The law was to be voted on by the people on the first Monday in April, and, if approved, was to be operative from and after May 1. If approved, County Commissioners could not grant licenses longer than to that date, &c.

The contest over the liquor question was short, but very excited. On April 5, the election took place. Ramsey county, strange to say, gave a majority in favor of the law. When this result was known, late in the evening, the church bells rang a peal of joy. The result in the Territory was for, 853; against, 662.

It was ardently hoped and expected, by the advocates of the law, that it would operate successfully, but, as in so many other cases, they were disappointed. In Ramsey county, the Commissioners construed the law to suit themselves, and granted licenses as before. Thus the liquor traffic in Saint Paul went on about as usual. In Stillwater, however, the law was enforced, and the saloons closed up.

Believing the law to be unconstitutional, its opponents took an early occasion to test it by a case occurring at Saint Anthony soon after. WILLIAM CONSTANS, a commission merchant on the levee, had in his warehouse several packages of liquor, stored there by or for another party, and Sheriff BROTT, being informed of the fact, made a descent on his place, to confiscate and destroy the liquor. CONSTANS and his friends resisted the process, offering to give the packages up, if BROTT would give a bond to indemnify him if the law was declared unconsitutional. This the Sheriff declined to do. and summoned a larger force from the crowd colleded there, as a *posse comitatus.* CONSTANS' friends also rallied. and. in the excited state of things. a riot, with serious results. might have occurred. if other parties had not advised a compromise, which was effeded. and the liquors left in CONSTANS' possession for the time.

The Saint Anthony case soon came before Judge H. Z. HAYNER, of the Supreme Court, who declared the liquor law null and void. inasmuch as the legislative power was vested by the Organic Ad in the Governor and Assembly solely, and they had no power to delegate their authority to the people, and the law in question, being an attempt to do so, was inoperative. This was a severe blow to the temperance element, but. nothing daunted, it set to work to procure the passage of another and better law the next session.

THE TOWN ELECTION

took place on May 6. The result was as follows :

President	*B. W. Lott*	227	Robert Kennedy	183
Recorder	*Louis M. Olivier*	237	B. B. Ford	171
Councilmen	*Chas. Bazille*	231	*Wm. Freeborn*	396
	Egidus Keller	228	Firman Cazeau	178
	John Rogers	221	A. Baker	175
	Lot Moffet	306	W. W. Hichcox	166

Those in *italics* eleded.

The total vote cast in both precincts into which the town was now divided. was 414, evincing a population of about 1.500.

SOME NOTES ON STEAMBOATING.

The steamboat interest now began to be quite a considerable one. and profitable, doubtless, as travel on the Upper Mississippi. under the flood of immigration pouring in. was becoming large, and freighting was also growing in importance.

On page 173 was given some note of the beginning of the old Galena Packet Company. The '' Senator" and '' Nominee" had been the regular "stand-by" packets, up to this season. During the past winter, (1851–2,) the "Ben Campbell" had been built for the trade. During the seasons of 1849, 1850, and 1851, the packet line only made two trips per week, each way. This year, it commenced tri-weekly trips. During the season, also, there was quite a rivalry in the steamboat trade. The HARRISES, SMITH and SCRIBE, ran a packet in opposition to the old line, but, ultimately, they consolidated with it. Capt. LOUIS ROBERT brought out the "Black Hawk" and "Greek Slave," this year—both new. There were "wild" boats, also, in the trade. Capt. KEELER HARRIS, who had commanded a new boat this year, called the "Saint Paul," died in August, aged 36 years.

BRIEF NOTES.

The *Pioneer*, of July 29, in a pretty pointed paragraph, compares the dearth of schools to the abundance of churches :

"Truth compels us to say, that there is not a building in all Saint Paul, fit to be called a district school house. The only building known as such, is hardly fit for a horse stable. There was another miserable substitute for a school house on Bench street, belonging to the upper district; but that was sold the other day, to satisfy a mortgage of less than $200. All this in an opulent town, swarming with children, little, untaught brats—swarming about the streets, and along the levee, in utter idleness, like wharf rats. All this in a town, too, that boasts of half-a-dozen steepled churches. If Saint Paul is not a priest-ridden town, it is in a fair way to be. This is a blunt, homely truth, but we are perfectly indifferent who dislikes it."

The *Pioneer*, of August 25, says: "The court-house is finished, and is an ornament to the town."

The same journal (September 16) says: "NEILL's church has got a fine organ, and the Cedar street church followed suit." It also adds, on the subject of church music : "now we have good choirs in all the churches, which would do honor to the most refined congregations in the States."

The *Pioneer*, of October 21, has a little item which shows that even at that early day our present system of water-works was thought of. It suggests supplying the city with water "from one of the lakes toward Little Canada."

On August 10, it was stated that the cars on the Galena road had commenced to run to Rockford. They did not reach the Mississippi for three years after this.

At this date, Minneapolis was not yet christened by that name, but is always referred to in the papers as "*All Saints.*"

Hotels seemed to be as ill-fated those days as they were a few years subsequently. On June 23, a large hotel just erected by DANIELS & WASSON, near the upper levee, burned.

The repeated reference by the editors to the need of a cemetery, led to the formation in March of an association, which procured 80 acres on what was, for many years, and perhaps is now, known as "Nigger Lake," a beautiful forest-covered hill to the right of Como avenue, and laid out a cemetery called "Oak Hill." Several burials were made there, when, for some reason, the scheme was abandoned and the property reverted to the original owners. It is unfortunate that the sites of the graves made there were afterwards obliterated, and cannot be recognized.

"LANGRISHE & ATWATER's Troupe" commenced a theatrical season at Mazurka Hall, on May 22, and played to good houses for two or three weeks.

RATIFICATION OF THE SIOUX TREATY.

During the early summer, the Sioux treaties of 1851 were before Congress for ratification, and, for some reason, delayed unnecessarily. The result was looked for with great interest by the people in Saint Paul. On June 26, the Senate, having ratified the principal treaty, (with the upper Sioux,) the news was received in Saint Paul, amid great rejoicings.

The newspapers issued extras, and in the evening bonfires blazed on the bluffs, while the Maine law was somewhat disregarded. Settlers had not waited for the formal ratification of the treaty before taking possession of "Suland," as it was slangishly termed. Good points for farms, mills and townsites had already been seized on, which have since become leading cities of our State.

MURDER OF ELIJAH S. TERRY BY THE SIOUX.

The doom of the Dakota race in this State was practically

sealed by the treaty, although they continued to hang around until 1862. During all those years, there were repeated murders of white people by them, which nearly all went unpunished. On June 25, the Sissetons, near Pembina, murdered, under the most outrageous circumstances, a young man named ELIJAH S. TERRY, a resident of Saint Paul, who had gone to that point to teach a mission school. He was a finely educated and religious young man, who had designed to devote his life to the elevation of the very savages who murdered him. He was a brother of JOHN C. TERRY, of this city, and of BENJ. S. TERRY, who, 10 years later, himself fell at Birch Coolie by a Sioux bullet.

WIFE MURDER.

On July 21, a man named CHAUNCY GODFREY, formerly of Baraboo, Wisconsin, while in a fit of jealousy and drunkenness, shot his wife through the heart with a pistol, killing her almost instantly. They were boarding at the Tremont House, a small frame hotel which stood on Bench street, where the rear of Bell's Block now stands. In the excitement that followed, GODFREY escaped, and was captured some days afterwards at Reed's Landing. He broke jail several weeks subsequently, and fled from the Territory. No effort to retake him was made, and he was never heard from again.

The newspapers of that day did not cultivate sensational reporting, as they do now. The murder did not make an item of over six or eight lines in either journal.

DEATH OF JAMES M. GOODHUE.

On August 5th, Mr. GOODHUE's serious illness was announced in his own journal, and referred to with apprehension by the other papers. He grew rapidly worse. About the 26th he rallied, and hopes were entertained of his recovery, but he relapsed again, and sank rapidly, expiring on the 27th.

JAMES M. GOODHUE was born in Hebron, New Hampshire, on March 31, 1810. He entered Amherst College at a youthful age, and, after a creditable course, graduated in 1832, in his 23d year. He at once entered upon the study of law, and was, for a time, associated with Judge

W. R. BEEBE, now of the firm of BEEBE & DONOHUE, New York. He
ultimately emigrated west, and finally settled in the lead region of
Wisconsin, then almost on the frontier of the Northwest, and comparatively unsettled. Here he began to practice his profession with vigor
and success, and was soon widely known in that region. A circumstance, however, changed the current of his life. He was invited to
take charge of the editorial columns of the *Wisconsin Herald*, published at Lancaster, during the temporary absence of the editor. He
found in the new vocation the very field that his restless activity, strong
discrimination and keen wit eminently qualified him for. The paper
doubled its interest during his occupancy of the tripod, and at length
it resulted in his becoming its editor.

In the spring of 1849, Mr. GOODHUE resolved to remove to Saint Paul.
and swiftly executed his design. On April 28, he issued, under discouraging circumstances, the first paper ever published in Minnesota.
which he continued with remarkable success until his death, three
years subsequently.

He became a man of mark and power in the new commonwealth.
He was one eminently fitted to impress the "elements of empire."
which were "plastic yet, and warm." His habits, temperament.
feelings and style, were all such as to give him influence in such a
population as the Territory then had. His journal was an *institution*
inseparably connected with the word Minnesota. In the early days of
the Territory it was a powerful immigration document. Thousands of
the present citizens of our State first heard of Minnesota in the columns
of the *Pioneer*, or by extracts from it in other journals, which were
widely circulated, and were attracted hither, by his bright and glowing
pictures of life in the new Territory. His paragraphs thus circulated, powerfully contributed to correct the prevalent errors in eastern
States as to our climate, soil, etc. He was unwearied in laboring for
good enterprises to advance the prosperity of his adopted State. His
faith in its future greatness was unbounded. He constantly predicted
its prosperous career, in paragraphs that now read as if he had been
gifted with prophetic ken. When any civil or political emergency
arose, he could summon the force, strength, nerve and daring of his
nature so promptly and powerfully as to astonish and confuse his opponents. His strength of will and purpose was remarkable.

In a paper prepared by Rev. E. D. NEILL, his intimate
friend and spiritual counselor, for the Historical Society, his
character is strikingly sketched :

"The editor of the *Pioneer*, was unlike other men. Every action.
and every line he wrote marked great individuality. Impetuous as the
whirlwind, with perceptive powers that gave to his mind the eye of a
lynx, with a vivid imagination that made the very stones of Minnesota

speak her praise; with an intellect as vigorous and elastic as a Damascene blade, he penned editorials which the people of this Territory can never blot out from memory. His wit, when it was chastened, caused ascetics to laugh. His sarcasm upon the foibles of society was paralyzing. His imagination produced a tale of fiction called 'Striking a Lead,' which has already become a part of the light literature of the west. When in the heat of partisan warfare, all the qualities of his mind were combined to defeat certain measures; the columns of his paper were like a terrific storm in mid-summer in the Alps.

"As a paragraphist, he was equalled by few living men. His sentences so leaped with life, that, when the distant reader perused his sheet, he seemed to hear the purling brooks and see the agate pavements and crystal waters of the lakes of Minnesota, and he longed to leave the sluggish stream, the deadly malaria, and worn-out farms, and begin life anew in the Territory of the sky-tinted waters."

JOSEPH R. BROWN, whose sagacity in reading and knowing men was scarcely equalled by any one in our State, thus wrote of him:

"Col. GOODHUE was a man of warm temperament, which occasionally betrayed him into an undue severity of comment upon those who differed with him in opinion upon political questions, and upon aspirants for office whom he deemed unworthy of public confidence. Many of his editorials would have done no discredit to the *New York Herald* in its most palmy days. They are replete with satiric humor. Indeed, his powers of sarcasm were limited only by his sense of propriety, and we can all testify to the effective mode in which they were exercised. In comparison with the ordinary controversial articles of the country press, his style of writing was as fine gold to lead. * * * He will be numbered with the small band of sturdy men who labored constantly and with iron resolution to establish the pillars of society in our Territory upon a sound moral basis. His press was always found on the side of law, order, temperance and virtue. Minnesota may well lament his death, and inscribe his name on the roll of her benefactors."

But GOODHUE did not live to finish the harvest of fame and wealth which his energy and ability had begun to reap, as indicated by the foregoing extracts. He was mysteriously cut off in the prime of life, with apparently years of usefulness to come. The slight illness with which he was at first attacked took an unfavorable turn, and, on August 27th, 1852, as the twilight shadows darkened around his home, his eyes closed forever on earth. The news of this sad event produced a feeling of gloom in the entire community. He was buried

22

on Sunday, August 29th, by the Masonic fraternity, from the First Presbyterian church, the pastor of which, Rev. E. D. NEILL, preached his funeral discourse to the largest audience which had ever gathered in the town. The Legislature of the following year very appropriately honored his memory, by bestowing his name on a new county, now one of the most flourishing in the State.

OUR TOWN SURVEYS.

GOODHUE had a broad and liberal view of public improvements. In his pride of our young city, and his strong desire for its success and welfare, he never ceased to importune for its social, physical, educational and commercial prosperity. His paper teems with advice to the people, which it would have been wisdom for them to have adopted. He deplored the building of houses on the bluff side of Bench and Third streets, and so have thousands since then. At that day it could have been avoided. The execrable manner in which the town was laid out was another horror to him. In one of his articles, just before his death, he says:

"The projectors of this town appear to have had but the smallest possible ideas of the growth and importance that awaited Saint Paul. The original plat was laid off in very good imitation of the old French part of Saint Louis, with crooked lanes for streets, irregular blocks, and little skewdangular lots, about as large as a stingy piece of gingerbread, broken in two diagonally, without a reservation fit to be called a public square—without a margin between the town and the river; without preserving a tree for shade, without permanent evidences of boundaries made by the survey. In fact, it was a survey without measurement, a plan without method, a volunteer crop of buildings, a sort of militia muster of tenements. So much for the old plat. Then came Rice and Irvine's Addition. This is laid out but little, if any, better. In fact, the two plats appear to have taken a running jump at each other, like two rival steamboats—which, having inextricably run into each other, the passengers and crews have concluded to knock down the railings and run along together, as one craft. Kittson's is laid off in smaller lots than any of the other additions, and its streets make no sort of coincidence with other streets in town. *It would save immense cost and prove an eternal blessing to Saint Paul*, if the whole site of the town could now be thrown into one common field, and platted as it ought to be, with large reservations of public grounds, with straight, wide, regular streets, and blocks and lots of uniform size."

ANOTHER HOMICIDE.

On the night of October 12, an affray occurred in the saloon of THOMAS H. CALDER, between Col. DANIEL BRECK, JAMES BRECK, SIMON DALTON and others, in which DALTON was fatally stabbed, dying a few hours afterwards. A coroner's jury tried to sift the case, but could come to no conclusion as to who gave DALTON his quietus. (May be he suicided?)

THE ELECTION

came off on October 12. The canvass of votes for Saint Paul precinct of Ramsey county, showed as follows:

	Democrat.	Opposition.
	Louis M. Olivier.395	J. R. Brown.......301
	Mich'l Cummings.354	*J. C. Ramsey*......366
Representatives....	*William Noot*....363	B. L. Sellers.......306
	Wm. P. Murray..355	D. F. Brawley.....317
	B. W. Lott......382	V. B. Barnum......301
County Commissioner..	*Louis Robert*.....179	George Irvine......188
Treasurer............	*Rob't Cummings*..179	Ira B. Kingsley....185
Judge of Probate.....	*W. H. Welch*.....179	Henry A. Lambert..182
Surveyor..............	*Wm. R. Marshall*.184	

Those in *italics* elected.

ANOTHER MURDER BY INDIANS.

Though the Sioux had received, in good faith, a large sum as a quit-claim for territory they had no more actual owner-ship of than the fowls of the air, they seemed unwilling to give peaceable possession of it to white people. On October 27, a party of German immigrants were traveling up the Min-nesota valley, near Holmesville, where some Indians met them, and used threatening actions and language. Finally, a Sioux buck raised his gun and shot a woman, named Mrs. KEENER. Her body was brought to Saint Paul, and buried. The Indians were pursued, and the murderer, *Yu-ha-zee*, ar-rested. He was taken to Fort Snelling, on Tuesday; indicted by the grand jury of Ramsey county, on Thursday; tried and convicted of murder in the first degree, on Friday; and, on

Saturday, sentenced, by Judge HAYNER, to be hung. Justice, those days, was speedy, (to Indians, that is.) The Statutes of the Territory then provided that a person sentenced to be hung, could not be executed for at least twelve months thereafter. So *Yu-ha-zee* was sent to jail to meditate on his latter end. He was not executed until December 31, 1854.

THE SPECULATIVE ERA

seems to have commenced as early as this. A correspondent of the *Pittsburg Token*, who visited Saint Paul in the fall of this year, writes of it:

" My ears, at every turn, are saluted with the everlasting din of land! land! money! speculation! saw mills! land warrants! town lots, &c., &c. I turn away sick and disgusted. Land at breakfast, land at dinner, land at supper, and until 11 o'clock, land; then land in bed, until their vocal organs are exhausted—then they dream and groan out land, land! Everything is artificial, floating—the excitement of trade, speculation and expectation is now running high, and will, perhaps, for a year or so—but it must have a reaction."

NECROLOGY OF 1852.

In addition to the death of Hon. H. L. TILDEN, JAMES M. GOODHUE, and ELIJAH S. TERRY, before mentioned, several other prominent citizens died this year.

On June 13, DANIEL HOPKINS, merchant, died on the steamboat " Dr. Franklin, No. 2," while returning from a business trip to Saint Louis, aged 65 years.

ROBERT HUGHES, a painter, fell over the bluff, on Bench street, June 14, and was killed. [Several deaths have since occurred in the same manner.]

On November 22, EGIDUS KELLER, a member of the Town Council, died of inflammation resulting from a frozen heel.

On December 9, J. Q. A. ALTMAN, a printer, formerly of Pennsylvania, died.

December 22, RICHARD O. WALKER, merchant, formerly of Philadelphia, died, aged 24.

CHAPTER XXIII.

EVENTS OF THE YEAR 1853.

A RETROSPECTIVE VIEW—IMPRISONMENT FOR DEBT—A SIOUX-CHIPPEWA FIGHT
ON THE STREET—CHANGE OF ADMINSTRATION—GOV. WILLIS A. GORMAN
ARRIVES—MAJ. FORBES APPOINTED POSTMASTER—THE NORTHERN PACIFIC
RAILROAD SURVEY—BUSINESS DIRECTORY—BRUTAL MURDER OF TWO MEN—
BALDWIN SCHOOL DEDICATED.

THE fourth Legislative Assembly met on January 5, in the two-story brick now located on Third street, corner of Minnesota. (The Capitol was not then completed.) The *Pioneer*, speaking of the legislative buildings about that time, said :

"Strangers inquire which of the three doors the front of the building used as the Capitol, leads to the lower house. The members themselves sometimes get puzzled."

The *Pioneer*, of January 11, notes the fact that Messrs. KITTSON, GINGRAS and ROLETTE, members from Pembina, *walked* the 500 miles from that place, on snow two feet deep, with snow-shoes.

Some delay was experienced in electing officers and organizing. Hon. MARTIN McLEOD was elected President of the Council with but little delay, but the House was not so harmonious. Day after day they balloted for Speaker, and it was not until January 25, on the 64th ballot, that a choice was made. Dr. DAVID DAY, then temporarily residing in Benton county, at present our honored postmaster, was elected, over B. W. LOTT, by one vote.

On January 26, Gov. RAMSEY delivered his annual message to the two houses and populace, in the court-house, then recently completed.

INKLINGS.

Capt. WM. B. DODD was engaged in the month of February

in getting up a subscription to lay out a road from Saint Paul to Traverse de Sioux. The amount needed was raised and the road laid out. It is known to this day as " the Dodd road." Capt. DODD fell by an Indian bullet while bravely defending New Ulm, in 1862.

The temperance element made strong efforts for another prohibitory law this session, and deluged the Legislature with petitions, without avail.

"The several Masonic Lodges of this Territory met in Convention in this city on the 23d ult., at which a Constitution was adopted, and a Grand Lodge formed."—[*Pioneer*, February 3.]

Venison was so cheap this winter that one hunter complained that he only got $11 for nine carcasses!

The *Pioneer*, of January 20, 1853, rejoices over the evidences that Saint Paul is becoming a city. He walked down Third street after dark. " when the lights gleam from the dwellings, in multitudinous twinklings, like fire-flies in a meadow. Then along Third street *for an eighth of a mile* [!]the shops are so illuminated as to give the same a city aspect." Three years ago last winter, (he continues,) there was scarcely a store on that street.

LOCAL LEGISLATION.

The Legislature adjourned on March 5th. Among the acts passed were the following, affecting Saint Paul and Ramsey county :

To incorporate the Saint Paul Fire and Marine Insurance Company.
To incorporate the Saint Paul and Saint Anthony Railroad Company.
To incorporate the Baldwin School of Saint Paul.
To incorporate the Mississippi and Lake Superior Railroad Company.
To incorporate Hennepin Lodge, No. 4, I. O. O. F.
To amend an act to incorporate the Town of Saint Paul. [To grade or pave any street by assessing property *pro rata*.]

DIVORCE LEGISLATION.

The *Minnesotian*, of March 14, " congratulates the friends of sound morality on the fact that no divorces were granted at the late session." Prior to that year, the Legislative Assembly had severed nuptial bonds quite freely. The petitions of the applicant were generally referred to a committee who took the testimony and reported. Concerning the visits of the committees to the female party in the suit, their questions concerning the evidence and other occurrences—the stories told by old settlers are too "amusing" to repeat here. The congratulations of the above journal were appropriate.

Perhaps, under this head may as well be related a good story that used to be told of a Justice of the Peace in early days—one whose rotund form was well known in our midst. A couple—French people—came to him. to be married. The knot was well and truly tied. the fee paid. and the certificate delivered. But next day. back came the parties and wanted the ceremony undone. Their brief trial of married life had convinced them that they were not suited to one another! The obliging justice informed them that for $5 he would divorce them. The fee was paid. whereupon *he tore up the marriage certificate and announced that they were free and single* again.

IMPRISONMENT FOR DEBT.

Another curious phase of our early Territorial days. was the law authorizing imprisonment for debt. which was in force about four years. (Section 2, article ix, of chapter 16, laws of 1849.)

Chapter 90 of the Revised Statutes, 1851, seemed to provide some relief for debtors confined in jail. under the foregoing law. It provided that such persons might be discharged after ten days' confinement. by giving notice, in writing, to the creditor, that application would be made to two justices of the peace for relief. He was then to show his inability to pay the execution. and the justices were to investigate the fact, pro and con. If they considered that he was not acting fraudulently. and was really unable to satisfy the judgment. he was to be discharged from custody. and not be liable to arrest or imprisonment for the same debt thereafter. But where the debtor undertook to satisfy the execution, he could not be discharged until he had paid all the charges for his support while in prison. and the charges and costs.

The marshalsea in which debtors were confined in this county, was the miserable little log jail, about fit for a pig-pen. Whether there were many committals under the statute or not, I cannot find out now, but it is asserted that there were some cases, at least. It is also stated that a Frenchman named Bou-LANGE, died in the jail, while a prisoner for debt. The old settlers, nearly all of whom belonged to the "poor but honest" class, were not very apt to deal harshly with an unfortunate brother who had come in debt to them.

A SIOUX-CHIPPEWA FIGHT ON THE STREET.

On April 27, an exciting incident occurred, viz. : a skirmish or fight between small squads of Sioux and Chippewas, in one of the most public streets of Saint Paul, resulting in the murder of a Sioux squaw. The particulars may be briefly related :

Early in April. the Ojibwas killed a Sioux near Shakopee. In revenge for this, the Sioux then made an expedition near Saint Croix Falls, killing an Ojibwa, and losing two sons of old LITTLE CROW.

Hearing of these events, the Ojibwas prepared for revenge. A party of some 18, led by a young chief named *A-luc-en-zis*, started for Saint Paul, determined to assassinate any unlucky Sioux found hanging around the town, as plenty always were. They stealthily entered town on the night of April 26, and concealed themselves until day-break, in an unfinished building in lower town. At daylight they scouted carefully along to the edge of the bank by the gas house, to watch for Sioux coming up from Kaposia in their canoes. Ere long, one hove in sight, making for the landing. It contained "Old BETS," her brother, "Wooden-legged JIM," and her sister. Soon as the Chippewas noted this, they sprang down the bank, and made tracks for the landing, designing to ambush the Sioux at that spot. The marsh between Fifth street and the river was then overflowed, and they could not cross it. They were thus compelled to strike over Baptist hill, which they did at a rapid dog-trot, but, to their great disappointment, as they arrived near the Merchants' Hotel, found that, owing to the delay, the Sioux had landed and were coming up Jackson street.   This street had been cut through the bluff, leaving a high bank of dirt on each side.   The Sioux advanced carelessly up the hill, suspecting no danger, and turned up the steps of the " Minnesota Outfit," a large frame trading house of the American Fur Company, which stood on the site of the present Prince's Block, and in charge of Wm. H. Forbes. The Chippewas, fearful of losing their prey, rushed forward and stood on the bank opposite the store, and on a level with it.   The Sioux had just entered the store, when they drew up their guns and fired a volley at them.   The sister of Old Bets fell mortally wounded.   There were several persons in the store at the time, and it is miraculous that they were not killed. The Chippewas jumped down the bank and rushed towards the store, determined to finish their work.   They were met at the door by Theodore Borup and George H. Oakes, who happened to be present, and who peremptorily commanded them to clear out—or they would get into trouble.   This brought them to a sense of their rashness, and they at once retired by the route they came.

The wounded woman proved to be dying, and, at her request, was put in the canoe and taken to Kaposia, where she died the same morning.

Meantime, the firing and excitement attracted a number of citizens, who, as soon as they learned what had taken place, pursued the retreating Chippewas, whether to arrest them, or for what purpose, no one hardly knew.   They soon overtook the pagans, who, turning calmly around and confronting them, said :   " White man, why do you pursue us?   This is none of your affair !   Do you mean to interfere in our fights?"   No one knew what reply to make, and, as they were unarmed, allowed the Chippewas to pass on unmolested.

But we had almost overlooked " Wooden-legged Jim," who in his day had been quite a famous fighter.   As soon as the Chippewa volley had been fired, he drew out an old pepper-box revolver he carried, and, rushing to the door, tried to fire at them, but not a barrel would go off.   Throwing it down, he picked up a loaded gun standing in the store, and pursued them a short distance, getting a shot at them, and (it is said) wounding their chief. The latter returned the salute, knocking a splinter out of Jim's wooden leg, after which the latter stumped back, defiantly yelling the war-whoop. (Mr. James died in 1859.)

Gov. Ramsey at once dispatched a courier to Fort Snelling for troops to pursue and punish the Chippewas. Lieut. W. B. Magruder soon appeared with a platoon of cavalry, ready for the pursuit.

A Sioux guide was procured, and off they went on a gallop. The guide tracked the Chippewas to Saint Croix Falls, where they were overtaken, at noon next day. Seeing they were pursued, the Chippewas retreated to the bush, when they fired on the dragoons. The latter charged them, and Lieut. Magruder shot one with his revolver. His scalp was brought back as a trophy, and thus ended this singular chapter of early scenes in Saint Paul.

The "Minnesota Outfit" building, where this occurred, was afterwards used as the *Pioneer* printing office, and, in 1860, moved to Eighth street, below Broadway, where it still stands, a neat dwelling. The words, "Minnesota Outfit," are still faintly discernable under the recoating of paint.

THE PIERCE ADMINISTRATION

came into power on March 4, and, consequently, all the Federal officers in the Territory were sent to the guillotine. Among the new appointees announced, were the following:

Willis A. Gorman,* of Indiana, as Governor, vice Ramsey; J. Travis Rosser, of Virginia, as Secretary, vice Wilkin; M. W. Ir-

---

* Willis A. Gorman was born January 12, 1816, near Flemingsburg, Kentucky. He received a good education, and subsequently studied law. At the age of 20, he was admitted to the bar; and, in August, 1835, removed to Bloomington, Indiana, where, "without money or friends," he began the practice of his profession. At the age of 23, he was elected a member of the Legislature, and continued to fill that position for several terms—until the Mexican War broke out, when he promptly volunteered, and was elected Major of a battalion of riflemen, which took a conspicuous part at Buena Vista and other battles. In May, 1847, his battalion was mustered out, and he at once recruited a regiment (Fourth Indiana) of which he was elected Colonel. This regiment took part in a number of battles, until the close of the war. In August, 1849, Col. Gorman was chosen as Congressman in his district, and re-elected in 1851, serving in Congress four years.

When Pierce became President, he appointed Col. Gorman Governor of Minnesota,

WIN, of Missouri, as Marshal, vice FURBER; WM. H. WELCH, of Minnesota, Chief Justice, vice HAYNER; A. G. CHATFIELD, of Wisconsin, Associate Justice, vice COOPER; MOSES SHERBURNE, of Maine, Associate Justice, vice MEEKER; DANIEL II. DUSTIN, of New York, District Attorney, vice MOSS.

Governor GORMAN arrived on May 13, and took his seat on the 15th. He soon announced the following appointments:

SOCRATES NELSON, Territorial Auditor; LAFAYETTE EMMETT, At-

THE CAPITOL.

torney General; GEO. W. PRESCOTT, Superintendent of Public Instruction; ROBERT A. SMITH,* State Librarian, and Private Secretary;

---

which position the latter accepted and filled until May, 1857. He then resumed the practice of law in Saint Paul, with much success. In 1857, he was elected a member of the Constitutional Convention, and was a candidate that winter for United States Senator. In April, 1861, when the First Regiment was raised, Gov. GORMAN was appointed its Colonel, and went with it to Virginia. Soon after Bull Run, he was promoted to a Brigadier General, and served as such until 1864, when he was mustered out of service, and returned to Saint Paul. He resumed the practice of law, in partnership with Capt. (since Governor) C. K. DAVIS, whom he had been associated with in the army. In April, 1869, he was elected City Attorney, and has been four times re-elected to the same office. Gov. GORMAN is one of the most efficient speakers of his party in the State, and if the political scale should turn, he would no doubt be elected to a position to which his ability and experience in public life entitle him.

* ROBERT A. SMITH was born in Indiana, June 13, 1827, and lived in that State until his removal to Minnesota. In 1850, he was elected Auditor of Warrick county, and served as such three years. He arrived in Saint Paul in May, 1853, and at once assumed the duties of Private Secretary to Governor GORMAN, and Territorial Librarian, the latter of which he filled until 1858. In May, 1856, he was appointed by the Ramsey

ROSWELL P. RUSSELL, Territorial Treasurer; S. B. LOWRY, Adjutant General; ANDREW J. WHITNEY, Clerk of Supreme Court.

Until the completion of the Capitol, the Governor's office was kept in the law office of RICE, HOLLINSHEAD & BECKER, on upper Third street. On July 21, the executive chamber in the Capitol was first occupied.

A NEW POSTMASTER.

With the incoming of PIERCE's administration, among the heads that fell into the basket, was that of Postmaster BASS. His successor was WILLIAM H. FORBES, his commission being dated March 18, but was not gazetted in Saint Paul until April 14. Mr. FORBES bought out the fixtures of BASS' office, and removed them to a one-story frame building, situated about where NELSON's brick block on Third street now is. The glass boxes of BASS' time were extended so as to reach across the room, and a door in the middle of this partition gave entrance to the duly sworn employees to the work-room in the rear. Mr. FORBES appointed as his Deputy JOHN C. TERRY, who retained his position as assistant during several changes of incumbency, and, in 1870, bade adieu to the postal service, after 18 years of faithful labor, to embark in a more healthy and profitable occupation. Mr. WALLACE B. WHITE was, if we remember right, employed a short time after Mr. FORBES' term began, and BOB TERRELL, a lad then, assisted for a time. After TERRELL left, ANDREW WELCH was employed. ANDY remained in the service until the winter of 1858–9, when he died of consumption.

The Saint Paul of 1853 was not the Saint Paul of 1875, by a considerable. Around the "post-office" of that time were hazel bushes and trees. Standing in the door of the office one day, in the fall of 1853, Mr. TERRY shot three prairie chickens which had lit about where the *Pioneer-Press* office now stands, and were scratching undisturbed by the presence

---

County Board, County Treasurer; and, in the fall of that year, elected for two years, and, subsequently, four more terms, serving until March, 1868—a period of 12 years. In 1866, he entered the banking business with WILLIAM DAWSON and H. K. STEVENS, and has since then been transacting a large financial business. He is one of the best financiers in Minnesota, and is deservedly popular, as his repeated election shows.

of man.   Contrast the silence of those days with the busy tide
of human life that whirls by that spot now.

MINOR TOPICS.

The Grand Lodge of Odd Fellows was instituted on May 5.

"SHORT ALLOWANCE.—The fresh meat market is as bare as a clean
bone.   Not an ounce of fresh beef, veal, pork or mutton can be found
in the market.   Our citizens are reduced to salt provisions and fish."—
[*Democrat,* May 4.]

"On June 6, WM. W. WARREN, an educated Chippewa half-blood.
author of several valuable papers on the history, customs and traditions
of the Chippewas, died."—[Ib.]

"Buildings are going up, new stores opening, immigrants arriving,
and improvements of all kinds going ahead to a greater extent than
ever before."—[Ib.]

"On July 4, a man named FRANCIS DUNN was thrown from a wagon
in which he had been excursing with his family, and was killed."—[Ib.]

This summer Bishop CRETIN built Saint Joseph's Hospital.
on Exchange street.   Part of the grounds were contributed by
Hon. H. M. RICE.   The Bishop also bought grounds for a
cemetery—the same now occupied by Saint Joseph's Academy.
on Nelson avenue—but it was used for only three years as a
• burying ground, the bodies being then removed to the new
cemetery on the Lake Como road. which was consecrated in
the fall of 1856.

During this year, also, " Oakland cemetery," that beautiful
and well-managed " city of the dead," was opened.   On June
23, the association was organized with the following corporators: Rev. J. G. RIHELDAFFER, Rev. T. WILCOXSON, Rev.
E. D. NEILL, GEO. W. FARRINGTON, ALEX. RAMSEY, JOHN
E. WARREN, HENRY A. LAMBERT, B. F. HOYT, SHERWOOD
HOUGH.   On August 23, the association purchased forty acres
of land, for $1,600.   The first year only two lots were sold.
and it was several years before it had many lot owners.   P. P.
FURBER was Actuary several years, succeeded by EDMUND
F. ELY, and latterly by MORRIS LANPHIER.   The grounds
have recently been extended to 80 acres, and greatly beautified.
Fine drives and walks are laid out over it, and many handsome

marble and granite monuments erected. The most elegant
and costly is that of SAMUEL MAYALL, erected at an expense
of $7,000. Up to the present year, about 3,000 interments
had been made.

The papers this season were well saturated with railroad
talk, and quite a fever was raised over the proposed survey of
the Northern Pacific route. Gov. ISAAC I. STEVENS and Lieut.
F. W. LANDER, charged with that work, arrived about the
last of May, and organized an expedition here, which explored
the northern route. Two volumes were subsequently published by the War Department, containing the reports of the
above survey, and are valuable documents.

BUSINESS HOUSES—1853.

From the city papers this year, we get the names of the
following business houses in 1853 :

General Dealers.—H. C. Sanford, A. L. Larpenteur, D. L. Fuller,
D. & P. Hopkins, Louis Robert, Wm. H. Forbes, Rey & May, Culver*
& Farrington.

Boots and Shoes.—Henry Buel, Luke Marvin, H. A. Schliek, Philip
Feldhauser.

Dry Goods.—J. H. & S. McClung, Edward Heenan, A. T. Chamblin,
Cathcart, Kern & Co., S. H. Sergeant, J. E. Fullerton, Elfelt Bros., •
Curran & Lawler, Louis Blum.

Books.—LeDuc & Rohrer, Wm. S. Combs, Dahl & Doull.

Furs.—Louis Robert, C. J. Kovitz.

Drugs.—W. H. Jarvis, Dr. J. H. Day, Bond & Kellogg.

---

*GEORGE CULVER, one of the pioneers of our State, was born in Cayuga county,
New York, September 19, 1818. He removed, in 1834, to Michigan, and lived there
until 1837, when he moved west again, and engaged in business in Clinton and Fayette
counties, Iowa. Fort Atkinson, being the principal station then in the Winnebago region, he remained there until 1848, when he removed to Long Prairie, Minnesota, in
charge of a part of the Winnebago Indians, (see page 186,) and, shortly after his
arrival, engaged in business with CHARLES & HENRY M. RICE, in the Indian trade.
He continued in this until 1853, when he left Long Prairie, and, settling in Saint Paul,
formed a partnership with JOHN FARRINGTON, Esq., the firm being "CULVER & FAR-
RINGTON." This house has remained in active operation 22 years, and is one of the
oldest firms in Minnesota. It was the first to open direct trade with Manitoba, and the
first to engage in pork-packing in Minnesota. They maintained, for some years, trading posts among several tribes. Recently Col. CULVER has become proprietor of the
Metropolitan Hotel, the finest one in the State. His life, up to 1853, was one of stirring
adventure and pioneer hardship. It would require a volume to do it justice. He is now
one of the "solid men" of Saint Paul, respected and esteemed by all.

Hardware, Iron, &c.—J. McCloud, Jr. & Bro., C. E. & J. Abbott, W. R. Marshall.

Hats and Caps.—R. O. Walker.

Lumber.—J. W. Bass.

Furniture.—Stees & Hunt.

Grocers.—Julius Georgii, Nat. E. Tyson, L. B. Wait & Co., J. W. Simpson, W. H. Stillman, B. Presley, Alex. Rey, J. A. Farmer, C. Sanford, B. W. Brunson.

Glass.—W. W. Hickcox, S. H. Axtell.

Stoves.—F. S. Newell, C. D. Bevans, J. H. Byers.

Clothing.—L. Hyneman.

China.—R. Marvin.

Tobacco.—J. Campbell.

Leather.—P. T. Bradley & Co., Martin Drew & Co., G. Scherer.

Furnishing Goods.—Thomson Ritchie.

Confectionery.—Renz & Karcher.

Jewelry.—H. Fowler, N. Spicer, A. D. Robinson, Wm. Illingworth.

Storage, Forwarding and Commission.—Edw. McLagan, Constans & Burbank, Spencer, Kilpatrick & Markley, H. M. Rice, M. Kellogg & Co.

Millinery.—Mrs. Marvin, Mrs. Stokes.

The papers about this date refer to the fact that most dealers were confining themselves to one branch of traffic, instead of combining different classes of merchandize in one house, as was done in the early days of the city.

BRIEF MENTION.

Whoever reads the files of Saint Paul papers of this summer, will find numerous references to a "MADISON SWEETZER," who had been a sort of Indian trader. Said SWEETZER had made charges of "frod" in the late payment of the Dakotas, and all the papers were worked up into a white heat, pro and con, over it. A Congressional committee finally investigated the allegations, and reported that they were unfounded. SWEETZER sank again into obscurity, and died at Fort Wayne, Indiana, February 25, 1875.

A military company, called the "City Guards," was organized this summer, probably the first militia company organized under the laws of Minnesota. "Capt. SIMPSON" was commander; R. C. KNOX, Orderly Sergeant.

LINDEN & UNDERHILL'S theatrical corps opened a short season of drama, at the court-house, on July 20.

Superior, Wisconsin, was laid out this season, by some of our citizens, among them R. F. SLAUGHTER, E. Y. SHELLEY, R. R. NELSON,* D. A. J. BAKER, D. A. ROBERTSON, and others, who were the pioneers of that town. At that time, a trip to that place had to be made on foot. There was not even a wagon road.

The market house was built this season. The papers refer to the " city hall" occupying its second story.

At this time there were five journals published in Minnesota, three in Saint Paul, and two at Saint Anthony.

On June 29, Col. ROBERTSON retired from the *Democrat,* and was succeeded by DAVID OLMSTED.

In October, the papers notice the removal of the Sioux to the Upper Minnesota Reservations.

On December 7, a low desperado, named THOMAS GRIEVES, made an attack, in a drunken fit, on HENRY CONSTANS, in his place of business on the levee, and CONSTANS was compelled to shoot him in self-defense. GRIEVES died of the injury.

ELECTION OF 1853.

Politics were again warm this year, but the issues were confined to a straight party fight, the Democrats and Administration party against the Whigs. The election took place on October 12. The following is the full result in Ramsey county:

---

* R. R. NELSON was born in Cooperstown, New York, May 12, 1826. He is a son of the late Judge SAMUEL NELSON, one of the Judges of the Supreme Court of the United States, an eminent jurist, who died in December, 1873. R. R. NELSON studied law in his father's office, and was admitted to practice in that State. He removed to Saint Paul in May, 1850, and soon became one of the prominent lawyers of Minnesota. On April 23, 1857, he was appointed, by President BUCHANAN, one of the Supreme Judges of Minnesota Territory. His term expired on the admission of the State, May 11, 1858, but President BUCHANAN soon after appointed him United States District Judge, the duties of which office he has executed for 17 years, with much ability, and to the cordial satisfaction of all who have had business in his court. Judge NELSON is no less honored for his learning, sound decisions, and urbanity, yet firmness, on the bench, than for the uprightness of his life, and his social characteristics—qualities which eminently fit him to fill his important office with success.

Very truly Yours,
R. R. Nelson

	Democrat.	Whig.
Councillors, 2d dist.	*Isaac Van Etten*...481	B. W. Brunson.....376
	Wm. P. Murray...421	J. K. Humphrey....237
Councillors, 4th dist..	*Wm. Freeborn*.....462	D. B. Loomis......338
Representatives...	*Levi Sloan*........404	*Dr. J. H. Day*....388
	Wm. Noot.........390	M. S. Wilkinson...383
	B. Rogers.........378	J. M. Marshall.....387
	Wm. Davis........413	Find. McCormick..375
	Louis Bartlett.....425	Alden Bryant......383
Sheriff..............	—— Leonard 506	*A. M. Fridley*.....650
Register of Deeds....	*Louis M. Olivier*...548	Wm. H. Tinker....523
Judge of Probate....	*J. M. Stone*.......667	Allen Pierse.......486
County Attorney	*D. C. Cooley*......600	D. A. Secombe.....537
County Treasurer....	A. L. Larpenteur..476	*Nat. E. Tyson*.....497
Surveyor.............	*J. D. Case*........578	Jno. T. Halsted....570
Coroner.............	—— Carey.......525	*J. E. Fullerton*...581
Assessors	Benj. Gervais......544	W. H. Stillman....560
	John O'Gorman...564	Caleb D. Dorr....570
	Robert Cummings..590	Jas. R. Clewett.....520

Those in *italics* elected.

Justices of the Peace elected.—First Precinct, Joseph Lemay, *D.*; Second Precinct, N. Gibbs, *D.*

The total vote for Delegate in Saint Paul, was, H. M. RICE, 883; ALEX. WILKIN, 292. The vote in the Territory stood—RICE, 2,149; WILKIN, 696.

BRUTAL MURDER OF TWO MEN.

On December 26th, two young men, named JOHN CLARK and PHILIP HULL, were brutally murdered, on the corner of Robert and Fifth streets. They were respectable and intelligent mechanics, and had been, during the evening, sitting in a saloon near by, where, in conversation, they unintentionally made some severe criticisms on political or religious subjects, which must have given great offense to some persons in their hearing. When they rose to go home, they were followed by parties unknown, and both attacked in the dark with slung-shots, or other weapons, and their skulls so severely fractured that they died in a few hours. The slightest clue to the assassins was never gained, notwithstanding the efforts of the officers, and a reward of $500 offered by Sheriff FRIDLEY; and the affair remains a mystery to this day. Old settlers used to assert very positively, however, who committed the act, but no proof could ever be procured.

BALDWIN SCHOOL DEDICATED.

" Baldwin School" was an educational institute, organized by Rev. E. D. NEILL and others, and a commodious building was erected during the summer of 1853 for its use. This building was dedicated on December 29, by a banquet, at which addresses were made by Rev. E. D. NEILL. CHARLES J. HENNIS, WM. HOLLINSHEAD, W. A. GORMAN, JOHN P. OWENS, T. M. NEWSON, M. S. WILKINSON. Rev. T. R. CRESSEY, GEO. L. BECKER. W. G. LEDUC, and others. The name Baldwin School was given to it, as a compliment to Hon. MATTHEW W. BALDWIN, of Philadelphia, the principal donor to the building fund.   It had, in January following, 71 pupils, and was in successful operation until the public schools of Saint Paul got well organized in 1857.   During that year the building was rented for the Saint Paul post-office, and used as such until 1862.   In 1864, it was leased by the Board of Education, and, in 1869, purchased by them, being still known as " Baldwin School."   After being used as a school for three or four years, the completion of the Madison School rendered its further occupancy unnecessary, and it was leased to the city for public offices.

As a historical note on the growth of traveling, and the vivid contrast between " then" and " now," the *Minnesotian,* of December, 1853, has just heard of " *sleeping cars,* in which one may rest as comfortably as anywhere!" Then there was not a yard of railroad within 200 miles of Minnesota.   The papers that very month report the Chicago and Rock Island Railroad finished to within 50 miles of the Mississippi River, where it rested for the winter, and was completed the following spring.   But of this anon.

Navigation closed this fall on November 22d, unusually late for those times.   There were 235 arrivals this year.

CHAPTER XXIV.

EVENTS OF THE YEAR 1854.

INCORPORATION OF THE CITY—THE FIRST CITY ELECTION—E. S. GOODRICH PUR-
CHASES THE "PIONEER"—THE GREAT RAILROAD EXCURSION—BALL AND FES-
TIVITIES AT THE CAPITOL—BURNING OF THE SINTOMINE HOTEL—EXTRAOR-
DINARY BUFFALO HUNT—EXECUTION OF YU-HA-ZEE FOR MURDER.

THE fifth session of the Minnesota Legislature assembled in the new Capitol for the first time. The year 1854 witnessed entirely new coalitions. Ramsey county was represented this year by WM. P. MURRAY* and ISAAC VAN ET-TEN,† in the Council; and WM. NOOT, WM. A. DAVIS, LOUIS BARTLETT, JOHN H. DAY, and LEVI SLOAN. in the House.

LEGISLATION AFFECTING SAINT PAUL.

Not much private legislation affecting Saint Paul was made during this session. Among the acts we notice the following :

To incorporate the German Reading Society. Approved, February 23.

---

* Hon. WM. P. MURRAY was born in Hamilton, Ohio, June 21, 1827. He attended the law school of Indiana University, and graduated in 1849, having also previously studied for that profession. He came to Saint Paul in December, 1849, and is now one of the oldest lawyers in Minnesota. He has also filled a number of official positions. He was a member of the Territorial House of 1852 and 1853, Council in 1854 and 1855, (the latter year President) of the House of 1857, and Constitutional Convention the same year, member of the House in 1863, Senate in 1866 and 1867, House in 1868, and Senate again in 1875 and 1876—eleven sessions in all. He has also been a County Commis-sioner, and member of the City Council continuously since 1859, except about 18 months, while he was absent in South America. No man in our county has been so honored with positions of this kind as Mr. MURRAY, and, it may be said, no man has been more faithful, attentive and hard-working as a legislator or alderman, than he, and fully deserves his remarkable popularity. In 1857, the now flourishing county of Murray was named for him. ·

† ISAAC VAN ETTEN was a native of Orange county, New York, and studied law with Judge WILKIN, father of Hon. W. WILKIN. He was admitted to the bar in 1851, and at once came to Minnesota. He was Adjutant General of the Territory from 1852 to 1858—a member of the Territorial Council 1853 and 1854, and State Senate 1857-8. He was a law partner for some time of Col. ALEX. WILKIN, and afterwards of MICHAEL E. AMES, and Capt. HARVEY OFFICER, until 1865, and subsequently of Judge L. EM-METT in 1872. He died December 29, 1873, aged 45 years.

To incorporate a Chapter of Royal Arch Masons in Saint Paul. Approved, March 3.

To incorporate the Saint Paul Bridge Company.   Approved, March 4.

But the most important law concerning our city was the

ACT OF INCORPORATION

of the " City of Saint Paul," approved March 4, 1854. The territory embraced in the corporate limits was but a small fraction of that ample territory to which it is now grown, being not over 2,400 acres in all. Three wards were created, and much the same officers and general regulations that our present city charter provides for.

THE FIRST CITY ELECTION

under the new charter was held on April 4. The following was the result:

	Democrat.		*Whig.*	
For Mayor	David Olmsted	269	W. R. Marshall	238
City Marshal	*W. R. Miller*	262	A. H. Cavender	241
Treasurer	D. L. Fuller	224	*D. Rohrer*	271
Police Justice	James Starkey	227	*O. Simons*	248

Those in *italics* elected.

Aldermen elected.—First Ward, R. C. Knox, 2 years; A. T. Chamblin and R. Marvin, 1 year.   Second Ward, A. L. Larpenteur, 2 years; T. Fanning and C. S. Cave, 1 year.   Third Ward, Geo. L. Becker, 2 years; Jno. R. Irvine and J. M. Stone, 1 year.

Justices of Peace elected.—First Ward, W. H. Tinker; Second Ward, Joseph Lemay; Third Ward, J. M. Winslow.

Assessors elected.—First Ward, W. H. Tinker; Second Ward, W. H. Stillman; Third Ward, H. Stillwell.

On Tuesday, April 11, the City Council organized. They elected officers as follows: President, GEO. L. BECKER; Clerk, SHERWOOD HOUGH; Comptroller, FINDLEY McCORMICK; Surveyor, S. P. FOLSOM; Attorney, D. C. COOLEY.

THE SEASON OF 1854

was one of unprecedented prosperity for the young city, as well as for the entire Territory. Navigation opened on April 6 this year, and a heavy immigration poured in. The population and business of the city increased rapidly, and the county outside also received large accessions of population. Roads were opened: farms smiled in the wilderness: the " squatter's cabin" was to be seen on every lake. Other portions of Minnesota were prospered as highly. Towns sprang up on every hand; mills clattered by the waterfall: the emigrant wagon whitened every road, and hardly had the yell of the retreating red man died away, ere the settler's axe echoed in its stead.

E. S. GOODRICH PURCHASES THE "PIONEER."

Journalism in Saint Paul took a high bound forward this year. In March, EARLE S. GOODRICH* purchased of JOSEPH R. BROWN, the *Minnesota Pioneer*, and became its editor and publisher.

Mr. GOODRICH had been engaged in journalism in Wisconsin, and, being in New York city in the latter part of February, 1854, fell in at the same hotel with Capt. ESTES, one of the pioneer steamboatmen of the Upper Mississippi. In the course of conversation, Capt. ESTES said he had just been up to Saint Paul, and had seen Jo. BROWN, who remarked he was anxious to sell out the *Pioneer* office, to go into some other business, and was then trying to find a suitable person to purchase, one who would edit an able paper, and build up the party in Minnesota. " There, GOODRICH," said Capt. E., " there is a good field for *you.* The *Pioneer* is doing well, and Saint Paul is

---

*EARLE S. GOODRICH was born in Genesee county, New York, July 27, 1827. In early life he resolved to enter the editorial profession, and preliminary to that learned the printing business, and also studied law, being admitted to practice. He afterwards removed to Sheboygan, Wisconsin, where, in 1848, he established a campaign paper, which ran for some months. He was also elected Clerk of the Court, but resigned and removed to Green Bay. He was County Clerk of Brown county from 1850 to 1854, and one year District Attorney. In March, 1854, he settled in Saint Paul, and published the *Pioneer* with great success for over 10 years, winning the reputation of being the most graceful, elegant, and caustic editorial writer we have ever had in Minnesota. In 1862, while in Washington, he was tendered a commission as Captain and Aid to General MCCLELLAN, which he accepted, but was, by a blunder of STANTON's, sent, instead, to the Shenandoah Valley, where he served some time, and was then ordered to Saint Paul. A disagreement with Gen. POPE, then in command here, led him to resign his commission. In 1865, he purchased the Saint Paul Gas Company, which he controlled for two years. He soon after engaged in railroad construction, in which he has been interested most of the time since.

a prosperous place. bound to grow, as also the Territory.
You ought to go up there and buy the concern." Capt. E.
urged the matter so strongly that (although Mr. GOODRICH

EARLE S. GOODRICH.

had hardly spent a moment's thought on Saint Paul before that
interview) he was quite in the notion of going.   Hon. BEN.
C. EASTMAN, a Member of Congress from Wisconsin, happened to arrive at the hotel the same time, and he, too, urged

Mr. GOODRICH to come. glowingly describing the prospects of success. and offering to give him letters of introduction to prominent men.   The result was. that Mr. GOODRICH was en route for Saint Paul within 24 hours.

On arriving here, (March 4.) he at once called on JOSEPH R. BROWN, and found a letter, written by Mr. EASTMAN in advance. had already reached Major BROWN, and that the latter had his mind made up to sell the *Pioneer* to Mr. GOOD-RICH.   The bargain was quickly closed. and Mr. G. left for New York next day, to secure material for a daily paper, to be issued on May 1.

The *Democrat* and the *Minnesotian* at once determined to follow suit. the former appearing on May 1, the same day as the *Daily Pioneer*, and the latter on May 12.   On May 15, the *Daily Times* made its appearance. edited and published by THOMAS M. NEWSON, who had for a year or more been engaged as a writer on the *Pioneer*.   With him was associated J. B. H. MITCHELL and M. J. CLUM.   Mr. NEWSON subsequently secured the interest of both these gentlemen, and continued the *Times*. with much success. until 1861. when it was purchased by Hon. W. R. MARSHALL. as more fully mentioned under that date.

THE GREAT RAILROAD EXCURSION.

Perhaps the most notable event of 1854, was " the Great Railroad Excursion." as it was generally termed. to celebrate the completion of the " Chicago and Rock Island Railroad," the first road to reach the Mississippi River in the Northwest. Messrs. SHEFFIELD & FARNHAM, the contractors who built the road. to commemorate the opening of that line. prepared a monster excursion.   Nearly one thousand guests were invited. mostly from the east.   They rendezvoused at Chicago. about June 3d, and excursed westward over the new road to Rock Island. where five large steamers conveyed them to Saint Paul. arriving here on the 8th.   The company proceeded to Saint Anthony, Minnehaha, &c., in such conveyances as they could find. and in the evening a grand reception was given at the Capitol.

The hall of the House of Representatives was used as a supper-room, while the Supreme Court chamber was appropriated for a ball-room. In the Senate chamber, a large crowd assembled to listen to speeches from ex-President FILL-MORE. GEO. BANCROFT, the historian, Governor GORMAN, and a number of others. The music, dancing, feasting and speaking continued until midnight, the hour set for the departure of the steamers, and the great excursion terminated.

The opening of this great line of travel largely increased the steamboat trade on the Upper Mississippi. The packet company put on three new and first-class packets this year.

BRIEF ITEMS.

September 6. CHARLES L. EMERSON succeeded DAVID OLMSTED, as publisher of the *Democrat.*

On June 26, W. W. HICKCOX, a druggist, who was engaged in business in the well-known old brick drug store, so long occupied by DAY & JENKS. corner of Third and Cedar streets, had an altercation with a drayman, named PELTIER, in which the latter struck him with a dray-pin, fracturing his skull. HICKCOX died on July 3. PELTIER was arrested and tried for homicide, but ultimately got clear on the ground of self-defense.

The Sintomine Hotel. a large and fine frame structure, built by N. W. KITTSON, near the corner of Sixth and John streets, was burned on October 3, just as it was completed, and ready to occupy. E. C. RICH and HOWARD WARD had just leased it. This was quite a loss to the town, which needed more hotel room.

The Winslow House had recently been got into running order by Capt. I. C. GEORGE, (who died in 1872,) and the International Hotel was about being put under contract. It was commenced this fall, (contract price, $75,000,) but not completed for some two years.

THE COUNTY ELECTION

this fall occurred on October 10. The following is a synopsis :

	Democrat.	Whig.
	Reuben Haus....463	J. E. Fullerton..... 376
	D. F. Brawley..461	Wm. Hollinshead.. 343
Representatives....	*C. S. Cave*......459	Wm. H. Randall... 349
	Joseph Lemay..430	J. M. Marshall..... 371
	Wm. Davis.....453	Findley McCormick 359

Co. Commissioner....Joseph Le Bonn. 80   *Abraham Bennett*..1056
Judge of Probate.....W. H. Stillman..285   Richard Fewer.... 604
                       S. M. Tracy.....173
County Treasurer....Louis Robert....564   *Allen Pierse* 576
Coroner .... *Wm. H. Jarvis*.342

Those in *italics* elected.

At this period. Saint Anthony. Rum River and Manomin. were the precincts outside of what is the present bounds of Ramsey county.

BRIEF MENTION.

The *Democrat*, of October 22, notes the rush of immigration as follows: " Six steamboats arrived yesterday and landed about 600 passengers."

The currency which was chiefly in circulation those days, was mostly composed of " Indiana wild-cat," or *free-bank* issues. This fall it depreciated about as badly as the " Glencoe" and " Owatonna" did in 1859, causing much trouble and loss to tradesmen. Several meetings of merchants were called to devise means to remedy the evil, which resulted in organizing a protective union under the name, " Board of Trade." W. R. MARSHALL, was President, THOS. FOSTER, Vice President. SAM. W. WALKER, Secretary, and A. H. CATHCART,* Treasurer. It does not seem to have done much except take measures to remedy the currency fraud.

Navigation closed this fall on November 25th, the season having been unusually long, and a very prosperous one for

---

* ALEX. H. CATHCART is a native of Toronto, Canada, where he was educated and learned the dry goods business. He afterwards lived in Montreal and New York, and emigrated to Saint Paul in 1851. Soon after, with his brother, JOHN WILSON CATH-CART, he established here a dry goods store, now the oldest in Minnesota. For 24 years continuously, Mr. CATHCART has carried on that trade in our city, part of the time being the largest wholesale house in the State. J. W. CATHCART leased a plantation near Vicksburg during the war, and was killed by guerillas on April 11, 1864. He was a highly estimable and noble man.

steamboatmen.   The number of arrivals were 256, a large increase over former years.

THE FIRST EXECUTION IN RAMSEY COUNTY

took place on December 29. *Yu-ha-zee,* the Sioux Indian, mentioned on page 331, was, after much delays of law, hung in public, on a gallows erected on Saint Anthony hill.   The execution was witnessed by a large crowd, who, according to the journals of the day, looked on it more as a joke than as a solemn act of justice.

NECROLOGY OF THE YEAR.

Died, January 8, JOHN G. COOLEY, a merchant of the city ; July 10, Col. DANIEL H. DUSTIN, United States District Attorney ; July 27, C. D. FILLMORE, brother of the ex-President ; November 22, Hon. LEVI SLOAN, merchant and member of Legislature of 1854.

CHAPTER XXV.

EVENTS OF THE YEAR 1855.

THE THIRD HOUSE, OR "SOVEREIGNS"—MAILS—STAGE AND EXPRESS ITEMS—BIRTH
OF OUR FIRE DEPARTMENT—THE PIONEER HOOK AND LADDER COMPANY—
IMMIGRATION—THE REAL ESTATE MANIA—POLITICAL MATTERS, &C., &C.

THE Legislature of 1855 assembled on January 3. Ramsey county, this year, was represented by WILLIAM P. MURRAY and ISAAC VAN ETTEN. in the Council, and WM. A. DAVIS. D. F. BRAWLEY. CHAS. S. CAVE, REUBEN HAUS and JOSEPH LEMAY. in the House. No unusual or noticeable events characterized the session. Some local legislation affecting Saint Paul. amending its charter. &c., was passed. but scarcely worthy of notice here.

It was. during this year. if we remember right, that some of the boys organized the " Third House" or *Sovereigns*. as a burlesque on the Legislatures of that day. They were continued several years, and produced great amusement. D. C. COOLEY, was Governor. and his " messages" were admirable specimens of sarcasm.

This winter there was only a tri-weekly mail between Saint Paul and Dubuque. by M. O. WALKER's line of stages. Those who remember the M. O. WALKER era of staging. have no very pleasant reminiscences concerning it. The stages were anything but commodious, and. with spavined stock and surly drivers, intensified the horrors of a winter trip to Galena, the nearest point where the eastern-bound traveler could strike a railroad. The trip was advertised for four days. but frequently took six. Storms and drifts on the prairies often snowed up the stages at some frontiersman's cabin for two or three days, and not unseldom was real suffering and privation the consequence.

BIRTH OF OUR FIRE DEPARTMENT.

On March 1, 1855, our Fire Department was organized, by the formation of the Pioneer Hook and Ladder Company, with 28 members. A subscription was raised to purchase a hook and ladder wagon. One which had been used by a company in Philadelphia was purchased, and brought out. It was used by the hook and ladder company up to within a year or two, and did good service. A small fire engine was also purchased by several citizens, and was for several years the only engine in use.

THE CITY ELECTION

took place on April 3d, resulting as follows:

Mayor	*Alexander Ramsey*	552	James Starkey	256
Treasurer	*Daniel Rohrer*	494	Louis Demeules	312
Marshal	*W. R. Miller*	564	John Trower	237

Those in *italics* elected.

Aldermen elected.—First Ward, Wm. H. Nobles, C. H. Schurmeier; Second Ward, C. S. Cave, A. L. Larpenteur; Third Ward, J. R. Irvine, A. G. Fuller.

The total number of votes cast at the election was 809, from which the newspapers claimed 5,000 population for Saint Paul, but, in point of fact, it was much less than that.

IMMIGRATION, IMPROVEMENTS, ETC.

Navigation opened on April 17, the old favorite "War Eagle" leading the van, with 814 passengers. The papers chronicle the immigration that spring as unprecedented. Seven boats arrived in one day, each having brought to Minnesota 200 to 600 passengers. Most of these came through to Saint Paul, and diverged hence to other parts of the Territory. It was estimated by the packet company that they brought 30,000 immigrants into Minnesota that season. Certainly, 1855, 1856 and 1857 were the three great years of immigration in our Territorial days. Nothing like it has been seen since.

With such a human flood pouring into and through it, Saint Paul was a busy place. The hotels and boarding houses were crowded, the stage lines worked night and day, people even camping on the streets, stores doing a perfect rush of business, livery stables coining money, saloons reaping brisk profits, real estate dealers fairly ecstatic, and mechanics not half able to keep up with the work pressing upon them. Perhaps not a city on the continent, the size of Saint Paul, was such a bustling bee-hive as it was that season. The fever of real estate speculation, which before was but feebly developed, this season seemed to attack all classes, and began to grow into the mania which a few months later almost rendered Saint Paul a by-word.

THE REAL ESTATE MANIA.

In some sense the real estate mania this year was excusable and natural, in view of the enormous and rapid profits made by shrewd and daring operators. For instance, the papers chronicle one movement made by HENRY McKENTY, the king of real estate dealers, and who was on the flood-tide of prosperity during 1855, 1856 and 1857. In 1854, he entered several thousand acres of prairie farming land in Washington county, by land warrants, at $1.25 per acre. In the spring of 1855, he sold the same land to a colony from Pennsylvania, at $5 per acre, clearing 300 per cent. His total net profits on this transaction was $23,000, which he at once invested in more land, on which he in turn made almost as great profits.

Right here the author will be pardoned for giving an incident of those days which well illustrates the profits of real estate dealers. PENNOCK PUSEY, Esq., our plain and sober-going friend, came to Saint Paul from Philadelphia in 1855, and got acquainted with McKENTY, who startled him one day by offering him three and one-half per cent. a month, or 42 per per cent. annum, for the use of some money Mr. PUSEY had. This seemed such an enormous premium to the latter gentleman, who had come from a region where six and seven per cent. is the established rate, that he declined the offer on the ground that McKENTY could not afford to pay it, and that it would be wrong to accept such an usurious rate. McKENTY soon demonstrated, however, that he would make large profits if he could get the money, and hence could pay the rate mentioned without trouble. The loan was made. McKenty entered some large tracts of land in Cottage Grove, at $1.25 an acre. and within a year Mr. Pusey himself bought a part of the lands, and gave McKenty $2.50 an acre for it! Thus, while Mr. Pusey made 42 per cent. on his money, McKenty cleared 58 per cent. over and above that amount off of the lender! Mr. Pusey afterwards sold the land to O. Dalrymple at $15 per acre, as part of his famous wheat farms.

ITEMS.

The census of 1855 was announced in the papers, as follows: Population of the Territory, 53.600; of Ramsey county, 9,475; of Saint Paul, 4,716.

Building was very brisk this year. The mechanics could not turn out the buildings fast enough for people to get shelter in. Street improvements, to a considerable extent, were made, also. Third, Fourth, Jackson, and other prominent streets were graded.

This season the post-office was moved to the old brick building, near the bridge, which, after passing through many changes, is now a saloon.

The election this year was somewhat triangular. There were three candidates for Delegate in the field—H. M. Rice, Wm. R. Marshall, and David Olmsted—and three county tickets to match. The election, (October 9,) resulted in the choice of the following officers: Councillor, John B. Brisbin; Representatives, Wm. H. Nobles, F. Knauft, R. Haus, Ross Wilkinson and B. W. Lott; Sheriff, A. W. Tullis; Register, Louis M. Olivier; Treasurer, Charles F. Stimson, (Saint Anthony;) Attorney, I. V. D. Heard; Surveyor, James A. Case; Probate Judge, A. C. Jones.

LOCAL TOPICS.

On October 4, the *Daily Free Press*, an evening paper, made its appearance as the organ of the Gorman Democracy, or "Nebraska wing" of that party. It was edited by Hon. A. C. Smith, now of Litchfield, and published by Samuel J. Albright & Co. Saint Paul now boasted of five daily papers—three morning and two evening. Not long, however. was such an abundance of journals to shed intelligence on this saintly city. On October 31. the *Democrat* was discontinued and merged with the *Daily Pioneer*, under the name of *Pioneer and Democrat*, which it bore for six years, and the following spring the *Free Press* was discontinued.

A man named E. Howitz, a book-dealer. committed a forgery on MARSHALL & Co.. this fall. and escaped with several hundred dollars of ill-gotten booty.

On the night of November 9. the grocery store of H. C. SANFORD. corner of Third and Wabasha streets. on the site of the present Warner Block. was burned down. SANFORD had a quantity of powder in store. When it went off, it shook things up lively in the vicinity. Dr. J. H. STEWART* was lying sick of typhoid fever in the building that stood where McQuillan's Block now does. The shock threw him out of bed on the floor, and cured his fever! He never recommended the remedy in his subsequent practice. however.

In the fall of 1855. Rev. E. D. NEILL organized a Presbyterian society known as the "House of Hope," now one of the most flourishing churches in the city. It used to worship that fall in the Walnut street school house.

On November 19. navigation closed. The total number of arrivals this year were 553.

As an evidence of the amount of travel and business on the river during the season of 1855. it was stated that the packet company declared dividends (net profits) of $100,000 on that season's business. The "War Eagle." which cost $20,000. cleared $44.000 alone : and the "City Belle." costing $11,000. cleared $30.000 profits.

---

* Dr. J. H. STEWART was born in Columbia county, New York, January 15, 1829. He graduated at the University of New York, in 1851, and practiced medicine at Peekskill, on the Hudson River, from 1851 to 1855. In May, of the latter year, he came to Saint Paul and established himself here—soon becoming one of the most popular and successful practitioners in the city. In 1859, he was elected State Senator, and served on important railroad committees. He was commissioned Surgeon of the First Minnesota Regiment in 1861, and was captured at Bull Run, July 21, being held as prisoner at Richmond some time, but finally exchanged. In 1864, he was elected Mayor of Saint Paul, and the following year appointed Postmaster, which position he held five years. In 1869, he was again elected Mayor, and re-elected in 1871, and again in 1873. But few gentlemen in our city have been so popular as Dr. STEWART, a fact owing to his fine abilities professionally, and his *bonhomie* socially.

NECROLOGY OF THE YEAR.

Died in January, at Providence, Rhode Island, (his former home,) JOSEPH WAKEFIELD, a talented lawyer.   May 9,

DR. J. H. STEWART.

HENRY P. PRATT, one of the publishers of the *Minnesotian.* July 4, by drowning, LUKE MARVIN, Jr., a promising young business man.   November 22, Rev. JOSHUA BRADLEY, pastor of the First Baptist church.   December 3, by an accident, CHARLES ROSS.

24

CHAPTER XXVI.

EVENTS OF THE YEAR 1856.

CHANGE IN THE COUNTY LINES—CREATION OF OUR BOARD OF EDUCATION—WIN-
TER TRAVELING AND BUSINESS—THE PIONEER GUARD—A POLICE FORCE
CREATED—CORNER-STONE LAYING—THE CITY HALL BUILT—BARON VON
GLAHN—THE REAL ESTATE MANIA—CRIME AND DISORDER—A VIGILANCE
COMMITTEE—THE FULLER HOUSE BUILT, &C.

On March 11, CHARLES S. CAVE was appointed postmaster, vice Major FORBES. Mr. CAVE held the office four years,
but left it poorer than he entered it. He now resides in
Missouri.

The Legislature adjourned on March 1. No bills were
passed materially affecting Saint Paul, unless we except the
act detaching Saint Anthony from Ramsey county, and adding
it to Hennepin county, with which its interests were more
nearly allied, though many now believe that in a few years
we will all be in the same corporation again.

This change left two officers of Ramsey county residing beyond the new limits, viz.: CHAS. F. STIMSON, Treasurer, and
J. P. WILSON, Commissioner. The Board of Commissioners,
on March 23, elected ROBERT A. SMITH, as County Treasurer, and, at a special election, EDMUND RICE was chosen as
County Commissioner.

A "Board of Education" was also created, for the city of
Saint Paul, to consist of six members, two from each ward.

The "Pioneer Guard," the finest volunteer military company which ever flourished in our State, was organized this
spring. It existed until 1861, when most of its members went
to the war, and it ceased to maintain an organization.

BRIEF NOTES.

On May 23, McClung and Stewart's Blocks, a row of frame

buildings where the present stone blocks of the same owners stand, were burned.

On May 30, the City Council authorized the appointment of four policemen. Hitherto, the City Marshal. " BILL MILLER." had been the only officer in the city, with powers equivalent to a policeman. The first appointees were JOHN GABEL. NICH-OLAS MILLER, M. C. HARDWIG and EDWARD MAHER.

On June 24, the corner-stones of the proposed hall for the Historical Society, and of a projected Masonic Hall, were laid with great ceremony. A large procession of civic socie-ties, military, &c., paraded through the city. Mayor BECKER delivered the oration over the corner-stone of the former insti-tution, and "Rev." JOHN PENMAN. Grand Chaplain of the Masons, did the trowel work. Neither of these buildings, commenced with such prodigious flourish, were ever built, or progressed beyond a partial foundation.

About the same date, the corner-stone of the cathedral. corner of Saint Peter and Sixth streets, was laid, with impos-ing ceremonies, by Bishop TIMON, of Buffalo. The excava-tion for this large edifice had been commenced in the fall of 1854, but the work progressed slowly, for want of funds. It was completed for use in 1857. During this spring, the corner-stone of (old) "Assumption church," on Exchange street, was laid, and the church itself completed and occupied the same season. Rev. DEMETRIUS MAROGNA, since deceased, was first priest, followed by Rev. CLEMENT STAUB. In 1872-3, the new "Assumption church," on Eighth street, was erect-ed—the largest and most expensive church in our city.

Among other structures built in 1856, was the Jackson Street Methodist Episcopal church.

This season the City Hall was erected. The money for its erection was borrowed from "BARON VON GLAHN," a capi-talist who used to flourish around here in those days, and after-wards moved to Chicago.

The real estate mania this year assumed alarming propor-tions. Speculation was red hot, and the inflation continued for some months, when the panic of 1857 caused the memor-able collapse in values.

THE CITY ELECTION

this spring resulted as follows :

	Democratic.	*Republican.*
Mayor	Geo. L. Becker 723	A. G. Fuller 524
Treasurer	. . .Lewis Demeules 505	Dan. Rohrer 620
Justice	.Joseph Lemay 480	O. Simons 717
Marshal	Wm. R. Miller, (no opposition,) 1224.	

Those in *italics* elected.

Aldermen elected.—First Ward—Three years, Wm. Branch; two years, C. H. Schurmeier.

Second Ward—Three years, Wm. B. McGrorty; two years, Charles Rauch.

Third Ward—Three years, Chas. L. Emerson; two years, Patrick Ryan.

The City Council shortly afterwards met and organized by electing the following :

City Clerk, L. P. Cotter; City Attorney, J. B. Brisbin; Comptroller. Geo. W. Armstrong; Surveyor, James A. Case; Physician, Dr. Samuel Willey.

A REIGN OF CRIME AND DISORDER.

The rush of immigration, and the fast habits induced by the speculative era, brought to our city numbers of thieves, gamblers and other abandoned characters. For several weeks during the summer, crime was rampant. On July 9. the dead body of Geo. R. McKenzie, proprietor of the Mansion House. was found in the river, having been robbed of money known to be in his possession previously, and a young man named Robert Johnson, was assaulted, robbed, and thrown over the bluff, one night, by highwaymen, dying of his injuries. Sometimes eight or ten boats would be in port at once, each with large crews of low ruffians, who would roam about the city maddened with liquor, and committing excesses, and the small police force. (four men,) were able to do but little. A public meeting was held, at which a secret police, or sort of vigilance committee, was appointed to aid the authorities. Our streets were carefully patroled at night for some time, a number of suspicious characters arrested and sent out of town, others tried for offenses committed, and punished, and security

and order established in a short time. Meantime, the police
force was increased to twelve men. HENRY GALVIN, our
veteran patrolman, was one of those appointed.

On September 25, the "Fuller House," just completed and
furnished, was opened with a grand ball. The cost of the
building was $110,000. ALPHEUS G. FULLER was the builder

FULLER HOUSE—(AFTERWARDS INTERNATIONAL.)

and owner. A bonus of $12,000 was raised for him at the
outset. J. W. BASS and WM. H. RANDALL contributed the
land as a bonus. STEPHEN and ED. LONG were the lessees.
The hotel commenced doing a splendid business at once. The
next week it was stated that, between Saturday evening and
Monday morning, there were 100 arrivals. That fall all the
hotels did a large business. The same paper states the arrivals at the four principal houses, (Fuller, Merchants, American and Winslow,) in one week, amounted to over 1,000, and
it was stated at the close of the season that the number of visitors registered at all the hotels was 28,000.

THE ELECTION

this fall, (October 14.) was with the following result:

	Republican.	Democrat.
House, 1st District	*William Branch*..246	A. T. Chamblin.... 324
	B. W. Brunson...187	Isaac Rose......... 215
House, 2d District	*J. C. Ramsey*.....607	Wm. P. Murray.... 696
	C. Bergfeld.......408	Wm. Costello....... 664
	Dr. C. Goring....198	J. G. McBean....... 436
Treasurer........	P. P. Furber......493	W. B. McGrorty.... 659
		R. A. Smith, (Ind.,) 671
Co. Commissioner	...Parker Paine......560	E. Rice............1232
Coroner............	W. H. Shelly 502	Dr. J. D. Goodrich.1174

Those in *italics* elected.

Ramsey county extended northward at that time as far as Crow Wing, and R. A. SMITH was elected by the votes at that place, the vote here being almost a tie.

The season of 1856 was very prosperous in many ways. The city grew wonderfully, almost doubled, indeed. Many fine buildings, especially residences, were erected, streets graded, churches built, and other improvements made, that changed the appearance of Saint Paul from a rough frontier town to a bustling and thriving city.

BRIEF ITEMS.

On October 15. the papers announce the arrival of Rev. JOHN MATTOCKS,* from Keeseville. New York, to become pastor of the First Presbyterian church.

*Rev. JNO. MATTOCKS was born in Peacham, Vermont, July 14, 1814. He was the son of Hon. JNO. MATTOCKS, of that State, once Governor, and Member of Congress two terms. He graduated at Middlebury College in 1832, and commenced the study of law, but, embracing religion soon after, resolved to become a clergyman, and graduated in the theological department of Yale College. He settled in 1838, over a congregation at Keeseville, New York, where he remained eighteen years, when he accepted a call to the First Presbyterian church of Saint Paul. He came here in August, 1856, and at his death was the senior pastor in our city. In March, 1860, he was elected Secretary of the School Board, and Superintendent of Schools—a post he filled until July, 1871. He was also a leading member of the Historical Society, &c. Mr. MATTOCKS was a scholar of fine ability. He was quite an antiquarian by taste, and very fond of the natural sciences. His information on these points was full and accurate, and he frequently lectured on geology, &c., with much success. He died suddenly on November 13, 1875, to the great sorrow of the community, and of his congregation, for whom he had labored so long and faithfully.

On November 16, the building on the northwest corner of Saint Anthony and Washington streets, known as the "Rice House." (on the site of the Third street front of the present Metropolitan Hotel,) was burned.   It was a three-story brick, and in the upper story, the Legislature of 1851 held its session. SANBORN & FRENCH, attorneys, had rooms above; KING &

REV. JOHN MATTOCKS.

RICH, upholsterers, and D. L. FULLER & COMPANY, merchants, occupied the lower story at the time of the fire.

The papers speak of the large increase of business this year.   The number of business firms, they report, doubled this season.   Several new banking houses were established— that of WM. L. BANNING* is specially referred to.

---

*WILLIAM L. BANNING is a native of Wilmington, Delaware.   In early life he adopted the profession of law, and removed to Philadelphia, where he was associated in that profession with the late WILLIAM HOLLINSHEAD.   During his residence in Phil-

Work was commenced on the Saint Paul bridge this winter. Piles for the piers were driven into the river bed. SANFORD A. HOOPER and J. &. J. NAPIER were the original contractors.

NECROLOGY OF THE YEAR.

Died, on January 27, J. S. BROWN. a prominent banker. February 14, CHAS. J. HENNISS. a journalist. December 1, at Scotland. Connecticut. (his former home.) DAVID L. FULLER, an early merchant of Saint Paul.

---

adelphia, (1845,) he was elected a member of the Pennsylvania Legislature. In 1855, he removed to Saint Paul, and soon after engaged in the banking business, which he continued with success until 1861, when he retired from it. In the fall of 1860, he was elected a member of the House of Representatives, and took a prominent part in financial and railroad questions. In 1861, Mr. BANNING was appointed a Commissary in the army, and served under General FREMONT, in Missouri, for about two years. In 1864, he engaged in the enterprise of building the Superior Railroad, and to his energy and ability, and influence in enlisting capital, the people of Saint Paul are indebted for that valuable highway. He was President of the road for seven years, and retired from it owing to his impaired health. Captain BANNING is a valuable member of the Chamber of Commerce, where his views on political economy and public matters have always had great influence.

CHAPTER XXVII.

EVENTS OF THE YEAR 1857.

An Atrocious Murder—Death of Bishop Cretin—Attempted Removal of the Capital—Jo. Rolette Makes off with the Bill—The Ink-pa-doo-tah Massacre—Another Murder—Incendiarism—Sunrise Expedition, &c.

THE year 1857 was marked by a number of important events, and was one of the most exciting and memorable of any in our career.

"We learn that a new parish has been organized in the eastern part of the city, by the Episcopalians. A handsome stone edifice will be erected during the coming season, on the corner of Ninth and Olive streets. Rev. Andrew Bell Paterson, of Salem, New Jersey, has been called to the rectorship.—[*Minnesotian*, January 1.]

Services were held for several months in the Washington school house.

On the morning of January 14, a German tailor, named Henry Wm. Schroeder, formerly of Louisville, Kentucky, who lived alone in a little shop on Third street, on the present site of "Maxfield's Block," was found dead in his shop, having been murdered by a blow on the head with an axe or hatchet. He was a single man, and was known to have had considerable money, which he was accustomed to keep about his person, or in his shop. No clue to the perpetrator of the atrocious act was ever discovered.

On February 22, Right Reverend Bishop Cretin died, to the great sorrow of his large congregation in this region. His body lay in state at the old brick church on Wabasha street until the 24th, when the funeral took place. Fully 1,500 people were in the procession. A memoir of him is given on page 311.

The first City Directory of Saint Paul was issued in February, by Goodrich, Somers & Co. It contained about 1,700 names of citizens. Not one in five of these are now living in the city, nor of the 158 business houses advertised in it, are there over half a dozen in existence now, and these with more or less change of firm.

REMOVAL OF THE CAPITAL.

During this session occurred a somewhat exciting event, frequently referred to—the passage by the Legislature of an act removing the Capital to Saint Peter. The bill was introduced on February 6, by W. D. Lowry, Councillor from Saint Cloud, and on the 12th passed the Council—ayes eight, nays seven. Among those who prominently opposed it were Hons. J. D. Ludden, H. N. Setzer, J. B. Brisbin, and B. F. Tillotson. In the House it was opposed by J. R. Brown, L. K. Stannard, Dr. W. W. Sweney, of Red Wing, Elam Greeley, John M. Berry, and "our own" W. P. Murray. The measure was also generally opposed by the press of the Territory. It, however, passed on the 18th, and the bill was sent back to the Senate to be enrolled.

About this time the odor of the mouse had so permeated the atmosphere, that one of the most obtuse olfactories could have perceived it. There were a few individuals hereabouts who came to the conclusion that, after some things had occurred which looked a little "heathen Chinee," almost any maneuver to defeat the bill would be legitimate. The member from Pembina, "Jo." Rolette, as he was generally called, dearly loved a joke, no matter at whose expense. He was chairman of the Committee on Enrolled Bills! A wink was as good to him as a nod. On the 27th, the original bill and enrolled copy was placed in Mr. Rolette's hand to compare.

Next day, February 28, Mr. Rolette was not in his seat! The other side now saw the mouse "floating in the air," and concluded, as the Irish orator said, "to nip him in the bud." St. A. D. Balcombe, of Winona, now editor of a journal at Omaha, moved resolutions calling on Rolette to report forthwith; and if he failed to do so, that the next member of the committee. (Mr. Wales.) be ordered to procure another enrolled copy, and report the same, &c.

Mr. BALCOMBE at once moved the previous question on the resolutions, but Mr. SETZER moved a call of the Council, which was ordered, and Mr. ROLETTE reported absent. BALCOMBE moved that further proceedings under the call be dispensed with, on which there were yeas nine, nays five. Two-thirds not voting for the motion, the Chair, (Hon. J. B. BRISBIN.) declared it lost, notwithstanding BALCOMBE eloquently protested that nine *was* two-thirds of fourteen! The Sergeant-at-Arms, JOHN M. LAMB, of White Bear Lake, was ordered to report Mr. ROLETTE in his seat, and started out to " find" him. He didn't find him that day. The Council, unable to adjourn, patiently (?) waited his return. The dinner hour passed, and messengers were dispatched to the hotels for a supply of food. Bed-time arrived, still the Sergeant-at-Arms came not with the missing member. Beds and bedding were sent for, and the members camped on the floor of the Senate. Next day, no tidings of either ROLETTE or the Sergeant-at-Arms. It was rumored that ROLETTE had been seen near Sauk Rapids, in his sledge drawn by dogs, flying swiftly homeward, with the enrolled bill sticking out of his pocket.

Others said, *bosh,* and declared ROLETTE was hid in an upper room of the Fuller House, playing poker and drinking punch. Anon it was reported that JOHN LAMB was " looking" for ROLETTE in every possible and impossible place in the city, armed with a rope, and threatening to bear ROLETTE to the Council, dead or alive. It was asserted by others, however, that this was pure " blow"—that LAMB was not looking for him to any great extent—that he had one eye closed, (and some say both,) and couldn't have " seen" ROLETTE if he had met him. Certain it is, that LAMB didn't find him, " either dead or alive," and ROLETTE continued his poker and punch, while the enrolled bill quietly reposed in the safe of TRUMAN M. SMITH, banker, on the first floor of the Fuller House.

The Council, meantime, continued in its dead-lock, with the call still pending. Another bill was procured and enrolled, but Mr. BRISBIN, President of the Council, and Mr. FURBER, Speaker of the House, refused to sign it in that shape, endorsing on it their reasons therefor. The bill was, however, sent to the Governor, signed by him, and printed in the laws of that year, with the endorsements mentioned.

After a continuous session of five days and nights, (or 123 hours,) the Council adjourned, the call still pending. At midnight, on March 5, the last night of the session, the President resumed the chair, and announced the Council adjourned *sine die.* The moment the doors were thrown open, in stalked Jo. ROLETTE, and commenced rallying his brother members, in his vivacious and pointed style, on the good joke he had played on them.

But little more remains to be recorded, to show the end of this singular chapter of Minnesota history, one which, now that 19 years have cooled the passions excited by the contest, is generally mentioned with a smile by both the former friends and opponents of the scheme. The first of these took the ground after the session was over, that the bill had become a law, a position scouted by the others. The Saint Peter Company, we believe, erected buildings to accommodate the Territorial officers and Legislature, and, on June 29, A. F. HOWES, President of the company, applied before Judge R. R. NELSON, of the Supreme Court, for a writ of mandamus to compel the Territorial officers to remove to Saint Peter. Judge NELSON took the motion under advisement, and, on July 12, filed an opinion. After reviewing, at considerable length, the evidence concerning the passage of the act, he decides: "We are of the opinion, therefore, that there has been no law passed by the Legislative power of the Territory, removing the Capital from Saint Paul to Saint Peter. The application for a mandamus is therefore refused."

BRIEF ITEMS.

There was no legislation at the last session especially affecting St. Paul, except the incorporation of the "Saint Paul Library Association." The incorporators were CHARLES E. MAYO, J. W. McCLUNG,* R. F. HOUSEWORTH, S. D. JACK-

---

* JOHN W. McCLUNG was born near Maysville, Kentucky, November 21, 1826. He studied law at Transylvania University, and graduated in 1847. He practiced law at Maysville until 1855, when he came to St. Paul and engaged in law and the real estate

SON, J. F. HOYT, E. INGALLS, A. R. CAPEHART, WM. A. CROFFUT, THOMPSON CONNOLLY and P. DEROCHEBRUNE.

On March 25, Messrs. DAY & GRACE, who had contracted to build the Ramsey county jail for $75,000, broke ground for the same. The building was finished that fall.

On April 13, news was received of the *Ink-pa-doo-tah*

JOHN W. McCLUNG.

massacre. Great excitement prevailed. The Pioneer Guard promptly volunteered to go to the protection of the frontier.

business. He was elected County Commissioner in 1860, and City Assessor in 1864, serving five years. He was also Clerk of the Board of Public Works in 1872. He was elected County Assessor in March, 1875. We can hardly say of Mr. McCLUNG, as we have of others, that he is a *popular* man, for any one filling the difficult and unpleasant office he holds, must necessarily be the subject of much censure and fault-finding. But he bears it like a philosopher, and works for the interests of Saint Paul with an untiring zeal that is worthy of imitation. He has also published a work, "Minnesota as it is in 1870," that has done our State great benefit.

but could get neither transportation or proper ammunition. Two of the female captives, who were rescued soon after, were brought to Saint Paul and presented with a purse by our citizens.

Hon. SAMUEL MEDARY, who had been appointed Governor of the Territory, arrived on April 22, and at once assumed the gubernatorial chair.

This spring two new volunteer companies were organized. One was the "Saint Paul Light Cavalry," Capt. JAMES STARKEY : the other was called the Shields' Guards, Capt. JOHN O'GORMAN.

On April 27, the extra session of the Legislature convened, and continued until May 25. Among the local acts passed, affecting Saint Paul, were : To incorporate the Saint Paul Water Company ; to extend Rice street ; to incorporate the Saint Paul Fuller House Company ; to incorporate the Saint Paul Dramatic Joint Stock Association ; to open and extend Seventh street, &c.

The spring of 1857 was one of the latest ever known. The "first boat" did not arrive at Saint Paul until the morning of May 1. Once the barrier was broken, however, the season was inaugurated with a fleet of boats. On May 4th, *eighteen* were at the levee at one time, and, a few days afterwards, *twenty-four*, the largest number ever seen at our landing. Each of these were crowded with passengers and their goods, so great was the rush of immigration that spring.

SCRAPS.

On May 5, the city election occurred, with the following result :

	Republican.		Democratic.	
Mayor	*John B. Brisbin*, (Democrat—had no opposition,)			..1876
Treasurer	.. Daniel Rohrer	961	Edward Heenan	858
Marshal	.... *Wm. R. Miller*	1143	John O'Gorman	735

Those in *italics* elected.

Aldermen elected.—First Ward, Luke Marvin ; Second Ward, A. L. Larpenteur ; Third Ward, H. J. Taylor.

On the night of May 10, a murder took place at the "Cave," a low sink of crime above town. A man, named PETER W.

TROTTER, was stabbed by a roustabout, named "MIKE SMITH," *alias* GOLDEN, and died in a few moments. The murderer escaped and was never detected, although Deputy Sheriff J. W. PRINCE pursued him to Saint Louis.

Saint Paul was well supplied with theatres this season. "SALLIE ST. CLAIR's Varieties" opened at Market Hall on May 20, with a very good company.

On June 27, H. VAN LIEW opened the " People's Theatre," in a frame structure, built for the purpose, on the northeast corner of Fourth and Saint Peter streets. VAN LIEW had a very good company, and ran his theatre that season, and also during the summers of 1858 and 1859. The building burned down September 8. 1859, during a political meeting, while SCHUYLER COLFAX and GALUSHA A. GROW were addressing it. The scenery of the People's Theatre was painted by AL-BERT COLGRAVE, the first scenic artist in Minnesota. He came from Columbus, Ohio, and was a young man of promising ability and talent. In 1862. he enlisted in the Sixth Regiment. and died at Glencoe. in March following—an untimely ending of a noble life.

A few days subsequent to the opening of the People's Theatre. a Mr. SCOTT brought a small company here, and opened a theatre in a hall in Irvine's Block. Thus there were three theatres going at one time, and all doing well. The panic. a few weeks later. soon closed them up. The hall used by SCOTT's troupe was subsequently used for a while by the House of Hope congregation.

The election for delegates to the Constitutional Convention occurred on June 1. The Democratic nominees were all elected, as follows :

Moses Sherburne, Geo. L. Becker, Michael E. Ames, D. A. J. Baker. John S. Prince, Patrick Nash, Lafayette Emmett, Wm. P. Murray, W. A. Gorman, Wm. H. Taylor, W. B. McGrorty, Paul Faber.

The total vote cast in the city was 2,820, which would have shown (if not fraudulent) a population of 17,000, or more, but one journal asserts that " several steamboat crews voted several times in each ward !"

WAIFS.

On August 4, a severe fire occurred on the north side of Third street, between Market and Saint Peter, which destroyed some twenty buildings and much of their contents. The fire was undoubtedly the work of an incendiary.

On August 18, another fire swept the west side of Robert street, between Third and Fourth, then occupied by frame business buildings. This fire was also, beyond doubt, the work of an incendiary.

These two fires, taken in connection with a number of burglaries, attempted and successful, and the presence of a gang of hard characters in the city, and the insufficiency of the small police force to properly guard so extensive an area as they were expected to protect, led to the formation of an organization similar to that of the preceding summer—a volunteer patrol, or vigilance committee. This was kept up for several weeks, and rendered good service in clearing the city of vagabonds and criminals. The fires also demonstrated the necessity of fire engines, and the City Council set about procuring them, though it was fully a year before they were received.

A "FAST" TOWN.

During the summer of 1857, Saint Paul was said by travelers, to be the fastest and liveliest town on the Mississippi River. Emigration was pouring in astonishingly, several boats landing daily loaded with passengers. Those intending to go back in the country, usually purchased their supplies here, and the stores were almost overtaxed, so profitable was their trade. The hotels and boarding houses were crowded to overflowing. The principal business streets fairly hummed with the rush of busy life. Building was never so brisk ; an army of workmen and mechanics labored night and day to keep up with the demand for dwellings and stores. Another small army was engaged in grading streets, and laying gas pipes, the air being continually shaken with the concussion of blasting rock. Saloons, of course, throve as they always do, be times flush or hard. That season they coined money ;

so, also, did the livery stables. The city was continually full
of tourists. speculators, sporting men. and even worse characters, all spending gold as though it was dross. Perhaps
this "floating" population amounted to two or three thousand
persons during most of the summer. until the crash scattered
them like leaves before an autumn gale.

THE SUNRISE EXPEDITION.

During the summer, settlers near Cambridge. Sunrise. &c..
complained that the Chippewas were very troublesome, stealing, &c. Gov. MEDARY ordered Capt. STARKEY to take a
part of his volunteer cavalry company, and proceed to the
spot, and arrest any Indians known to be committing depredations. or order them to return to their Reservation. Capt.
STARKEY took 20 men, and, on August 24, started for the
settlements named. On August 28, they overtook six Indians
near Washington, and, while talking to them, the Indians
broke away and ran. Capt. STARKEY ordered one of his men,
FRANK DONNELLY, to head them off and tell them to stop.
DONNELLY did so, when one of the Indians, named *Sha-go-
ba*. shot DONNELLY. killing him instantly. The other cavalry-
men fired on the Indians, killing one and wounding another.
Securing the four Indians, and putting the other two, together
with DONNELLY's body, in a wagon, the cavalry returned to
Saint Paul. arriving on the 29th. The scene, when DON-
NELLY's bloody corpse was left at his house. can better be
imagined than described.

The funeral of DONNELLY took place on Sunday, August
30, from the Jackson Street Methodist Episcopal church.
"Rev." JOHN PENMAN preached the discourse from the text:
"To live is Christ, and to die is gain." (This was a subject
well suited to the piety of that holy and eloquent divine!)
The military of the city did the accustomed honors to their
fallen comrade.

The Indians were kept in confinement for several days.
when they were released by Judge NELSON, on a writ of
habeas corpus. brought by Maj. CULLEN. Superintendent of
Indian Affairs. *Sha-go-ba* was sent to Chisago county. to be

25

tried for the murder of DONNELLY, but soon cut his way out
of the "jail" with a knife, and escaped.

ITEMS.

On August 31, the Washington school house, which had
been built that season, was dedicated. This was the first
school house built by the Board of Education, and cost $8,433.

On September 3, the City Council subscribed $50,000 to-
ward the Saint Paul bridge, which had been commenced the
previous winter, and stopped for want of funds. The work
was now pushed forward night and day, to complete the piers
before frost, and the wood work was built during the winter.

On September 7, the District Court, second judicial district,
assembled, Judge R. R. NELSON presiding. There were 400
cases on the calendar, no term of the court having been held
for two years.

On September 16, the "Mercantile Library Association"
was organized. It maintained its organization quite successfully for several years, accumulating a considerable library,
keeping up a good reading room, and getting up two or three
interesting courses of lectures. In 1863, its library was united
with the Young Men's Christian Association, and formed our
present well-managed and excellent "Saint Paul Library."

This fall, the Milwaukee and Prairie du Chien Railroad was
completed. The nearest railroad connection east had hitherto
been at Dunleith. Step by step, the iron horse was advancing
toward our city.

CHAPTER XXVIII.

EVENTS OF THE YEAR 1857.—Continued.

The Real Estate Mania—The Period of the "Flush Times"—The Panic—
The Real Estate Market Ruined—Hard Times—The Census—Election—Currency Troubles—Perilous Balloon Ascension, &c., &c.

THE real estate mania, before mentioned, was now at its
height.   No description that can be given of this singular era of our history can convey an idea of it.   Only those
who lived through the "flush times" will ever know what
they were.

Everybody seemed inoculated with the mania, from the
moneyed capitalist to the humble laborer who could merely
squat on a quarter section, and hold it for a rise.   The buying
of real estate, often at the most insane prices, and without
regard to its real value, infected all classes, and almost absorbed every other passion and pursuit.   Town-sites and
additions to towns were laid out by the score.*   Many of
these town-sites were purely imaginary, and had never been
surveyed at all.   Lots in these paper cities were sold by the
hundred east, at exorbitant prices.   Agriculture was neglected, and breadstuffs enough for home consumption were not
raised.   Their import formed a large branch of trade.   Honest
labor was thrown aside for more rapid means of wealth.
Farmers, mechanics, laborers, even, forsook their occupations
to become operators in real estate, and grow suddenly rich, as
they supposed.

"Real estate dealers"—some of them honorable men, like
HENRY MCKENTY, but many without character or conscience,

---

* D. C. Cooley, "Governor of the Sovereigns," in one of his inimitable messages to
the Third House, recommended, with bitter irony, that a small portion of the land be
reserved for agriculture, and not all laid out in town lots.   There was almost some
grounds for the advice.

mere shysters—flourished in Saint Paul by the score. A large
share of them were purely street sharpers, having no office
but the sidewalk, and no capital but a roll of town-site maps,
and a package of blank deeds, yet all fairly coining money,
and spending it, in many cases, as rapidly as made, on fast
horses, fast women, wine and cards. These operators would
board boats, on their arrival, or hang around hotels, and, by a
little sharp maneuvering, as "confidence men," find out and
manipulate unsuspecting strangers, who had money, and fleece
them of their means, by selling them lots in moonshine towns,
for several hundred dollars each, not actually worth as many
cents, even if they got a title at all. Such operations were
repeated by the score, until Saint Paul and Minnesota got a
name abroad anything but enviable.

This mad, crazy, reckless spirit of speculation, which characterized those times, was appalling, to look on it now from a
soberer stand-point. Perhaps in no city of America, was the
real estate mania, and reckless trading and speculation, so
wild and extravagant, as in Saint Paul. It could not last, and
must soon bring its own punishment in general ruin. Indeed,
the storm was near at hand.

THE BUBBLE BURSTS.

On August 24, occurred the failure of the Ohio Life Insurance and Trust Company, of New York, which gave rise to
the memorable panic or financial revulsion of that year.

To Saint Paul, this pricking of the bubble of speculation
was more ruinous and dire in its consequences than perhaps
to any other city in the west. Everything had been so inflated and unreal—values purely fictitious, all classes in debt,
with but little real wealth, honest industry neglected, and
everything speculative and feverish—that the blow fell with
ruinous force. Business was paralyzed, real estate actually
valueless and unsaleable at any price, and but little good
money in circulation. Ruin stared all classes in the face.
The notes secured by mortgages must be paid, but all values
were destroyed. No device would raise money, for no one
had any to lend. Everybody was struggling to save himself.

The banking houses closed their doors—nearly all the mercantile firms suspended or made assignments. All works of improvement ceased, and general gloom and despondency settled down on the community. In a few days, from the top wave of prosperity. it was plunged into the slough of despond.

And now the " hard times" commenced in earnest. No description of this terrible and gloomy period will convey any idea of it. With many, even those who had but shortly before imagined themselves wealthy. there was a terrible struggle between pride and want. But few had saved anything, so generally had the reckless spirit of the times infested all classes. The humble poor. of course, suffered : but the keenest suffering was among those who experienced the fall from affluence to poverty.

The papers were crowded for months with foreclosures of mortgages, executions. and other results of the crash. Not one in five of the business houses or firms weathered the storm. despite the most desperate struggles. The population of the city fell off almost 50 per cent.. and stores would scarcely rent at any price.

BREVITIES.

On September 19. the gas works having been completed, and got in running order. gas was for the first time let on the city.

On September 21, A. C. JONES. Deputy Marshal, commenced to take the census of Ramsey county, pursuant to section four, of the Enabling Act. the object being to ascertain the population of the State when admitted, and fix its representation in Congress. The census was completed in about six weeks, and showed the population to be as follows : Of Saint Paul. 9.973 : of Ramsey county. 12,747, and of the Territory. 150,037. [It was the wish of the writer to have given the *names* of adult male citizens in this census. but the length of such a list precluded the attempt. after the list was prepared. and alphabetically arranged.]

THE FIRST STATE ELECTION

occurred on October 13. The State had not yet been admitted, though it was supposed this would be done in December, and State officers were therefore elected.   The vote in Ramsey county was as follows:

	Republican.	Democratic.
District Judge	E. C. Palmer, (Ind.,) 1936	Wm. P. Murray...1253
Senators	J. W. Selby.........1143	*Isaac Van Etten*..2040
	Martin D. Clark.....1048	*Charles S. Cave*..1690
	J. M. Marshall......1156	*Wm. Sprigg Hall*.1754
Representatives	James Day..........1297	*John W. Crosby*..2076
	Daniel Rohrer......1224	*Wm. Davern*.....1986
	Charles Colter......1073	*Wm. B. McGrorty*.1676
	B. F. Irvine.........1125	*Charles Rauch*....2037
	A. Varenne.........1088	*James Starkey*....2024
	V. B. Barnum.......1078	*Geo. L. Otis*......2079
Probate Judge.	C. T. Cotton........ 973	"Rev." J. Penman 1291
		A. C. Jones, (Ind.,) 691
Clerk of Court	E. Ingalls........... 986	*R. F. Houseworth*.2016
Sheriff	J. W. Prince, (Ind.,). 684	*J. Y. Caldwell*...1698
	R. B. Galusha, (Ind.,) 382	
Treasurer	*R. A. Smith,* (no opposition,)...............2659	
Attorney	*I. V. D. Heard,* (no opposition,)............3196	
Register Deeds.	Louis Demeules..... 370	*Edward Heenan*...1285
	S. Hough, (Ind.,)... 622	
Coroner	J. M. Castner........ 948	*Dr. J. V. Wren*...1708
Surveyor	James A. Case...... 303	*W. F. Duffy*......1236

Those in *italics* elected.

CURRENCY TROUBLES.

Toward winter, the stringency increased severely.   The currency which had been in use before the crash had about all gone up, or been withdrawn.   There was a limited amount of specie in circulation, but this was soon hoarded up.   Exchange on the east was 10 per cent. !   To devise some measures for relief, meetings of the merchants were held, and various measures recommended to the Legislature—a stay law, general banking system, &c.   The city and county boards were advised to issue " denominational scrip," to use as currency.   This scheme was soon after put in operation, and the *scrip* was in circulation for two or three years.   Every old settler remembers it—not with pleasure, perhaps.   But it was of some use.

In the midst of these troubles came a call from Stearns and other counties, asking relief for poor settlers, whose crops had been destroyed by grasshoppers. A considerable amount was subscribed in this city, poor as everybody was. Our own home destitute were also cared for, and public improvements were projected to give them employment.

The City Council this summer ordered two new fire engines, for the use of the city. In anticipation of this, two fire companies were organized—"Hope Engine Company, No. 1," on September 14, and "Minnehaha Engine Company, No. 2," on December 4. Of the former, M. LEVOY, R. C. WILEY, JAMES HERY, JOHN H. DODGE, and others, were the organizers: and of the latter, H. P. GRANT, M. J. O'CONNOR, R. G. SHARPE, L. E. CLARKE, J. B. OLIVIER, S. T. RAGUET, &c.

WILLIAM MARKOE built a handsome balloon this summer, and made two ascensions. The last was on October 8, at the Territorial Fair, in the Capitol grounds. S. S. EATON and H. H. BROWN went with him. The balloon descended on Rice Creek, about 18 miles northward, throwing Mr. EATON out, and breaking the valve ropes off in the neck of the balloon. The balloon shot up rapidly, and when a mile high, Mr. BROWN climbed up to the neck of the balloon by the netting, and secured the cords ! It was a perilous feat, but saved their lives.

From a report made to the Chamber of Commerce, it was ascertained that 343 buildings, costing $591,500, had been erected this season. Among them were several churches, a county jail, a school house, bridge, &c. For street improvements, sewers, &c., $133,153 had been expended.

CHAPTER XXIX.

EVENTS OF THE YEAR 1858.

THE "FIVE MILLION LOAN BILL"—CREATION OF THE FOURTH WARD—ADMIS-
SION OF THE STATE—DULLNESS OF BUSINESS—CABLE CELEBRATION—FIRE
ENGINES ARRIVE—HOMICIDE—DEDICATION OF SCHOOL HOUSES—ELECTION
STATISTICS.

ONE of the most noticeable events in 1858, was the "Five Million Loan," which was passed this spring, by the Legislature. and was voted on April 15. The debate on its merits was short, but somewhat acrimonious. Meetings were held, pro and con, handbills circulated, &c. R. O. SWEENY prepared an amusing caricature, which was lithographed by the opponents of the measure, and made much merriment. When the loan measure was voted on, it was carried by a majority that was surprising. In the city. the vote was, ayes 4,051, noes 183 !

In common with other cities of the country. Saint Paul was, that winter, visited by sweeping revivals of religion.

Navigation opened on March 25—one of the earliest dates on record—but travel and business on the river were painfully dull. The Northern Line Packet Company was put on this season.

The papers about this period frequently mention the " Sons of Malta." One of our citizens rose to the high rank of Cardinal in this ancient order.

The Fourth Ward was created by the Legislature this winter. out of the Third Ward.

THE CITY ELECTION

occurred on April 4. It was not a straight party contest. the Republicans making no nominations as such. The result was :

	Independent.	Democratic.
Mayor	Moses Sherburne.....1546	*N. W. Kittson*.....1788
Treasurer	*Daniel Rohrer*.......1936	Mich. Cummings...1334
City Justice.	{ *Orlando Simons*......1193	Thomas Howard....1191
		Nelson Gibbs........ 857
Comptroller	..*T. M. Metcalf*,.......1615	C. W. Williams.....1520

Those in *italics* elected.

Aldermen elected.—First Ward, C. H. Schurmeier; Second Ward, P. O'Gorman; Third Ward, Nicholas Gross, three years; Wm. H. Wolff, two years; Thomas Grace, one year; Fourth Ward, Henry M. Dodge.

BRIEF MENTION.

The LaCrosse and Milwaukee Railroad was completed this spring to LaCrosse. Little by little the iron horse was approaching our city.

On May 14. the papers announced that the State was admitted, but no demonstrations were made over the event. . The State officers were quietly sworn in on the 24th.

Business was depressingly dull all the season. Still. a number of buildings were built. and public improvements carried on. ' The scarcity of a good currency was a great drawback to trade.

During July, at an adjourned session of the Legislature, an attempt was made to remove the Capital to Nicollet Island, but it did not meet with much favor.

On September 1, Saint Paul. with other cities of the Union, celebrated the successful laying of the Atlantic Cable to England. The celebration was carried out with much spirit and enthusiasm—a procession, orations, music, &c., and at night fireworks and general illumination.

Our Fire Department were gladdened, this fall, by the arrival of two new engines, which the city had procured at Philadelphia. They were formally delivered to Hope Engine Company, No. 1, and Minnehaha. No. 2, on November 1, and did good service for some ten years, when steamers were substituted. This summer, also, Fort Snelling was abandoned by the Government, and Hon. JOHN S. PRINCE* purchased the

---

* Hon. JOHN S. PRINCE was born in Cincinnati, May 7, 1821, and resided in that city until 1840, being, during the latter part of that period, in the commission business. He

post engine, and presented it to a company formed of employees of his mill, called, "Rotary Mill Company, No. 1," so that we had now a well-equipped Fire Department.

On October 18, an old man, named JAMES McCLAY, was killed at a disreputable shanty, near the jail, by two roughs, named "Chicago JACK" and CORMACK MALLOY. They escaped without any punishment, by some technicality.

On November 13, Adams school was dedicated, and, soon after, Jefferson school. The latter burned down about nine years subsequently, and has been rebuilt on another site. Saint Paul had now three good school houses, and a good corps of teachers.

On December 22, "House of Hope," on Walnut street, was dedicated.

THE ELECTION

that fall was only for County Auditor and Representatives, the latter useless after all, as the session [of 1859] was never called. The following was the vote :

	Democratic.		Independent.	
	John B. Brisbin..1770		H. J. Taylor.....	941
	W. A. Gorman...1150		Wm. Branch.....	864
	E. D. Cobb.......1301		M. Groff.........	615
Representatives....	*Wm. Von Hamm*.1436		W. B. Quinn.....	87
	Wm. P. Murray..1209		T. M. Metcalf....	377
	John S. Prince...1523		W. II. Nobles....1061
County Auditor.......*L. P. Cotter*......1026			*Alex. Buchanan*..1084

Those in *italics* elected.

The business and financial outlook this fall was very discouraging. Trade was almost paralyzed. The harvest had been poor. There was no immigration. Some "Glencoe" money,

then entered the employ of the American Fur Company, at Evansville, Indiana, and after the company suspended in 1842, he engaged with PIERRE CHOUTEAU, Jr., & Co., who assumed the business, and became their purchasing agent, throughout Ohio, Indiana, Illinois, Michigan and Wisconsin. In 1854, he came to Saint Paul, to look after their real estate here. Connected with it was a saw mill, long known by early residents as the Rotary Mill. This was carried on by Mr. PRINCE for 15 years. He also dealt largely in real estate, on his own account. Personally, no gentleman in our city has been more popular than Mr. PRINCE. He was a member from Ramsey county, in the Constitutional Convention, and has been elected Mayor five times, being one of the most faithful and valuable municipal officers our city ever had.

based on the State railroad bonds, began to circulate, but they were looked on with distrust.   State scrip circulated for a while, but it soon ran down to forty cents on the dollar, and all classes were in bad financial straits.

NECROLOGY OF THE YEAR.

July 11, by drowning, Hon. Wm. Costello, ex-member of the Legislature, from this county.   November 23, M. W. Irwin, formerly United States Marshal for Minnesota.   December 4, John H. Brownson, a lawyer, (by falling from a window.)

CHAPTER XXX.

EVENTS OF THE YEAR 1859.

MURDER OF MRS. LALIYER—G. L. LUMSDEN CONVICTED OF MAIL ROBBERY—THE
BILANSKI MURDER CASE—WRIGHT COUNTY WAR—SKETCH OF BISHOP GRACE—
DEATH OF DOCTOR BORUP.

NO session of the Legislature was held this winter. Members had been elected, but the session was not called together by the Governor, it having been left for him to decide whether it was necessary or not.

CRIME.

During January, a man, named LAWRENCE LALIYER, was arrested at Prairie du Chien, on charge of having murdered his wife, in Mounds View township, in 1856. Her remains were found buried under an old ice house. LALIYER was tried for murder in the first degree twice, and, on the second hearing, convicted of murder in the second degree, and sentenced to a short term in the penitentiary.

On February 12, GEO. L. LUMSDEN, a clerk in the Saint Paul post-office, was arrested on charge of stealing a land warrant out of the mail, and selling it to HENRY McKENTY. He was convicted, and soon after sentenced to ten years' imprisonment in the State's prison. LUMSDEN was pardoned, in 1864, on condition that he would enlist in the army, which he did, and, in a few days afterwards, was killed at the battle of Nashville.

On March 11, STANISLAUS BILANSKI, a Polander by birth, of whom some account is given on page 121, died at his residence on the Stillwater road. He was married at the time to a woman whose name had been ANNIE EVARDS, formerly of Fayetteville, North Carolina, with whom he had had but little previous acquaintance, and of whose past life, what was

known, was not creditable.   BILANSKI's last illness was short,
and his symptoms thought suspicious by several persons who
visited him.   After his burial, a girl, who had been employed
in the family during BILANSKI's illness, reported that she had
purchased arsenic at Mrs. B.'s request, and mentioned other
circumstances fully sufficient to warrant the belief that BILAN-
SKI was the victim of a design to murder him on the part of
his wife.   Mrs. BILANSKI was at once arrested, and the body
of B. being exhumed, the stomach was subjected to analysis.
This was made by Dr. WM. H. MORTON, and revealed strong
and unmistakable proofs of arsenic, and, on May 15, Mrs. BI-
LANSKI was indicted for murder in the first degree.   On her
trial she was ably defended, but, on June 3d, was found guilty.
On December 9, she was sentenced to be hung, and March
23d was fixed by the Governor as the date.

"THE WRIGHT COUNTY WAR."

Many of the readers of this book may have heard of the
Wright County War, but do not know to what it refers.   In
the fall of 1858, one H. A. WALLACE was murdered in
Wright county, and a neighbor, named OSCAR F. JACKSON,
was tried for the offense, in the spring of 1859, but acquitted
by the jury.   On April 25, a crowd of men assembled, and
hung JACKSON to the gable end of WALLACE's cabin.   It was
a most wicked and inexcusable outrage.   Governor SIBLEY
offered a reward for the conviction of any of the lynchers.
Not long afterwards, one EMERY MOORE was arrested on the
charge of aiding in the affair, and taken to Wright county for
trial, but was rescued by a mob.   Governor SIBLEY at once
decided to take vigorous measures to maintain the majesty of
the law.   A military force was called out, and three companies dispatched (August 5) to Monticello, to arrest the rioters
and reinforce the law.   The Pioneer Guard headed the column, which was in command of Colonel JOHN S. PRINCE.
A few special officers and detectives accompanied the force.
The military proceeded to Monticello, reinforced the civil
authorities, arrested eleven lynchers and rescuers, and turned
them over to the Wright county officers.   Having subdued

the "rebellion," they returned on August 11—the "Wright County War," as it is facetiously termed, having fortunately ended without bloodshed.

THE CITY ELECTION

took place on May 3, resulting as follows:

Republican.		*Democratic.*	
Mayor........Henry J. Howe......1514		*D. A. Robertson*......1755	
Comptroller...F. Willius..........1468		*Wm. Von Hamm*......1801	
Treasurer....Daniel Rohrer.......1411		*C. A. Morgan*........1851	

Those in *italics* elected.

Aldermen elected.—First Ward, Wm. Branch; Second Ward, M. J. O'Connor; Third Ward, R. C. Wiley; Fourth Ward, Peter Berkey.

On May 23, Dr. J. F. HEYWARD, a capitalist of the city, died, leaving a large estate.

On July 1, Col. WILBUR M. HAYWARD, a lawyer of Saint Paul, died at Taylor's Falls.

On July 6, Dr. CHARLES W. BORUP, one of the first and most prominent bankers of the city, of the firm of BORUP & OAKES, died suddenly. He was a native of Denmark, came to America when young, and was engaged in the fur trade on Lake Superior for many years. He came to Saint Paul in 1849, and had been, since that date, one of the most influential and wealthiest citizens.

During August, the hearts of our Catholic population were gladdened by the arrival of Rt. Rev. THOMAS L. GRACE,* who

---

* Rt. Rev. THOMAS L. GRACE was born in Charleston, South Carolina, November 15, 1814. He commenced his studies, preparatory to the priesthood, under Bishop FENWICK, in the Seminary of Cincinnati, in 1828. A year later, he went to the Dominican Convent of Saint Rose, Kentucky, where he became a member of the Dominican order, continuing there his studies until 1837. In that year he went to Rome, and studied at the Minerva until 1844. He was ordained priest in Rome, December 21, 1839. On his return to America, in 1844, he was for two years engaged in the ministry in Kentucky, and for 13 years in Memphis, Tennessee. While in Memphis, he built the very fine church of Saints Peter and Paul, the Convent of Saint Agnes, Orphan Asylum, &c. On July 24, 1859, he was consecrated Bishop of Saint Paul, and arrived here shortly after. He has had great success in his zealous labors in this city and State, increasing the church greatly, procuring large additions to the clergy, opening schools, establishing charitable institutions, and multiplying churches. He is warmly beloved by his large congregation, and respected by other sects, for his learning, piety, amiable character and benevolence. He is regarded as one of the ablest prelates in America.

had recently been ordained Bishop of the diocese of Saint Paul.

The State election took place on October 11. WM. SPRIGG HALL, C. N. MACKUBIN and Dr. J. H. STEWART were elected Senators; and GEO. MITSCH. OSCAR STEPHENSON. J. B. OLIVIER. D. A. ROBERTSON. JOHN B. SANBORN and HENRY ACKER. Representatives; A. W. TULLIS. Sheriff; SHERWOOD HOUGH. Register; I. V. D. HEARD,* County Attorney; R. A. SMITH, Treasurer: J. F. HOYT. Probate Judge.

On December 5. a fire destroyed several frame buildings on the north side of Third street. where McCargar's Block now stands, and thence to the corner above.

On December 14, the two organs of the party. the *Minnesotian* and the *Times*, were united into one journal, and the joint proprietors, "NEWSON, MOORE, FOSTER & Co.," were elected State printers. This firm was not a happy family, and the union was soon dissolved.

The year 1859. closed with somewhat better prospects financially. The harvest had been abundant, and somewhat enlivened business. The people of the State were confident that the panic had spent its force, and that matters were now on the mend. For the first time this fall, grain had been exported from the State. and the people began to get on a foundation of *real* prosperity.

---

* ISAAC V. D. HEARD was born at Goshen, New York, August 31, 1834. He came to Saint Paul in May, 1852, when 18 years of age, studied law, and was admitted to practice. He was elected City Attorney in 1856, and again in 1865, 1866 and 1867. He was appointed County Attorney in 1857, elected the same fall for two years, and re-elected in 1859 and 1861, serving over six years. He was elected State Senator from Ramsey county, in 1871. Mr. HEARD volunteered, during the Sioux War, in an independent cavalry company; was Judge Advocate during the trial of the 303 Indian murderers the same fall, and afterwards wrote a valuable work on the Sioux War.

CHAPTER XXXI.

EVENTS OF THE YEAR 1860.

SUPPOSED UXORICIDE—DESTRUCTIVE FIRES—EXECUTION OF MRS. BILANSKI—
PRICES, BUSINESS, &C.—THE DOUGLAS AND LINCOLN CAMPAIGN—SUICIDE OF
WM. C. GRAY.

ON January 26. the wife of a shoemaker. named WM.
O'NEILL. was found dead in their hovel, in the swamp.
near the corner of Seventh and Cedar streets.   It was uncertain whether she had died by accident. or her husband murdered her in a drunken fit.   He was tried for it. at any rate, and sentenced to Stillwater for five years.

February 25. THEODORE FRENCH. a leading lawyer of the city, died.

On March 16. most of the buildings on both sides of Third street. from Robert to Jackson. were destroyed by fire.   It commenced in the clothing store of a well-known character. named ISAAC ANSELL.   Some 25 or 30 business houses were broken up by this calamity.

These fires. of which there were several very destructive ones, from 1857 to 1861. always produced great discouragement.   But from the ashes of despair ever grew the plant of new hope and courage.   The fires really did good.   Most of the buildings destroyed were old shells. and in their places fine and valuable. blocks were built.   Old settlers have seen Third street swept by flames nearly from one end to the other. and rebuilt again.

On March 22. the appointment of W. M. CORCORAN. a lawyer and real estate dealer, as postmaster, was announced. He held the office about a year.   He resides now in Maryland.

THE EXECUTION OF MRS. BILANSKI.

A strong effort was made by a few members of the Legislature, opposed to capital punishment, to commute the death-sentence of Mrs. BILANSKI, to imprisonment for life. A bill to accomplish this was passed early in March, but Governor RAMSEY promptly vetoed it, on the grounds of unconstitutionality, and that it was a case not calling for any show of clemency. The law, therefore, took its course.

The execution of the unfortunate woman took place at ten o'clock, on March 23d. The scaffold was erected in the enclosed yard adjoining the jail, and alongside the old hook and ladder house. An immense crowd, several thousand in number, were present. The Pioneer Guards, with loaded muskets and fixed bayonets, were placed in line in front of the jail, to preserve order. Mrs. BILANSKI, who had spent the whole morning in devotional exercises, with Father CAILLET and another clergyman, walked with a firm step to the gallows, cheerfully bidding her acquaintances good-bye. Before the fatal noose was adjusted, she spoke a few words, to the effect that she had not had justice in her trial, and conveying the impression that she was innocent. She then kissed the crucifix, the black cap was put on, and the noose adjusted. The bolt was then drawn, and the body fell. After hanging a short time, it was taken down and buried in the Catholic cemetery.

THE CITY ELECTION

this spring resulted as follows:

Democratic.		Republican.	
Mayor.........*John S. Prince*.....1148		C. D. Gilfillan.........1133	
Treasurer ....*Chas. A. Morgan*...1257		Geo. C. Mott..........1012	
Comptroller...*Wm. Von Hamm*...1262		T. M. Metcalf.........1012	
City Justice...*Nelson Gibbs*.......1285		Luke Marvin.......... 997	

Those in *italics* elected.

County Commissioners elected.—J. C. Burbank, J. R. Irvine, John Smith, J. W. McClung, John Nicols.

Aldermen elected.—First Ward, R. H. Fitz; Second Ward, H. P. Grant; Third Ward, C. M. Daily; Fourth Ward, W. M. Corcoran.

"Ingersoll's Block" was this year built by D. W. Ingersoll.*

---

*DANIEL W. INGERSOLL was born at Newton, New Jersey, June 12, 1812. At quite an early age he entered the mercantile business, in the employ of a friend, at Newton,

26

It supplied a great want in the matter of a public hall for meetings, &c. It was used for some 14 years for that purpose. and. a few months ago, converted into offices.

PRICES—BUSINESS—IMMIGRATION.

Some improvement in business. &c., was noticeable during this spring, and immigration commenced. Much of the splendid wholesale trade of our city dates from this time, and was one of the good results of the commercial revulsion. Country dealers. unable to buy large stocks east, on long credit. as formerly, could purchase small lots in Saint Paul for cash. and many of our merchants thus had a wholesale trade thrust on them. without seeking it. which has grown into huge proportions, and now employs an immense capital. Thus, out of the nettle disaster. we plucked the flower prosperity.

Prices had, about this date, touched their lowest ebb. Produce and provisions, fuel, rents. &c.. were so low that even a little money would go a great ways in the " pursuit of happiness." The *Minnesotian*, of June 2. mentions that houses. that in 1856 or 1857 rented for $18 and $20 per month, then only brought $5 and $6. Potatoes were 15 and 18 cents a bushel ; wood, $4 per cord, and other necessaries in proportion. Even whisky could be had for 25 cents a gallon. Alas ! that those halcyon days should have fled forever !

FRAGMENTS.

On April 7, Rogers'* Block was destroyed by fire.

who not long after removed to Burlington, Vermont, and Mr. INGERSOLL accompanied him to that place, ultimately becoming his partner. In 1837, Mr. INGERSOLL removed to New York, and engaged in trade there, remaining until 1855, when he came to Saint Paul. He established his dry goods house here the following year, which has continued one of the leading establishments of Minnesota since that year. Mr. INGERSOLL was never elected to any position except the School Board, in which he has given valuable labor for education, and is now its President, but has held many honorary appointments, being President of the State Reform School Board of Managers, President of the State Temperance Association, &c., and member of a number of charitable, religious, and similar bodies. He is one of our most faithful and energetic workers in every good cause.

* HIRAM ROGERS was born in Bucks county, Pennsylvania, April 7, 1806. He subsequently went to Philadelphia, where he was engaged in the manufacture of morocco, &c., which he carried on extensively for some years. In 1836, he removed to Zanesville,

The census was taken in June, by John M. Lamb, Deputy Marshal. The result was reported: Population of the city,

D. W. INGERSOLL.

10,279; of the county. 12,150; native born, (in city,) 5,620; foreign born, 4,659.

Ohio, where he carried on leather, and boot and shoe manufacturing, for about 20 years. In 1856, he came to Saint Paul, investing a large amount of capital here, and erecting several fine blocks of buildings, &c. He has also, in connection with his son, Wm. D. Rogers, carried on the manufacture of boot-packs, &c., quite extensively, and in other ways added to the trade and prosperity of our city.

This season. Capt. DAVIDSON started a line of packets from Saint Paul to LaCrosse, with three small boats, and thus laid the foundation of his present marine corporation. The presidential campaign of 1860 was a memorable one, and was hotly contested in Saint Paul. The Republicans had a large club, called the "Wide Awakes," commanded by Capt. WM. H. ACKER,* and the DOUGLAS Democrats had a similar club, called the "Little Giants," commanded by Capt. ALEX. WILKIN. Both were finely drilled.

On August 9, the telegraph from Saint Paul to LaCrosse being completed, the first message was sent, being addressed to Hon. WM. H. SEWARD.

On November 10, WM. C. GRAY, once a prominent broker and real estate dealer, committed suicide, by leaping over the bridge into the river. A sheriff had arrested him for forgery, when GRAY broke away from him, ran to the bridge, and committed the desperate act, in full sight of a number of persons.

The county election (November 6) resulted as follows:

	Republican.	Democratic.
Auditor	T. M. Metcalf..1510	C. W. Griggs...... 943
Court Commissioner	O. Malmros....1288	Greenleaf Clark....1169
Surveyor	D. L. Curtice..1251	C. M. Boyle.......1214
Senate	*Jas. Smith, Jr.*. 703	J. C. Burbank..... 673
	Jno. B. Sanborn 581	Alex. Wilkin....... 506
House	*Andrew Nessel.†* 677	J. P. Kidder........ 679
	Henry Acker... 726	John S. Prince..... 663
	W. L. Banning. 501	Thomas Daly...... 447

Those in *italics* elected.

---

* Captain WILLIAM H. ACKER was born in Clyde, Wayne county, New York, December 5, 1833. He was a son of Hon. HENRY ACKER, deceased, who held several important offices in this county at various times. WM. H. spent most of his youth in Michigan, coming to Saint Paul in 1854. He was book-keeper in the banking house of W. R. MARSHALL, for several years. In 1856, he was one of the organizers of the Pioneer Guard, the first military company in Minnesota, and was afterwards its Captain. He was very fond of military exercises, and was a fine drill-master. On March 19, 1860, Governor RAMSEY appointed him Adjutant General of the State, but when the war broke out in 1861, General ACKER resigned, and recruited a company, which became Company C, First Regiment. He was wounded at Bull Run, and afterwards commissioned a Captain in the Sixteenth Regulars. He fell at Shiloh, April 6, 1862. His death created profound sorrow in this city, where he was warmly esteemed. His remains now repose in Oakland cemetery.

† NESSEL contested KIDDER's seat and gained it.

On December 25, WM. HOLLINSHEAD, one of the ablest lawyers of the city, died.

The *Daily Times* was this month sold to WM. R. MAR-SHALL, who, on January 1, issued it as the *Daily Press.*

CAPT. WILLIAM H. ACKER.

The year 1860 closed under gloomy circumstances. The disunion cloud was darkening the southern horizon, and the mutterings of war were heard in the distance. Trade was again depressed, currency depreciated, and gloom and forebodings rested on all.

CHAPTER XXXII.

EVENTS OF THE WAR PERIOD.—1861 TO 1865.

THE DISUNION PERIOD—OPENING OF THE WAR—THE FIRST REGIMENT RAISED—
OFFICERS OF THE VARIOUS REGIMENTS—OUR RAILROAD SYSTEM BEGUN—THE
SAINT PAUL AND PACIFIC RAILROAD—OVERLAND EMIGRATION—THE CALL FOR
600,000 MEN—THE SIOUX OUTBREAK—BIRCH COOLIE—ORIGIN OF OUR BANKING
SYSTEM—SAINT PAUL AND SIOUX CITY RAILROAD—CASUALTIES AND CRIMES—
THE SANITARY FAIR—END OF THE WAR—CELEBRATION—RETURN OF OUR
REGIMENTS—OUR QUOTA, &C.

THE year 1861 was marked in history by the opening of
the great struggle between the Northern and Southern
States. The disunion movement, which began in the fall of
1860, steadily advanced, and in its course the depression of
business, the failure of banks, and gloomy forebodings of
trouble, were the results. In Saint Paul this was especially so.

At the municipal election, (April 2,) the following vote
was cast:

	Republican.		*Democratic.*	
Mayor	Dr. J. H. Stewart	881	*John S. Prince*	1121
Comptroller	Findley McCormick	860	*Wm. Von Hamm*	1135

Those in *italics* elected.

Aldermen elected.—First Ward, J. E. Thompson; Second Ward,
Wm. P. Murray; Third Ward, N. Gross; Fourth Ward, L. H. Eddy.

During this month, the appointment of CHARLES NICHOLS,
as postmaster, was announced; also GEO. W. MOORE, Collector of the Port; Hon. AARON GOODRICH, Secretary of
Legation to Brussels. &c.

On April 13, the telegraph brought the sad news of the fall
of Sumter, and the call for 75,000 troops. Great excitement
prevailed for some days, and war was the only theme of conversation. Capt. WM. H. ACKER and Capt. ALEX. WILKIN,
at once commenced recruiting companies for the First Minnesota Regiment, and war meetings were held to encourage en-

listments.   Gen. JOHN B. SANBORN* was appointed Adjutant
General of the State, vice ACKER, resigned.

In four days, Capt. ACKER's Company (C) was full, and ac-
cepted, with the following officers : Captain, WM. H. ACKER ;
First Lieutenant, WILSON B. FARRELL ; Second Lieutenant,
SAMUEL T. RAGUET.   On the 22d, Capt. WILKIN's Company
" A," (Pioneer Guard,) was accepted—First Lieutenant,
HARRY C. COATES ; Second Lieutenant, H. ZIERENBERG.
Ex-Governor GORMAN was commissioned Colonel of the Regi-
ment, with Dr. J. H. STEWART as Surgeon, and Rev. E. D.
NEILL as Chaplain.   The Regiment was mustered in at Fort
Snelling on April 29, and on June 22, left for Washington.
In the meantime a

SECOND REGIMENT

had been accepted.   " The Western Zouaves" was recruited
in Saint Paul by Capt. H. H. WESTERN, and became Company D.   The Regiment was mustered in on June 26.   Among

---

* Gen. JOHN B. SANBORN was born December 5, 1826, in Merrimac county, New
Hampshire.   Determining upon the profession of law, after preparatory schooling, he
studied three years, and was admitted to practice in July, 1854.   In December, of the
same year, he removed to Saint Paul, and at once began a successful practice here, in
the well-known law firm of early days—" SANBORN, FRENCH & LUND."

In 1859, he was elected a member of the House of Representatives.   The next year
he was elected to the Senate of 1861.   Hardly had his term closed, when the war broke
out, and he was appointed Adjutant General of the State.   Very heavy labor now de-
volved on him, in the organizing, arming and equipping of the four regiments raised that
year.   When the Fourth Regiment was filled, the command was tendered to him, and
he accepted it (December.)   He remained in command of Fort Snelling that winter,
and early in the spring of 1862, his regiment was sent to Mississippi, when it at once
entered the Corinth campaign.   Col. SANBORN was placed in command of a demi-
brigade, and subsequently of a brigade, afterwards part of the famous 17th army corps.
On September 19, at Iuka, he lost 600 out of 2,200 of his men, and, for his gallant conduct, was promoted to Brigadier General.   He was also in the battles of Port Gibson,
Raymond, Jackson, Champion Hills, and the assault on Vicksburg.   After the surrender of the latter post, he was assigned to the command of the southwest district of
Missouri, where, after the campaign against PRICE, he was, upon recommendation of
Gen. ROSECRANS, promoted to Brevet Major General, for "gallant and meritorious
services."

After the close of the war, he performed other important duties, civil and military, for
some months.   In September, 1866, he was appointed one of the special "Peace Commission," along with Generals SHERMAN, HARNEY, TERRY, and Senator HENDER-
SON, to negotiate treaties with the principal tribes of the central plains.   The commission
was engaged 18 months on this important labor.

On his return home, he resumed the practice of his profession.   In 1872, he again
served as a member of the Legislature.

our citizens who, at various times, held rank and commissions on its rolls, are the following :

Alex. Wilkin, Lieut. Colonel; Dr. W. L. Armington, Assistant Surgeon; John D. Wilson, (Company D,) Sergeant-Major; Webster D. Hoover, (Company D,) Quartermaster Sergeant; Brewer Mattocks, Hospital Steward; Michael Esch, Band Leader, (died, July 10, 1873;) Calvin S. Uline, Second Lieutenant, Company I, afterwards Captain, Major and Lieut. Colonel; John B. Davis, Captain, Company F, and afterwards Major; John Moulton, Company D, promoted Lieutenant, Captain and Major; Horace H. Western, Captain, Company D; Moses C. Tuttle, First Lieutenant, Company D, promoted Captain; S. P. Jennison, Second Lieutenant, Company D, promoted First Lieutenant and Adjutant; C. F. Meyer, Second Lieutenant, Company G, promoted First Lieutenant and Adjutant; James W. Wood, Second Lieutenant, Company I, promoted First Lieutenant and Adjutant; Geo. W. Shurman, Adjutant, and promoted Captain, Company D; Samuel G. Trimble, Company D, promoted Second Lieutenant and First Lieutenant, (killed at Mission Ridge, November 25, 1863;) Hiram Lobdell, Company D, promoted Second Lieutenant and First Lieutenant; Jacob T. McCoy, Company D, promoted Second Lieutenant and First Lieutenant; Isaac W. Stuart, Company D, promoted Second Lieutenant; John S. Livingston, Second Lieutenant, Company F, promoted First Lieutenant and Captain; Andrew R. Kiefer, Captain, Company G; Jacob Mainzer, First Lieutenant, Company G; Henning Von Rumohr, Second Lieutenant, Company G, promoted First Lieutenant and Captain; Charles Rampe, promoted Second Lieutenant, Company G; Fred. Lambrecht, promoted Second Lieutenant, Company G; Jacob J. Noah, Captain, Company K; E. Allen Otis, Second Lieutenant, Company K, promoted Staff.

The Second Regiment left Fort Snelling for the seat of war October 14.

Congress, which assembled July 4, having authorized the raising of 500,000 troops, a Third, Fourth and Fifth Regiments were apportioned to Minnesota's quota, besides one or two companies of Cavalry and Batteries of Light Artillery, Sharpshooters, &c.

THE THIRD REGIMENT

was completed in October, and remained at Fort Snelling until March. Among the citizens of Saint Paul who served in its ranks, the following gained commissions :

Ephraim Pierce, Second Lieutenant, promoted First Lieutenant, Adjutant and Captain, Company F; Otto F. Dreher, First Lieutenant, Company F, promoted Captain, Company A; John C. Devereux, Second Lieutenant, Company G, promoted First Lieutenant and Captain; Damon Greenleaf, Second Lieutenant, Company I, promoted First Lieutenant and Captain; Hiram D. Gates, First Lieutenant, Company K.

THE FOURTH REGIMENT

was organized in December.   Saint Paul was largely represented in its officers, as follows:

John B. Sanborn, Colonel, afterwards Brigadier and Major General: D. M. G. Murphy, Quartermaster, promoted Captain, Company B: Dr. John H. Murphy, Surgeon; Geo. M. D. Lambert, Hospital Steward, promoted Assistant Surgeon; Rev. Asa S. Fiske, Chaplain; Frank E. Collins, Quartermaster Sergeant; Thomas P. Wilson, Commissary Sergeant, (afterwards Major of another regiment;) Wm. F. Wheeler, First Lieutenant, Company F, promoted Captain; James Drysdale, Second Lieutenant, Company F, promoted First Lieutenant; John G. Janicke, Second Lieutenant, Company G, promoted First Lieutenant; Edward H. Foster, Second Lieutenant. Company I; L. B. Martin, First Lieutenant, Company K, promoted Captain; Frank S. DeMers, Second Lieutenant, promoted Adjutant; Cheeseman Gould, Second Lieutenant, Company B, promoted First Lieutenant and Captain.

THE FIFTH REGIMENT

was recruited mostly during the winter of 1861–2, and was not mustered in until March, 1862. Our citizens who bore commissions in that Battalion, are as follows:

John C. Becht, Captain, Company E, promoted Major; Wm. B. Mc-Grorty, Quartermaster; Dr. J. A. Vervais, Surgeon; Rev. John Ireland,*

---

* Right Reverend JOHN IRELAND, D. D., was born at Burnchurch, Kilkenny county, Ireland, September 11, 1838. His parents came to America in 1849, settling at Chicago, where he attended school at "Saint Mary's of the Lake." Three years later, his father, RICHARD IRELAND, Esq., settled in Saint Paul, where he has since resided. In 1853, under the auspices of Bishop CRETIN, Dr. IRELAND left for France, to complete his studies, in company with Rev. THOMAS O'GORMAN, now of Rochester, Minnesota, and Rev. A. RAVOUX. The latter placed them at Meximeux, Ain, where Dr. IRELAND passed four years of preparatory study, and another four years with the Marist Fathers of Hyeres, Var, where he completed his theological course. In 1861, he returned to Saint Paul, and was ordained priest, by Bishop GRACE, on December 21. The next year he was commissioned Chaplain of the Fifth Minnesota Volunteers, and remained in service a year, resigning on account of ill-health. Since that date he has been pastor of the cathedral parish. On February 12, 1875, he was appointed by the Sovereign Pon-

Chaplain; F. A. Cariveau, First Lieutenant, Company D; Killian Six, Second Lieutenant, Company E; Ross Wilkinson, First Lieutenant, Company F, promoted Captain; David O. Oakes,'Second ,Lieutenant, Company F, (killed, May 28th, 1862, at Corinth;) W. A. Van Slyke, Second Lieutenant, Company G; Luther E. Clark, Captain, Company I; Alpheus R. French, Second Lieutenant, Company I, promoted First Lieutenant and Captain; Patrick Ryan, First Lieutenant, Company I; James Farrell, First Lieutenant, Company I.

BRACKETT'S BATTALION.

originally three companies, attached to the Fifth Iowa Cavalry, was recruited in the fall of 1861. Commissioned officers from Saint Paul as follows:

Alfred B. Brackett, Captain, Company C, promoted Major and Lieut. Colonel; Henning Von Minden, Captain Company A, promoted Major; Albert T. Phelps, Captain, Company A; August Matheus, Captain, Company A; Gustave Leue, Second Lieutenant, Company A; Joseph J. Buck, Second Lieutenant, Company A; Geo. A. Freudenrich, Second Lieutenant, Company A; Adam Lindig, Second Lieutenant, Company A; Wm. Smith, Second Lieutenant, Company B, promoted Captain; Erwin Y. Shelley, First Lieutenant, Company C, promoted Captain; Mortimer Neeley, Second Lieutenant, Company C, promoted First Lieutenant and Captain; R. W. Peckham, Second Lieutenant, Company C; Charles H. Osgood, Second Lieutenant, Company C; Andrew J. Church, Second Lieutenant, Company C; Wm. B. McGeorge, Second Lieutenant, Company C, promoted First Lieutenant and Adjutant.

At the election, on October 9. the following officers were chosen: Senators.—JAMES SMITH. Jr.. and J. R. IRVINE. Representatives.—HENRY L. CARVER. PHILIP ROHR. N. GROSS. Sheriff.—D. A. ROBERTSON. Treasurer.—R. A. SMITH. Register.—CHARLES PASSAVANT. Clerk of Court.— GEO. W. PRESCOTT. Attorney.—I. V. D. HEARD. Probate Judge.—J. F. HOYT. (HOYT resigned in1 862, when E. C. LAMBERT was elected.)

---

tiff, Bishop of Maronea, *in partibus infidelium*, and Vicar Apostolic of Nebraska, but, at the solicitation of Bishop GRACE, this appointment was recalled, and Dr. IRELAND was appointed to the Coadjutorship of the See of Saint Paul—consecrated December 21, 1875. Dr. IRELAND, since his priesthood began, has labored untiringly for the welfare of his flock, and is looked up to by them with the deepest affection. His labors in the cause of temperance, which have been blessed with remarkable success, have gained him the gratitude of every good citizen. He is zealous in all good works, is an impressive and eloquent preacher, and, having attained a rank but few prelates reach at his age, a career of extensive usefulness is yet before him.

EVENTS OF THE YEAR 1862.

The year 1862, was marked by several important events— among which were the Sioux massacre, the heavy levies of troops, the beginning of our railroad system, &c.

The principal legislation of the winter, affecting Saint Paul. was the creation of the Fifth Ward.

The second company of Sharpshooters was recruited this spring. Capt. WM. J. RUSSELL, First Lieut. EMIL A. BURGER, and Second Lieut. JOHN A. W. JONES, were citizens of Saint Paul.

The Legislature of 1862, did a work of great importance by infusing life into our dead railroads. The franchises, which the State secured by foreclosure sale in 1860, were conveyed to new corporations. Work was commenced vigorously on the Saint Paul and Pacific Road, between Saint Paul and Saint Anthony, by Messrs. WINTERS & DRAKE.* and iron arrived early in the summer, sufficient to lay the track to Saint Anthony.

THE SAINT PAUL AND PACIFIC RAILROAD

may truly be called a Saint Paul institution, and as such it has always been regarded. It was projected and started by Saint Paul citizens, and has been almost exclusively managed and officered by them. The company was first chartered by the Legislature, May 22, 1857, and endowed with a part of the Congressional land grant, under the name "Minnesota and Pacific Railroad," and authorized to construct a line "from Stillwater via Saint Paul and Saint Anthony to Breckenridge, on the Sioux Wood River, with a branch from Saint Anthony via

---

* ELIAS F. DRAKE, one of the pioneer railroad men of Minnesota, is a native of Ohio, in which State he lived until he came to St. Paul, in 1861. In early life he studied law, and practiced awhile, but was more interested in finance than law, and was appointed cashier of the State Bank of Ohio, which position he filled ten years. During that period he served three terms as member of the Legislature, one of which he was Speaker. He was largely interested in works of internal improvement, embarking capital in several of them. Mr. DRAKE, in company with two other capitalists, (HIRSHMAN & WINTERS,) in 1862, built the first railroad in Minnesota, from Saint Paul to Saint Anthony, which gave a start to our present splendid railroad system. Soon after, he, with some associates, took hold of the Minnesota Valley Railroad, and, in the face of great obstacles, completed it to Sioux City, Iowa, in 1872. Mr. DRAKE represented his county in the State Senate in 1874-5, with marked ability, and advantage to the State. He is known as one of the most able, sagacious, hard-working and resolute business men in our State.

Anoka, Saint Cloud and Crow Wing, to Saint Vincent, near the mouth of the Pembina River," &c. Among the names of the first Board of Directors (named in the act) were ALEX. RAMSEY, EDMUND RICE, R. R. NELSON, WM. L. AMES, CHARLES H. OAKES, F. R. DELANO, and other past and present citizens of Saint Paul. EDMUND RICE was first President. The line was surveyed in 1857, and some grading done by SELAH CHAMBERLAIN that fall, but the panic, then raging, prevented much active work being done.

When the five million loan bill was passed, in 1858, work was resumed vigorously, and most of the bed between Saint Paul and Saint Anthony graded, when the failure of the loan scheme again compelled a stoppage of work.

In 1860, the mortgage given by the road to the State, as security for its aid, was foreclosed, and the bed, franchises, &c., became the property of the State, and so remained until March, 10, 1862, when the Legislature conferred them on EDMUND RICE, R. R. NELSON, E. A. C. HATCH, J. E. THOMPSON, WM. LEE, and others, with provisos that certain portions should be constructed by specified dates. The name of the corporation was also changed to "Saint Paul and Pacific Railroad Company."

A contract was soon entered into, (March 11, 1862,) with Messrs. E. F. DRAKE and V. WINTERS, to construct the road from Saint Paul to Saint Anthony, and it was completed and running on June 28, of that year. The first locomotive was the "William Crooks,"* named in honor of the Chief Engineer of the road: it was run by WEBSTER C. GARDNER, who still runs on the same road; and J. B. RICE, at present Assistant Superintendent, was the conductor of the first train. Hon. E. RICE, the President, about that time, went to England, where he enlisted capitalists in the construction of the road, and sent back 3,000 tons of rails for its construction. Work was steadily pushed on the road during the ensuing year. On February 6, 1864, the road was divided into two companies—the part from Saint Paul to Breckenridge, and the Branch Line to Watab, being called the "First Division," under the presidency of GEO. L. BECKER, and the remaining portion, (Saint Cloud to Saint Vincent, Saint Paul to Winona, &c.,) being

---

* WILLIAM CROOKS was born in New York City, June 20, 1832. He attended West Point Military Academy, and learned the profession of Civil Engineer. He came to Saint Paul in 1857, as Chief Engineer of the Saint Paul and Pacific Railroad, and was one of the men who helped carry through that enterprise in its dark and trying days. In honor of his services, the first engine which ever turned a wheel in Minnesota, (1862,) was named for him. Col. CROOKS volunteered in the Sixth Regiment, in 1862; was commissioned Colonel, and commanded that fine battalion two years, resigning October, 1864. He then aided Hon. E. RICE in starting the "River Road," making two trips to Europe, &c. Col. CROOKS was a member of the Legislature in 1875, and has been re-elected for another term. He also served a term as member of the Board of Public Works of Saint Paul.

called the "Saint Paul and Pacific." Recently, the Saint Vincent branch has been leased to the "First Division" for 99 years, and thus is now again virtually one organization.

On the Branch Line, the road was completed to Elk River, 39 miles.

E. F. DRAKE.

in 1864, and, on September 1, 1866, to Saint Cloud, 74 miles.   On the Main Line it was completed to Wayzata in 1867; to Willmar in 1869; to Benson in 1870, and to Breckenridge, 217 miles from Saint Paul, in October, 1871.   The road from Saint Cloud to Melrose, 35 miles, has also been completed, and from Glyndon to Crookston, 84 miles, &c.

The officers of the Saint Paul and Pacific, (including both divisions at the various dates,) have been :   Presidents.—1857 to 1871, Hon. ED. RICE; 1864 to 1875, (First Division,) Hon. GEO. L. BECKER, (the latter also Land Commissioner.)   Vice Presidents.—Hon. R. R. NELSON, to 1864, and W. B. LITCHFIELD, thence.   Secretaries.—J. W. TAYLOR, HENRY ACKER, S. S. BREED, (1864 to 1875.)   Treasurer and present Land Commissioner.—HERMAN TROTT. Superintendents.—First, WM. CROOKS; second, W. B. LITCHFIELD; third, F. R. DELANO; fourth, E. Q. SEWALL.   Chief Engineers.—First, D. C. SHEPARD; second, WM. CROOKS; third, CHAS. A. F. MORRIS.   General Ticket Agent.— 1862 to 1875, JOHN H. RANDALL.   General Freight Agent.—1862 to 1875, JAMES W. DORAN.   Attorney.—HENRY F. MASTERSON. ' The names of some of the old and faithful officers of this pioneer road have been very appropriately given to the flourishing towns along the main line.

THE SAINT PAUL AND CHICAGO RAILWAY.

Section 25 of the original charter of the Minnesota and Pacific Railroad, authorized a line from Saint Paul to Winona.   On March 6, 1863, a grant of swamp lands was made to it by the State.   The city of Saint Paul subsequently gave a bonus of $50,000 to the line, and, on March 19, 1867, the Directors of the Saint Paul and Pacific Railroad resolved that it should be called the "Saint Paul and Chicago Railway." In 1864, Hon. E. RICE, President of the Saint Paul and Pacific Railroad, commenced active efforts to build the road.   He went to England, enlisted the aid of capitalists, procured an enlargement of the land grant, and, in a few months, the road was under way, and progressed steadily until completed to LaCrescent, in 1872.   Through eastern trains commenced running in September, 1872, via Winona.   The road bed was sold to the Saint Paul and Milwaukee road, of which it is the "River Division."   The officers of the road have been :   President.—EDMUND RICE, 1864 to 1875.   Chief Engineers.—C. A. F. MORRIS, WILLIAM CROOKS, D. C. SHEPARD, and, at present, JOSEPH G. DODGE.   Secretary.—HENRY ACKER, &c.

The city election took place on April 1, with the following result :

Republican.		Democratic.	
Mayor........D. W. Ingersoll.........853		*John S. Prince*.....1197	
Comptroller ..Edw. Zimmerman......815		*Wm. Von Hamm*....1216	
Treasurer.. ..A. Armstrong, (Ind.,)..869		*C. A. Morgan*......1174	
City Justice ..A. McElrath 925		*N. Gibbs*...........1106	

Those in *italics* elected.

This summer, an important movement was inaugurated, that ultimately led the way for the Northern Pacific Railroad, by calling public attention to the desirability of the route via the Upper Missouri.   A party of citizens formed an expedition to go to the gold mines in Idaho and Montana, overland, and started on May 14.   They arrived safely.   Meantime Congress appropriated a small amount for guidance and protection to emigrant trains.   Capt. JAMES L. FISK was appointed to command an expedition, and another train left on June 16, getting through safely.   Most of our citizens who accompanied these expeditions, ultimately returned.

The call ·for 600,000 men, in July, was very disheartening, coming after the disasters in Virginia, but was bravely met. Meetings were called, funds subscribed to encourage enlistments, the city voted a monthly bounty to the families of volunteers, and with this stimulus five regiments were raised in a few days.   Among our citizens who held official rank in these regiments were :

SIXTH REGIMENT.

William Crooks, Colonel; Hiram P. Grant, Captain, Company A. promoted Major and Lieut. Colonel; F. E. Snow, Adjutant; Alonzo P. Connolly, First Lieutenant, promoted Adjutant; H. L. Carver, Quartermaster; H. H. Gilbert, Second Lieutenant, Company G, promoted First Lieutenant and Quartermaster; Dr. A. Wharton, Surgeon; Dr. J. W. McMasters, Assistant Surgeon; Harry Gillham, First Lieutenant, Company A, promoted Captain; Wm. T. Barnes, First Lieutenant. Company A; Jacob E. Baldwin, Second Lieutenant, (died; December 10, 1863;) Dana White, First Lieutenant, Company C, promoted Captain; R. Schœnemann, Captain, Company E: Christian Exel, First Lieutenant, Company E; Matthias Holl, Second Lieutenant, Company E, promoted First Lieutenant; Justus B. Bell, Second Lieutenant. Company E; D. H. Valentine, Captain, Company G; Chas. J. Stees, Second Lieutenant, Company G, promoted Captain; Geo. W. Prescott, First Lieutenant, Company G; A. C. Helmkamp, Second Lieutenant, Company G, (died, September 24, 1864, at Saint Paul;) E. O. Zimmerman, Second Lieutenant, Company G; Fred. Norwood, Sergeant-Major; D. H. McCloud, Sergeant-Major; H. D. Tenney, Quartermaster Sergeant; Wm. S. McCauley, Commissary Sergeant; John H. Gillis, Hospital Steward, (died, April 8, 1864, at Saint Peter;) George L. Van Solen, Hospital Steward.

SEVENTH REGIMENT.

Wm. R. Marshall, Colonel, promoted Brigadier General; Dr. Brewer

Mattocks, Assistant Surgeon; Wm. H. Burt, Captain, Company C; Frank H. Pratt, Second Lieutenant, Company C, promoted First Lieutenant and Captain; Stephen C. Miller, Second Lieutenant, Company F, promoted Captain; James Gilfillan, Captain, Company H, promoted Colonel, Eleventh Regiment; S. Lee Davis, Second Lieutenant, Company H, promoted First Lieutenant.

EIGHTH REGIMENT.

Dr. F. Rieger, Surgeon; Wm. Paist, Second Lieutenant, Company H, promoted Captain; Egbert E. Hughson, First Lieutenant, Company H; John G. McGregor, Second Lieutenant, Company I, promoted First Lieutenant and Captain; Wm. T. Rockwood, Captain, Company K; John I. Salter, First Lieutenant, Company K; Benj. W. Brunson. First Lieutenant, Company K; William Helsper, Second Lieutenant. Company K; R. Goodhart, Sergeant-Major; Edgar W. Bass, Quartermaster Sergeant.

NINTH REGIMENT.

Alex. Wilkin, Colonel, (killed at Tupelo, July 14, 1864;) John P. Owens, Quartermaster, brevetted Colonel; Dr. John J. Dewey, Assistant Surgeon; S. P. Tomlinson, Hospital Steward; Thomas Van Etten, Second Lieutenant, Company I, promoted First Lieutenant and Captain.

TENTH REGIMENT.

Samuel P. Jennison, Lieutenant Colonel; Cyrus A. Brooks, Assistant Surgeon; M. R. Prendergast, Commissary Sergeant; M. H. Sullivan, Captain, Company H; M. J. O'Connor, Captain, Company K.

Hardly were these regiments raised, when the fearful Sioux massacre occurred on our frontier. The news of this event was received here on August 20. A volunteer cavalry company was at once raised by our citizens, and started, with other troops, toward the scene of the massacre. Some of this company afterwards fell at Birch Coolie. Large numbers of fugitives from the western counties fled to Saint Paul for safety, destitute and panic-stricken, and many of them suffering from wounds.

On September 2d, occurred the tragic affair at Birch Coolie. The news was received here on the 6th, and it was truly one of the blackest days in the many gloomy ones of that year of disaster and trouble. In the conflict at Birch Coolie, 23 men were killed and 60 wounded. Among the Saint Paul men

who lost their lives were : BENJ. S. TERRY, FRED. S. BEN-
EKEN, GEORGE COLTER, WM. M. COBB, WM. IRVINE, WM.
RUSSELL, JOHN COLLEDGE, H. WHETSLER, ROBERT BAX-
TER, ROBERT GIBBENS.   The bodies of these men were
afterwards disinterred and brought to Saint Paul, where they
were buried with appropriate honors.

ITEMS.

The *Daily Union* was established this fall, by F. DRISCOLL.
In the spring of 1863, it was consolidated with the *Daily Press*.
The post-office was removed, in December, to the stone
building on Third street, above Market.
On October 10, the Winslow House was burned down.
The election this fall, November 2, resulted as follows :
Representatives.—WM. P. MURRAY, J. P. KIDDER, J. B.
BRISBIN.   Auditor.—WM. H. FORBES.   Probate Judge.—E.
C. LAMBERT.   Coroner.—O. F. FORD.

NECROLOGY OF 1862.

Died, January 4, at Saint Paul, MICHAEL E. AMES, a well-
known lawyer of our city.   April 8, at Shiloh, Captain WM.
H. ACKER, of Saint Paul.   May 19, ALEX. BUCHANAN, ex-
County Auditor.   May 28, at Corinth, Captain DAVID O.
OAKES.   August 24, in Canada, LOUIS M. OLIVIER, formerly
Register of Deeds.   September 12, LAWRENCE P. COTTER,
City Clerk.   December 22, at Saint Louis, EDWARD HEENAN,
formerly County Auditor.

EVENTS OF THE YEAR 1863.

The city election (April 7) resulted as follows :

	Union.		*Democratic.*	
Mayor	J. H. Stewart	838	*John Esaias Warren*	920
Comptroller	T. M. Metcalf	736	C. H. Lienau	1024
Assessor	C. T. Whitney	796	*John J. Soens*	938
Surveyor	G. A. Johnson	805	C. M. Boyle	957
Street Com'r	G. Rank	807	*John Dowlan*	938
Attorney	S. M. Flint, (on both tickets,)			1730

Those in *italics* elected.

27

This season commenced the memorable drought which extended over the years 1863 and 1864. The low water was the worst result, seriously affecting trade on the river.

Gen. SIBLEY's expedition to the Missouri occurred this year. Col. MILLER was in command of the headquarters here. In July, LITTLE CROW was reported killed.

On July 6, a torch-light procession, fireworks, illumination, &c., took place in honor of the victory of Gettysburg.

HATCH'S BATTALION

was organized during this summer. The following citizens of Saint Paul bore commissions:

E. A. C. Hatch, Major; Charles H. Mix, First Lieutenant, Company A, promoted Captain; Allen T. Chamblin, Captain, Company A; Geo. A. Freudenreich, Second Lieutenant, Company A; Wm. H. Ensign, First Lieutenant, Company B; James E. Cochrane, Second Lieutenant, Company C, promoted First Lieutenant; Mark T. Berry, First Lieutenant, Company E.

THE SECOND CAVALRY

also bore on its rolls the following names of our citizens:

Andrew J. Whitney, Commissary; Dr. J. A. Vervais, Surgeon; Dr. Charles J. Farley, Assistant Surgeon; Joseph S. Thompson, Sergeant-Major; Horace W. Moore, Hospital Steward; John Ledden, Second Lieutenant, Company H; Frank C. Griswold, Second Lieutenant, Company M.

Captain H. H. WESTERN was commissioned in June, First Lieutenant of the Third Battery.

ORIGIN OF OUR BANKING SYSTEM.

The year 1863 was marked in our financial history, by the establishment of the First National Bank, on December 8. This, the pioneer national bank of our State, was one of the earliest established in the country. Its original stockholders were: J. E. THOMPSON,* President; HORACE THOMPSON,

---

* JAMES E. and HORACE THOMPSON were born in Poultney, Vermont, in 1822 and 1827, respectively. While young men, they removed to Georgia, and entered into business there, remaining until 1859, when they settled in Saint Paul, and engaged in the banking business, with great success, becoming the leading bankers of Minnesota.

Cashier; T. A. HARRISON, Vice President; CHARLES SCHEF-
FER, Assistant Cashier; W. M. and H. G. HARRISON, and
J. C. BURBANK, Directors. H. P. UPHAM was appointed

L. E. REED.

Teller, and WM. H. KELLY, Book-keeper. Its present officers
are: H. THOMPSON. President; L. E. REED,* Vice Presi-

JAMES E. THOMPSON was suddenly cut off, in the prime of life, on May 28, 1870, but
not until he had established a reputation as one of the best financiers in Minnesota, and
one of the first men in our city. HORACE THOMPSON is also one of the ablest and most
influential capitalists in our State, and one of our most liberal and public-spirited citizens.

* L. E. REED was born in Massachusetts, in 1830. His parents removed to Ravenna,
Ohio, when he was three years old, and he lived there until 1851, when he came to Saint
Paul. Mr. REED engaged in the banking business, in our city, at a very early day,
being connected with the THOMPSON BROTHERS in 1862, and, subsequently, with the
First National Bank, when it was established, in 1863. He afterwards became a partner of WM. DAWSON, under the name of "DAWSON & COMPANY", and continued four
years, after which he was Vice President of the City Bank, for three years. In 1873, he
was elected Vice President of the First National Bank. Mr. REED, though a modest

dent; H. P. UPHAM, Cashier; W. W. HOYT. Paying Teller. Capital, $1,000,000. Surplus, $250,000.

The Second National Bank was established April 10, 1865. Its officers are: E. S. EDGERTON, President; D. A. MONFORT, Vice President; G. R. MONFORT, Cashier: W. B. BELL. Teller. Capital, $200,000.

The National Marine Bank was next organized. O. B. TURRELL, President; W. R. MARSHALL. Vice President: F. C. HOWES. Cashier. Capital, $100,000.

The Merchants National Bank, organized in 1870. M. AUERBACH, President; WALTER MANN. Vice President: W. R. MERRIAM. Cashier. Capital, $500,000.

The other banking houses of our city are as follows: German American Bank. FERDINAND WILLIUS, President; J. B. SANBORN. Vice President; GUSTAV WILLIUS. Cashier. Capital, $200,000.

Farmers and Mechanics Bank. JOHN FARRINGTON, President; Dr. A. WHARTON, Vice President; C. A. MORTON. Cashier. Capital, $50,000.

Savings Bank of Saint Paul. W. R. MARSHALL. President; H. SAHLGAARD. Vice President; JOHN S. PRINCE. Cashier.

DAWSON & COMPANY. [WILLIAM DAWSON. R. A. SMITH and ALBERT SCHEFFER.]

The total capital employed by the above banking houses, is over $2,000,000, and are all managed by men of acknowledged financial ability and experience.

The enrollment for the draft was made this summer, and as threats of resistance were made, and trouble was anticipated similar to that in other cities, a provost guard was stationed in the city for some weeks.

The election this fall was closely contested, the " Union League," a secret political organization, playing a conspicuous part. EDMUND RICE and JOHN NICOLS were elected Senators : and R. H. FITZ. J. P. KIDDER, and A. R. KIEFER.

and unassuming gentleman, in private life, is one of the ablest financiers in our State, and his judgment and sagacity are proverbial. He wields an influence in money circles greater than almost any man in Minnesota.

Representatives: D. A. ROBERTSON, Sheriff; R. A. SMITH. Treasurer: C. A. PASSAVANT, Register of Deeds; H. J. HORN,* Attorney; R. F. CROWELL, Judge of Probate: G. A. JOHNSON, Surveyor; PHILIP SCHEIG, Coroner, &c.

In October, the Seventh, Ninth and Tenth Regiments left for "Dixie."

December 20. the American House was destroyed by fire.

NECROLOGY OF 1863.

Died, April 12, at the residence of Hon. JOHN S. PRINCE, GABRIEL FRANCHERE, a 'pioneer of the Northwest. July 3, by a railroad accident, Capt. ABRAM BENNETT. July 10, CHARLES N. MACKUBIN, formerly a banker, legislator, &c. July 3, at Gettysburg, Capt. W. B. FARRELL. August 7, Capt. CHARLES KOCH, Fifth Regiment. November 9, HENRY A. LAMBERT, formerly Probate Judge. December 16, at Washington, ROBERT F. FISK.

PRINCIPAL EVENTS OF 1864.

The early part of this year was marked by the return of a number of our regiments on veteran furlough, and the entertainments given them by our citizens.

The city election this spring went Republican, for the first time, by the following vote:

Republican.		Democratic.	
Mayor........Dr. *J. H. Stewart*....1100		Geo. Culver........	784
City Justice...A. McElrath..........1140		F. F. Strother......	707
Comptroller ..H. Schiffbauer........1000		C. H. Lienau.......	859
Treasurer.....C. T. Whitney, (no opposition,)................			1875

Those in *italics* elected.

While the events of the war, the large levies of troops, the suffering, among the destitute families of absent soldiers, the

---

* HENRY J. HORN, (we had almost written "HARRY HORN," as his intimate friends call him,) was born in Philadelphia, in 1821. He studied law with HENRY D. GILPIN, and was admitted to the bar in 1849. In 1855, he came to Saint Paul, and has actively practiced his profession ever since. He was elected City Attorney in 1857, and re-elected in 1858 and 1859; elected County Attorney in 1863; member of School Board in 1857 and 1858, and is at present Corporation Counsel. His legal services to the city and county have been of great value, and he has been zealous in promoting every good work. No man has more warm friends than Mr. HORN, or is more respected and confided in.

mourning in thousands of households "over the unreturning
braves," and other incidents of the strife, sometimes caused
gloom, still there was remarkable courage and hopefulness
among the people. Financially, matters were curious. The
rise in gold, and the inflation produced by the enormous issues
of currency, created a buoyancy in business matters that gave
a silver edge to the cloud. Even real estate looked up, the
population increased, and our railroads were now in actual
progress. Security was restored to the frontier, and immigration recommenced.

SAINT PAUL AND SIOUX CITY RAILROAD.

This road was incorporated in 1857, as one of the lines of the Root
River Valley and Southern Minnesota Railroad, and separated from that
corporation in 1864, into a new line, called the "Minnesota Valley
Railroad." Under the five million loan impetus, a few miles of the road
from Mendota to Shakopee was partially graded, in 1858. Nothing
more was done until after the act of 1864. Messrs. E. F. DRAKE, JNO.
L. MERRIAM, HORACE THOMPSON, A. H. WILDER, H. H. SIBLEY, JNO.
S. PRINCE, J. C. BURBANK, W. F. DAVIDSON, CHAS. H. BIGELOW, GEO.
A. HAMILTON, Capt. R. BLAKELEY, and others, became incorporators
and stockholders, and furnished means to construct and equip a part
of the road. From this time on, its building was steadily pushed.
The line from Mendota to Shakopee was opened November 16, 1865;
from Saint Paul to Mendota, August 24, 1866; completed from Saint
Paul to Belle Plaine, November 19, 1866; to LeSueur, December 5,
1867; Saint Peter, August 17, 1868; Mankato, October 12, 1868; Lake
Crystal, December 13, 1869; Madelia, September 5, 1870; Saint James,
November 1, 1870; Worthington, 1871; Sioux City, 1872. [From
Sioux City, Iowa, to Saint James, Minnesota, the line is called "The
Sioux City and Saint Paul Railroad."]

This road is one of our home institutions. It was projected, constructed, and is still owned and operated and controlled by Saint Paul
men, who, by their expenditure of capital, and by their labor and
energy, have thus given the State this important and valuable highway
of commerce.

The officers of this road, since its period of active life, have been:
President and Land Commissioner.—Hon. E. F. DRAKE.   Vice Presi-
dent.—Hon. JNO. L. MERRIAM.   Secretary.—GEO. A. HAMILTON.
Chief Engineers.—First, JOHN B. FISH; second, CHARLES MCNAMARA;
third, J. W. BISHOP; fourth, T. P. GERE.   Superintendents.—First,
J. H. GARDNER; second, JNO. F. LINCOLN.   Treasurer.—H. THOMP-
SON.   General Manager.—J. W. BISHOP.   Secretary of Land Depart-

ment.—EDWARD SAWYER.   General Ticket and Freight Agent.—J. C. BOYDEN.

On June 14, the Sixth Regiment left for the South.

The draft, to fill calls previously made, commenced at the Provost Marshal's office, Mackubin's Block, on May 26.   Saint Paul had filled her quota previously, but several townships were drawn on.

On July 18, the call for 500,000 men was received.   The quota of Saint Paul was 160 men, she having already furnished 1,180.   This number was raised only by special exertions, the city giving $30,000 as bounties, besides large sums raised by subscription.

THE ELEVENTH REGIMENT

was organized from the men obtained under this call.   Among our citizens holding official position in it were:

James Gilfillan, Colonel; Peter Gabrielson, Assistant Surgeon; Robert L. Morris, Assistant Surgeon; Franklin Paine, Captain, Company B; John S. Moulton, First Lieutenant, Company E; Jason W. Gardner, Quartermaster Sergeant; Wilford C. Wilson, Hospital Steward.

The Eleventh Regiment departed for the front on September 22.

The political campaign of 1864 was "red-hot," McCLELLAN and LINCOLN being candidates for the presidency.   Public meetings, torch-light parades, &c., kept the excitement at fever heat.   The vote on county officers was:

	Union.	Democratic.
Legislature	James Smith, Jr..744	Wm. P. Murray......750
	C. D. Gilfillan...779	*John A. Peckham*....772
	A. R. Kiefer.....517	*John M. Gilman*.....561
District Judge	J. P. Kidder.....1116	*W. Wilkin*.........1520
Auditor	W. H. Kelley....1248	*J. F. Hoyt*.........1406
Judge of Probate	*R. F. Crowell*...1322	E. C. Lambert......1311

Those in *italics* elected.

On September 28, a soldier of Hatch's Battalion, named MINER, had both arms blown off, while firing a salute, by the premature explosion of a cannon.   The following day, another soldier, named LAFLESH, had his right hand blown off in the same way.   A liberal purse was raised for the unfortunate men.

On November 4. a terrible casualty occurred in front of our lower levee. The boiler of the steamer "John Rumsey" blew up, just as she was coming into port, blowing the boat to pieces, and killing seven men. also badly injuring others. Nearly every house in the city was shaken by the concussion. The boat was owned by Mr. RUMSEY. of LaCrosse, but leased by W. F. DAVIDSON, and the latter party. after several years' litigation. ultimately paid over $30,000 to the families of the men killed by the accident.

On December 19. another call for 300.000 men had been made, making the quota of Saint Paul 200 men. It seemed almost impossible to raise this number, but by special subscriptions raised by ward committees. in addition to the Government bounties, it was at length accomplished. The

FIRST REGIMENT MINNESOTA HEAVY ARTILLERY

was raised from the men obtained under this call. Among our citizens honored with commissions, were the following:

Dr. Clinton G. Stees, Surgeon; George Powers. Hospital Steward; E. D. K. Randall, Senior First Lieutenant, Company A; E. J. Van Slyke, Junior First Lieutenant, Company A; William Colter, Junior Second Lieutenant, Company A; Wm. M. Leyde, Captain, Company B; James J. Egan, Junior First Lieutenant, Company B: R. G. Daniels, Junior First Lieutenant, Company C; Harvey Officer, Captain, Company E; B. N. Cushway, Junior First Lieutenant, Company E: James K. Wilson, Senior Second Lieutenant, Company H; Henry C. Collins, Junior Second Lieutenant, Company I; Harry H. Wilson. Junior Second Lieutenant, Company K; James P. Allen, Captain, Company L; Harrison Allen, Senior Second Lieutenant, Company L.

The Heavy Artillery was the last body of troops which left our State for the war.

On December 22. a married woman, named ELEANOR STELZER, living on Summit avenue. while laboring under insanity. killed two of her children with a hatchet. attempted to kill a third, and cut her own throat, dying in a few moments.

NECROLOGY OF 1864.

Died, January 8, at Saint Louis, Rev. F. R. NEWELL. a Unitarian clergyman of Saint Paul, then temporarily in the em-

ploy of the Sanitary Commission. January 20, Capt. T. M.
SAUNDERS, Third United States Artillery, and Quartermaster
at Saint Paul. April 11, near Vicksburg, Mississippi, JOHN
W. CATHCART. He was buried at Saint Paul, May 12. May
16, CHARLES L. EMERSON, formerly editor of the *Saint Paul
Democrat*, for several years Surveyor General, Alderman of
the city, &c. June 15, LOUIS BUECHNER, the first lithographer
in Saint Paul. July 14, at Tupelo, Mississippi, Col. ALEX.
WILKIN, of the Ninth Regiment. September 1. MATTHEW
BROOME, a trader and capitalist of the city. November 12.
C. A. GATES, was accidentally killed on the Des Moines
River, where he was hunting.

THE SANITARY FAIR.

On January 9. 1865, the ladies and other patriotic citizens
of Saint Paul, gave a fair at Mozart Hall, (Mackubin's Block,)
the object being to raise money for the destitute families of soldiers, of which there were a large number in our city. The
fair remained open four days and evenings, and was crowded
to excess all the time, the citizens spending their money with
lavish generosity. At the close, the entire receipts were found
to be $13,000, leaving $10,000 after paying all expenses. A
contest for a sword, to be given to a Minnesota officer, was
one feature. Col. C. S. ULINE carrying it off by 2,300 votes
over all competitors.

In addition to this amount, our citizens had, during the war
period, given lavishly to the Sanitary and Christian commissions, to hospital funds and other war charities, to the families
of soldiers, and to numerous special cases of distress, &c.
Mayor PRINCE reported, in the summer of 1865, that in the
preceding four years, $225,000 had been raised and expended
by our citizens. A noble and patriotic record, truly, and one
that we may point to with pride.

On February 5, a young man, named JOHN McHUGH, was
fatally stabbed in an affray in a saloon on upper Third street.

On March 14, 1865, Dr. J. H. STEWART was appointed
postmaster, holding that office for five years.

In the spring of 1865, after four years of dreadful conflict,

which can only be briefly hinted at here, the clouds of war
seemed lifting. Glorious news was received from Petersburg,
and the Shenandoah, and from SHERMAN. Soon came the
news of the evacuation of Richmond, and the end then seemed
near. A general celebration was arranged, to commemorate
the Union victories. It took place on April 8. An artillery
salute, a procession, civic and military, a general decoration
of buildings with flags, &c., were the principal features. At
the International Hotel, addresses were made by Gov. MILLER,
JOHN M. GILMAN, Judge GOODRICH, T. J. GALBRAITH, J. W.
TAYLOR, S. LUDVIGH, and even "President JONES." All
were enthused with joy, and when Gen. SIBLEY, president of
the day, read from the balcony a telegram announcing the surrender of LEE and his army, the crowd fairly exploded with
delirious excitement. At night a general illumination and a
torch-light parade took place.

The city election, on April 4, resulted as follows :

	Democratic.		Republican.
Mayor	*John S. Prince*	867	Charles E. Mayo..702
Attorney	*I. V. D. Heard*	900	E. C. Palmer.....666
Street Commissioner.	*John Dowlan*	1567	(No opposition.)

Those in *italics* elected.

The exultation at the Union victories, was somewhat chilled
by the sad news of the death of President LINCOLN, on April
15. It created profound gloom and sorrow, and, on April 19,
the day of his funeral, all business was suspended in the city—
the bells tolled, and funeral sermons were preached in nearly
all the churches, to large audiences.

The spring and summer of this year was marked by the
return of our regiments from the South, to Fort Snelling, to
be mustered out. Each of them was received here with the
most cordial demonstrations of joy, and escorted to the Capitol, where an ovation was given them by the ladies and citizens generally, and speeches of welcome made by prominent
officials. These receptions were a feature of the summer.

Altogether, our city had furnished to the army of the Republic, 1.470 men ; but of this number, *one hundred and
twenty-four* brave men returned not. Many of them lie in

unrecorded graves on battle-fields where they fell, or heaped in the burial-trench of some prison-pen, the victims of disease and starvation. It is not creditable to our city, so generous and liberal, that a monument to the memory of these martyrs to liberty, our friends and fellow citizens, has not been erected, as has been done in many other places.

CHAPTER XXXIII.

EVENTS OF THE PERIOD, 1865 TO 1870.

A New Era of Prosperity—The Census of 1865—December Steamboat Excursions—The Lake Superior Railroad—A Singular "Accident"—The State Reform School—Supposed Uxoricide—Destructive Fires—Court of Common Pleas—Supposed Murder of Dr. Harcourt—Attempted Removal of the Capital—The City Water Works—Another Murder—Completion of Railroads, &c.

A NEW era seemed to have commenced with the close of the war. Our city entered on a career of unusual prosperity. Money was abundant, capital came in from abroad; business never was more flourishing; real estate buoyant; immigration increasing; employment plenty for all classes; every branch of trade and manufacture brisk, and everything presented a vivid contrast to the despondent days from 1857 to 1862.

From this period may be dated the most rapid growth of Saint Paul. Her railroad system, had now become well advanced. Building had never been so brisk. The population increased very rapidly. In short, the struggles and drawbacks of infancy over, Saint Paul began to assume the vigor, the energy, the strength, of maturity.

The census taken this summer showed a considerable increase of population, despite all drawbacks. The population of the city was reported at 12,976, and of the county at 15,107.

On August 24, the body of a man was found in the river, below Dayton's Bluff, tied by a rope around the neck to a heavy stone at the bottom. The body was much decayed, and was not recognized, but it was evident that a murder had been committed, and its concealment attempted. The body of the stranger was buried by the Coroner, but was destined to ere long play an important part in the criminal annals of the county.

The autumn of 1865 was remarkable for its lateness and

uniform mildness. Nothing approaching it had been known in the weather records of our city. That year, the first of December steamboat excursions were inaugurated, by Colonel HEWITT.*

This fall will also be remembered as the period of the Vermillion gold excitement, in which many of our citizens were interested.

THE LAKE SUPERIOR AND MISSISSIPPI RAILROAD.

During the year 1865, the grading on this road was pushed quite vigorously, and completed to Wyoming, 30 miles.

This road was first incorporated in 1857, under the name of the "Nebraska and Lake Superior Railroad," and the name was changed by the Legislature of 1861, to its present title. LYMAN DAYTON and others, were made corporators. But little was done in actual construction for some three or four years. Meantime, Capt. WM. L. BANNING, L. DAYTON, JAMES SMITH, Jr.,† WM. BRANCH, Dr. STEWART, ROBERT A. SMITH, PARKER PAINE, and one or two others, took hold of the enterprise and put in enough money to grade 30 miles. On October 20, 1865, the President of the road, LYMAN DAYTON, died. Capt. BANNING succeeded him, and, after much trouble, got some Philadelphia capitalists to build and equip the road. It was not completed to Duluth until 1870, and the Stillwater branch was built the same year.

The early officers of the road were: LYMAN DAYTON, President, to his death in 1865; 1865 to 1870, Capt. WM. L. BANNING; FRANK H. CLARK, 1870 to 1873; and J. P. ILSLEY, to the present time. GATES

---

* GIRART HEWITT, one of the most active real estate dealers of the city, was born in Hollidaysburg, Pennsylvania, in 1825. He studied law, and removed to Alabama in 1845, remaining there twelve years. He came to Minnesota for health, in 1856, and has since that date been a prominent citizen. Col. HEWITT's specialty has been immigration and December steamboat excursions. His "pamphlet" on Minnesota and its advantages to immigrants, has been circulated in the United States and Europe by the hundred thousand, and passed through twenty editions. He says he never held any office except School Inspector, and was beat the only time he ever ran for Alderman, and that, too, after his services in the Indian War of 1862!

† Hon. JAMES SMITH, Jr., was born at Mount Vernon, Ohio, October 29, 1815. While young, his eye-sight was seriously impaired by sickness, but he accomplished his education and read law, being admitted to practice in 1839. He was a partner of the late Col. J. W. VANCE, killed on Banks' Expedition. He remained at Mount Vernon until 1856, when he settled in Saint Paul, and was a partner first of Judge L. EMMETT, and afterwards of Hon. JOHN M. GILMAN. For ten years or more past, he has been Attorney of the Lake Superior Railroad. Mr. SMITH was a member of the State Senate in 1861, 1862 and 1863, and has just been elected for another term—the last time without opposition, a fact that evinces the high esteem in which he is held by his fellow citizens.

A. JOHNSON* was Chief Engineer through the period of construction, in connection, part of the time, with J. S. SEWALL, and was then Superintendent for two or three years, succeeded by W. W. HUNGERFORD, and more recently by GEO. II. SMITH. THOMAS BRENNAN, who laid all the iron on the road, is, at present, Assistant Superintendent. The first Secretary was CHARLES ST. CLAIR : next. CHARLES BREWSTER.

HON. JAMES SMITH, JR.

succeeded by ROBERT P. LEWIS ; then R. II. LAMBORN, and the present Secretary, THOS. M. DAVIS. Hon. JAMES SMITH, Jr., has been Attorney from the inception of the road until the present time.

On November 8, the *Daily Pioneer* was sold to II. P. HALL and JOHN X. DAVIDSON.

---

* GATES A. JOHNSON was born at Plattsburg, New York, 1826. He adopted the profession of engineer, and in 1855 removed to Saint Paul. He pursued his calling with much success for several years, being elected City Engineer in 1860, and County Surveyor in 1863. He was also elected Chief Engineer of the Superior Railroad in 1861, and remained until the completion of the road. In 1871, he was elected Alderman, and has given faithful attention to the interests of the city.

There were no well-defined issues in politics this year. Two old settlers, WM. R. MARSHALL and HENRY M. RICE, were candidates for Governor, the former gaining the day, but the county election was dull. The following officers were elected:

D. A. ROBERTSON, Sheriff; ALBERT ARMSTRONG, Clerk of Court; S. M. FLINT, District Attorney; J. MAINZER, Register of Deeds; O. F. FORD, Coroner; Dr. JOHN STEELE, County Commissioner; W. P. MURRAY and GEO. L. OTIS, Senators; PARKER PAINE. WILLIAM BRANCH and HERMAN TROTT, Representatives.

NECROLOGY OF 1865.

Died, January 2, WILLIAM HARTSHORN, one of the earliest pioneers of our city. February 16. M. L. TEMPLE, a merchant of this city, and Capt. W. B. McGRORTY, a well-known public man, were drowned at LaCrosse. April —, in Virginia. JOHN W. CROSBY, formerly Chief of Police of Saint Paul. April 11, JEREMIAH W. SELBY, an old and esteemed citizen. May 22, Hon. JOHN A. PECKHAM, banker, alderman, legislator, &c. July 21, at Homer, Louisiana, Dr. EBENEZER MILLER, formerly Deputy Sheriff. October 1. SOLOMON COGGSWELL. an old resident. October 4, DESIRE MICHAUD, for many years a merchant. October 14, Captain EMIL A. BURGER, an ex-officer. October 20, LYMAN DAYTON, one of the early settlers of the city. October 25, JOSEPH R. ATKINS, a prominent fireman. November 2, CHARLES T. WHITNEY, a well-known real estate dealer, formerly County Commissioner and City Treasurer. November 11, at Evansville, Indiana. Capt. R. M. SPENCER, an early steamboatman.

PRINCIPAL EVENTS OF 1866.

The year 1866 was one of great ease financially, the enormous expenditures of Government in settling up its war claims, making money plenty.

On March 1. ground was broken for the Opera House.

On May 25. the Cosmopolitan Hotel and ten other buildings. were destroyed by fire.

The city election this spring was not much contested. The following officers were elected : Mayor.—JOHN S. PRINCE. Treasurer.—NICHOLAS GROSS. Justice.—E. C. LAMBERT. Surveyor.—C. M. BOYLE. K. T. FRIEND was elected by the Council, City Clerk. Comptroller.—JOHN W. ROCHE. City Physician.—Dr. A. G. BRISBINE.

The cholera having threatened to pay the city a visit, a quarantine was established at Pig's Eye.

June 20. Rev. J. D. POPE. for ten years pastor of the First Baptist church, resigns.

June 30, Jefferson school house burned.

July 1, Capt. JOHN JONES appointed Chief of Police. vice TURNBULL. resigned.

July 29. Capt. H. L. CARVER. C. W. NASH and others. purchase the *Pioneer*.

August 11. the first steam fire engine, " City of Saint Paul." received by our firemen. and assigned to Hope Engine Company, No. 1.

August 21. a curious " accident" occurred at the Mansion House, a hotel which stood where the Custom House now is. A man, named HAWKES, from Chicago, who was boarding there. while cleaning a revolver, shot his wife. killing her instantly. As it afterwards transpired that he had taken a policy of insurance on her life for $10,000, not long before. the facts seemed to warrant his prosecution for murder. He was consequently tried on that charge, but acquitted. The county was the only sufferer, the trial costing $4,000.

INSTITUTION OF A STATE REFORM SCHOOL.

During the year 1866, one of the most useful of our State institutions. a Reform School for juvenile culprits, was instituted. and soon after got into operation. adjoining what is now the corporate limits of our city, on the road to Minneapolis. This institution had its origin in the following circumstances :

During 1865, Hon. I. V. D. HEARD. City Attorney. was frequently called on to prosecute young boys, some of them mere children, for larceny and other petty crimes. Their confessions as to their own acts. and those of their companions. were deplorable, and exhibited an amount of depravity among the boys of the city, that alarmed Mr. HEARD and excited his sympathies. There seemed but one way to check and cure the evil—a juvenile reformatory.

After several communications to the daily papers on the necessity of such an institution in or near our city, Mr. HEARD

EDWARD ZIMMERMAN.*

on November 9, 1865, addressed an official communication to the City Council, urging that body to take steps to secure a juvenile reformatory.

---

* EDWARD ZIMMERMAN was born in Strasbourg, (then in France,) April 26, 1821, and resided in the Department of Alsace until 1848, when the revolutionary troubles induced him to seek a home in the new world. He came to New York that year, and to Saint Paul in 1855, and entered mercantile business here, in which he was widely known, and highly respected. He was, also, an active and useful member of the Board of Education for several years. He died on July 27, 1866.

28

The communication was referred to a special committee. who reported, on January 2, strongly urging that Mr. HEARD's proposal be concurred in, and means taken to secure such an institution as was proposed. A committee was appointed to secure the proper legislation, and an appropriation from the State for the purpose, and sufficient aid pledged by the city to ensure its organization, conditioned that the institution was located in or near the latter.

The Legislature of 1866, on a proper representation of the facts, established by enactment, a " House of Refuge," and appropriated for the purchase of grounds, &c., in Ramsey county, $5,000. on condition that the city of Saint Paul would contribute a similar sum, which was done. Messrs. D. W. INGERSOLL. S. J. R. McMILLAN. A. T. HALE and Rev. J. G. RIHELDAFFER, were appointed managers. A very suitable location, near the city, called the Burt Farm, was purchased for $10,000, and, in a few months, the institution was in successful operation. Mr. RIHELDAFFER having been appointed as Superintendent. Its name was subsequently changed to the " State Reform School."

On January 1, 1875, the Superintendent reported that since the opening, 253 inmates had been received, and 145 of these had been discharged, all of whom were, (so far as known,) doing well, and many holding positions of trust and responsibility, and leading moral lives. The amount of good such an institution does, no one can tell, for its main power is in preventing rather than remedying.

October 18, two servant girls, named LENA BODEN and SOPHIA MARTIN, at Mrs. STOKES' boarding house, on the site of the present Metropolitan Hotel, were burned so badly by the explosion of kerosene, with which they were lighting a fire, that they died within a few days.

November 3. J. D. WILLIAMS, who, for a number of years, had kept " Williams' Ferry," above the city, was murdered near Fort Snelling.

December 19, the Chamber of Commerce, which, for almost 10 years, had been dormant, was reorganized, and became one of our most important institutions.

The election, this fall, resulted in the choice of the following officers: Senator.—WM. P. MURRAY. Representatives.— C. H. LIENAU, EDMUND RICE, and C. K. DAVIS. Judge of Probate.—R. F. CROWELL. Auditor.—S. LEE DAVIS.

NECROLOGY OF 1866.

Died, February 5, BERT MULLER. a pioneer hotel keeper, policeman, &c. February 20, at Burlington, Iowa, R. FRANK HOUSEWORTH, an old resident, Clerk of the Ramsey county Court. member of School Board, &c. March 2. at Prairie du Chien. Rev. LUCIEN GALTIER, first priest of Saint Paul. March 21, Dr. WM. H. MORTON. a well-known physician. April 7. J. WATSON WEBB, a merchant. May 4. AMABLE TURPIN. father of Mrs. LOUIS ROBERT. aged 100 years. June 3. PERRY SLOAN, by accidentally falling from the third story of Merchants' Hotel. August 13, at the Iowa Insane Hospital, DEWITT C. MARVIN, a well-known auctioneer of Saint Paul. August 23, at Philadelphia, WM. H. WOLFF, for many years a druggist in Saint Paul, Alderman. &c. October, 15, KENNEDY T. FRIEND. City Clerk. December 14, GEORGE G. STRONG. formerly of Second Regiment.

PRINCIPAL EVENTS OF THE YEAR 1867.

The congregation of Christ church, Protestant Episcopal, (Rev. S. Y. McMASTERS,* rector,) which had for about 16 years worshipped in the old chapel on Cedar street, completed their new and fine edifice, corner of Fourth and Franklin streets. early in January.   On the 13th, it was used for service,

---

* Dr. STERLING Y. McMASTERS was born at Guilford Court House, North Carolina, December 9, 1813, and graduated at the University of that State. He studied medicine in early life, but subsequently studied theology, and was ordained a clergyman in the Protestant Episcopal church. In 1846, he became rector of Christ church, at Alton, Illinois. In 1858, he became President of Saint Paul's College, Palmyra, Missouri. Three years later, this was broken up by the war, and he became Chaplain of the Twenty-seventh Illinois Regiment. In 1863, he came to Saint Paul for his health, and became rector of Christ church, ministering to that society for 12 years. He soon attained a high reputation in our State as a fine scholar, a skilled theologian, an earnest, active, faithful clergyman, and a Christian gentleman of the finest culture. He was a member of the State Normal Board, of the Minnesota Historical Society, and was Commissioner to the Vienna Exposition in 1873. He was a Free Mason of the 33d degree. He died November 5, 1875, sincerely lamented.

and, two Sabbaths later, caught fire from the furnace, and was destroyed, all except the bare walls. It was soon rebuilt.

January 25, the "Mansion House," corner of Wabasha and Fifth streets, was destroyed by fire, the fifteenth hotel, the papers remarked, that had been burned in our city. In this case, it was ultimately of some benefit to the public. It led the way to the purchase, a few days subsequently, of the ground for the site of the Custom House and Post-office.

The great increase of business in the District Court of Ramsey county, for some months prior to this date, clearly rendered an additional court necessary. The bar, at meetings held in 1866, decided to secure the same, and the Legislature of 1867, established the "Court of Common Pleas" for Ramsey county. At a city election held April 2, Hon. WILLIAM SPRIGG HALL* was elected as Judge.

Several very destructive fires [besides those noticed] occurred this season. On February 22, WEIDE & BRO.'s wholesale grocery store, on Third street, burned down. June 22, the machine and car shops of the Saint Paul and Pacific Railroad were destroyed—loss $150,000. May 23, several buildings on the south side of Third street, above Cedar, were destroyed, including an old landmark, the "Saint Paul House," on Bench street.

The municipal election, this spring, resulted in the choice of the following officers: Mayor.—Hon. GEO. L. OTIS.†

---

* WILLIAM SPRIGG HALL, one of the most respected jurists that Ramsey county ever had, was born July 9, 1832, in Anne Arundel county, Maryland. He was educated at Saint John's College, in that State, and studied law, being admitted to practice in 1854. He came to Saint Paul in October of that year, and formed a law partnership with HARWOOD IGLEHART, formerly of Annapolis, Maryland. In 1856, he was appointed Superintendent of the Common Schools of Minnesota, which office he filled two years. In 1857, he was elected to the State Senate, in which he showed high ability. In 1867, he was elected Judge of the Court of Common Pleas, and re-elected in 1874, for seven years more. His health failed rapidly about that period, and he took an European tour without much benefit. On February 25, 1875, he died on a railroad car, while on his way home from the east.

† GEO. L. OTIS was born in New York, October 7, 1829. He removed to Michigan in 1837, and lived there until 1855, in the meantime studying law and was admitted to practice. In October, 1855, he came to Saint Paul, and has practiced his profession here since that date, with eminent success. He was elected a member of the Legislature (House) of 1857-8, and of the Senate in 1866, performing valuable services on the Judiciary Committee during the first named session. Mr. OTIS was elected Mayor of Saint Paul in

Street Commissioner.—JOHN DOWLAN.   Attorney.—HARVEY
OFFICER.   The Council elected B. W. LOTT. City Clerk ; J.
W. ROCHE, Comptroller : Dr. B. MATTOCKS. City Physician.

GEO. L. OTIS.

On April 27, Hope Hose Company, No. 1, was organized.

1867, and in 1869 was the nominee of his party for Governor, but they were too greatly
in the minority to succeed.   Mr. OTIS has also given several years' service to the public
as one of the Managers of the State Reform School.   He is one of the ablest members
of the Ramsey county bar, and in the Masonic order has attained a high rank.

July 28. Saint Mary's church, (Catholic.) was dedicated. Rev. L. CAILLET has been its priest since that date.

September 10. ground was broken for the Custom House.

November 14, a young woman, named MAGGIE MURPHY. burned to death at Gen. SIBLEY's residence by the explosion of a kerosene lamp.

THE SUPPOSED MURDER OF DR. HENRY HARCOURT.

During the fall of this year occurred one of the most interesting criminal trials that has ever taken place in the history of the Northwest. and rivalling, in some features, the celebrated cases of EUGENE ARAM or Dr. WEBSTER.

On page 420. was mentioned the finding of the body of an unknown man, evidently murdered. A curious chain of circumstances led to the arrest, at Chicago, on September 23. 1866, of a young man named GEO. L. VAN SOLEN. for some years a resident of Saint Paul. as the murderer of the unknown man, who was subsequently proven (as was supposed) to be Dr. HENRY HARCOURT, of England—more latterly of Saint Louis, Missouri. VAN SOLEN had known HARCOURT in Saint Louis, in 1864 and 1865, and shortly afterwards the former returned to Saint Paul. HARCOURT soon after received a letter from a person unknown to him. offering him a situation, as surgeon to an expedition, if he would come to Saint · Paul. and giving VAN SOLEN as a reference. Dr. HARCOURT came to Saint Paul with a surgeon's outfit, about August 15. and stopped at VAN SOLEN's house. The two went hunting at Pig's Eye. on August 19. VAN SOLEN returned alone. stating that HARCOURT had run away from him, and the latter was never seen alive after that day. His friends in England. alarmed at not hearing from him. investigated his whereabouts, which led to VAN SOLEN's arrest, as stated. He was tried on the charge, in December, and ably defended by Hon. C. K. DAVIS* and Hon. I. V. D. HEARD. The theory of the

---

* CUSHMAN K. DAVIS was born in Henderson, New York, June 16, 1838. While an infant, his parents removed to Waukesha, Wisconsin, where he attended Carroll College, but subsequently graduated at the University of Michigan, in 1857. He studied law with Hon. A. W. RANDALL, and, after the election of that gentleman as Governor, he appointed Mr. DAVIS as State Librarian. He was admitted to the bar in 1859, and

CUSHMAN K. DAVIS.

defense was, that the body of the unknown man, found in the

removed to Milwaukee, where he practiced some time, but ultimately returned to Waukesha, at which place, in 1862, he enlisted in the Twenty-eighth Wisconsin Volunteers.
He was, not long after, promoted to First Lieutenant, and was put on the staff of Gen.
GORMAN, with the rank of Assistant Adjutant General. When Gen. GORMAN retired from
the service, Capt. DAVIS returned to his command, and was made Judge Advocate of
the Department. After several months' service, illness compelled him to withdraw from
the army. He settled in Saint Paul in 1864, engaging in the practice of law with great
success. In 1866, he was elected to the Legislature, and, in 1868, appointed United States
District Attorney. In November, 1873, he was elected Governor, and has filled that
office with acknowledged ability. He is one of the most scholarly and ready speakers
in our State.

river, was not that of HARCOURT. The prosecution. Judge
S. M. FLINT and H. J. HORN, Esq.. had the body exhumed.
and endeavored to prove, by its size. &c., and articles found
on it, that it was HARCOURT's body. The jury. on the first .
trial, disagreed, and, on a second trial, in the spring of 1868,
VAN SOLEN was acquitted. The *Pioneer*. in commenting
on the case, said : " It is a case painful as it is mysterious,
and one of the dark riddles that occur more frequently in real
life than in the attractive pages of fiction."

The election this fall resulted in the choice of the following
officers :

Senator.—GEO. L. BECKER. Representatives.—WM. P.
MURRAY, D. C. JONES and C. H. LIENAU. Sheriff.—D. A.
ROBERTSON. Treasurer.—C. S. ULINE. Register. —J.
MAINZER. Attorney.—S. M. FLINT, &c.

NECROLOGY OF 1867.

Died, January 5, JACOB BECK. an ex-soldier. Turner, &c.
January 20. BENSON GALLOWAY, for some years a merchant
on Third street. March 20, D. C. MURRAY, an old resident.
April 2, at Waconia, B. RODECK, a prominent fireman. April
26. JAMES WILEY, a well-known citizen. June 7. MICHAEL
DORNIDEN, member of City Council. June 19. Dr. WM.
CAINE, homœpathic physician since 1858. July 5. CHARLES
PATTEN, a resident since 1852. July 7. WILLIAM PERKINS.
an early settler. August 4. Capt. SAMUEL T. RAGUET, late
of the First Minnesota Volunteers. a prominent fireman,
merchant, &c.

PRINCIPAL EVENTS OF THE YEAR 1868.

On January 9, a row of frame buildings. on the northeast
corner of Third and Wabasha streets, burned down. J. L.
FOREPAUGH, that year, erected on the site, his fine block. now
the property of P. F. McQUILLAN, by whose name it is
known. It is the largest and finest business block in our city.

On February 29. the *Daily Dispatch*. an evening journal.
was issued by H. P. HALL and DAVID RAMALEY.

April 21, Mackubin's Block burned. Total loss. $120,000.
The city election this spring, resulted:
Mayor.—Dr. J. H. STEWART. City Justice.—O. MALM-
ROS. Comptroller.—J. W. ROCHE. Treasurer.—NICHOLAS
GROSS. The Council elected JOHN J. WILLIAMS as City
Clerk, &c.

McQUILLAN BLOCK.

May 22, the Rotary Mill, an old landmark, burned.
August 8, old Christ church, (Cedar street,) burned.
The post-office was removed to the Opera House this season.
At the State election, this fall, the following officers were
chosen: Representatives.—JOHN M. GILMAN,* JAMES J.

---

* JOHN M. GILMAN was born in Vermont, September 7, 1824. He was admitted to
the practice of law in that State, and removed to Ohio in 1846, settling at New Lisbon.
He was a member of the Legislature of that State in 1849-50. He removed to Saint
Paul in September, 1857, and soon afterwards formed a law partnership with Hon. JAS.
SMITH, Jr., which continued some years. He is now a member of the firm of " GILMAN,
CLOUGH & LANE." Mr. GILMAN has been three times a member of the Legislature
from this county, and has rendered the State valuable service in that capacity.

EGAN and PAUL FABER. Judge of Probate.—O. STEPHEN-
SON. County Auditor.—S. LEE DAVIS.

NECROLOGY OF 1868.

Died, January 15. SAMUEL L. VAWTER, a prominent merchant. February 2. ELIAB L. WHITNEY, an early real estate
dealer. February 3, in Hennepin county. JAMES DAY, a pioneer builder of Saint Paul. February 21. GEORGE H. OAKES,
a well-known early resident. February 26, at Toronto, Canada, H. HOLMES, an early surveyor of Saint Paul, afterwards
a General in the Confederate States Army. March 14. Rev.
J. E. DIXON, a teacher. March 29, at Orono, Judge MOSES
SHERBURNE, one of the early jurists of Minnesota. April
10. RUDOLPH H. FITZ, a pioneer builder, Alderman, &c.
April 10, THOMAS H. CALDER, a well-known character
of early days. April 21, S. R. CHAMPLIN, a merchant
for many years. April 27, at Chicago, by suicide. WM.
WOOD, of the firm of MEHAFFEY & BLACK, in 1856. May
20, JIM LORD, a relic of early days. July 12, Capt. EUGENE
H. FALES, an ex-army officer. August 4, SIMON POWERS, a
pioneer stage line operator. August 30, at Louisville, " President" JONES, an eccentric character, who lived at Saint Paul
for several years. September 19, MICHAEL J. WISE, an old
resident. October 10. Dr. J. A. VERVAIS, a pioneer physician. November 6, Rev. T. H. N. GERRY, a Protestant
Episcopal clergyman. December 25, THOMAS WALL, well
known in political circles.

PRINCIPAL EVENTS OF 1869.

January 1. Jubilee of colored citizens at Ingersoll Hall,
to celebrate the amendment to the State Constitution conferring
on them the elective franchise.

January 12. Masonic Hall, in McQuillan's Block, dedicated.

February 3. The International Hotel burned. This fire
commenced about two o'clock a. m. There were over 200
guests in the house, but all escaped without injury. The loss
was stated at $125,000. [See page 365.]

During the Legislative session of 1869, a bill was intro-

duced, by Hon. C. H. CLARKE, of Hennepin county, to remove the Capital to Kandiyohi county, on one of the sections
of land called "Capital lands." The bill passed both houses,
with very little opposition—probably being regarded in the nature of a joke. When presented to Gov. MARSHALL for his sig-
nature, he declined to approve it, and returned the bill, with his
reasons for vetoing it, which were probably satisfactory, as a
motion to pass it over his veto failed to carry. The same, or
substantially the same, measure was introduced again in 1872,
but met with no favor.

The city election this spring resulted in the choice of the
following officers: Mayor.—JAMES T. MAXFIELD. Comptroller.—J. W. ROCHE. Attorney.—W. A. GORMAN. Assessor.—CHARLES PASSAVANT. Surveyor.—D. L. CURTICE.
Street Commissioner.—FRANK DECK. The City Council
elected JOHN J. WILLIAMS, City Clerk: Dr. MATTOCKS,
Health Officer, &c.

THE CITY WATER WORKS.

An important event of this year was the completion of the
city water works, by the "Saint Paul Water Company."
This company was first chartered in 1857, but nothing was
done by the parties holding the franchises, until about 1864 or
1865, when C. D. GILFILLAN, and others, took hold of the enterprise, and, after much labor and expenditure, completed the
works. The water was turned on from Lake Phelan, the res-
ervoir, on August 23. There has been in all, 17 miles of pipe
laid, three miles of canals built, and 1,100 buildings are now
supplied with water. The works have a capacity of 4,300,000
gallons every 24 hours. In all, $340,000 have been invested
in the works. To the energy, perseverance and enterprise of
Hon. CHARLES D. GILFILLAN,* president of the company,

---

* CHARLES D. GILFILLAN was born near Utica, New York, July 4, 1831. He was
educated at Hamilton College, and removed to Missouri, in 1850. In April, 1851, he
came to Saint Paul, then removed to Stillwater, where he practiced law three years,
returning to Saint Paul in 1854, and continuing his profession here. He was elected to
the Legislature in 1864 and 1865. At the close of the latter term, he began the construction of the Saint Paul Water Works, which will always entitle him to the rank of
one of the benefactors of our city He has just been elected a third time to the Legislature.

Saint Paul is indebted for this valuable improvement: and perhaps no city in the Union is more cheaply or easily supplied with water than Saint Paul.

The State election. (November 2.) was somewhat more closely contested than usual this year. Hon. GEO. L. OTIS, one of our most popular and esteemed citizens, was a candidate for Governor, and, although his party throughout the State was in a hopeless minority, he received a vote in this

CHARLES D. GILFILLAN.

county that was a generous compliment to him, the result being: for HORACE AUSTIN, 778: for Mr. OTIS, 2847! The county officers elected were: Senator.—GEO. L. BECKER, (no opposition.) Representatives.—JOHN M. GILMAN, PAUL FABER, JNO. L. MERRIAM. Clerk of Court.—ALBERT ARMSTRONG. Sheriff.—JOHN GRACE. Treasurer.—C. S. ULINE.

Register.—Jacob Mainzer. County Attorney.—Harvey Officer.

The newspapers reported that 509 buildings were built this year, at a total cost of $1,500,000.

NECROLOGY OF 1869.

Died, near Princeton, Minnesota, January 7, from a gun-shot wound, Geo. W. Thompson, an early resident. January 14. Robert P. Patterson, a brick-mason, well-known in the city. January 26. at Chicago, Richard Marshall, formerly proprietor of the City Mills. February 22, near Omaha, by freezing. H. H. Gilbert, formerly Deputy State Treasurer, and Quartermaster of the Sixth Regiment. March 19. Charles Creek, an early settler. March 27. Rev. Demetrius Marogna, priest of Assumption church. April 11. Nelson Gibbs, for several years City Justice, &c. May 8. Julius Schmidt, well known to theatre-goers. May 28, Asa Goodrich, for several years president of the gas company. June 29, Geo. C. Mott. since 1861, clerk in the Surveyor General's office. July 10. at Chicago, Mason M. Forsythe, a well-known business man of Saint Paul. July 14. Joseph Campbell, an old settler. August 10. Col. Henry McKenty, once the largest and most prominent real estate dealer in Minnesota. October 30, Andy L. Shearer, for some years a "banker" on Jackson street. November 12. Louis C. Jones, a capitalist. November 22. Jacob B. Braden, a highly respected merchant. November 22. Orrin Curtis, formerly Mayor of Saint Anthony, a well-known insurance agent. November 25, David Stuart, Jr., an old resident. December 30. Thomas Daly, well known in political circles.

PRINCIPAL EVENTS OF THE YEAR 1870.

During the rebuilding of part of the Saint Paul bridge, this winter, a young man, named James Nolan, fell about 100 feet on the ice, and was killed.

At the spring election, only one ticket was in the field, being elected as follows: Mayor.—William Lee.* Comp-

---

* William Lee, one of the oldest wholesale merchants of Minnesota, was born in Milford, Hunterdon county, New Jersey, April 14, 1822. After completing his educa-

troller.—JOHN W. ROCHE. City Justice:—THOMAS HOWARD.
Treasurer.—MICHAEL ESCH. Surveyor.—D. L. CURTICE.
The City Council elected WM. RHODES. President; M. J.
O'CONNOR, City Clerk ; Dr. MATTOCKS, Health Officer.

The river was on a freshet this spring, being the highest
water for 20 years.

May 4, JOSEPH A. WHEELOCK was appointed postmaster.

May 19, Concert Hall Block burned. A young lady, named
MCLELLAN, was burned to death ; and two brothers, named
MUELLER, tailors, saved their lives only by leaping from the
windows in the rear to the foot of the bluff, receiving frightful
injuries. The fire spread across the street, consuming several
buildings. The total loss was $50,000.

June 1, the corner-stone of the new Merchants' Hotel was
laid by the Old Settlers' Association, with appropriate ceremonies.

On June 27, the Metropolitan Hotel was opened, GILBERT
DUTCHER, proprietor.

The census of 1870 showed a rapid growth of the city since
1865. The total population of the city was reported at
20,030 ; county, 23,085.

An atrocious murder was committed, on September 2, in
Rose township. A man, named JOSEPH STEHLE, of Saint
Anthony, was enticed away from home by a tramp, named
DANIEL GUNDY, who murdered and robbed him. GUNDY
was convicted of the crime in March following, and sentenced
to imprisonment for life.

The Lake Superior and Mississippi Railroad was completed
and opened to Duluth in August, this year, thus giving our
city a connection with the great lake system, which has been
of incalculable advantage to its commerce.

The State election this fall resulted in the choice of the following officers : Representatives.—H. H. SIBLEY, JOHN L.

---

tion, he engaged in mercantile business at Easton, Pennsylvania, and, in 1859, removed
to Saint Paul, where he established what is now one of the leading jobbing houses in
our city. Mr. LEE was twice elected Mayor, and is at present County Commissioner,
serving the public with fidelity and ability. While devoted to his business, he finds
time to engage in politics, simply (as he asserts, and the writer believes,) as a recreation
from business cares!

MERRIAM, CHRIS. STAHLMAN.   Probate Judge.—O. STE-
PHENSON.   County Auditor.—HIRAM J. TAYLOR.

Navigation remained open this fall unprecedentedly late.   A
steamboat excursion in aid of the Home of the Friendless,
came off on December 17—the latest on record.

NECROLOGY OF 1870.

Died, April 11, CHARLES A. MORGAN, for several years
City Treasurer.   May 12, at Hebron, Illinois, JOHN McCON-
KEY, a former railroad man.   May 21, THOMAS THOMAS, a
pioneer builder.   May 28, JAMES E. THOMPSON, President of
the First National Bank.   May 30, J. W. SIMPSON, one of the
pioneers of the city.   June 6, ISAAC A. BANKER, one of the
earlier surveyors and real estate dealers.   June 4, EDWARD
COLES LAMBERT, for many years Probate Judge, City Justice,
&c.   June 23, WILLIAM ILLINGWORTH, town-clock builder.
June 16, at Charleston, Illinois, JONATHAN FROST, one of the
early merchants.   July 11, Lieutenant CHARLES RAMPE, formerly of the Second Regiment.   October 6, by suicide, WIL-
LIAM YUNG.   October 29, F. SCHWARTZ, a well-known
German citizen.   November 11, VETAL GUERIN, the oldest
living settler.   November 16, HENRY BUEL, for many years a
well-known merchant.   December 9, WILLIAM J. CULLEN, a
prominent public man.   December 28, LOT MOFFET, builder
and proprietor of "Moffet's Castle," or the Temperance House.

CHAPTER XXXIV.

EVENTS OF THE YEARS. 1871 TO 1875.

ADVANCE IN REAL ESTATE—THE PRAIRIE FIRES—RELIEF FOR CHICAGO SUFFER-
ERS—CHANGES IN CITY CHARTER—BOARD OF PUBLIC WORKS CREATED—PUB-
LIC PARK PURCHASED—STREET RAILWAY BUILT—MORE STEAMERS SECURED—
THE GREAT STORM OF 1873—CUSTOM HOUSE COMPLETED—THE JAY COOKE
PANIC—ANNEXATION OF WEST SAINT PAUL—A CARNIVAL OF CRIME—THE
CENSUS OF 1875—CONCLUSION.

THE events of the period from 1870 to the present date.
can only be briefly noted. as they are too recent, and not
sufficiently " historical" to bear chronicling at much length.

PRINCIPAL EVENTS OF 1871.

One of the noticeable features of this year. was the rapid
and decided advance in real estate.   The demand was better.
and sales more ready. than for several years—perhaps. better
than since the fatal 1857.   Woodland Park. and a number of
other additions. were. about this date. got into market. and
the rapid advance in prices—sometimes doubling in a few
weeks—almost reminded one of the kiting days before the
memorable collapse.   It set the real estate market all ablaze,
and gave it an impetus which continued until the JAY COOKE
disaster of September, 1873, again checked it.

The city election this spring resulted in the following choice :
Mayor.—WILLIAM LEE, re-elected.   Attorney. — W. A.
GORMAN.   Comptroller.—JOHN W. ROCHE.   Surveyor.—D.
L. CURTICE.

July 5. the Minnesota State Sabbath School Convention
assembled in a temporary building. opposite the Capitol.

The State Fair took place at the Driving Park. September
26. 27, 28 and 29.

The fall of this year was memorable for the destructive fires
in the Northwest—Wisconsin. Michigan. and our own prairie
region were swept by the flames.   The crowning disaster was

the great fire of Chicago, October 8th and 9th. Our City Council, as soon as it could be called together, appropriated $20,000 for the relief of the sufferers of that city, and the amount was taken to Chicago the same evening. A considerable amount in money, provisions and clothing, was also sent to the sufferers by our prairie fires.

On October 24, 25 and 26, occurred the excursion of the Old Settlers' Association of Minnesota, to the Red River of the North, to celebrate the completion of the Saint Paul and Pacific Railroad to that river.

The State election this fall, (November,) resulted in the following choice: District Judge.—WESTCOTT WILKIN. Treasurer.—CAL. S. ULINE. Sheriff.—JOHN GRACE. Register of Deeds.—JACOB MAINZER. County Attorney.—W. W. ERWIN. Surveyor.—C. M. BOYLE. Court Commissioner.—G. SIEGENTHALER. Senators.—JOHN NICOLS and ISAAC V. D. HEARD. Representatives.—JOHN B. SANBORN, PETER BERKEY,* JAMES C. BURBANK, H. M. SMYTHE and EDMUND RICE.

December 15, the Ramsey County Pioneer Association was organized. This society was designed to include all who settled in this county prior to the admission of the State, (May 11, 1858,) and who were of age at the date of the organization of the society.

The newspapers reported that 832 buildings were built during 1871, at a total cost of $1,735,761.

Died, January 9, WM. BEAUMETTE, one of the earliest settlers in Saint Paul. (1838.) January 11, at Santa Barbara, California, Major H. A. KIMBALL, a lawyer of this city.

---

* Capt. PETER BERKEY, one of the self-made men of our city, was born in Somerset county, Pennsylvania, in 1822. His early life was one of hard labor, privation, and but little opportunity for education. To his own pluck and industry he owes his present respected position in our community. In early days, he struggled with fortune on the canals, railroads and stage roads of his native State. He and SELAH CHAMBERLAIN stood by the track of the Pennsylvania Railroad, in 1836, and saw the first train go by. He came to Minnesota in 1855, and has since been engaged in the hardware, iron, railroad, livery, insurance and banking business, at various dates. He is now President of the Saint Paul, Stillwater and Taylor's Falls Railroad, Director of the Second National Bank, &c. He has given the city and county years of valuable service, as Alderman, County Commissioner, member of the Legislature, and other offices, and in all good enterprises is a most valuable and reliable citizen.

29

January 28, at Cottage Grove, PIERCE P. FURBER, for many years actuary of Oakland cemetery, and Justice of the Peace. First Ward. March 3, WM. R. WOOD. a draughtsman in the Surveyor General's office. March 4. JOHN AUSTIN, a well-known English resident. March 20. at Little Canada, PIERRE GERVAIS, a resident here. 1838 to 1845. April 7. CHARLES · WEED. a well-known railroad agent. April 11. Major NATHANIEL McLEAN. ex-editor and public officer : a settler of 1849. April 16, at Saint Peter, ROBERT F. SLAUGHTER, an early real estate dealer. June 13, at Waterford, Pennsylvania, JOHN CURTIS, for many years a hotel keeper and hardware dealer. June 20, JOHN B. LAHR. August 4. AMOS W. PEARSON. a manufacturer of this city. August 30, C. G. WYCKOFF, a public officer, prominent Mason, &c. September 22. GEORGE LOWRY, for many years a saddler. October 2, JOHN C. RAGUET, a prominent merchant. November 27. at Saint Cloud. MASON H. MILLS. December 25. HENNING VON MINDEN. an officer during the war, engineer, &c.

EVENTS OF THE YEAR 1872.

Some very important amendments were made to the charter of the city by the Legislature this winter. One was, providing that the city election should be held (after 1872) the same day as the State election, and terms of officers expiring in the spring of 1873 should continue until 1874. Each ward was also divided into two election precincts. and the limits of the city largely extended.

A " Board of Public Works" was also created, to consist of five members, one from each ward. They are charged with the control and supervision of public improvements generally. The Board has performed a large amount of work in improving our streets, sewerage, &c., though at considerable expense.

Another important act was the one authorizing the purchase of a public park. Five commissioners were to be appointed by the District Judge. to purchase a suitable tract for that purpose. Judge WILKIN soon after appointed H. H. SIBLEY. J. A. WHEELOCK, SAMUEL COLHOUN. W. P. MURRAY, and J. C. BURBANK. After some months of inquiry and survey, a very fine tract bordering on Lake Como, containing about 260 acres, was purchased for $100,000, the bonds for which were issued by the City Council.

The last spring city election was held on April 2. resulting in the following choice: Mayor.—Dr. J. H. STEWART. Treasurer.—MICHAEL ESCH. Justice.—ARCHIBALD McELRATH. Commissioners.—CASPER H. SCHURMEIER. PETER BERKEY.

On February 10. the "Saint Paul, Stillwater and Taylor's Falls Railroad" was formally opened by an excursion. and on February 14, the West Wisconsin Railroad, a new route to Chicago, was dedicated to business by an excursion.

During this year, the first street railway was chartered and constructed. On July 14. two miles were opened to travel. The following year a branch line was built.

On July 2. two new steam fire engines were ordered by the City Council, and soon after received, making four in all in use by our Fire Department, which is now one of the best managed and most efficient in the country.

On July 24, the Sheriff of Crow Wing county, fearing trouble with the Chippewas. owing to the lynching of two of their number, at Brainerd, telegraphed for a military force from this city. Although this was late at night, by daylight next morning, two military companies were under arms, and en route for Brainerd. Fortunately the expedition was a bloodless one, and is now generally known as the " Blueberry War."

At the State election this fall, the following officers were chosen: Senator.—EDMUND RICE. Representatives.—J. N. ROGERS, HUBERT H. MILLER, GEO. BENZ, HENRY A. CASTLE, H. J. BRAINARD. Auditor.—J. B. OLIVIER. Probate Judge.—H. R. BRILL. Mr. OLIVIER resigned soon after, and was elected Abstract Clerk. S. LEE DAVIS was elected as Auditor.

The winter of 1872, set in unusually early and severe, and a "fuel famine" added to its discomfort.

December 21, "Warner's Corner," as it was long known, burned down. together with the building adjoining, then occu-

pied by A. T. C. Pierson. In the latter, a young man, named
John H. Dowling, was burned to death.

The season of 1872. was remarkable for the number of fine
buildings erected. The papers reported 932 buildings built
during the year. at a cost of $2,346,487.

Died, January 12. Baron Von Freudenreich. a native of
Germany. a resident since 1856. January 14. at Memphis, R.
McLagan, an early settler. January 27, Wm. B. Newcomb,
a prominent merchant. January 28. Capt. John O'Gorman.
formerly Chief of Police. January 30. J. A. Chaffee. merchant. February 1, at Chaska, James Houghton, pioneer
steamboatman. February 10. at Carver, Geo. P. Holmes,
formerly of Saint Paul. February 16. Thomas Shearan,
Alderman Second Ward. February 28. David Hart, a well-
known tobacconist. April 4. Marshall Sellers. an old
resident. April 22, George P. Peabody, a prominent merchant. May 2, Walter Kittredge. many years in the hotel
business. May 3, at Elgin. Illinois. Walter W. Webb. a
young merchant. May 20, at Lakeville. Patrick O'Gorman.
for several years an Alderman. June 3. Rodney Parker. a
pioneer hotel keeper. June 19. J. R. Brewster. June 26.
I. C. George. a well-known railroad man. July 7, Capt.
Chas. G. Pettys, an early real estate dealer. August 3, August Von Beeck. formerly of Fifth Regiment. August 9.
at San Jose, California, Judson A. Russell, several years
clerk of the *Press* office. August 26. at Cleveland, Ohio.
Andrew Spencer, formerly a Saint Paul hotel keeper. September 12, Luther H. Eddy, for several years Alderman.
Chief of Police, &c. September 21, John H. Carrier. September 23, at Chicago, C. N. Pease, formerly a bookseller
here. October 9, Allan Campbell, an editor of *Daily Dispatch*. October 25, Rev. J. R. Balme, an Englishman by
birth, used to preach on the levee, &c. November 6. Wm.
Towlerton. November 9, Butler Comstock, a pine land
operator. November 21, Dr. Samuel Willey, a prominent physician for many years. Nov. 27, John P. Kilroy,
well-known in Second Ward politics. December 12. at Ti-
conderoga. New York, R. W. Delano, for several years a

member of Saint Paul School Board.   December 31. Wm.
Branch, railroad builder. public man. &c.

PRINCIPAL EVENTS OF 1873.

The year 1873, opened with a storm, unequalled in severity
and destructiveness by any which had ever occurred in the
memory of man.   On January 7. a "polar wave" swept over
the State. lasting some 36 hours, during which time. the wind
blew an icy gale, and the air was filled with fine snow.   In a
report made by Gov. Austin to the Legislature. on the subject. it is stated that 70 persons died from exposure. a large
number were maimed. and about 300 cattle. horses. &c..
perished.

January 29. Odd Fellows' Hall. in Semper's Block. was
burned.

On February 9. the Saint Paul Custom House was so far
completed, that the post-office was removed to it—a change
hailed with joy.   The Custom House had occupied five years
in construction. and cost $350.000.   The engraving accompa-
nying this. shows its fine proportions and architecture—a
building that is truly an ornament to our city.

On September 19, the news was circulated of the failure of
Jay Cooke.   Those who remembered the disastrous failure
of the Ohio Life and Trust Company. in 1857. (page 380.)
were apprehensive that history was about to repeat itself. and
that another financial revulsion would occur.   While to some
extent it did occur in the manufacturing districts and money
centers of the east. it was scarcely felt here, beyond a slight
stringency of the money market, and a dullness in real estate.
Not a failure of any mercantile or banking house occurred as
a consequence. nor did any manufacturing establishment close
its doors.   How vastly different was our condition in 1857.
when a similar flurry utterly wrecked every branch of business and every enterprise.   Then. there was no real wealth.
no actual capital, no solvent business, no production to create
exchange, and a currency not worth the paper used in its issue.
Everything was fictitious and unreal.   Now. how changed.
Twenty million bushels of wheat marketed per annum. had

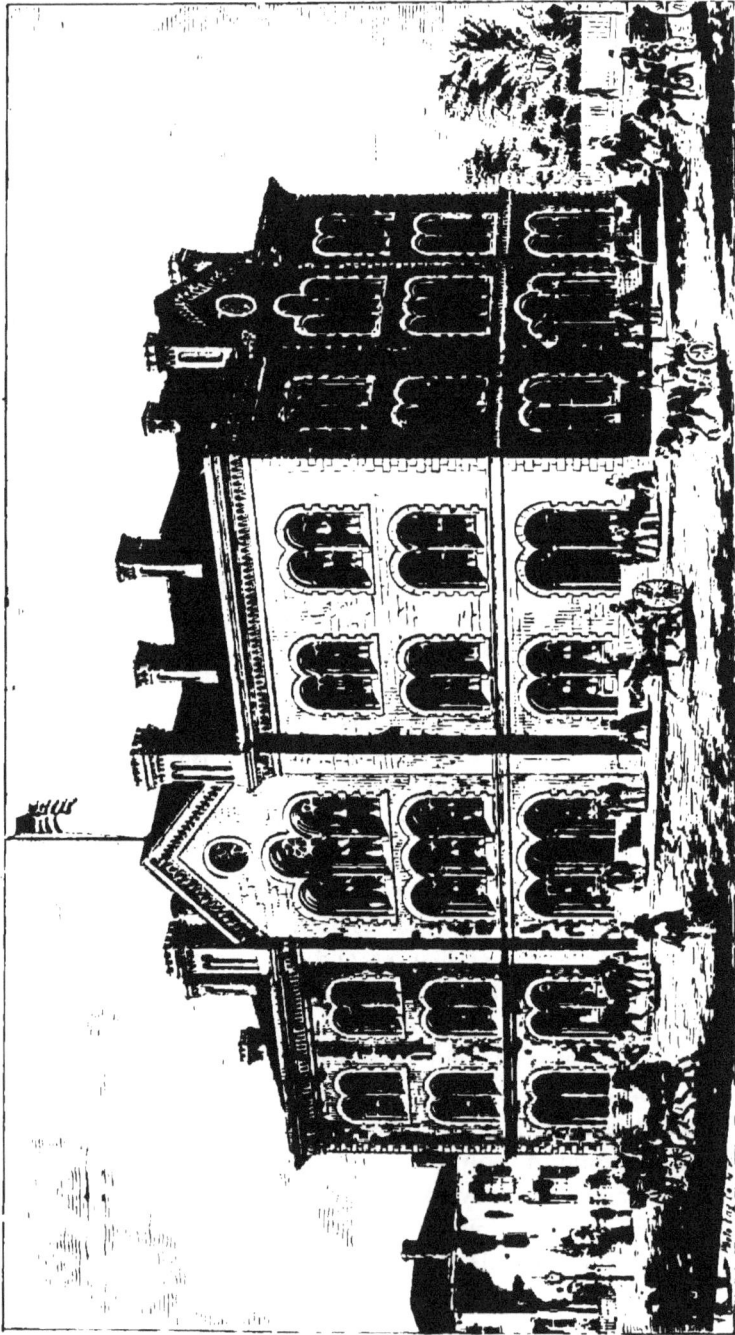

CUSTOM HOUSE.

created real financial strength and profitable trade. Wealth and capital had accumulated. Few or none were in debt, and all in a condition to laugh at panics. Sixteen years had built up from the soil a new commonwealth, strong in its own resources, with capital accumulated from ,honest industry and trade, and with reserve means to weather even severer financial storms unscathed.

The election on November 4, combined, for the first time. the city with the State tickets, making a lengthy list of officers elected, as follows: Senator.—E. F. Drake. Representatives.—L. Hoyt, Geo. Benz, T. M. Metcalf.* John X. Davidson, H. Meyerding. Treasurer.—Calvin S. Uline. Sheriff.—John Grace. Register.—Theo. Sander. Attorney.—C. D. O'Brien. Surveyor.—C. M. Boyle. Clerk of Court.—A. Armstrong. Coroner.—P. Gabrielsen. For the city: Mayor.—J. H. Stewart. Treasurer.—F. A. Renz. Attorney.—W. A. Gorman.

This fall, a moving appeal for aid was received from the frontier counties, which had been ravaged by the grasshoppers. Large donations in money, food and clothing were sent to the sufferers, with that lavish generosity that has always characterized our city.

Died, February 8. William L. Ames, an early resident. February 27, F. J. Metzgar, an early resident. March 13. Casper H. Schurmeier, a prominent German citizen. March 25. Judge Sherman Finch. a much respected lawyer. May 5, John H. Grindall, a well-known builder. May 9. Michael Harris, a prominent fireman. May 14, at Baraboo. Wisconsin, Lieut. Edwin J. Van Slyke, formerly of the Heavy Artillery. May 16. at Chicago, Oscar R. Cowles. better known as " King Cole." a well-known sporting man in Saint Paul, 1855 to 1858. May 31, H. Herwegen, a merchant. June 24. at Denver, Gustave Hancke. a well-known

---

* Tracy M. Metcalf was born in Homer, New York, 1827. In 1852, he removed to Michigan, where he was engaged in the Paymaster's Department, of the Southern Michigan Railroad, until 1854, when he came to Saint Paul. Mr. Metcalf was City Comptroller, from 1857 to 1859; County Auditor, in 1861 and 1862, and member of the Legislature in 1874. He was also Chief Clerk in the Provost Marshal's office in this district, from 1862 to 1865. For the past ten years he has been in the real estate business.

and popular musician. July 10, MICHAEL ESCH, City Treasurer. July 13, HOWARD A. HUNT, merchant. July 25, at Minneapolis, CONRAD ZENZIUS, director of the Musical Society. July 29, JOHN NICOLS, iron merchant, several years Senator from this county. &c. August 6, Major ROBERT WHITACRE, capitalist and real estate operator. September 5, Lieut. HARRY H. WILSON, formerly of the Heavy Artillery. September 20, HUGO PETZHOLD, a German politician. October 1. GILBERT DUTCHER, proprietor of the Metropolitan Hotel. September 26, at the Insane Asylum, Saint Peter, GEORGE MORTON, for several years Captain of Police. October 13, JOHN SIMS. December 25, A. W. GRENIER. December 26. ISAAC VAN ETTEN, a prominent lawyer.

PRINCIPAL EVENTS OF 1874.

At the Legislative session this winter, several acts affecting this city and county were passed. One was the revised and consolidated city charter—a ponderous document of 100 pages. Another important act was the one authorizing a change of the county line between Dakota and Ramsey counties, so as to annex West Saint Paul to this city and county. This proposed change was to be voted on at the next general election, and, if approved by a majority of the people of the two counties, should become a law.

April 2d, the newspapers reported a daring forgery on two of our banks, by which the perpetrator gained $7.400. No certain clue to the bold rascal was ever gained.

This season, the old Pioneer Hook and Ladder building was converted into court rooms and offices for the county.

April 22, the *Daily Pioneer* became the property of Hon. DAVID BLAKELY.

August 12, Prof. S. S. TAYLOR, shot and seriously wounded by a burglar, whom he surprised in his house.

September 9, serious fire on Third street; HUNTINGTON'S photograph gallery, and other parties, burned out.

The State election this year, (November 3,) resulted in the choice of the following officers: Auditor.— S. LEE DAVIS. Probate Judge.—O. STEPHENSON. Senator.—W. P. MUR-

RAY. Representatives.—WM. CROOKS, H. H. MILLER,
GEORGE BENZ, F. R. DELANO, LORENZO HOYT. County
Commissioners.—WM. LEE and E. S. BLASDELL.. The total
vote cast in the city at the election, was 5,017. On change of
county line, the vote stood—yeas. 4,700; nays, 53. Dakota
county also voted in favor of it. Due proclamation of the
ratification of the Legislative act, was made by the Governor.
on November 16, and West Saint Paul became a part of our
city. being designated as the Sixth Ward. By this annexation. about 2,800 acres were added to the area of Saint Paul.
making in all an area within our city limits of 13,583 acres.
or twenty-one and one-fifth square miles. One of the immediate results of the annexation was, abolishing tolls on the
Saint Paul bridge, and it was thrown open to free use on November 4.

This year was characterized by an unusual amount of crime.
On August 3, near the head of Rice street, a man, named
MICHAEL KELLEY stabbed BARNEY LAMB, during an alterca-
tion, killing him almost instantly. KELLEY was tried twice.
and, on the second trial, found guilty, and sentenced to the
State's prison for life.

On November 1, JOSEPH LICK and his wife, ULRICA, were
attacked in the yard of their residence, No. 59 West Tenth
street. late at night, by some parties armed with a hatchet and
knife. Mrs. LICK was killed, and her husband severely injured. Three persons, Mr. and Mrs. FRANK RAPP and GEO.
LAUTENSCHLAGER, were arrested for the act, and subsequently
found guilty of murder in the first degree—the latter being
condemned to suffer the death-penalty. Mr. and Mrs. RAPP
were sentenced to the State's prison for life, and an appeal to
the Supreme Court. in the case of LAUTENSCHLAGER, is now
pending.

On November 10, a man, named JOHN H. ROSE, shot PAT-
RICK O'CONNOR, a respectable and industrious contractor.
with a gun. in broad daylight, on a public street. O'CONNOR
died in a day or two. ROSE was convicted the following
summer of murder in the first degree, and sentenced to the
State's prison for life.

The municipal election was held this year, (under the revised charter,) separate from the State election, on December 6. There was only one ticket nominated for city officers, and they were elected, as follows: Mayor.—JAMES T. MAXFIELD.* Comptroller.—JOHN W. ROCHE. City Justice.—S. M. FLINT. The Sixth Ward, for the first time, joined in our city election. •

Died, January 10, MARTIN WHELAN, an old resident. January 19, J. J. PRENDERGAST, a prominent fireman. January 27, by accident, TIMOTHY MCCARTHY. March 29, EDWARD HOGAN, for many years a well-known dry goods merchant. March 30, DAVID GUERIN, one of the first white children born in Saint Paul. April 6, at Chicago, A. VON GLAHN, a capitalist of Saint Paul in early years. April 9, CHARLES SYMONDS, the first ice dealer in Saint Paul. April 28, ROBERT TERRY, an old settler. May 11, Capt. LOUIS ROBERT, a pioneer of Minnesota, for many years a prominent trader, &c. June 5, (at Dixon, Illinois,) WM. KENNEDY, for sixteen years Superintendent of the Saint Paul Gas Company. June 11, JOHN L. STRYKER, a well-known real estate owner. August 31, Hon. HENRY ACKER, formerly member of the Legislature, Federal officer, County Superintendent of Schools, &c. October 6, Dr. THOMAS R. POTTS, City Physician, an old settler. October 12, Capt. WM. PAIST, Secretary of the State Agricultural Society, State Grange, &c. November 1, (at Chicago,) S. K: PUTNAM, formerly Alderman. October 31, HENRY SHEARAN, for several years a policeman. November 25, at Newport, Minnesota, WM. R. BROWN, for many years a resident of the city.

PRINCIPAL EVENTS OF 1875.

The months of January and February were characterized by intense and unusually protracted cold weather.

---

* JAMES T. MAXFIELD was born in Norwich, Ohio, March 7, 1827, and lived in that city until 23 years of age, when he went to Goshen, Indiana, of which State he remained a resident eight years, being a member of the Indiana Legislature in 1852-3. He then removed to Detroit, subsequently to Cleveland, and became a resident of Saint Paul in 1864. Mr. MAXFIELD is known as one of our most enterprising, public-spirited and valuable citizens. He has been three times elected Mayor, and has labored hard and successfully for the welfare of our city.

February 19. Judge S. J. R. McMillan. elected United States Senator.

March 1. H. R. Brill. appointed Common Pleas Judge. vice Hall..

FIRST BAPTIST CHURCH.

March 15. Orlando Simons. appointed Common Pleas Judge.

April 1, C. H. Bigelow's house burned.

April 11. the *Pioneer* and *Press* consolidated.

May 30, dedication of the First Baptist church, the finest church edifice in Minnesota.

June 1, Dr. DAVID DAY appointed postmaster.

The months of September and October were characterized by a great revival of religion, aided by Messrs. WHITTLE.and BLISS, two lay evangelists.

November 27, OLIVER BEAUDOIN, killed by a railroad accident, at the lower levee.

December 21, consecration of Rt. Rev. JOHN IRELAND, as Coadjutor Bishop.

The census of Saint Paul and Ramsey county was completed this month, showing as follows: Population of city, 33,178; county, 36,333. The tax duplicate was also returned, showing the total valuation of the city to be $27,755,926, having, in five years, fully trebled. Contrast this with the first census of Saint Paul (1849) giving a population of 840, and the first tax roll, showing a total valuation of $85,000! In the appendix will be found a compendium of the various census and assessment rolls.

Died, January 4, ALANSON WILDER, a resident since 1864. January 15, JAMES GOODING, ex-Chief of Police. January 17, JOHN B. WAGNER. January 23, JOHN GRAHAM, a manufacturer. January 31; MICHAEL FETSCH, a leading fireman. February 24, Hon. WM. SPRIGG HALL, Judge of Common Pleas Court. March 1, Capt. JAMES R. LUCAS, Deputy State Auditor. March 11, HENRY SCHIFFBAUER, ex-City Comptroller. March 22, GEO. NATHAN. March 26, at San Francisco, California, JAMES WYLIE, for many years a carpet merchant here. June 1, AUGUSTUS BOYDEN. June 6, JARED VAN SOLEN, an old resident. June 19, WM. M. DWINNELS, one of our earliest settlers. July 20, at Fort Totten, Dakota Territory, WM. H. FORBES, a pioneer. July 2, PATRICK H. BUTLER, an old resident. August 8, Hon. CHARLES SCHEFFER, State Treasurer for several years, a leading wholesale merchant, president of the Musical Society, &c. August 17, PARKER PAINE, for many years a banker, &c. August 18, THEODORE SCHLEIF. August 29, H. BERRY. September 3, BENJAMIN F. HOYT, a pioneer of our city. September 23, ROBERT WILEY, an old resident. November 5, Rev. S. Y. McMASTERS, D. D., rector of Christ church. November 8, at Bass Lake. SAMUEL McCULLOUGH. November 13. Rev. JOHN MATTOCKS, pastor of First Presbyterian church. for twelve years Superintendent of Schools. &c. November 23. JOHN G. IRVINE, a much esteemed young citizen. November 28. Judge J. J. SCARBOROUGH, formerly of Georgia. &c.

CONCLUSION.

And here the writer must lay down the pen of the historian. His task is done. and he closes it with satisfaction, and with pardonable pride in the goodly subject on which he has labored so long. with no other motive than to place on the enduring page of history, those facts concerning the early days of Saint Paul which might else be lost, if not recorded in time.

He has. in these imperfect and poorly written annals, traced the career of our city from the dimly remembered days of 1838. when a single bark-roofed hovel formed its only civilized landmark. an unknown point in the wilderness surrounding it—through the perils of its infancy and pioneer days, its struggles to secure and retain the Capital. its period of wild inflation and speculation, its financial reverses and dark days, its later years of success and prosperity, fairly won by the enterprise of its citizens—until we reach the Saint Paul of 1875—a prosperous, populous, opulent city, the capital of a great and flourishing State, the commercial emporium of the valley of the Upper Mississippi.

The period mentioned is but a brief span, after all—about one average generation—but what great results those few years have seen accomplished.   Let the mind take in our city now, with its 33,000 inhabitants, and taxable property of $27,000.-000—its long miles of splendid, smooth. well-paved avenues. lined with solid business blocks and public buildings. or palatial mansions. and underlaid with water and gas pipes. and a well-arranged system of sewerage—her levee. with the commerce of the greatest river in the world. and its tributaries. connecting us with 35,000 miles of inland navigation—her eight railroads, with nearly a hundred trains arriving and departing daily.   Her numerous manufactories, warehouses, elevators, &c., banking houses with millions of capital in the aggregate, and large wholesale houses doing a trade of millions annually—her numerous large and elegant churches, commodious first-class hotels, well managed public schools, orphan asylums, hospitals, and other charitable and reformatory institutions—a splendidly drilled and efficient fire department and police force—public libraries and academies of art and science—in a word, all the numerous institutions which are the outgrowth of civilization and refinement, aided by wealth, and the remarkable progress of our city will be apparent, inspiring us with the hope that the *future* of a community which has achieved such wonders in the past, will be still more brilliant and glorious.

CHAPTER XXXV.

A QUARTER CENTURY'S RETROSPECT.

The Unparalleled Growth of our City—A Century's Work Compressed in 25 Years—The Social Condition of our City 25 Years Ago, Contrasted with Now—Money vs. Culture and Social Refinement—Our Æstheti-cal Growth—Education, Literature, Music and Art.

[For this interesting chapter—a fitting close to our civic history—the writer is indebted to Col. Earle S. Goodrich. Indeed, this acknowledgment is scarcely necessary—his graceful and polished.style would be recognized without it.]

THE past quarter of a century stands by itself in the importance and variety of the results achieved in all departments of knowledge and enterprise. The happy marriage of the mechanic arts with science, has produced and perfected a series of remarkable inventions, which, in ministering to the demands of commerce, manufactures, and the social needs and luxuries, have revolutionized trade, created new and expanded old industries, refined the conditions of labor, and by their influence upon habits of thought and methods of life, have affected the structure as well as changed the surface of society, and almost created a new race in a single generation. These transformations, clearly enough seen in old communities, are most vividly revealed in the new and frontier sections. For whereas, in the older States, twenty-five years ago, there were in existence all known methods which produce wealth, and all the culture and ease which are the fruit of it, here, at the Northwest, civil society was just in process of organization, and all things were as wild and untamed as nature itself. There, in the older communities, nature was already subdued, and country as well as town showed the marks of refined living, so that the influence of the quarter century's progress is revealed more in the inner and higher life of the people than in physical manifestations; while here, on the border, whatever lies between the first turning of the sod and the last achievement of art, had to be wrought from crude nature, and by men gathered together by chance, and exhibiting not merely every grade of culture, but every phase of the lack of it. Here, then, has been furnished the most tangible and striking revelation of the wonderful progress which has marked the third quarter of the present century.

In selecting out of this frontier region a point to serve as an example of the remarkable development of the last twenty-five years, and which shall cover not merely increase of business and access of population, but growth in those mental, moral, and æsthetic directions which make up culture, and are the flowering of a high civilization, we can, without being invidious, choose our own city of Saint Paul. The history, which closed with the last chapter, certainly presents a record in which our citizens may take a justifiable pride. It shows the work of a century compressed into a quarter of the time. The simple record of the organization of our religious societies, embracing almost every sect ; of the beginning and spread of our educational system ; of societies devoted to art and science, as well as to charity and reform ; of our public libraries ; and of scores of other beneficent organizations, having for their object the improvement of our people in intelligence and worth ; this simple record reveals more forcibly our progress in culture than any mere generalizing can show ; for all these things not only sustain culture, but grow out of it, and are the best and highest indications of its quality and strength.

The social condition twenty-five years ago and now, presents as strong a contrast as anything shown in our history. A small population, joining together to form a community, but mingling only in business intercourse ; divided into cliques which represented every nationality ; this made up an unpromising composition to mould into shapely and attractive social form. Yet, the very heterogeneousness of the character of our early settlers, through the wearing but smoothing effect of years of friction, and under gradually improving conditions, has developed a society more cosmopolitan, and with greater variety and breadth of culture, than can be found in many cities of quadruple our age and population. Freedom from insularity marks our habits and manners as it does our position ; the representatives of many lands have contributed their graces and refinements; until, if we were to calculate our age by the ordinary growth of social tone and breeding, we might without vanity count by decades instead of years.

This change in the social condition is due greatly to the difference, then and now, in the prime objects of life and effort. The accumulation of wealth is everywhere and at all times the moving spring of energy, not always for the gratification of a sordid desire for gain, but for the comfort which it brings, and the good which may be done with it. With our first settlers, making money seemed the sole aim and end of living. And while that passion continued the dominant one, the possession of money was the touchstone of influence; the man who gained the most of it was the man most regarded—with little reference, during the earlier years, to the means by which it was obtained, or to the mental or moral qualities of its possessor. Under the impulse of this spirit there could, of course, be little society worth its name, for the general tendency was toward narrowness, selfishness and vulgarity. It must be understood, however, that these sweeping remarks apply to society in the mass, and are held to be true of it only in that sense. For no one, whose residence dates back to our earliest days, can fail to recall many homes, in Saint Paul and vicinity, which were the seats of an elegant hospitality, and from which proceeded the most elevating influences. These cannot be remembered with more gratitude than is their due; they were the leaven that leavened the whole lump; and the air of graceful refinement that pervaded them, remains with us as the purest and best of the social atmosphere of to-day. We are still sordid enough, without doubt, but our growth has been in the right direction, and we can now see more in life than the gathering of a fortune. There is to-day more pride in the possession of a good name than in great riches; and there exists a healthily growing respect for social position and family repute, which are the fruits of good conduct and virtuous living. These things as tangibly mark right development as do the substitution of the opera and drama for the Indian dance and pow-wow, the popular lecture-room for the public gambling-hall, and the music of MOZART, BEETHOVEN and WAGNER for the grotesque mouthings of negro minstrelsy.

In public architecture, the progress is seen at a glance, by comparing the Mission of Saint Paul, (of which an engraving is given in this history,) with Saint Mary's, the First Baptist church, or the German Catholic cathedral: while scattered over the city are hundreds of elegant residences, which show that in domestic architecture, no stereotype forms have been used, but that expression has been given to cultivated individual tastes, in which lies the peculiar charm and beauty of any structure named, and used as, a home. Many of these are beauty spots upon the face of the city, reflecting a refining influence upon all who see them, and holding within their walls, in pictures and libraries, such treasures of art and knowledge as prove that all is not done for outward show, but that very much is the legitimate expression of enlightened sentiment and cultured taste.

The strictly material progress of Saint Paul during the quarter century past, does not come within the purview of this chapter. In those preceding, the details of its growth in trade, commerce, population, manufactures, and all the industries which go to make up a prosperous community, have been as fully presented and discussed, as could be suitably done in such a work. But this may be said, that, coupling the substantial character of our development with its rapidity, the result is quite without example, even in this region and during this period of marvelous growth. We cannot, however, contemplate this picture of progress, pleasing as it is, without noticing that ghostly shadows fall upon it, day by day, as one by one of those who laid the foundations of our prosperity, pass away from our midst. The majority of the men who, twenty-five years ago, were influential in the political, financial, and commercial enterprises of the little town just christened after its mission chapel, and whose names and deeds are recorded in this book, sleep now in one or another of the pleasant cemeteries that lie on the outskirts of the city which they founded. The many are taken ; the few are left. May these few linger among us during long years to come, enjoying the prosperity which they helped to create, and receiving the benediction of every worthy citizen of our beautiful Saint Paul !

APPENDIX.

LIST OF FEDERAL, COUNTY AND CITY OFFICERS SINCE 1849.

FEDERAL OFFICERS.

Postmaster:
April 7, 1846—Henry Jackson.
July 5, 1849—Jacob W. Bass.
March 15, 1853—Wm. H. Forbes.
March 11, 1856—Charles S. Cave.
March 12, 1860—W. M. Corcoran.
April 12, 1861—Charles Nichols.
March 14, 1865—Dr. J. H. Stewart.
May 4, 1870—J. A. Wheelock.
June 1, 1875—Dr. David Day.

Collector of the Port:
1851-53—Charles J. Henniss.
1853-55—Robert Kennedy.
1855-57—L. B. Wait.
1857-59—James Mills.
1859-61—E. A. C. Hatch.
1861-76—George W. Moore.

COUNTY OFFICERS.

Register of Deeds:
1849-52—David Day.
1852-54—M. S. Wilkinson.
1854-58—L. M. Olivier.
1858-60—Edward Heenan.
1860-62—S. Hough.
1862-66—Charles Passavant.
1866-74—Jacob Mainzer.
1874-76—Theodore Sander.
1876-78—Alex. Johnston.

Sheriff:
1849-52—C. P. V. Lull.
1852-54—George F. Brott.
1854-56—A. M. Fridley.
1856-58—Aaron W. Tullis.
1858-60—J. Y. Caldwell.
1860-62—A. W. Tullis.
1862-70—D. A. Robertson.

Sheriff:
1870-76—John Grace.
1876-78—John C. Becht.

Judge of Probate:
1849-52—Henry A. Lambert.
1852—Ira B. Kingsley.
1853—Henry A. Lambert.
1854—Jesse M. Stone.
1855—Richard Fewer.
1856-58—A. C. Jones.
1858-60—John Penman.
1860-62—J. F. Hoyt, (res. Ap. 12, '62.)
1862—R. F. Crowell.
1863—E. C. Lambert.
1864-69—R. F. Crowell.
1869-73—Oscar Stephenson.
1873-75—Hascall R. Brill.
1875-76—Oscar Stephenson.

Treasurer:

1849-52—James W. Simpson.
1852—S. H. Sergeant.
1853—Robert Cummings.
1854—Nathaniel E. Tyson.
1855—Allen Pierse.
1856—(to March 23,) C. F. Stimson.
1856-68—Robert A. Smith.
1868-76—Calvin S. Uline.

County Attorney:

1849-53—W. D. Phillips.
1853-56—D. C. Cooley.
1856-64—Isaac V. D. Heard.
1864-66—Henry J. Horn.
1866-70—S. M. Flint.
1870-72—Harvey Officer.
1872-74—W. W. Erwin.
1874-76—C. D. O'Brien.

County Surveyor:

1852-53—S. P. Folsom.
1853—W. R. Marshall.
1854-58—J. A. Case.
1858-60—Wilbur F. Duffy.
1860—D. S. Kenney.
1861-64—D. L. Curtice.
1864-66—Gates A. Johnson.
1866-72—(No election.)
1872-76—Charles M. Boyle.

Coroner:

1854—J. E. Fullerton.
1855-57—Dr. W. H. Jarvis.
1857—Dr. J. D. Goodrich.
1858-60—Dr. J. V. Wren.
1860-62—James M. Castner.
1862-64—O. F. Ford.
1864-66—Philip Scheig.
1866-68—O. F. Ford.
1868-70—J. P. Melancon.
1878-72—Dr. A. Guernon.
1872-74—P. McEvoy.
1874-76—Dr. P. Gabrielsen.

Clerk of Court:

1850-53—J. K. Humphrey.
1853-54—A. J. Whitney.
1854-58—George W. Prescott
1858-62—R. F. Houseworth.
1862-66—George W. Prescott.
1866-76—Albert Armstrong

Auditor:

1859-61—Alexander Buchanan.
1861-63—Tracy M. Metcalf.
1863-65—William H. Forbes.
1865-67—J. F. Hoyt.
1867-71—S. Lee Davis.

Auditor:

1871-73—Hiram J. Taylor.
1873—John B. Olivier, (resigned.)
1873-76—S. Lee Davis.

Court Commissioner:

1861-67—Oscar Malmros.
1867-71—Henry M. Dodge.
1872-76—G. Siegenthaler.

District Judge:

1858-64—E. C. Palmer.
1864-78—Westcott Wilkin.

Common Pleas Judges:

1866-75—William Sprigg Hall.
1875-82—O. Simons.
1875-82—H. R. Brill.

County Commissioners.

Acker Henry, 1869-71.
Baker D. A. J., 1858 to '61.
Barney T. J., 1871-73.
Bennett Abr., 1855 to '58.
Berkey Peter, 1863-72-75.
Betz J. G., 1861-63.
Blasdell E. S., 1874-5.
Brainerd H. J., 1868-75.
Branch Wm., 1858-9.
Burbank, J. C., 1860.
Clark Martin D., 1858 to '60.
Davern Wm., 1858-9.
Emerson C. L., 1858-9.
Godfrey Ard., Nov. 1849 to Jan. 1850.
Gervais Benj., 1850-1.
Hale H., 1862 from 5th July.
Hammond George, 1862-7.
Holland John, 1864-9.
Howard Thomas, 1867-71.
Hoyt L., 1871-3.
Irvine J. R., 1860.
Kelly Dan., 1871-5.
Kilroy John P., 1862-66.
Lambert John S., 1858 to '60.
Larpenteur A. L., 1859.
LeBonne Joseph, 1852-4.
Lee William, 1875.
Lindeke William, 1873-5.
McClung J. W., 1860.
McGrorty William B., 1858-9.
McLean N., 1856 to '59.
Marvin L., 1859.
Morgan Charles A., 1865 from Sept 9.
Murray James F., 1858-9.
Nicols John, 1860-1, 1871-3.
O'Connor M. J., 1861.
Parker A. F., 1861-2.
Prince John S., 1871-2.

County Commissioners:
Rice Edmund, 1856 to '58.
Robert Louis, Nov. 1849 to Jan. 1856.
Russell R. P., 1850-3.
Ryan Patrick, 1864-6.
Schiller ——, 1859.
Schurmeier C. H., 1872-3.
Selby J. W., 1862.
Smith John, 1860-1.
Spiel, Joseph, 1867-72.
Stahlman C., 1870-1.
Steele John, 1866-8.
Stees W. M., 1859.
Taylor H. J., 1859.
Welch Wm., 1871-5.
Whitney C. T., 1863-5.
Wilkinson Ross, 1859.
Wilson J. P., Jan. 1854 to April 1856.
Wolff Wm. H., 1858 to '60.

Senate.
Becker George L., 1868-9-70-1.
Boal James McC., 1849-51.
Brisbin John B., 1856-7.
Cave Charles S., 1858.
Drake E. F., 1874-5.
Farrington George W., 1852-3.
Forbes William H., 1849-51-2-3.
Hall Wm. Sprigg, 1858-60.
Heard I. V. D., 1872.
Irvine John R., 1862-3.
Mackubin C. N., 1860.
Murray William P., 1854-5-66-7-75-6.
Nicols John, 1864-5-72-3.
Otis George L., 1866.
Rice Edmund, 1864-5-73-4.
Sanborn John B., 1861.
Smith James, Jr., 1861-2-3-76.
Stewart J. H., 1860.
Van Etten Isaac, 1854-5-8.

House of Representatives:
Acker Henry, 1860-1.
Banning William L., 1861.
Bartlett Louis, 1854.
Benz George, 1873-4-5.
Berkey Peter, 1872.
Brainard H. J., 1873.
Branch William, 1857-66.
Brawley Daniel F., 1855.
Brisbin John B , 1863.
Brunson Benjamin W., 1849-51.
Burbank James C., 1872.
Carver H. L. 1862.
Castle Henry A., 1873.
Cave Charles S., 1852-5.

House of Representatives:
Chamblin A. T., 1857.
Costello William, 1857.
Crooks William, 1875-6.
Crosby John W., 1858.
Davern William, 1858.
Davidson John X., 1874.
Davis C. K., 1867.
Davis W. A., 1854-5.
Day John H., 1854.
Delano F. R., 1875.
•Dewey John J., 1849.
Egan James J., 1869.
Faber Paul, 1869-70.
Findley Samuel J., 1852.
Fitz R. H., 1864.
Fullerton J. E., 1852.
Gilfillan Charles D., 1865-76.
Gilman John M., 1865-9-70.
Gross Nicholas, 1862.
Haus Reuben, 1855-6.
Hoyt Lorenzo, 1874-5.
Jackson Henry, 1849.
Johnson Parsons K., 1849.
Jones D. C., 1869.
Kidder Jefferson P., 1863-4.
Kiefer Andrew R., 1864.
Knauft F., 1856.
Lemay Joseph, 1855.
Lienau Charles H., 1867-8.
Lott Bushrod W., 1853-6.
Lunkenheimer John, 1876.
McGrorty William B., 1858.
Merriam John L., 1870-71.
Metcalf Tracy M., 1874.
Meyerding Henry, 1874.
Miller H. H., 1873-5.
Mitsch George, 1860.
Murray William P., 1852-3-7-67-8.•
Nessel Andrew, 1861.
Nobles William H., 1856.
Noot William, 1853-4.
Olivier John B., 1860.
Olivier Louis M., 1853.
Otis George L., 1858.
Paine Parker, 1866.
Peckham John A., 1865.
Ramsey Justus C., 1851-3-7.
Rauch Charles, 1858.
Rice Edmund, 1851-67-72.
Richter Fred., 1876.
Robertson, D. A., 1866.
Rogers J. N., 1873.

* Elected, but did not take his seat.

House of Representatives:
Rohr Philip, 1862.
Sanborn John B., 1860-74.
Selby Jeremiah W., 1852.
Sibley H. H., 1871.
Sloan Levi, 1854.
Smythe H. M., 1872.
Stahlman Christopher, 1871.

House of. Representatives:
Starkey James, 1858.
Stephenson Oscar, 1860.
Tilden H. L., 1851.
Trott Herman, 1866.
Webber William, 1870.
Wilkinson Ross, 1856.

CITY OFFICERS.

Mayor:
1854—David Olmsted.
1855—Alex. Ramsey.
1856—George L. Becker.
1857—J. B. Brisbin.
1858—N. W. Kittson.
1859—D. A. Robertson.
1860-63—John S. Prince.
1863—J. E. Warren.
1864—Dr. J. H. Stewart.
1865-67—J. S. Prince.
1867—George L. Otis.
1868—Dr. J. H. Stewart.
1869—J. T. Maxfield.
1870-72—Wm. Lee.
1872-75—Dr. J. H. Stewart.
1875-76—J. T. Maxfield.

City Treasurer:
1854-59—Daniel Roher.
1859-64—Charles A. Morgan.
1864-66—C. T. Whitney.
1866-70—N. Gross.
1870 to July 10, 1873—M. Esch.
1873-76—F. A. Renz.

City Justice:
1854-60—Orlando Simons.
1860-64—Nelson Gibbs.
1864-66—A McElrath.
1866 68—E C. Lambert.
1868-70—O. Malmros.
1870-72—Thomas Howard.
1872-75—A. McElrath.
1875—S. M. Flint.

City Clerk:
1854-56—Sherwood Hough.
1856-58—L P. Cotter.
1858—A. J. Whitney, (Resigned.)
1858—Isaac H. Conway.
1859-61—John H. Dodge.
1861 (to Sept. 12)—L. P. Cotter.

City Clerk:
1862, (Sept 12,) to Oct. 15, 1866—K. T. Friend
1866 (Oct. 15)-68—B W. Lott.
1868-70—John J. Williams.
1870-76—M. J. O'Connor.

Comptroller:
1854-56—F. McCormick.
1856—G. W. Armstrong.
1857 { A. T. Chamblin, resigned.
       Sher. Hough, resigned (July 21)
       T. M. Metcalf.
1859-63—Wm. Von Hamm.
1863—C. H. Lienau.
1864—Henry Schiffbauer.
1865-76—John W. Roche.

Attorney:
1854—D. C. Cooley.
1855—J. B. Brisbin.
1856—I. V. D. Heard.
1857—C. J. Pennington, resigned.
       H. J. Horn.
1860—S. R. Bond.
1861-65—S M. Flint.
1865-67—I V. D. Heard
1867-69—Harvey Officer.
1869-76—W. A. Gorman.

Engineer:
1854—Simeon P. Folsom.
1855-57—J. A. Case.
1857—J. T. Halsted.
1858—D. L. Curtice.
1859—F. Wipperman.
1860—Gates A Johnson.
1861-63—Charles A. F. Morris.
1863-69—Charles M Boyle.
1869-74—D. L Curtice.
1874-76—D. I. Wellman.

Chief of Police:*

1854-58—William R. Miller.
1858-60—John W. Crosby.
1860—John O'Gorman.
1861—H. H. Western.
1862—James Gooding.
1863—Michael Cummings, Jr.
1864—J. R. Cleveland.
1865-6—G. W. Turnbull (res July,'66)
1866-67—John Jones.
1867-70—J. P. McIlrath.
1870-72—L. H. Eddy.
1872-75—J. P. McIlrath.
1875—James King.

Physician and Health Officer:

1856—Samuel Willey.
1857-59—J. V. Wren.
1859—J. A. Vervais.
1860-62—T. R. Potts.
1862 to June, 1866—A. G. Brisbine.
1866—T. R. Potts.
1867-71—Brewer Mattocks.
1871—M. Hagan.
1872-74—T. R. Potts.
1874-76—Brewer Mattocks.

Wharfmaster:

1858—S. R. Champlin.
1859—Andrew R. Kiefer.
1860—Louis Semper.
1861—James J. Hill.
1862—John B. Cook.
1863— { James Hall.
         { Paul Faber.
1864—T. K. Danforth.
1865—Henry Constans.
1866—Louis Krieger.
1867—John O'Connor.
1868—G. A. Borup.
1869-72—Patrick Butler.
1872—H. D. Mathews.

Market Master.

1859-61—N. J. March.
1861—Jacob Heck.
1862-65—Michael Cummings, Sr.
1865-68—N. Gibbs.
1868-70—John O'Connor.
1870—John Lunkenheimer.
1871-75—P. McManus.

Chief Engineer Fire Department:

1854—W. M. Stees.
1855-59—C. H. Williams.

* From 1854 to 1858 this office was called City Marshal.

Chief Engineer Fire Department:

1859—J. B. Irvine.
1860-62—J. E. Missen.
1862—W. T. Donaldson.
1863—L. H. Eddy.
1864—J. C. A. Pickett.
1865—C. H. Williams.
1866-69—B. Presley.
1869-70—Frank Breuer.
1870-72—J. C. Prendergast.
1872—R. O. Strong.
1873-76—M. B. Farrell.

Superintendent of Schools:

1856-59—E. D. Neill.
1859—B. Drew.
1860-72—John Mattocks.
1872-74—Geo. M. Gage.
1874-76—L. M. Burrington.

Street Commissioner:

1860—R. C. Knox.
1861-63—Patrick Murnane.
1863-69—John Dowlan.
1869—Frank Deck.

City Council:

Bazille Charles, 1854-6.
Beaumont J. I., 1865-7.
Becker George L., 1854-6.
Berkey Peter, 1859-62, 1864-5, 1868-71.
Betz John G., 1863-5.
Branch William, 1856-61.
Breuer F., 1870-71.
Cave Charles S., 1854-7.
Chamblin A. T., 1854-7.
Corcoran William M., 1860-2.
Cummings Michael, Jr., 1868-72.
Dailey C. M., 1860-2.
Dawson William, 1865-8.
Demeules Louis, 1874-7.
Dodge H. M., 1858-61.
Dorniden M., 1864-7.
Dowlan John, 1874-7.
Eddy Luther H., 1861-4, 1869-72.
Emerson Charles L., 1856-9.
Fanning Thomas, 1854.
Farrell M. B., 1869.
Finck Adam, 1862-5.
Fisher J. W., 1871-5.
Fitz R. H., 1860-3, 1865-8.
Fuller A. G., 1855.
Galbraith Thomas J., 1865.
Gies William, 1866-7.
Golcher William, 1872-75.
Grace Thomas, 1858-9, 1869-79.
Grant C. L., 1867-8.

Board of Education :
Houseworth R. F., 1865-6.
Howard Thomas, 1867-70.
Ingersoll D. W., 1865-77.
Kiefer John, 1865-68.
Kelly W. H., 1862-7.
King T. J., 1863-5.
Lambert E. C., 1861-7.
Lambert Henry A., 1861-3.
Langford N. P., 1859.
Little George, 1859-60.
Lott B. W., 1858-60.
Lumsden G. L., 1857-8.
McCormick F., 1858-9-
McNamee Francis P., 1863-9.
Mann C. A., 1866-9.
Marshall William R., 1856-7.
Mason W. F., 1866-7.
Mathews James H., 1866-8.
Mattocks John, 1859-72.
Merrill D. D., 1865-8.
Meyerding Henry, 1869-79.
Minor John, 1872.
Moody A. C., 1864.
Mott George C., 1858-9.
Mueller B., 1874-5.
Murphy J. H., 1876-9.
Neill E. D., 1856-60.
Nicols John, 1862-5.
Noah Jacob J., 1860-61.
Paine Parker, 1856-74.
Palmer E. C., 1856-7.

Board of Education :
Peckham J. A., 1862-5.
Phillips J. B., 1860-61.
Pond J. P , 1857-8, 1869-62.
Pope John D., 1862.
Potts Thomas R., 1860-62, 1862-3.
Prescott George W., 1862, 1865-8.
Putnam S. K., 1860-62.
Ramaley David, 1862-5.
Robertson D. A., 1862-69.
Rogers John, 1869-72.
Scheffer Albert, 1875-8.
Selby J. W., 1861-3.
Sheire Monroe, 1868-75.
Sibley H. H., 1868-70.
St. Peter I., 1875-6.
Starkey James, 1857-8.
Stewart J. H., 1858-61.
Strong C. D., 1862-3.
Studdart I. F. A., 1871-5, 1876-9.
Terry J. C., 1876-9.
Torbet A. M., 1856-7.
Trott Herman, 1869-72.
Von Minden H., 1871.
Ward J. Q. A., 1862-5.
Watson George, 1876-9.
Wedelstaedt H., 1868-71.
Williams J. Fletcher, 1864-7, 1869-71.
Wolff Albert, 1872-5.
Zenzius Conrad, 1865-8.
Zimmerman Edward, 1862-6.

31

GROWTH OF WEALTH AND POPULATION.

The first assessment made in Saint Paul, in 1849, gave a valuation of $85,000. In 1853, this had risen to $723,534; and, in 1854, almost doubled, being $1,300,000. In 1856, it rose to $3,287,220, which, in one year more, (1857,) had increased nearly 100 per cent., being $6,437,285. This valuation of the "flush times" shrank, with everything else, and, in 1860, had declined $1,691,176. From this on, the following table gives the quinquennial increase:

	1860.	1865.	1870.	1875.
First Ward—Real Estate.	$877,592	$450,644	$1,342,159	$3,592,743
Personal Property.........	241,933	286,475	321,290	1,185,005
	1,119,525	737,019	1,663,449	4,777,748
Second Ward—Real Estate	1,219,100	747,312	2,143,926	4,106,751
Personal Property.........	297,209	896,028	779,942	3,526,734
	1,516,309	1,643,340	2,933,868	7,633,485
Third Ward—Real Estate.	818,149	616,479	1,194,181	3,069,274
Personal Property.........	267,963	366,657	285,012	724,674
	1,086,112	983,326	1,479,193	3,793,948
Fourth Ward—Real Estate	926,685	685,951	1,262,041	[5,897,943
Personal Property.........	98,488	266,974	143,209	772,270
	1,024,173	952,925	1,405,250	6,670,213
Fifth Ward—Real Estate.	....	421,663	1,129,215	3,939,525
Personal Property.........	....	518,997	145,032	676,012
	....	940,660	1,274,247	4,618,137
Sixth Ward—Real Estate.	....	....	....	230,474
Personal Property.........	....	....	....	32,927
	....	....	....	263,401
Total, (city,)..........	$4,746,119	$5,257,370	$9,315,507	$27,755,926
McLean—Real Estate.....	72,909	73,015	78,777	$182,235
Personal Property.........	5,112	46,807	35,936	16,587
	78,012	168,663	171,463	210,888
Mounds View—Real Estate	68,642	71,614	46,294	104,713
Personal Property.........	3,296	1,511	3,922	8,768
	71,938	73,125	50,216	113,481
New Canada—Real Estate	290,998	128,204	230,642	568,420
Personal Property.........	16,888	19,265	27,975	91,817
	307,886	198,712	307,156	721,127
Reserve—Real Estate.....	199,668	116,352	169,723	427,065
Personal Property.........	8,008	32,101	24,876	32,013
	207,676	198,408	221,019	491,858
Rose—Real Estate........	346,665	218,667	247,314	621,924
Personal Property.........	6,943	25,950	25,892	19,623
	353,608	331,208	341,951	789,890
White Bear—Real Estate.	60,642	64,591	71,554	161,142
Personal Property.........	1,718	10,349	13,487	20,354
	62,360	80,662	85,041	199,496
Total, (county,).......	$5,827,599	$6,308,058	$11,492,353	$30,282,666

COMPENDIUM OF CENSUSES.

	1850.	1855.	1860.	1865.	1870.	1875.
First Ward................	....	....	3,419	2,348	3,426	4,762
Second Ward...............	....	....	2,401	2,893	3,466	4,609
Third Ward................	....	....	2,049	2,715	3,956	5,236
Fourth Ward...............	....	....	2,532	2,874	4,775	10,175
Fifth Ward................	....	....	....	2,146	4,408	6,893
Sixth Ward................	....	....	....	....	....	1,503
Total City................	1,083	4,716	10,401	12,976	20,030	33,178
Mound's View Township.......	....	....	99	115	215	295
White Bear Township...........	....	....	267	278	430	647
New Canada Township........	....	....	511	565	789	799
Reserve Township.............	....	....	249	350	429	388
McLean Township.............	....	....	124	328	442	316
Rose Township...............	....	....	499	495	750	710
Total County...............	2,227	9,495	12,150	15,107	23,085	36,333

NOTE.—The first census taken in Saint Paul was in June, 1849, simply an enumera-
tion of the inhabitants, which were reported at 840. The census of 1850 and 1855, were
not taken by wards, but the city and county given as a total.

NATIVITIES OF THE POPULATION.

The census of 1875, gives the nativities of the population of Ramsey county as follows :

Native Born.		*Foreign Born.*	
Minnesota	11,805	Canada	1,309
Connecticut	160	England	662
Illinois	644	Ireland	2,662
Indiana	207	Scotland	131
Iowa	154	Wales	19
Kentucky	120	Sweden	1,437
Maine	285	Norway	565
Massachusetts	394	Denmark	159
Michigan	214	Holland	30
Missouri	328	France	126
New Hampshire	140	Switzerland	168
New Jersey	89	Austria	162
New York	1,789	Bohemia	665
Ohio	619	Wirtemberg	8
Pennsylvania	723	Baden	35
Vermont	216	Bavaria	175
Virginia and West Virginia	152	Hanover	31
Wisconsin	739	Prussia	1,850
Other States and Territories	1,284	Germany	3,837
		Other Countries	333

Total native born............20,122

Total foreign born............14,364

Unknown, 1,847. Total, 36,333. Percentage of native born, 58.4; of foreign born and unknown, 41.6.

INDEX.

32

www.ingramcontent.com/pod-product-compliance
Lightning Source LLC
Chambersburg PA
CBHW031811270326
41932CB00008B/378